THE EXPERIENCES OF FACE VEIL WEARERS IN EUROPE AND THE LAW

One of the most remarkable aspects pertaining to the legal bans and societal debates on the face veil in Europe is that they rely on assumptions that lack any factual basis. To rectify this, Eva Brems researched the experiences of women who wear the face veil in Belgium, and brought her research results together with those of colleagues who did the same in four other European countries. Their findings, which are outlined in this volume, move the current discussion on face veil bans forward by providing a much-needed insider perspective. In addition, a number of legal and social science scholars comment on the empirical findings and on the face veil issue more generally.

EVA BREMS is a professor of human rights law at the Human Rights Centre, Ghent University, Belgium, where her research covers most areas of human rights law with a specific interest in minority issues and women's rights.

CAMBRIDGE STUDIES IN LAW AND SOCIETY

Cambridge Studies in Law and Society aims to publish the best scholarly work on legal discourse and practice in its social and institutional contexts, combining theoretical insights and empirical research.

The fields that it covers are: studies of law in action; the sociology of law; the anthropology of law; cultural studies of law, including the role of legal discourses in social formations; law and economics; law and politics; and studies of governance. The books consider all forms of legal discourse across societies, rather than being limited to lawyers' discourses alone.

The series editors come from a range of disciplines: academic law; socio-legal studies; sociology; and anthropology. All have been actively involved in teaching and writing about law in context.

Series editors

Chris Arup
Monash University, Victoria
Sally Engle Merry
New York University
Susan Silbey
Massachusetts Institute of Technology

A list of books in the series can be found at the back of this book.

THE EXPERIENCES OF FACE VEIL WEARERS IN EUROPE AND THE LAW

Edited by

Eva Brems

CAMBRIDGE
UNIVERSITY PRESS

University Printing House, Cambridge CB2 8BS, United Kingdom

Cambridge University Press is part of the University of Cambridge.

It furthers the University's mission by disseminating knowledge in the pursuit of education, learning and research at the highest international levels of excellence.

www.cambridge.org
Information on this title: www.cambridge.org/9781107058309

© Cambridge University Press 2014

First published 2014

Printed in the United Kingdom by Clays, St Ives plc

A catalogue record for this publication is available from the British Library

Library of Congress Cataloguing in Publication data
The experiences of face veil wearers in Europe and the law / edited by Eva Brems.
   pages cm – (Cambridge studies in law and society)
ISBN 978-1-107-05830-9 (hardback)
1. Muslim women – Legal status, laws, etc. – Europe, Western.   2. Hijab (Islamic clothing) – Law and legislation – Europe, Western.   3. Islamic clothing and dress – Social aspects – Europe, Western.   I. Brems, Eva, editor of compilation.
KJC5144.M56E98   2014
342.408′52975674–dc23

2014003927

ISBN 978-1-107-05830-9 Hardback

CONTENTS

CONTRIBUTORS

Rim-Sarah Alouane is a teaching assistant in public law at the Institut Maurice Hauriou, France.

Schirin Amir-Moazami is an assistant professor in the Department of Islamic Studies at Free University Berlin.

Naima Bouteldja is a French journalist and co-director of documentary film company, Red Rag Productions.

Emmanuelle Bribosia is a professor at the Institute for European Studies and Director of the Legal Department of the Institute for European Studies, Université Libre de Bruxelles, Belgium.

Eva Brems is a professor of human rights law at the Human Rights Centre, Ghent University, Belgium.

Susan Edwards is University Dean of Research, University of Buckingham, UK.

Nadia Fadil is an assistant professor at KU Leuven, Belgium.

Erica Howard is a reader in law, at Middlesex University, London.

Yaiza Janssens is doctoral researcher and teaching assistant at the Human Rights Centre, Ghent University, Belgium.

Kim Lecoyer is doctoral researcher at the Human Rights Centre, Ghent University, Belgium.

Maleiha Malik is a professor of law, King's College London.

Annelies Moors is a professor in the Department of Anthropology and Sociology at the University of Amsterdam.

Saïla Ouald Chaib is doctoral researcher at the Human Rights Centre, Ghent University, Belgium.

Kate Østergaard is a Ph.D. freelance consultant researcher and part-time lecturer at the University of Copenhagen.

Isabelle Rorive is a professor at the Institute for European Studies and Centre Perelman for Legal Philosophy, Université Libre de Bruxelles, Belgium.

Birgitte Schepelern Johansen is a postdoctoral fellow at the Centre for European Islamic Thought, University of Copenhagen.

Dolores Morondo Taramundi is a research fellow at the Institute of Human Rights, University of Deusto, Spain.

Victoria Vandersteen is research collaborator at the Human Rights Centre, Ghent University, Belgium.

Jogchum Vrielink is a postdoctoral researcher and Research Coordinator, Discrimination Law, Research Centre on Equality Policies, University of Leuven.

Margit Warburg is a professor in sociology of religion at the University of Copenhagen.

ACKNOWLEDGEMENTS

My research for this book was funded by a Starting Grant of the European Research Council. Thanks are due to Victoria Vandersteen, who managed to gain access to Belgian face veil wearers, to Saïla Ouald Chaib and Jogchum Vrielink with whom I have been exchanging views and writing papers on this issue for several years now, and to Yaiza Janssens and Kim Lecoyer who helped with Nvivo coding. As always, a special word of thank is due to Martine Dewulf for administrative and editorial assistance. Thanks also to Finola O'Sullivan and Elizabeth Spicer at Cambridge University Press for their warm and professional support.

INTRODUCTION TO THE VOLUME

Eva Brems

1. WHY STUDY FACE VEIL WEARERS?

In Belgium, as in France, legal restrictions on religious dress worn by Muslim women have been on the agenda for over two decades. Yet until a few years ago, this debate was almost exclusively focused on the headscarf. Despite being heavily involved in the debate on headscarf bans both as an academic and as a human rights activist, I hardly spent a thought on the Islamic face veil, until local governments in my country began to ban it. When the federal Parliament started in earnest to talk about a nationwide ban, many in the human rights world were baffled. The issue seemed to fall out of thin air, as the estimated 200 to 300 face veil wearers in Belgium had never caused any noticeable trouble. Even more disturbing was the swift rise of a hardly contested political and societal consensus around the need for a ban. Not only debate was lacking, it seemed that nobody bothered to gain any knowledge about the practice of the face veil, let alone about the views and experiences of the women who wore it. Critical voices were heard only from human rights organizations[1] and from a small number of scholars. At the Human Rights Centre of Ghent University we

---

[1] At the time of the vote, only Amnesty International (AI) had issued a press release, arguing that the ban would violate religious freedom: Amnesty International, 'Een algemeen verbod op gezichtssluiers is in strijd met de mensenrechten', 21 April 2010. At the time, I was the chair of the Flemish section of AI. The explicit position by the International Secretariat of AI came as a surprise to me and to many in the organization, as this (as well as headscarf bans!) was a topic that AI had not yet worked on before. Later, other human rights organizations would follow, e.g. Human Rights Watch: L. Gerntholtz and G. Van Gulik, 'Beyond the Burqa' (www.hrw.org).

started with traditional legal research, detailing how and why the proposed ban would violate the European Convention on Human Rights (Vrielink *et al.* 2011, 2013). Yet disturbed by the lynch mob atmosphere that surrounded the topic and by the absence of any insider perspective, we decided to interview face veil wearers in Belgium. We teamed up with Dr Jogchum Vrielink at Leuven University, who had experience with field research of this type, aimed at assessing whether legislation realizes its stated purpose. By the time the research was completed, the ban had been adopted. Yet the way the legislative process proceeded[2] – fast and almost in unison – does not suggest that the availability of our empirical data at the time of deliberation would have persuaded any Members of Parliament to vote differently. The presentation of our results to two Flemish newspaper journalists did however move a small stone in the river, as it resulted in an editorial concluding that the legislator had been wrong.[3] A lot more significantly, the Danish experience (see below and Chapter 3 in this volume) – giving up the idea of a ban after learning about empirical reality) – shows that empirical data can have an impact on opinion makers and politicians.

This creates some hope at a time when political pressure to ban face veils continues to build in several countries (see below), and as a challenge to the French face veil ban is pending before a Grand Chamber of the European Court of Human Rights.[4]

2. BRINGING INSIDER REALITIES INTO THE FACE VEIL DEBATE

One of the most remarkable aspects pertaining to these bans and debates is the fact that they proceed on the basis of assumptions about women wearing the face veil, that lack any basis in knowledge. At the time the bans in Belgium and France were adopted, no empirical research was available that would document the experiences and

---

[2] Although I had not been active in politics before, I was asked to participate in the 2010 elections and was elected to the federal Chamber of Representatives. As such, I participated in the (second round of) discussions and vote on the Belgian face veil ban.

[3] Wouter Verschelden, 'Boerkaverbod', De Morgen, 26 May 2012, www.demorgen.be/dm/nl/2462/Standpunt/article/detail/1444441/2012/05/26/Boerkaverbod.dhtml

[4] Application no. 43835/11, *SAS v. France*. The Human Rights Centre of Ghent University introduced a third-party intervention in this case. This is available at www.ugent.be/re/publiekrecht/en/department/human-rights/publications/sas.pdf

motives of the women concerned. Nor was any effort undertaken to consult those women in the process leading up to the ban (with the exception of one woman who was heard by the French Gérin commission at her own request – see below). The bans are thus almost entirely based on outsider experiences and views. The same holds to a large extent for the academic debates on the matter and even for NGO positions.

Yet in recent years, qualitative research into the experiences of women wearing the face veil has been conducted in no fewer than five European countries: France, Belgium, the Netherlands, the United Kingdom and Denmark. The present volume in Part I presents the main findings of this exceptional research. The choice of countries covered in Part I has thus been determined by the availability of empirical research. Some of these research results have not been published before (UK data), or have not been published in English (Netherlands and Denmark data). In all cases, this volume offers an original analysis of the data that has not been published before.

For Part II, a number of legal and social science scholars with expertise in minority rights, discrimination, women's rights and/or Islam were invited to comment on the situation of face veil wearers in Europe today, as well as on the legal bans that affect them, engaging with the results of the empirical research. Building on the lived experiences of face veil wearers, these comments thus situate the face veil issue in the wider debates on the role of religion in the public life of European societies, the marginalization of minority women in societies that otherwise champion women's autonomy, and the marginalization and demonization of Islam in Europe.

In this manner, the book attempts to fill a gap in the current literature discussing face veil bans: the gap of the insider perspective.

As the legal interventions to ban or restrict the wearing of face veils are a central focus, especially in Part II, it is useful to first present an overview of such interventions across Europe. This will be done in the next section. But first a note on terminology. Such legal interventions are widely labelled 'burqa bans'. However this term is inaccurate for various reasons. In the first place, 'burqa' tends to be taken to refer to the (mostly blue) piece of clothing covering the entire female body, including the head, except for a small region around the eyes, which is covered by a concealing net or grille. Such face veils (also called chadris) are typical of areas in Pakistan and Afghanistan. They are (virtually) never worn, however, in Western Europe. To the extent that face veils are worn here, these generally concern the so-called 'niqab': a face veil that may or may not cover the eyes but does cover the rest of the face. A second reason why the reference to 'burqa bans' is not entirely correct is that as a rule these bans are – at least formally – not focused on the face veil, but rather prohibit face covering and concealment in general (see below).

3. LEGAL SITUATION IN EUROPE

3.1 Starting small: local bans

Until 2011, no countrywide face-covering bans existed in Europe.[5] Yet in several countries, local bans were in place restricting at least certain facial concealments in certain contexts. Some were specifically introduced when niqab wearers appeared in local streets, others that had long been on the books were rediscovered and applied to this new situation.

Local face-covering bans exist in Belgium, the Netherlands, Italy and Spain; albeit in varying degrees. In Belgium the 'geographical coverage' of these local prohibitions appears to be the widest, with virtually all major cities and towns having a prohibition in place. One category of local Belgian bans prohibits 'disguises', 'masks' and 'costumes' that cover one's face. These bans date back to the nineteenth century, with festivities and carnival in particular in mind, and was (re)interpreted to include face veils as of 2004 and 2005. A second category was introduced around the latter time, to target face veils specifically. It uses wording such as 'appearing in public unidentifiably' or 'with concealed or covered face'. Municipalities confronted with women wearing face veils had requested the assistance of superior regional authorities in dealing with the issue. In response, the latter proffered model provisions enabling municipalities to prohibit face veils should they wish to do so.[6] Generally, exceptions apply, for temporary authorizations by the mayor, or for certain periods, holidays or situations (e.g. carnival and Halloween). In Belgium, contradictory case law on the application of local bans to face veils was one of the reasons for the enactment of the general ban.[7]

[5] See Brems et al. (2013); Vrielink et al. (2013).
[6] Such a model provision was drafted in Flanders in 2004, by the administrative services of Home Affairs.
[7] See, respectively: Police Court Brussels, 26 January 2011, www.legalworld.be; Police Court Tongeren (Maaseik department), 12 June 2006.

In the Netherlands such local bans are quite rare. As in Belgium, they tend to be worded in neutral and general terms.[8] Despite the absence of case law, the legality and constitutionality of these provisions is widely considered controversial,[9] and as such they hardly seem to be enforced in practice.

In Italy, local bans can be found particularly in the north and northeast of the country. Initially, the regulations tended to be general (rather than contextual) in nature, and municipalities based them on article 5 of the 1975 Public Order Protection Act (POPA), prohibiting any means intended to render the identification of a person difficult in spaces open to the public. The POPA originated in the 1970s during Italy's so-called Years of Lead (*Anni di piombo*), and was aimed at suppressing violent political activism; it had led a dormant existence since that time, until the appearance of face veils led to its 'rediscovery'.[10] In two cases, these local prohibitions gave rise to litigation and case law,[11] which basically led to the finding that the POPA could not be regarded as grounds for prohibiting face veils in public space in general, since the traditional, religious nature of these garments either provides a reasonable justification for wearing them, or that the garment at least is not intended to prevent its wearer being recognized. As such, this case law excluded the possibility for municipalities to issue bans specifically targeting face veils. However, according to some interpretations it did not exclude local prohibitions limited to certain places or situations.[12] Since then some municipalities have issued ordinances that amount to more contextual prohibitions of (*inter alia*) face veils, limited to certain municipal buildings and institutions.[13]

Finally, in Spain a relatively small number of towns and cities in Catalonia (including, most notably, Barcelona), started as of 2010 to

---

[8] E.g. providing a 'prohibition, without authorization by the Mayor, to appear in a publicly accessible place, while being masked, disguised or otherwise unrecognizable' (Art. 2.4.26 §1 Municipal Regulations of Maastricht). Other examples of municipalities in which such regulations are in place, include: Borsele, Doetinchem, Goedereede, Middelharnis, Roermond and Valkenburg (B. P. Vermeulen *et al.*, *Overwegingen bij een boerka verbod* [Considerations Concerning a Burqa Ban], The Hague, 2006, 55).

[9] The reasons being that the Dutch constitution requires a formal law in order for rights and freedoms to be curtailed (*ibid.*).

[10] Möschel (2011).

[11] For the first (administrative) case, see: Administrative Tribunal Trieste 16 October 2006, no. 645 (*Giurisprudenza di merito* 2007, 2423); Council of State 19 June 2008, VI Chamber, no. 3076. A second case was dealt with at the criminal level: Criminal Tribunal of Trevio, Proceeding no. 8533/04 RG MOD.21 (see extensively Möschel 2011).

[12] Möschel (2011: 10).

[13] R. Owen, 'Italian police fine woman for wearing burqa in public', *The Times*, 5 May 2010.

pass regulations banning face covering in municipal buildings.[14] One of these bans, issued by the municipality of Lleida,[15] was appealed by a Muslim association that claimed it violated basic rights. The Catalan Superior Court of Justice upheld the ban, accepting that it was required for identification and security purposes.[16]

3.2 Nationwide bans: France and Belgium

The general bans in France and Belgium are both of a 'neutral' nature, that is: they are not specifically aimed at face veils, but rather at covering one's face (in public) in general. That being said, the background of the bans as well as the reasons advanced to support them unambiguously indicate that in both states the legislators were primarily concerned with the Islamic face veil, the neutral drafting being chosen mainly in an attempt to avoid claims of (direct) discrimination.

3.2.1 France

The first legislative proposal to ban the face veil in France dates from 2006, when Jacques Myard – an MP for the centre-right UMP – tabled a bill aimed at, *inter alia*, criminalizing the wearing of face veils, claiming they amounted to a 'violation of the dignity of women'.[17] The bill was not discussed. In July 2008, the French Conseil d'Etat upheld a decree that denied French citizenship to Ms. Machbour, the Moroccan spouse of a French citizen, on grounds of insufficient assimilation (*défaut d'assimilation*) due to 'the radical practice of her religion, incompatible with the essential values of the French community, in particular with the principle of sex equality'.[18] Among the different elements that made up that practice or could constitute its radicalism, media comments first, and scientific literature after, drew general attention (and public opinion) to the fact that Ms. Machbour wore a face veil.

In the wake of that debate, Myard reintroduced his bill in September 2008, but it again failed to be debated.[19]

---

[14] W. Fautré, 'Is the burqa compatible with women's rights? The "burqa issue" in the EU', paper presented at the conference Burqa and Women's Rights and the European Parliament, Brussels, 10 June 2010.
[15] The city was the first municipality to introduce this type of ban in 2010.
[16] Catalan Superior Court of Justice, 9 June 2011.
[17] Proposition de loi visant à lutter contre les atteintes à la dignité de la femme résultant de certaines pratiques religieuses, parliamentary document no. 3056, 4 October 2006.
[18] Conseil d'Etat, 27 juin 2008, Mme Machbour, no. 286798.
[19] Proposition de loi visant à lutter contre les atteintes à la dignité de la femme résultant de certaines pratiques religieuses, parliamentary document no. 1121, 30 September 2008.

The effective move towards a general ban in France began not long after MP André Gérin, along with others, filed a resolution on 9 June 2009 aimed at establishing a commission of inquiry concerning the face veil on French territory.[20] Not long afterwards, President Nicolas Sarkozy, in a speech on 22 June 2009 stated that such veils were not welcome in France, and that legislation was necessary 'to protect women from being forced to cover their faces and to uphold France's secular values'.[21] The French Parliament subsequently initiated an inquiry into the issue, led by the said André Gérin. The commission of inquiry consisted of thirty-two members, representing all parliamentary groups. It heard witnesses and experts, and it sent out questionnaires to several French embassies. The results of these inquiries were published on 26 January 2010. The report concluded that the face veil constituted an infringement of the three principles constitutive of the French Republic: liberty, equality and brotherhood. More specifically, the report considered the face veil to constitute an infringement on the freedom and the dignity of women (liberty); a denial of gender equality and of a mixed society (equality); and a rejection of 'the common will to live together' (brotherhood). The majority of the commission therefore recommended, first, that Parliament adopt a resolution declaring that the wearing of the full veil is contrary to the values of the Republic, and that, second, a general ban of the face veil in public spaces be adopted. President Sarkozy subsequently, in April 2010, suggested that Parliament debate a ban. On 11 May Parliament unanimously adopted a resolution declaring the face veil an affront to French values, and calling for the practice to be prohibited on French territory.[22] This paved the way for the general ban. The bill leading up to it, which was submitted by the government on 19 May, was passed in both houses of Parliament with an overwhelming majority, in the summer of 2010.[23] Doing so, it overruled the advice of the Council of State that estimated that 'no incontestable

---

[20] W. Fautré, 'Is the burqa compatible with women's rights? The "burqa issue" in the EU', paper presented at the conference Burqa and Women's Rights and the European Parliament, Brussels, 10 June 2010.

[21] C. Gabizon, 'Sarkozy: "la burqa n'est pas la bienvenue"', *Le Figaro*, 26 June 2009.

[22] Résolution réaffirmant la prééminence des valeurs républicaines sur les pratiques communautaristes et condamnant le port du voile intégral comme contraire à ces valeurs, Assemblée nationale, no. 2272.

[23] In the lower house the bill received 335 ayes, only 1 nay and 221 abstentions (13 July 2010). In the Senate there were 246 ayes, 1 nay and 100 abstentions (14 September 2010).

legal basis' could be provided for a general ban.[24] On 7 October 2010, the Constitutional Council upheld the constitutionality of the ban, with only minor reservations. Most notably the Council determined that the ban could not be enforced in places of worship.[25]

Act no. 2010–1192 of 11 October 2010 prohibiting the concealment of the face in public subsequently came into force on 11 April 2011. It states: 'No one may, in spaces open to the public, wear a garment that has the effect of hiding the face' (art. 1). Exceptions apply when 'clothing [is] prescribed or authorized by legal or regulatory provisions', when the clothing 'is justified by reasons of health or professional motives', or when the clothing is 'part of sports activities, festivities or artistic or traditional manifestations' (art. 2, II).

Sanctions consist in fines for the wearer of up to €150, and/or participation in a citizenship course. Additionally, the Act penalizes anyone who forces another 'through threats, violence, constraint, abuse of authority or power for reason of their gender' to wear face coverings, with a fine of €30,000 and one year's imprisonment. The latter penalties can be doubled if the victim is a minor.

3.2.2 Belgium

In Belgium, the face veil issue had been on the political agenda longer than in France. The first proposal dates back to the beginning of 2004, and was submitted by the right-wing extremist Vlaams Blok party.[26] At the time, it did not lead to parliamentary discussion.

During the 2007–10 legislature various bills were submitted with the purpose of introducing a general ban. One of these was approved almost unanimously by the plenary Chamber at that time.[27] This briefly made it seem as though Belgium were poised to become the first European country to have a 'burqa ban', but the premature fall of the government meant that it did not come to this: the Senate had 'evoked'[28] the bill,

---

[24] Rapport Assemblée générale plénière du Conseil d'Etat, Etude relative aux possibilités juridiques d'interdiction du port du voile integral, 25 March 2010.

[25] Constitutional Council, 7 October 2010, no. 2010-613 DC, §5.

[26] Parliamentary documents, Senate 2003–4, no. 3-463/1 (Van dermeersch) and Chamber 2003–4, no. 51-880/1 (Van Steenberge, De Man and Laeremans).

[27] More specifically it concerned 136 ayes, 0 nays and 2 abstentions.

[28] The majority of legislative proposals in Belgium are 'optionally bicameral'. Regarding such proposals, the governing principle is that the Chamber of Representatives has the authority to approve a bill autonomously but the Senate has the right to 'evoke' the approved bill and discuss it. This so-called 'right of evocation' must be invoked within a certain term and it requires a minimum number of members.

and its approval was precluded by early dissolution of the chambers on 7 May 2010.

Various legislative proposals were once again submitted after the elections. Three of these proposals were combined and discussed.[29] The bill was approved with an overwhelming majority[30] – only by the Chamber of Representatives: the Senate opted against even discussing the bill. A large majority voted against parliamentary hearings on the matter and against the referral of the bill for advice to the Council of State.

The Act of 1 June 2011 'to institute a prohibition on wearing clothing that covers the face, or a large part of it' was published in the *Belgian Official Journal* on 13 July and entered into force ten days later. Concretely, it inserts an Article 563*bis* into the Belgian Criminal Code. In practical terms and 'subject to legal provisions to the contrary', the Article punishes persons 'who appear in places accessible to the public with their faces covered or concealed, in whole or in part, in such a manner that they are not recognizable' with a monetary fine of €15 to €25[31] and/or a prison sentence of one to seven days.[32] An exception applies when face covering is permitted or imposed by 'labour regulations or municipal ordinances due to festivities'. The law moreover enables continued application of local bans imposing administrative sanctions in this field (see above).

In Belgium too, the law was unsuccessfully challenged before the Constitutional Court, which, like the French Constitutional Council made only a minor reservation for places of worship.[33]

3.3 Developments elsewhere
In addition to the general and local bans already in place, there is a growing movement among the public and politicians in European countries to call for (general) burqa bans.

Developments towards a general country-wide ban, in the wake of France and Belgium, seem to have progressed most in Italy. After it

---

[29] I.e.: Parliamentary documents, Chamber BZ 2010, no. 53-85/1; Parliamentary documents, Chamber 2010–11, no. 53-754/1; Parliamentary documents, Chamber BZ 2010, no. 53-219/1–2.

[30] In the plenary Chamber, there were 129 ayes, 1 nay and 2 abstentions.

[31] Increased with the legal surcharge factor (i.e. multiplied by 5.5).

[32] This is a theoretical option. In the extremely unlikely event that a judge would pronounce a prison sentence rather than a fine, it would not be executed, as is the case for all prison sentences under six months in Belgium.

[33] Belgian Constitutional Court, 6 December 2012, no. 145/2012.

became apparent that the local bans could not be justified in the light of existing legislation, a number of draft laws have been tabled since 2007. The parliamentary commission on constitutional affairs approved one of these bills on 2 August 2011. This draft law would prohibit persons from being in public wearing any garment that covers the face, punishable with fines of €100 to €300. As in France, the ban would also punish individuals who force others to conceal their faces in public, with fines of €30,000 and up to twelve months in prison.[34] The bill remains pending.

In the Netherlands, the political discussion on the face veil first surfaced in response to local Belgian cases making the news in the Netherlands,[35] which led to a parliamentary motion being voted in December 2005, calling for a general ban of 'the public use of the burqa in the Netherlands'.[36] Additional motions on the issue, were adopted in October 2006 and November 2007.[37] In April 2006, the government – in pursuance to the initial motion – appointed a commission of (legal) experts.[38] Their report, published in November 2006, largely cautioned against the introduction of a general ban.[39] Nonetheless, the government at that point announced that a law on face covering would be enacted. This commitment was reaffirmed (*inter alia*) in the 2007 Government Agreement, without giving rise to legislative initiatives by government however. Bills by individual MPs were introduced in July 2007 and in November 2007,[40] but neither of these led to parliamentary debate. The subsequent Government Agreement of September 2010 again announced that the government would 'submit a

---

[34] Anonymous, 'The burqa, the law and other EU countries', www.france24.com; House of Representatives, Commission for Constitutional Affairs, draft law aimed at prohibiting the wearing of full-face veils such as the burka and the niqab. ('Divieto di indossare gli indumenti denominati burqa e niqab'), AC no. 627-A, 24 October 2011, www.camera.it/701?leg=16& file=AC0378C; see Möschel (2014).

[35] Prior to this, in 2003, the issue of the face veil had attracted some media attention when a school banned students from wearing it (Moors 2009: 396).

[36] Parliamentary documents, Chamber of Representatives, 2005–6, 29 754, no. 41; *Parliamentary Reports*, Chamber of Representatives, 2005–6, no. 36, 2546.

[37] Parliamentary documents, Chamber of Representatives, 2006–7, 29754, no. 88; Parliamentary documents, Chamber of Representatives, 2006–7, 29754, 30 545, no. 25.

[38] Parliamentary documents, Chamber of Representatives, 2006–7, 29754, no. 71.

[39] See: B. P. Vermeulen *et al.*, *Overwegingen bij een boerkaverbod* [Considerations Concerning a Burqa Ban], The Hague, 2006.

[40] The former was introduced by right-wing MP Geert Wilders (and Sietse Fritsma), and it was aimed at a 'non-neutral', general ban of the face veil only, while the latter was submitted by Liberal MP Henk Kamp, and it was aimed at a neutral, general ban. See respectively: parliamentary documents, Chamber of Representatives, 2006–7, 31 108, no. 2 (Wilders and Fritsma); Parliamentary documents, Chamber of Representatives, 2007–8, 31 331, no. 2 (Kamp).

bill concerning a general prohibition on face-covering clothing, such as burqas'.[41] A bill was introduced in Parliament in early 2012, and as in France, a negative advice of the Council of State could not deter the political majority to pursue it.[42] This was however prevented by the fall of the cabinet in April 2012 followed by elections. The new coalition included in its agreement a set of functional face-covering bans rather than a general ban.[43]

A functional ban is in existence in the German state of Hessen with respect to public servants.[44]

In Spain, the Senate, by a narrow vote, approved a motion to ban face veils and other face-covering garments in June 2010.[45] The Socialist government of Prime Minister Zapatero did not support the motion, favouring educational measures instead.[46] In July 2010, however, Spain's lower house of Parliament rejected a bill to effectively ban the wearing of face-covering garments in public.[47] At the regional level, the Catalan Parliament rejected two motions aiming to introduce a face veil ban in public spaces presented by the Popular Party on 1 July 2010 in the Plenary and on 5 April 2011 in the Commission on Welfare and Immigration.[48]

Debate is also prevalent in some Nordic countries, most notably in Denmark, with the emphasis being strongly on the principle of gender equality. In 2009 a discussion on a ban in public places erupted, after the spokesperson of one of the parties in the government coalition stated that he favoured such a ban. The Minister of the Interior subsequently set up an ad hoc committee. As discussed in Chapter 3 in this volume, the findings of the empirical research commissioned in that

---

[41] Government Agreement VVD [Liberals] – CDA [Christian Democrats], Vrijheid en verantwoordelijkheid, 29 September 2010, 26.

[42] Parliamentary document TK 33165 no. 2, 3 February 2012 (bill); the advice of the Council of State (dated 28 November 2011) is available as TK 33165 nr 4.

[43] Bans are proposed in the fields of education, health care and public transportation, as well as for access to government buildings. Those wearing face coverings are also obliged to show the face for identification purposes and are excluded from welfare payments (see coalition agreement, 29 October 2012, www.rijksoverheid.nl/documenten-en-publicaties/rapporten/2012/10/29/regeerakkoord.html).

[44] M. Mahlmann, 'Flash-report – Prohibition of the burka in the Land Hessen', available at www.non-discrimination.net/content/media/DE-29–2011%20Burqa.pdf

[45] The vote consisted of 131 ayes and 129 nays.

[46] R. Minder, 'Spain's Senate votes to ban burqa', New York Times, 24 June 2010.

[47] By a vote of 183 nays to 162 ayes, with two abstentions.

[48] Amnesty International (2012: 98).

context – namely that the number of women wearing the face veil was very small, and that many were Danish converts – put an end to plans for a ban. Yet the penalty for anyone who forces someone else to cover his or her face has been increased to four years' imprisonment.[49]

Switzerland likewise refrained from legislating on the issue, at least at the federal level. In September 2012, the Swiss Senate rejected by 93 votes to 87 an initiative aiming at banning full face veiling from public spaces, an initiative that was proposed by the canton of Aargau.[50] Yet the canton of Ticino voted in a referendum in September 2013 to ban face covering in public.[51] Yet proposed bans were rejected in the cantonal parliaments of Basel City, Bern, Schwyz, Solothurn and Fribourg.[52]

In Austria as well, prominent politicians have called to ban face veils.[53] Yet thus far no legislative initiatives have been taken in the country that would lead to a ban.

Even in the United Kingdom, a private member's bill to ban face covering in public was discussed in Parliament in autumn 2013. While the issue does not fail to generate vigorous debate in the UK, the case for a ban never gathered broad political support, as described in Chapter 5 this volume.

4. THE EMPIRICAL STUDIES AND THEIR PRESENTATION IN THIS VOLUME

Part I of this book presents the results of empirical research among women who wear/wore a face veil in five European countries: Belgium, Denmark, France, the Netherlands and the United Kingdom. These studies were conducted by different research teams at different times and in different contexts. The Danish and Dutch studies were commissioned by the government of those countries in a context in which they were considering the possible adoption of a ban on face covering. Both reports

---

[49] W. Fautré, 'Is the Burqa Compatible with Women's Rights? The "Burqa Issue" in the EU', paper presented at the conference Burqa and Women's Rights and the European Parliament, Brussels, 10 June 2010.

[50] Swissinfo.ch Swiss news World Wide, 28 September 2012.

[51] The referendum obtained a 65.4 per cent majority. The federal Parliament will have to decide on the constitutionality of the rule. www.swissinfo.ch/ita/politica/Il_Ticino_mette_al_bando_il_burqa_nella_costituzione.html?cid=36936130

[52] Swissinfo.ch Swiss news worldwide, 12 August 2013.

[53] Anonymous, 'Minister Hahn möchte die Burka verbieten: Für Verbannung aus dem öffentlichen Raum', News.at, 18 April 2008.

were published in 2009. The French study was an initiative of the Open Society Foundations' at Home in Europe Project, reacting to (the process leading up to) the face veil ban in France. The research began in October 2010 and the results were presented in April 2011, the month in which the ban entered into effect. The Belgian study was likewise a reaction – this time by an academic actor – to the political rush towards a face veil ban in that country. The interviews in Belgium were conducted between September 2010 and September 2011. The study was presented in May 2012. Finally, the UK study was another initiative of the Open Society Foundations, conducted in 2011, and not yet published at the time of writing (end 2013). While both the research questions and the context were thus slightly different for each study – in particular with respect to the existence or imminence of a ban – the methodologies are similar, based mainly on qualitative analysis of semi-structured interviews, as is common in socio-legal research.

The raw data from the interviews in the five countries show very strong similarities. This is first of all the case with respect to the background of the women who wear the face veil. Contrary to what a section of public opinion seems to assume, these are not recent immigrants who had been wearing the face veil in their countries of origin. The large majority of the interviewees are women who are born in Europe or who have lived there for most of their lives, with a significant number of converts among them. Moreover, the similarities among the research results are striking in a number of crucial fields. One concerns the credible assertion by all interviewees that they wear the face veil as a matter of free choice in their personal religious journey. Another is the finding that the face veil does not indicate a withdrawal from society. These women interact not only with family, friends and neighbours, they do not shy away from interactions with teachers, shop-keepers and any other people they come across in daily life. Mention should be made however of the recurring testimonies of harassment and abuse of women who wear the face veil in public places by anonymous people. Such experiences were frequent already before the 'burqa ban' debates, yet appear to have increased since. Finally, across the countries, niqabis express their frustration at their misrepresentation in public and political discourse, in particular concerning the assumption of submission.

In some respects, the data on the United Kingdom show differences from those of Belgium, Denmark, France and the Netherlands. In the latter countries, the decision to start wearing a face veil is generally a highly individual one, as many women did not know any niqabis personally before starting to cover their face. Moreover, these decisions are often met with disapproval in their close environment. In the United Kingdom, most niqabis had relatives or friends who wore the face veil before they did, and hence met with less disapproval. Moreover – probably as a result of a more tolerant environment – niqabis in the UK show significantly higher levels of education and of employment than those in the other countries.

While the substance of the empirical findings is thus very similar for the five countries that were studied, the presentation in this book is not. Opting against repetitiveness, the authors were invited to present their research in context and from the angle they judged most relevant. Hence, all empirical chapters include very pertinent information on the political context surrounding the 'burqa debate' in the respective countries. Moreover, building on the strengths and the broader work of each researcher or research team, each chapter comes with its own extras. The Danish chapter includes a reflection on quantitative research attempting to count Denmark's niqabis. The Dutch chapter includes Annelies Moors's analysis of the public and political debates about face veiling in the Netherlands as contestations about the definition of Dutchness. The chapter on Belgium confronts the experiences of niqabis with the assumptions of the Belgian legislator. And the chapter by Naima Bouteldja compares the experiences of women wearing a face veil in France and England.

For Part II, scholars who were working on the face issue – without having knowledge of the empirical data – were invited to write a comment on the face veil debate after familiarizing themselves with these data. Each author adopts a different angle, in line with her or his expertise and previous work on the matter. All contributors reject general face veil bans, albeit not all for the same reasons. Indeed, even without access to empirical data about the motives and experiences of women who wear the face veil, the very large majority of scholars working on this issue reject such bans. The confrontation with the empirical material led some authors to put the gap between empirical reality and public or political discourse at the heart of their analysis. Others refer to the empirical findings in support of some of their arguments or use them as a canvas on which to draw their critique. Together, these comments offer a fine sample of scholarly arguments rejecting face veil bans, and of the relevance of insider arguments for such arguments.

For legal scholars and theorists, empirical data allow the authors to improve the accuracy and pertinence of their arguments. Yet what the volume in its entirety makes clear above all is that the real challenge is addressed to policy makers. Policy making on the basis of unchecked assumptions and in disregard of reality may – and in the 'burqa ban' experience does – result in policies that are ineffective, counterproductive and at odds with the fundamental rights and values they claim to advance.

REFERENCES

Amnesty International. 2012. 'Choice and Prejudice: Discrimination against Muslims in Europe', at: www.amnesty.org/en/library/info/EUR01/001/2012.

Brems, Eva, Ouald Chaib, Saïla and Vrielink, Jogchum 2013. 'Uncovering French and Belgian Face Covering Bans', *Journal of Law, Religion and State* 2, 69–99.

Moors, A. 2009. 'The Dutch and the Face-veil: The Politics of Discomfort', *Social Anthropology/Antropologie Sociale* 17(4): 393–406.

Möschel, M. 2011. 'Veiled Issues in European Courts', in Giulia Calvi and Nadia Fadil (eds.), *Politics of Diversity. Sexual and Religious Self – Fashioning in Contemporary and Historical Contexts* EUI Working Papers, HEC 2011/01, 8–9.

2014. 'La burqa en Italie: d'une politique locale à une législation nationale', in O. Roy and D. Koussens (eds.), *Quand la burqa passe à l'Ouest. Enjeux éthiques, politiques et juridiques*, Presses universitaires de Rennes, coll. Sciences religieuses, pp. 237–50.

Vrielink, Jogchum, Ouald Chaib, Saïla and Brems, Eva 2011. 'Boerkaverbod. Juridische aspecten van lokale en algemene verboden op gezichtsverhulling in België', *Nieuw Juridisch Weekblad* 244: 398–414.

Vrielink, Jogchum, Ouald Chaib, Saïla and Brems, Eva 2013. 'The Belgian 'Burqa Ban': Legal Aspects of Local and General Prohibitions on Covering and Concealing One's Face in Belgium', in Alessandro Ferrari and Sabrina Pastorelli (eds.), *The Burqa Affair across Europe: Between Public and Private Space*. Farnham: Ashgate, pp. 143–70.

PART I

WEARING THE FACE VEIL IN EUROPE

2

FACE VEILING IN THE NETHERLANDS: PUBLIC DEBATES AND WOMEN'S NARRATIVES

Annelies Moors

In the course of the last decade, many countries in Europe have witnessed debates about face veiling and in some cases efforts have been made to implement local, functional or general bans.[1] The Netherlands is a particularly interesting case. It was the first country in Europe where in December 2005 a parliamentary majority voted in favour of banning face coverings from all public space. Whereas such strong position against face veiling may have been expected in France, where in 2004 the wearing of headscarves in public schools had already been prohibited, by contrast, in the Netherlands such a ban was without any related precedent and all the more unexpected for that.[2] In this contribution, I start with a brief summary that traces how face veiling has emerged in the Netherlands as an issue that has evoked strong anxieties.[3] Next to the unexpected and rapid emergence of face veiling as a topic of public debate and policy making, there is also another element that needs to be considered. Those voicing strong opinions about the undesirability of face veiling in public would often simultaneously state that they had no idea who these women were or

---

[1] For an overview, see Grillo and Shah (2012). France implemented a ban on wearing face coverings in public on 11 April 2011 and Belgium did so on 23 July 2011.

[2] There are considerable differences in how the state governs Islam in the Netherlands and in France. Whereas in the Dutch case girls are allowed to wear headscarves in public schools because it may be considered a religious practice, in France they are not allowed to do so because headscarves are seen as an ostentatious religious sign (Scott 2007; Bowen 2007).

[3] Moors (2009a) describes and analyses face-veiling cases and debates in the Netherlands in more detail.

what motivated them to wear a face veil. The main part of this contribution then focuses on how the narratives of women who, at the time, engaged in face veiling, relate to assumptions about face veiling in public and political debate.[4] After a brief note on the backgrounds of the women concerned, I turn to two fields of debate that were the central focus of contestations between policy makers and face-veiling women. These were, first, the ways in which Islam was presented in relation to 'the position of women', and, second, how references to 'subjective feelings' evoked by face veiling have been employed in law making.

1. FACE VEILING AND THE CULTURALIZATION OF POLITICS

Between 2000 and 2005 the Netherlands witnessed dramatic shifts in policy making about face veiling, both in terms of the substance and scope of bans on face veiling and with respect to the motivations for such legal restrictions. One way to trace such transformations is by analysing the advisory rulings of the Equal Treatment Commission and the subsequent attempts at policy making at the national level.[5] The turn of the millennium functions as a convenient baseline for such an analysis, as it was in the year 2000 that the Equal Treatment Commission produced its first ruling about face coverings. In this case, concerning a student enrolled in a training programme for pharmacy assistants, the Commission concluded that there was no objective justification for a prohibition, as wearing a face veil 'leaves sufficient possibilities for communication' (including non-verbal forms). To this the Commission added that the school should take into consideration that 'in a multicultural society as the Netherlands not all groups in society

---

[4] This contribution builds on a Dutch-language report (Moors 2009b) that was subsidized by the Ministry of Housing, Communities and Integration. The report was made publicly available as a parliamentary document on 4 November 2009 (https://zoek.officielebekendmakingen.nl/blg-38040.html). Methods used were a discourse analysis of newspaper articles, official documents and political talk as well as ethnographic fieldwork with policy makers and face-veiling women. Unless mentioned otherwise, all websites mentioned in this chapter were last accessed on 20 March 2013.

[5] The Equal Treatment Commission monitored compliance with the Dutch Equal Treatment Act, which prohibits discrimination in education and employment on grounds such as religion, sex, race and political orientation. It does so by responding to complaints in the format of a non-binding ruling that carries considerable weight in court cases. On 2 October 2012 this Commission became part of the Netherlands Institute for Human Rights www.mensenrechten.nl.

show their feelings through facial expression'.[6] Neither the media nor politicians paid particular attention to this case and there was no public or political debate.

Within three years this had dramatically changed. In January 2003 face veiling became an issue of intense public debate when three Moroccan-Dutch students who had started to wear a face veil were refused entry to a school for vocation training and adult education.[7] This time, the Equal Treatment Commission came to a very different conclusion. It supported the line of argumentation of the school that its ruling did not target a particular religion, because it prohibited *any type* of face covering and accepted its objective justifications that it impedes communication, hinders identification and hence poses a security risk, and strongly diminishes the girls' chances for internships and future employment.[8] Political parties on the right and on the left as well as Muslim associations supported the right of individual schools to include a ban on face coverings in their regulations.

Whereas at the time no one had indicated that there were moves afoot to proscribe face coverings in public at the national level, a good two years later, the situation was again very different. In December 2005, when Geert Wilders tabled a resolution 'to prohibit the public use of the burqa in the Netherlands', a parliamentary majority consisting of right-wing parties and the Christian Democrats voted in favour of this resolution.[9] The arguments Wilders presented to justify such a ban also differed substantially from those used in the case of the Amsterdam educational institution in 2003. They included that the burqa is a symbol of women's oppression and hence inhumane, that it is unacceptable that people appear in public who cannot be identified, and that it widens the gap between the native Dutch and others.[10] Although a commission of experts, installed to investigate whether such a law could be enacted expressed strong doubts, with the possible exception of a proportional ban on face coverings in the case of a security threat, in November 2006 the then Minister of Alien Affairs and Integration

---

[6] CGB case no. 2000-63, www.mensenrechten.nl/publicaties/oordelen/2000-63. All translations from the Dutch are the author's.

[7] For an analysis of how face-veiling became media hype at particular moments, see Moors (2009a).

[8] CGB case no. 2003-40, www.mensenrechten.nl/publicaties/oordelen/2000–40.

[9] Wilders did so as an independent MP. By then he had left the right-wing Liberal Party (VVD), because the latter had, in his eyes, not taken a sufficiently strong stance against negotiations with Turkey about EU membership.

[10] Parliamentary document TK 29754, no. 41.

expressed her intention to implement a general ban as soon as possible.[11] These actions of politicians in 2005 and 2006 drew tremendous media attention and made face veiling a main topic of public and political debate.

How did face veiling, a practice that only a few hundred women engaged in and a non-issue at the turn of the millennium, turn into such a major national concern? To better understand this rapid change, a longer-term perspective is called for. Attempts to ban the face veil are part of an ongoing process of the culturalization of politics. Next to the long-standing European history of distrust of Islam, two trends that occurred almost simultaneously in the course of the 1980s need to be mentioned briefly. Whereas by then it had become evident that the 'guest workers' of the 1960s had come to stay, family reunification coincided with economic restructuring, and a rapid increase in unemployment especially in those sectors in which migrants had been employed. Hence, their presence was no longer seen as a solution to labour shortages but had become a societal problem. At roughly the same time, Islamic revivalist movements had emerged on a global scale – as evident in the Islamic Revolution in Iran in 1979 – and Islam was becoming a more important societal force. As a result, post-migrants from Muslim-majority countries such as Turkey and Morocco were increasingly addressed as Muslims, with some also self-defining as such. Such a religious identification was deemed particularly problematic in the Netherlands, because of its late but very rapid process of deconfessionalization of the 1960s. The public presence of Islam signified for some a return to the ancient regime of a pillarized society they felt they or their parents had freed themselves from (Van der Veer 2006).[12]

An effect of these two trends – migrants considered as a problem and increasingly defined as Muslims – was that Islam came to be seen as the root cause of a wide range of societal problems. In the course of the 1990s some mainstream politicians in the Netherlands had already started to

---

[11] The commission of experts concluded that a general or specific prohibition on the burqa would be discriminatory, that a *general* prohibition on all face coverings could not be justified on objective grounds, as there were already sufficient options to forbid face coverings in particular settings and circumstances. It added that a prohibition might also have the effect of stigmatizing Muslims and polarizing the relations between Muslims and non-Muslims (Vermeulen 2006).

[12] 'Pillarization' refers to the segregation of society along confessional and ideological lines ('pillars'), with the elites from each pillar cooperating in political administration (Lijphart 1968).

publicly speak about Islam as incompatible with European values.[13] Moreover, it was by the end of the twentieth century that a populist, neo-nationalist anti-Islam movement started to gain ground, arguing that the way of life of the majority population was under threat of Islamization. Its protagonists, distancing themselves from the Dutch consensual form of governance and from what they called multicultural political correctness, introduced a far more confrontational political style, through which they claimed to express the emotions and senti-ments of 'ordinary autochthonous (native Dutch) people'. Pim Fortuyn was an early exponent of this trend, whose popularity skyrocketed after the 9/11 terror attacks that were the starting point of the global 'war on terror'.[14] His murder in May 2002 by an animal rights activist a few days before the national elections, and the enormous election victory of the List Pim Fortuyn, caused a political landslide. In the years to come, mainstream political parties also increasingly took up an anti-Islam stance.

Simultaneously, the first years of the twenty-first century also marked a major turn in Dutch security discourse and policy making. It is true that already in the 1990s the Netherlands had started to witness a gradual securitization of society with a shift from objective measures towards subjective feelings of security (De Graaf 2011; Cesari 2009), whereas with the fall of the Berlin Wall Islam had already replaced communism as a major global threat in the eyes of the Western powers. Still, it was the terrorist attacks of 9/11 that placed security issues on top of the political agenda, foregrounding the threat of Islam. After the murder of Theo van Gogh in November 2004 by a Moroccan-Dutch young man who claimed to have done so on religious grounds, and other major terrorist incidents in Europe, a host of anti-terrorist meas-ures were very rapidly enacted. It was no coincidence that Geert Wilders made his first statement in Parliament about a general ban on face

---

[13] A major turning point was Frits Bolkestein's speech at the Liberal International in Luzern in 1991, in which he asserted the incompatibility of Islam and Western, liberal values (NRC, 21 September 1991), another was Paul Scheffer's article 'The multicultural drama' in which this prominent Labour Party ideologue considers Islam as the main reason for the failure of the integration of minorities (NRC, 29 January 2000).

[14] Pim Fortuyn had already published his *Tegen de Islamisering van onze samenleving* ('Against the Islamization of our society') in 1997. Half a decade after his murder, two members of the right-wing Liberal party each started their own political movement. Geert Wilders established his Party for Freedom in February 2006 and Rita Verdonk her movement Proud of the Netherlands in October 2007.

veiling during a debate on the radicalization of Muslims.[15] In other words, the rapid escalation of an anti face-veiling discourse and the sweeping attempts to ban these, need to be seen in a context that had become increasingly Muslim unfriendly, with the relations between Muslims and non-Muslims strongly polarized and increasingly framed by the securitization of Islam.

Still, it would take another seven years before a law to ban face coverings from all public space was ready to be presented in Parliament. In early 2007 new elections had brought a centre-left coalition cabinet to power. This coalition government did not support the idea of a general ban, but instead worked towards a number of functional bans (in education, health, public transport and for civil servants) using as its main argument the need for open communication to maintain the rule of law. The fact that also this centre-left cabinet persisted in implementing multiple functional bans at the national level (rather than leaving it up to the authorities concerned) points to the impact of the rapidly growing anti-Islam neo-nationalist parties on mainstream politics.[16] At the same time, this continued preoccupation with face veiling also needs to be located in the broader context of shifts in Dutch identity making. In the course of the last decade, Dutch policy makers on the right and on the left have increasingly agreed on the fact that post-migrants will only integrate if the Dutch national identity is more firmly established. The net result is that public discourse and national policy making have become more explicitly assimilationist, placing increasingly high demands on Muslims in particular to prove their belonging to the nation and their loyalty to the state.[17] When a new centre-right minority government came to power in 2010, after concluding an agreement of support with Geert Wilders's Party for

[15] Parliamentary document TK 29754, no. 41, 19 October 2005. At the time, face veils were not yet a topic of public debate. When in September 2005 Wilders stated in an interview that he was planning to table his resolution, the reporter added, 'Until now there has not been a discussion about face-veils on the streets' (*De Telegraaf*, 10 September 2005).

[16] Wilders's Party for Freedom was one of the main winners of the 2007 elections, while Rita Verdonk had started Proud of the Netherlands in October 2007 and rapidly gained a large following. Polls held in April 2008 indicated that if there had been elections then her party would have been one of the largest in Parliament. *De Volkskrant* (5 April 2008) summarized her party programme with a headline over the full width of the front page as 'The death penalty, the *burqa*, and more highways'. For the turn to neo-nationalism in Europe, see Gingrich (2006).

[17] Citizenship was increasingly defined in terms of shared values rather than with respect to legal rights and obligations. For the culturalization of citizenship in the Netherlands, see, for instance, Geschiere (2009); Verkaaik (2010).

Freedom (at the time the third largest political party), a general ban on face coverings was again included in the coalition agreement. This cabinet's 2011 Memorandum of Integration officially declared the end of Dutch multicultural society.[18] It considered Dutch society as a community of citizens with a shared language, values and beliefs, that is grounded in a fundamental continuity of values, beliefs, institutions and habits, which shape 'the leading culture', and to which those who settle in the Netherlands need to adapt. Face veiling is considered a cause of discomfort and hence an issue where the legislature needs to act normatively. In spite of strongly negative advice from the Council of State, by February 2012 the cabinet agreed on a ban on face coverings in all public space to start on 1 January 2013.[19] However, new elections brought a new coalition government to power, that includes the social democrats who previously had expressed a preference for functional bans. Instead of a general ban, the latest coalition agreement includes a more extensive version of such functional bans.[20]

2. A NOTE ON THE WOMEN CONCERNED: NUMBERS AND CHARACTERISTICS

When policy makers and those participating in public debate turned their attention to the women wearing a face veil, their first concern was the number of women concerned. References were often made to numbers that were already circulating, which generally ranged from 50–100 to 200–400.[21] On the basis of my extensive search for face-veiling women, it is indeed likely that at the time the range was somewhere between 100–400. This may seem a wide margin of error, but it is well worth realizing that even if the number were 500, this still means that on average only 3 in 100,000

[18] For a critique of the idea of a 'singular, coherent and consistent Dutch multicultural model', see Duyvendak and Scholten (2012: 277).

[19] The draft law entails a general prohibition on face coverings, parliamentary document TK 33165 no. 2 (3 February 2012); the advice of the Council of State (dated 28 November 2011) and the reaction of the cabinet are available as TK 33165 nr 4.

[20] Bans are proposed in the fields of education, health care and public transportation, as well as in access to government buildings. Those wearing face coverings are also obliged to show the face for identification purposes and are excluded from welfare payments (see coalition agreement, 29 October 2012, www.rijksoverheid.nl/documenten-en-publicaties/rapporten/2012/10/29/regeer akkoord.html).

[21] The estimate of 50–100 is mentioned in the Vermeulen (2006) report, the estimate of 200–400 is mentioned in an article by Samira Dahri (who wears a face veil herself) and her husband Suhayb Salam (a well-known salafi preacher), dated 15 December 2006 (www.niqaab.org, downloaded 15 January 2009).

inhabitants of the Netherlands wear a face veil. Moreover, it is likely that the difference between the lower and higher estimate depends on how the category of face-veiling women is delineated. Individual women wear face veils with different levels of consistency. Whereas they generally acknowledge the rule that a woman needs to wear a face veil if in the company of non-mahram men, only a small number is willing or able to follow this rule consistently; many more recognize that they do not always do so. Some wear a face veil most of the time, but allow for exceptions, such as, for instance, when they visit their parents, or when their school or employer prohibits face veiling. Others only wear a face veil at particular occasions, such as when they visit the mosque. The lower estimate would then only include those who wear it fairly consistently, whereas the higher also includes the part-timers.[22]

In debates about face veiling, time and again politicians made a host of statements about the women concerned, yet also recognized, sometimes in the very same sentence, that they did not know who these women were. In general, they tended to assume that face-veiling women were recent migrants from disadvantaged backgrounds, unable to speak Dutch and poorly educated. On the basis of my research, it is evident that many face-veiling women did not fit this picture. It is, of course, impossible to claim that such vulnerable migrants were absent among face-veiling women. Neither is it possible to draw a representative sample, as the total population of face-veiling women is unknown.[23] However, because of the relatively large number of women I was able to trace, both off-line and on-line, it is evident that many of them had a very different background.

The large majority of the women I talked with had either converted to Islam ('new Muslims') or were Moroccan-Dutch women who had largely been raised and educated in the Netherlands. In addition to white, ethnically Dutch women, the category of the converts also included women whose parents had come from Suriname, the Caribbean, Latin

[22] Moreover, for many women wearing a face veil is a particular phase in their religious life cycle. Some only do it for a very brief period, 'for fun' or to try it out, and do not continue. Others move more consistently towards increasingly covered styles of dress, with a face veil as the last item added. Some may at a certain moment again move away from fully covering.

[23] Instead, I used a modified snowball sample, with the first women interviewed referring me to others in their off-line and on-line networks. This also gave me a sense of whether and how they were connected to each other. Aware of the risk that the women interviewed would be a particular subcategory of the total population, I tried to speak with as broad a range of women as possible, working with my personal and professional networks but also approaching them directly on-line. I had extensive conversations with over twenty women. In many cases, we also had contact through email, and I was able to follow some of them on-line.

America or South-East Asia. This fits well with the results of other research projects, with the information face-veiling women themselves presented to me, and with the information I gathered on-line.[24] It is true that references were also made to Egyptian, Somali, Turkish, Tunisian, Pakistani and Afghan women wearing a face veil, but in comparison to the converts and the Moroccan-Dutch women, their number was very small. Occasionally someone would refer to a new migrant wearing a face veil, but they were few and far between. It is far more common for women who wore a face veil in their country of origin, such as, for instance, Yemen, to take it off when travelling to Europe (Moors 2007). Whereas they often would wear a face veil back home because this was common practice in their social circle, doing so in the Netherlands had the very opposite effect of drawing a host of unwanted attention and making one stand out in the crowd.

As the face-veiling women I talked with had mostly grown up in the Netherlands, their knowledge of Dutch was not an issue. Their level of education varied widely, about one-third had university-level education, about one-quarter had no more than the lowest level of vocational training, and the remainder fitted somewhere in between. Their current or, more often, earlier fields of employment similarly varied from unskilled work in agriculture and production or services such as cleaning and call-centre work, to various forms of administrative work, and professional employment as legal clerks or educational trainers. They varied in age from 17 to 40, with about half between 21 and 30, about one-third under 21 and a few above 30. Half of them were married at the time of research, one-quarter was single and one-quarter divorced; a little over half of them were responsible for young children. Most of them were from a working-class or lower middle-class background, a few had Moroccan-Dutch fathers who were self-employed, and a few converts were from an upper middle-class background. Most of the new Muslims had parents who had grown up in a Christian or Jewish environment but were no longer actively practising their religion. Most born Muslims referred to their parents as 'cultural Muslims', whose religiosity was, in their eyes, far more structured through the

---

[24] Fakhrunissa (2005a) did a small pilot project as junior fellow at ISIM (International Institute for the Study of Islam in the Modern World). Most of the women she talked with were also either Dutch converts or Moroccan-Dutch women. Vroon-Najem's ongoing work on women converts indicates that next to white, ethnically Dutch women, there is a considerable group of post-colonial and other migrants present among converts.

culture of their country of origin than by knowledge of the foundational texts. The women often lived in migrant neighbourhoods, not only in the large cities of Amsterdam, Rotterdam and The Hague, but also in smaller towns in the middle and the south of the country. All in all, these women can hardly be considered as a specific social category. There was, however, one element they had in common. To them wearing a face veil was part and parcel of their commitment to become a better Muslim.

3. ISLAM AND WOMEN'S SUBORDINATION

Before elaborating on how the women concerned consider face veiling as part of their religious project, I first analyse how Islam figures in public debates and policy making. In the 2003 Amsterdam case those arguing in favour of a ban on school premises were very careful not to make any references to religion. Rather than using face veil or a specifically Islamic term, such as niqab or burqa, they opted for the neutral term 'face coverings', a term that also includes secular practices, such as the use of visor helmets. Also their lines of argumentation, referring to face coverings as an obstacle to communication and a security risk, purposely did not touch upon religion. Such a neutral language of a ban on face coverings was used, because otherwise it would infringe on the constitutional right of freedom of religion.[25]

This reluctance to link face coverings to Islam in official texts came to an abrupt end when Geert Wilders tabled his resolution in 2005, and explicitly referred to the burqa and the niqab rather than to face coverings in general. Moreover, Muslim women's oppression was a central argument he provided for a ban. In his 2007 proposal for a law, he elaborated further on this, stating that he considered the burqa as 'an expression of the rejection of essential Western values, including the equality of men and women', as 'a symbol of the oppression of women, irrespective whether the burqa or the niqab is worn by force or by choice', and as 'an obstacle for the emancipation and integration of women in Dutch society.' In his view, then, 'a prohibition of the burqa

[25] If the school had used a term referring to the Islamic face veil, it would be a case of *direct* discrimination on the basis of religion, for which no justification is allowed. It is true that when the secular term face coverings is used, this may still be considered *indirect* discrimination on the basis of religion, as it disproportionately affects those who adhere to a particular religious conviction. Indirect discrimination, however, is allowed if an 'objective justification' makes such a ruling necessary.

advances the emancipation and autonomy of Muslim women', and can put an end to the 'social pressure' that their social environment may exert on them.[26]

Emphasizing the link between the proposed ban and Muslim women's subordination, Wilders made explicit what were, in fact, commonly held assumptions about face veiling. It is evident that face coverings had been turned into a political issue because Muslim women were involved, as it is this link between act and actor that turns covering the face into a sign of gender inequality. And it was not only Geert Wilders who linked the face veil to women's subordination. In its 2008 letter to Parliament, in which it proposed functional bans, the cabinet stated that face coverings are 'often considered as woman-unfriendly and to many these are a symbol of a fundamentalist Islam that does not suit Dutch society'.[27] The Explanatory Memorandum to the Draft Law of 2012, prohibiting face coverings in all public space, further elaborates on the relation between face coverings, Islam, and women's subordination. It briefly mentions that 'certain orthodox trends', 'a small minority in Islam', may consider covering the face as a religious requirement (2012: 5).[28] It then claims that a ban is nonetheless legitimate because it protects an important element of public order, the equivalence of men and women. The fact that women (and not men) need to conceal themselves is seen as an expression of a non-equivalent position in public life, as 'in our society covering the face is a symbol of women's subordination to men'. Moreover, covering the face would hinder women's participation in society and is an obstacle for women to exert their social and economic human rights on an equal footing with men. In addition, as the memorandum stated, a prohibition will also protect those women who may cover their faces because of physical or social pressure from their environment.[29]

---

[26] Parliamentary document TK 2007/08 31 108 (12 July 2007). These arguments are similar to those used in France in 2004 to prohibit headscarves in public schools (Asad 2006; Bowen 2007: 208ff.). Wilders presented his draft law as he considered the functional bans the cabinet was planning to propose as too limited.

[27] Parliamentary document TK 2007/08 31 200 VII, no. 48, 8 February 2008.

[28] In an earlier public statement, Minister Donner had argued that he considered face veiling as a cultural or regional style of dress, rather than one related to Islam, apparently following the French President Sarkozy who in his speech to Parliament in 2009, stated that the burqa is 'not a sign of religion, it is a sign of subservience'. As such, direct state interference in the substance of a religion goes, however, against the grain of Dutch secularism (see Moors 2011a); this line of argumentation was quickly abandoned.

[29] Parliamentary document TK 33165 no. 3, 6 February 2012.

In short, two interrelated moves are evident in the ways in which Islam and gender are at stake in public and political debate. The first attempts to ban face veiling (the 2003 Amsterdam school) purposely left Islam out of the equation and no references were made to women's subjugation. Within a few years that had changed. Islam was explicitly targeted and face veiling had turned into a symbol, sign or tool for women's subjugation. In the years to come such references to Islam have remained there to stay. It is evident that whereas the 2012 Draft Law used the secular term face coverings, it has incorporated many of the arguments Wilders had presented earlier against wearing 'the Islamic burqa and niqab'.

In the narratives of the women themselves, in contrast, religion is not only central stage but also linked to highly positive connotations. As the women themselves explained, it is true that young girls sometimes put on the face veil 'for fun' and to try out its effects, but if that is their only motivation, they also quickly give it up again. For those who wear a face veil with some level of consistency, Islam is a strong motivation force. Whereas their narratives differed in terms of their specific sartorial practices and the speed with which they had changed their public appearance, they all used a strongly religious discourse to explain how they had moved towards longer, looser and more covering styles of dress, with the face veil as 'the last step' or 'something extra'.

Discussing the relation between Islam and dress, the women themselves consider wearing covered styles of dress, including a face veil, not so much an expression of an Islamic identity (although it may be that too), but first and foremost as a recommended or obligatory religious practice. To them such sartorial changes were part of a longer-term process in which piety becomes increasingly central in their lives. Moreover, taking up face veiling could not simply be reduced to the desire to conceal one's body from the gaze of men. The women underlined that to them wearing a face veil is above all an act of worship and a means to express their love for God. 'It is a way to get closer to God, it is a way to experience again the intense feeling of being in love with Islam', explained one of the Dutch converts. 'At some moment I wanted to do more, something extra, to experience again that intense feeling of being in love with Islam. I thought I would get that again with a face veil.' Wearing a face veil had a strong positive effect on them. Some used a highly spiritual language to describe this, using terms such as experiencing a sense of 'floating through the air', or referring to 'experiencing a feeling of inner peace'. Others would point to how wearing a face veil made them feel good, 'I felt really, wow, this is it. I felt strong.' The latter may also refer to having been able to overcome many obstacles. At the same time, they also explained how they experienced face veiling as a self-disciplinary practice, as a means to produce particular feelings and sensations and to shape their actions. As a Moroccan-Dutch woman said, 'when you wear a face veil you are not only more at peace with yourself, more quiet, but you also act that way'. After all, 'if you wear a *niqab* you should not hang around and talk loudly, that does not go together with wearing a face veil, even if there are some sisters who do so'.[30]

Talking about their move towards face veiling, the women strongly distanced themselves from any suggestion of physical or social pressure. Instead they framed their motivations in terms of affective experiences as well as with reference to the importance of acquiring Islamic knowledge. Some women stated that they had started to cover and then to wear the face veil because of an intensely felt need to do so, that they could not explain, 'that is why it is called belief, not knowledge'. For others it was through learning about Islam that they understood that they needed to change their styles of dress. As one of them said, 'I always said, it is important that religion is in the heart. Now I know that what is in the heart is also reflected in your appearance. It starts with the heart, but if the interior is fully committed to religion, then your appearance will follow suit.' Whereas some appreciated a literalist interpretation of the central texts and followed the opinions of salafi religious scholars, they all agreed that, because there is a difference of opinion among Islamic scholars whether wearing a face veil is obligatory or not, they had to use their own judgement about this issue and to evaluate the evidence themselves. Yet, as many said, 'even if it is not obligatory, it is a good deed'. Moreover, it is because many consider it as recommended rather than obligatory, that they experience face veiling as 'doing something extra'. ✈

Many – not only the new Muslims but also the born Muslims – highlighted that they had gone through a 'process of conversion' in order to find true Islam. They pointed out that it was crucially important that in order for face veiling to work as an act of worship, one needed to wear it with a pure intention. In the words of one of them, 'Everything you do, needs to be based on a pure intention, that means that you only

---

[30] Compare Mahmood (2005) for women in the piety movement in Egypt.

do it for Allah and not, for instance, because of social pressure or because it is a trend.' Such an emphasis on the importance of acting with the right intention and on the basis of religious conviction tallies with the liberal discourse of wearing a face veil as a conscious choice, and stands in stark contrast with the portrayal of face-veiling women as doing so because of pressure from their environment. In fact, their narratives time and again highlight how their families as well as their husbands try to convince them not to cover their face, sometimes because they fear for their safety. The women themselves find this often hard to deal with because they consider having a good relation with (and some would say being obedient to) one's parents and husband as important Islamic virtues. Still one's obedience to God is more important. In order to reconcile their desire to wear a face veil as a form of worship with the reluctance of their kin and husbands, they develop a wide range of in-between forms. Some simply do not wear the face veil if they visit their parents. As a Dutch convert said, 'It was already difficult enough for them that I had become Muslim, it really would have been too much if I showed up wearing a face veil'. Or they adapted their styles of dress in another way. 'You will never see a Dutch Muslima wearing black when she visits her parents, we all wear lighter colours then.'

At the same time, they also complicate notions of freedom and emancipation when they point to the double standards that prevail in secular arguments about face veils as a sign or mechanism of women's oppression. Whereas the 2012 Explanatory Memorandum states that face veiling hinders women's exertion of their social and economic human rights and their participation in society, the women concerned are of the opinion that, on the contrary, prohibiting face veiling is not only an infringement of their freedom of religion, but also of their right as women to choose how to appear in the public. When discussing policy makers' argument that a ban would support women who are forced to wear a face veil, they do not only argue that forcing a woman to cover would not have any religious merit, but they join other participants in the debate who argue that such a ban would only marginalize these women further, excluding them from access to education, health care, public transport or, in the case of a general ban, all public space. Moreover, they consider themselves as active participants in society. It is true that for many of them, care for the family, especially when they have small children, and gaining more religious knowledge are more important than outside employment and a career. However, as they point out, there are other categories of women who similarly opt not to work outside the house when they have small children and for whom immaterial, religious values are more important than paid employment, yet they are not similarly targeted.

4. THE SHIFT TO SUBJECTIVE FEELINGS

Although references to Muslim women's subjugation were common in public debate, they were not the most central argument used in parliamentary deliberations. In that case concerns about security and communication were the most prevalent. Already in the 2003 case at the Amsterdam school security risks and problems with communication were used as objective grounds to ban face coverings. Both Wilders and the right-wing liberal party had not agreed with the new cabinet's plans for functional bans and came with their own proposals to implement a general ban on face covering. Yet whereas Wilders used Islamic terms and linked wearing a face veil to women's oppression in his draft law, the right-wing liberal party used the secular term face coverings and focused on covering the face as a security threat when it proposed to change the law on identification in order to bring about a general prohibition in all public space.[31] The arguments used were that people wearing face coverings made camera surveillance far less effective, and more generally, hindered the detection and prosecution of those involved in criminal acts, as they made it impossible for others to recognize, identify or describe them. The implication of such a position is that people should not have the right to remain anonymous in public, as they are already a priori constituted as suspects of criminal acts.

The argument that face coverings formed an objective threat to security did, however, not really work for law-making. It is true that it was mentioned as the only possible legal ground for a general ban in the Commission of Experts' report of 2006, but neither the Dutch security services nor the police nor the public transportation sector supported this line of argumentation. On the contrary, they generally argued against such attempts at banning face veils, considering them irrelevant (there is no problem with face-veiling women), unnecessary (existing measures suffice) or even counterproductive (being provocative). The women themselves by and large considered identification a non-issue. Whereas they strongly disliked being compared with those intending to

[31] Parliamentary document TK II 2007/08 31 331.

engage in criminal acts, they also recognized the need to show one's face at moments when photographic ID is required, such as when crossing borders or when engaging in financial transactions. As one of them said, 'I understand that if I want to use my public transportation card, I may need to show my face. But I do not understand why I need to do that for the remainder of the trip.' Some may prefer to show their face in the presence of a female officer, but they would generally take a pragmatic stance and also do so if only a man were available.

At the same time, the women strongly objected to the biased way in which the argument of security was employed. They do not only strongly oppose the fact that in public debate they are automatically slotted into the categories of radical or extremist, because they wear a face veil. The main issue they raised is that rather than being the potential perpetrators of acts of aggression, they are, instead, the targets of violent acts of others. Most of them had regularly been confronted with people who scolded, insulted or spat at them, because they were wearing a face veil. Some also mentioned being physically threatened, with cars attempting to hit them, people throwing things at them or trying to pull off the face veil. They reported that especially when politicians had raised the issue of banning face veils, that people seemed to feel confident or even entitled to engage in such acts. The fear these forms of violence evoke is one of the reasons why their families or husbands tried to keep them from wearing the face veil.

The women responded in a variety of ways: they tried to ignore it, speak back, withdraw as much as possible from appearing in public, or considered moving abroad to a more Islam-friendly environment. Some use humour to make things easier, 'I was walking with my friend down town, then you hear them say ninja or zorro, so I said, "watch out for my ninja-star", everyone laughs, you can also get angry, but these people are only ignorant'. Most try not to heed the comments, and point out that patience and restraint are Islamic values. But some also admit that that does not always work. As a Moroccan-Dutch woman said, 'Sometimes I do a supplication, let me be deaf and blind to their comments. But at other times, I do not care, I am also proud to be a Muslim, I do not think that because you are a Muslim, you should let people walk over you. Then I talk back.' Many try to avoid situations in which they expect problems. 'Because of security, I take the car and my husband rides a bike to work', but some make a point of continuing what they used to so, 'I was known here in town as the niqabi on a bike'. Many feel under pressure, of continually having to bear in mind how others will react to their presence. Talking about the future, they often discuss the idea of emigrating to an Islamic country (to do *hijra*), also because they worry about how their children may be affected negatively when they grow up.

The 2007 proposal to change the law on identification did, however, not only focus on security 'in objective terms', it also explicitly referred to 'subjective feelings of insecurity' as an argument to ban face veiling. A similar shift from objective obstacles to subjective feelings is evident in how the term communication has been employed in law-making about face veiling. When in the 2003 Amsterdam school case, face coverings were considered an obstacle to communication, this referred to face-to-face contact in an educational institution. The main concern was with problems of sensory perception in educational settings. The February 2008 cabinet letter added the adjective 'open' to 'communication', bringing in subjective experiences of sociability. In this letter, the cabinet considers open communication 'of fundamental importance for smooth and easy interaction between people in society. The mutual acceptance of difference and commonality emerges when people are able to get to know and relate to each other without hindrance.' Face coverings are considered a strong obstacle to open communication, with Islamic face veils also evoking in many 'a feeling of anxiety and unsafety'.[32]

The Explanatory Memorandum to the 2012 Draft Law brings together the turn to subjective feelings of insecurity and the need for open communication. As this memorandum points out, covering the face makes it impossible to gauge someone's intentions, produces a sense of discomfort and makes people feel 'less at home'. The objective of the general ban is 'to promote open communication between citizens and to hamper concealing one's identity'. Postulating that 'recognizability and open communication are essential characteristics of our society', it states that what matters is 'not the quantity of the phenomenon, but its fundamental incompatibility with the social order in our country'. In short, in the course of the last decade, 'objective security' (pertaining to public order) and identification have been extended to and replaced by the more all-encompassing notions of 'recognizability' and open communication, as central for maintaining the social order and morality. In this way, a stance against face veiling has become a matter of principle.

[32] Parliamentary document TK 2007/08 31 200 VII, no. 48, 8 February 2008.

Such arguments about communication have often been taken for granted, also in educational settings, based on the assumption that non-verbal, visual communication works more directly and is less 'mediated' than verbal interaction.[33] However, this overlooks the fact that non-verbal forms of communication are also learned and that facial expressions may reveal as well as conceal one's inner state of being. Moreover, an argument can also be made that, particularly in educational settings, what ought to count is the substance of the work that students present, rather than how they appear in the classroom. In discussions with university teachers who were in favour of a ban in the classroom, there was an interesting divergence in the ways in which they discussed their concrete classroom experiences and how they talked about face veiling in the abstract. They did not feel that face veils were a serious obstacle to personal face-to-face communication, but they expressed a strong concern that face-veiling students refused 'to accept our values', that they did not want 'to make an effort to integrate in society' and that they 'purposely and provocatively set themselves apart'.[34] In other words, face veiling is not so much a technical obstacle to communication, but produces a feeling of discomfort.

The women themselves point to the importance of context when discussing the effects of face veiling in public spaces. They differentiate between forms of face-to-face interaction and more generally appearing in public space. In the case of face-to-face interaction, they often express their awareness that face veiling may make communication more diffi-cult, and point out that both parties need to make it work. Many recognized that they also need to try to defuse the sense of discomfort their counterparts may experience, such as, for example, by immediately greeting others. As one of them, who had been told by her physician that her niqab frightened the other patients, explained, 'When I step into the office, I always greet everyone politely, good morning, good afternoon. Everyone always returns my greetings. I keep my hands in sight, so they can see them and do not need to worry, what is she doing there. My eyes

[33] Yet, non-verbal forms of communication are also learned; they may reveal as well as conceal. See also the 2000 ruling of the Equal Treatment Commission, mentioned before. For more on this case, see Herrera and Moors (2003).

[34] These quotations are from discussions with those teaching in departments where one or two face-veiling students were present. When talking about this issue in the abstract, some would point to face veiling as an obstacle to communication. Those who actually had face-veiling students in class, did not complain about such direct problems in communication, but rather used a culturalist vocabulary, pointing to a sense of discomfort.

are visible. I speak loud and clearly Dutch to my children, even exaggerating it a bit, so they can easily understand me.'

Talking about simply being present in public space, their take is different. In that case they again tend to focus on the double standards they are confronted with. They recognize that their veiled appearance in public may create for some a sense of discomfort and discourage communication. But they also point out that there is a wide range of sartorial practices, forms of body language or behaviour that does not invite open communication, such as wearing sunglasses, especially reflecting ones that make it impossible to 'look each other in the eye', or may cause a sense of discomfort for others. It is, however, only in the case of face veiling that such feelings become a ground for legislation. It is no surprise then that many expressed nostalgia for those days in which different ways of appearing in public were celebrated as evidence of Dutch open-mindedness and tolerance. When they speak about the Netherlands, they also consider it their country, but they regret that 'the Netherlands as it used to be, where people were free to live their own lives' is rapidly disappearing. 'The Netherlands, as I know it, is the country where you are allowed to be who you are, as long as you do not bother others, and I do not do that'. The Moroccan-Dutch women were as outspoken about this as were the Dutch converts. As one of them said, 'The neighbourhood where I live is, as they say, a Moroccan neighbourhood. I am only living here because it is close to the Islamic school. They consider me there too Dutch. That is because I want my children in bed on time, I want them to eat whatever I have prepared for them, and if other children bother us, I go and talk to their mothers. Look, the Dutch mentality is much closer to Islam than the traditional Moroccan mentality. Do not bother other people, for instance.' Another woman succinctly expressed her stance as, 'I consciously choose to wear a niqab, I say, let me do my thing, this is the Netherlands!'

5. CONCLUSION

To understand the very rapid and extreme shift in policy making about face coverings in the Netherlands, the historical contextual needs to be taken into account. The turn from guest workers to Muslims (starting in the 1980s), the shift from the red (communist) to the green (Islamic) threat (1989), and the emergence of the notion of Islam as an obstacle to integration (starting in the 1990s), all preceded the turnabout of the early 2000s. This culturalization of politics then gained force with the rapid growth of anti-Islam neo-nationalist parties and movements (led by Fortuyn, Verdonk and Wilders) that also affected mainstream politics both in substance and style. It is within this context that arguments about face covering as a threat to security and an obstacle to communication shifted from 'objective problems' to 'subjective feelings', converging in an emphasis on a generalized 'sense of discomfort'. With integration increasingly defined in assimilationist terms, the call for the production of a strong Dutch identity became increasingly vocal. The hypervisibility of face-veiling women made them a highly convenient target for those politicians who wanted to show their support for such a strong Dutch identity and their willingness to set limits to behaviour, which had now come to be labelled as deviant.[35]

Although policy makers used and still use a secular language to restrict face veiling – employing the term face coverings rather than face veils or niqab – it is hard to overlook that what mattered most was that the actors were Muslim women. To define face veils as a symbol or tool of women's subordination, Islam is the missing link. Such an association of face veiling with women's subordination can be traced to a colonial discourse that considered veiling as the most visible symbol of Muslim women's oppression by their own men (Ahmed 1982; Yeğenoğlu 1998). Whereas the notion that face coverings produce subjective feelings of insecurity and discomfort may seem a neutral observation, its framing in relation to radical or fundamentalist Islam and women's active refusal to accept Dutch values, indicate that also these arguments are intrinsically linked to the fact that the actors are Muslim women.

Whereas participants in political debate hold strong views on face veiling, they also often admit that they have no idea about the backgrounds and motivations of the women concerned.[36] Turning to the women's narratives, striking differences with the perspectives presented in public and political debates are evident. Face-veiling women emphasize that they engage in this sartorial practice because they consider it religiously recommended if not obligatory practice. Yet whereas their motivations are religiously grounded (in more multilayered ways than is recognized in public debate), their arguments against a ban on face

---

[35] In Moors (2009a) I have shown that in most cases (except for the 2003 case) politicians started the public debate about face veiling.

[36] This is very similar to the point Leila Ahmed (1982: 522) makes about how Americans would simultaneously state that they did not know anything about Islam and that Muslim women were terribly oppressed.

veiling fit very well in a liberal–secular discourse, that includes the freedom of religion, support for human rights and the rejection of discrimination. Their main bone of contention is the use of double standards. When 'objective security' is discussed, no attention is paid to the fact that face-veiling women are not the perpetrators of violent acts, but instead are its targeted victims. When women's oppression is discussed, there is no recognition of the fact that rather than being forced to cover, they are far more often prohibited from doing so, by their own families as well as by state institutions. Discussions about subjective feelings of security and discomfort do not only overlook how political debates affect their feelings of security, but such discussions are also strongly biased, as only particular kinds of feelings of discomfort are deemed legitimate and worthy of legislative action, while others are not. It is evident that there are others who do not 'participate in society', who obviously do not want to communicate, and who produce a sense of discomfort through their style of dress, yet they are not similarly targeted.

Public and political debates about face veiling then are contestations about the definition of Dutchness. Face-veiling women – both Moroccan-Dutch women who have grown up in the Netherlands, and ethnically Dutch new Muslims – highlight the fact that they are also part of the Dutch nation. Politicians have carved out new strong notions of Dutchness in opposition to the older pillarized system and to 'multicultural tolerance', resulting in a strongly normative secularism, with a ban on face coverings as a matter of principle. Face-veiling women, in contrast, do not position themselves in opposition to these traditions, but employ elements of both discourses, arguing for the right to practise their religion in orthodox ways and for the right to present an alternative lifestyle in public, while simultaneously pointing to the desirability of pragmatic solutions. Rather than placing themselves outside of the folds of the Dutch nation, this is what being Dutch means to them.

REFERENCES

Ahmed, L. 1982. 'Western Ethnocentrism and Perceptions of the Harem', *Feminist Studies*, 8(3): 521–34.
Asad, T. 2006. 'Trying to Understand French Secularism', in H. de Vries (ed.), *Political Theologies*, New York: Fordham University Press, 494–526.

Bowen, J. 2007. *Why the French Don't Like Headscarves*. Princeton, NJ and Oxford: Princeton University Press.

Cesari, J. 2009. 'The Securitisation of Islam in Europe', Changing Landscape of European Liberty and Security, paper no. 15 (www.ceps.eu).

De Graaf, B. 2011. 'Religion bites: religieuze orthodoxie op de nationale veiligheidsagenda', *Tijdschift voor Religie, Recht en Beleid*, 2(2): 62–80.

Duyvendak, J. and Scholten, P. 2012. 'Deconstructing the Dutch Multicultural Model: A Frame Perspective on Dutch Immigrant Integration Policymaking', *Comparative European Politics*, 10(3): 266–82.

Fakhrunissa, E. (2005), 'Face-veiling women in the Netherlands'. Leiden: ISIM, unpublished report.

Geschiere, P. 2009. *The Perils of Belonging: Autochthony, Citizenship, and Exclusion in Africa and Europe*. University of Chicago Press.

Gingrich, A. 2006. 'Neo-nationalism and the Reconfiguring of Europe', *Social Anthropology*, 14(2): 195–217.

Grillo, R. and Prakash, S. 2012. *Reasons to Ban? The Anti-Burqa Movement in Western Europe*. Gottingen: Working paper Max Planck Institute for the study of religious and ethnic diversity.

Herrera, L. and Moors, A. 2003. 'Banning the Face-Veil: The Boundaries of Liberal Education', *ISIM-Newsletter*, 13: 16–17.

Lijphart, A. 1968. *The Politics of Accommodation: Pluralism and Democracy in the Netherlands*. Berkeley, CA: University of California Press.

Mahmood, S. 2005. *Politics of Piety: The Islamic Revival and the Feminist Subject*. Princeton University Press.

Moors, A. 2007. 'Fashionable Muslims: Notions of Self, Religion and Society in San'a', *Fashion Theory*, 11(2/3): 319–47.

  2009a. 'The Dutch and the Face-Veil: The Politics of Discomfort', *Social Anthropology*, 17(4): 393–409.

  2009b. *Gezichtssluiers: Draagsters en debatten*. University of Amsterdam.

  2011. 'Minister Donner as Mufti: New Developments in the Dutch "Burqa" Debates' (at: http://religionresearch.org/martijn/2011/09/21/minister-donner-as-mufti-new-developments-in-the-dutch-%E2%80%98burqa-debates%E2%80%99/).

  2012. 'The Affective Power of the Face-Veil: Between Disgust and Fascination', in B. Meyer and D. Houtman (eds.), *Things: Material Religion and the Topography of Divine Spaces*. New York: Fordham University Press, 282–95.

Scott, J. 2007. *The Politics of the Veil*. Princeton, NJ and Oxford: Princeton University Press.

Van der Veer, P. 2006. 'Pim Fortuyn, Theo van Gogh, and the Politics of Tolerance in the Netherlands', *Public Culture*, 18(1): 111–24.

Verkaaik, O. 2010. 'The Cachet Dilemma: Ritual and Agency in New Dutch Nationalism', *American Ethnologist*, 37(1): 69–82.

Vermeulen, B. 2006. *Overwegingen bij een boerka verbod*. The Hague (parliamentary publication 29754, no. 91).

Yeğenoğlu, M. 1998. *Colonial Fantasies: Towards a Feminist Reading of Orientalism*. Cambridge University Press.

3

NIQABIS IN DENMARK: WHEN POLITICIANS ASK FOR A QUALITATIVE AND QUANTITATIVE PROFILE OF A VERY SMALL AND ELUSIVE SUBCULTURE

Kate Østergaard, Margit Warburg and Birgitte Schepelern Johansen

This chapter presents the results of a study commissioned by the Danish government in connection with the political discussions on a ban of face veils in Denmark in 2009. Both the qualitative and the quantitative results challenged the political and public discourse at that time, and in the end the work fulfilled its purpose of giving a well-founded basis for political decision making. As such, the results are of general empirical interest, and they – by and large – demonstrated that the prevalence and motives of wearing face veils in Denmark are in line with what is known from other European studies.

What also makes the study of general interest is the way in which we emphasized and addressed the methodological challenges of researching the small subculture of Muslim women wearing face veils in Denmark. These challenges were further augmented by the fact that the time allotted for the study was indeed limited, and that it was carried out in a politically tense atmosphere. The methodological issues, which make up a recurrent part of the discussion in the chapter, are relevant for a range of similar studies in the sociology of religion and also pertinent for the reliability of the conclusions, which in this case had to stand up against public prejudices and political spin.

The face veil is found in different forms and varieties among Muslim women living in Western countries. We have chosen to use the term niqab as the common denominator for Muslim face-covering clothing, since this is the prevalent form worn by Muslim women in the West. A niqab is a face covering that leaves the part around the eyes clear if not worn together with an eye veil. The niqab is usually part of a full-body black covering. In public, burqa has become the favourite term for such clothing, but the burqa (i.e., the blue version with a net in front of the eyes), as it is known in Afghanistan, is very rarely, if at all, worn in Denmark. Furthermore, we use the term niqabi as a designation for women wearing the niqab since this term is often used in Muslim environments in the West.

The chapter is organized so that it first presents the background for and terms of the study. This is followed by a presentation and discussion of the methodological challenges of the study and in particular our strategy for reaching persons belonging to the niqabi subculture in order to conduct our qualitative interviews. In connection with the methodological discussion, the background of the niqabis and the form of their Islam are elaborated on because these topics were part of the assignment and also have methodological implications. The results of the interviews make up the middle part of the chapter, and this is followed by further considerations of the methods applied for studying the niqabis in Denmark from a combined qualitative and quantitative perspective. The results of the quantitative study and the detailed methodological discussion connected with obtaining a reasonably reli-able estimate of the number of niqabis in Denmark have recently been published in another article (Warburg et al. 2013). This part of the chapter will therefore only be summarized here, highlighting the most significant results. The chapter ends with reflections on the political outcome of what became known as the burqa affair in Denmark and the role of the researcher working with a politically controversial question.

1. THE BACKGROUND FOR AND TERMS OF THE STUDY

The politically heated debate about some Muslim women wearing face-covering clothing began several years ago in a number of European countries (Bakht 2012; Byng 2013; Chesler 2010; Kiliç et al. 2008; Lettinga and Saharso 2012; Moors 2009b, Saharso and Lettinga 2008).[1]

In Denmark, the debate began in 2009, when the junior party in the Danish Liberal–Conservative government announced that they would 'work for a ban against burqas'.[2] This policy was part of the party's integration agenda 'Democratic Integration'. The ban was justified as a measure against 'religious oppression', and by the position that the sight

---

[1] For further details, see the Introduction to this volume.
[2] www.konservative.dk/nytogdebat/nyheder/2009/august/sider/integrationsudspil.aspx, p. 4.

of women concealed by a burqa or niqab was not compatible with an open society. The leader of the Conservative Party later explained at the party's conference that the burqa 'is a symbol of militant and fundamental extremism'.[3]

The issue of a possible ban was then deferred for a closer study in an ad hoc committee under the Ministry of the Interior. As part of the committee work, the ministry asked the University of Copenhagen to investigate and report on the use of burqas and other types of face-covering clothing among Muslims in Denmark. The terms of reference from the ministry specified the topics of the report and the time allotted for this study, which was one month for the data collection. The ministry wanted the researchers to give a general overview of the Muslim tradition of wearing face-covering clothing and more specifically to investigate the background and motives of these women and to give a sound estimate of the number of niqabis in Denmark. This meant that we had to address both qualitative and quantitative issues related to the wearing of face-covering clothing.

The context of the study, and its specifications, must be understood in the light of the current political debate at that time. The request from the ministry reflected the politicians' wish to map the magnitude of what was considered a problem and whether wearing a burqa symbolized the oppression of women and anti-democratic values. The results and conclusions were reported to the ministry in late 2009 and released to the public three months later.[4]

2. PROFILING NIQABIS: A METHODOLOGICAL CHALLENGE

The methodological approaches for studying niqabis are in some respects different from studies of large social groups, because niqabis constitute a very small percentage of the general population. Niqabis make up a small minority within the minority of religiously active persons within the minority of Muslims in Denmark. Furthermore, the niqabis share the characteristics of elusive or hidden populations, which may be defined in terms of two characteristics, namely that there is privacy on membership because it involves stigmatized or illegal behaviour and that the size and boundaries of the population are unknown in advance (Heckathorn

[3] http://jyllands-posten.dk/politik/article4173467.ece?page=1
[4] *Rapport om brugen af niqab og burka* (2009).

1997, 2002). These populations are therefore elusive in the sense that members are difficult to find because they are not organized; rather they belong to different communities through social relations and loose networks. Niqabis are, for example, not members of a hypothetical Danish Association for the Promotion of Niqab, which would be able to provide a more or less complete list of its members. A significant methodological challenge in researching hidden groups is thus that it is difficult to get systematic access to its individual members as well as to get access to information regarding the number of members and/or their prevalence among the general population (Faugier and Sargeant 1997; Lambert 1990).

Furthermore, the circumstances surrounding our research included a public discourse which stigmatized the wearing of niqab and labelled its use as oppressive of women and as un-Danish behaviour (e.g. Gjersten 2009). Even though the behaviour is visible because it is public, the population practising this behaviour is hidden in the sense that it was difficult to locate and gain access to interviewees. In addition, members who are reached under such circumstances often refuse to cooperate, or provide unreliable information to protect themselves and others (Heckathorn, 1997, 2002). In the present study the research was directly linked to a political controversy, and it was likely that we would be met with scepticism towards participation, not only among the niqabis themselves but also among informants acquainted with this highly politicized minority group (Johansen and Spielhaus 2012).

Members of rare groups who are not organized cannot successfully be contacted through standard random sampling of the relevant sub-population – in this case Muslim women in general. The statistical probability of reaching a sufficient number of niqabis is simply too small. Alternative *stratified* sampling strategies are often used to increase the probability of contacting the target population. Stratified sampling is where sampling is concentrated in strata such as certain geographical areas or among particular segments known or assumed beforehand to have an above average representation of the group (Kalton 2001; Sudman *et al.* 1988). For example, converts of Danish ethnic background constitute a relatively high proportion of niqabis (Jensen and Østergaard 2007b). However, stratified sampling implies a risk of bias.

A common risk of bias, called under-coverage bias, in stratified sampling arises from the assumption that the group is so sparsely represented outside the selected strata that these unselected strata can be ignored. For example, in our study we concentrated on the three largest cities, Copenhagen, Aarhus and Odense, because the majority of Danish Muslims live in these cities, and because the wearing of a niqab seems to be an urban phenomenon. We explain later how we dealt with this under-coverage bias in the estimate of the total number of niqabis in Denmark.

Having selected relevant strata, the further sampling strategies for rare and hidden groups are often key informant, snowballing and location sampling. Key informants are people known in advance to have a special knowledge about the group, or have privileged access to many of the group members. Key informants are often useful in helping to locate informants, and can function as gatekeepers, thus providing access to interviewees. Relying on key informants implies the risk, however, that the information may be distorted because of personal and institutional bias among a usually limited number of key informants (Heckathorn 1997, 2002). Snowballing uses initial informants to facilitate contact to new respondents from their networks, whereas location sampling entails getting access to people who frequent specific locations. In snowballing sampling, one advantage is that it often leads to contacts also outside of established organizations, because snowballing makes use of the informants' own networks as a gateway to reach potential new informants. However, snowballing runs the risk of bias that isolated individuals in the target group are not reached (Erickson 1979). Another risk of bias of particular importance for qualitative studies arises where, if by accident, all the individuals reached belong to the same social cluster or network within the population. This may lead to a situation where important qualitative aspects of the population are not represented among the interviewees. In the next section we elaborate on how we used these strategies and addressed the built-in risks of bias.

3. ACCESS TO AND SELECTION OF NIQABIS FOR QUALITATIVE INTERVIEWS

Since our work was a directly commissioned work from the government, it is no surprise that we were met with some suspicion regarding the nature of the project and who we were seen to represent. This came on top of the fact that many Muslims feel despised and misrepresented by both journalists and politicians (Jensen and Østergaard 2007b), and this feeling which was exacerbated by the ongoing discussions on legislation being introduced to ban face veiling in public.

A further challenge was that we had just one month for data-collection and therefore very little time to build up sufficient trust among most of the key informants' networks to obtain acceptance from potential interviewees. Furthermore, the period of research was in the fasting month of Ramadan, and it is probable that this did not ease the accessibility of the highly religious informants, as they were occupied with their spiritual life and being with friends and family.

We experienced time and again that women who had at first agreed to be interviewed, later withdrew just before the interview would take place. We tried to find interviewees through other researchers, Muslim private schools and leading maternity visiting nurses but in vain. In one case it was possible to find an interviewee through a journalist in Aarhus. In all other cases it was necessary to get access through gatekeepers from Muslim communities with whom we had established a trusting relationship from previous studies (Østergaard 2006; Jensen and Østergaard 2007b).

The problem was, however, that these gatekeepers often did not have personal ties to niqabis because niqabis rarely attend activities in the larger established Muslim organizations. We were able to reach only two of the women through one of the largest youth organizations and one of the biggest mosque congregations in Copenhagen. In the first case, the gatekeeper knew of only one woman, who was a former niqabi, in the entire organization. In the other case, the gatekeeper knew of four niqabis in the congregation and was able to facilitate contact to one of them. This information on the relatively few niqabis in established milieus was consistent with observations from earlier field observations of the range of activities in the two organizations (Jensen and Østergaard 2007b). The majority of the interviewees were reached through snow-balling in informal networks and location sampling.

In the end we managed to interview seven women from different Muslim backgrounds. For this analysis we include here an additional interview conducted a year after the initial fieldwork in connection with a study on Salafi groupings in Denmark (Jensen and Østergaard 2011).

Table 3.1 gives an overview of the eight interviewees and the different routes of access. Four of the interviewees (Khadija, Hanna, Hakima and Amina) were reached through four different independent key informants and were not acquainted with each other. Hakima became the first link in a small snowballing chain which reached Zeinab. Hakima also made possible a location sampling in connection with an Eid (the feast after the Ramadan fasting month) charity party for the

TABLE 3.1 Overview of the eight interviewees

Access to interviewee	'Name'	Date, place	Ethnicity, age	Religious affiliation	Remarks
Earlier informant from Muslim Youth Organization	Khadija	24/9/2009, CPH	Iraqi, 24	Sufi, former Shia	Earlier niqabi
Journalist, non-Muslim	Hanna	28/9/2009, Aarhus	Danish, 23	Salafi, former Lutheran	
Earlier informant outside organized groups	Hakima	4/10/2009, CPH	Somali, 29	'Spiritual', former Salafi	Earlier niqabi
Earlier informant from Sunni mosque	Amina	6/10/2009, CPH	Egyptian, 46	Muslim Brotherhood/ Salafi	No niqab in classes
Hakima (see above)	Zeinab	6/11/2009, CPH	Somali, 30	Salafi	Earlier niqabi
Hakima (see above)	Halima	3/10/2009, CPH	Danish, 21	Salafi	Interviews at Eid charity event
	Busra		Danish, 30	Salafi	
	Iman		Somali, 36	Salafi	

benefit of children who had been orphaned as a result of the war in Iraq. The event took place in a venue called the Dawa centre, which belonged to a new loosely organized Salafi grouping.[5] The event was however attended not only by regular participants at the centre, but by a broader group of women who supported the cause rather than the specific ideology of the centre. A significant number of the about fifty participants wore the niqab although this was difficult to estimate accurately since they unveiled at the gathering. The number of participants correspond approximately to half of the estimated about one hundred devout Salafis in Copenhagen (Jensen and Østergaard 2011a).

Through participation at this event we reached a group of three women (Halima, Busra and Iman). The three women all frequented the centre from time to time, Busra on a more regular basis to participate in various lessons and Halima and Iman only occasionally for bigger events. All of the three women also participated in different private networks from which Halima and Busra knew each other. Hakima, who facilitated the contacts in the first place, knew Iman in advance. Zeinab, who is also connected to Hakima's network, used to occasionally frequent the Dawa centre as well as the largest Arab Sunni mosque in Copenhagen.

The study is thus biased in the sense that we have several women from the same loosely connected networks. The Salafi milieu in Copenhagen consists of a few study circles around sheikhs, the Dawa centre and several private networks but they are all intertwined and a charity party will attract women from the different circles and networks. The Salafi networks are however the only milieu known to support the niqab and due to the scale of the Salafi milieu it is very unlikely that anybody could make contact with distinct and separate groups as you might in larger urban areas.

---

[5] The specific centre will be elaborated on below. Here it should be noted that the term Salafism is the most widespread term, but not all agree on it. The term is used here as Vincent Wictorowicz, explains it. Salafism is different networks originating from Saudi Arabia but what unites these different networks is a common creed, *aqida*. Central to the creed is that the Prophet Muhammad and the first generations of Muslims (the Salafs) are the only models of proper Islamic behaviour. All ideas and actions that cannot be traced back to the Quran and Sunnah are rejected as innovation, *bid'a*, and are considered the worst sin, namely idolatry, *shirk*, and hence a violation of the unity of God, *tawhid*. There is a widespread tendency in these communities to identify opponents as infidels, *kuffar*, on whom, in principle, there is an obligation to fight. Moreover, Salafis understand the authoritative Islamic texts as self-explanatory. The scholarly task is therefore to find the truth in the texts and try to avoid human reason, which is seen as dependent on human desires and interests rather than the divine will (Wictorowicz 2006).

We have, as mentioned, tried to address this challenge by getting access to niqabis through other routes of contacts.

Five of the interviews lasted several hours and took place in private homes. The three interviews obtained at the location sampling at the *Eid* charity event lasted approximately half an hour each and took place in private in a small adjoining room.

The interviews were semi-structured and centred on a broad opening question about how they came to wear the niqab. The women were also asked to elaborate on this theme and sometimes nudged by additional questions. The additional questions typically concerned the religious affiliation of the niqabis and what consequences the women experienced as a result of wearing niqab. We did not directly ask about the issue of coercion, but chose instead to let the interview centre around the women's accounts of wearing the veil. Very often they addressed the issue of coercion by themselves and if they did not, they were asked questions such as what was your family's, husband's, friends', etc. opinion about wearing the veil. The eight women included three ethnic Danish women, three Somali women, an Iraqi woman and an Egyptian woman. This distribution of niqabis, according to ethnicity, is consistent with the opinion of researchers and informants from Muslim communities that niqabis in Denmark have mainly Danish, Somali and, to a lesser extent, Arabic backgrounds.

Furthermore, this was confirmed by our own field observations from earlier and later field studies among Muslims in the Copenhagen area (Jensen and Østergaard 2007b; Jensen and Østergaard 2011a).

We were satisfied with the diversity of different Muslim environments approached. The sample counted both organized and non-organized women, present niqabis and former niqabis as well as women with different ethnic backgrounds and connected to different religious affiliations. The desirability of including former niqabis is, however, not obvious.

4. DEFECTORS AS INFORMANTS ON HIDDEN GROUPS

Three of the eight women interviewed considered themselves former niqabis. Among the other five, Amina who removed the veil when she attended classes, regarded herself as niqabi, and she wore her niqab on a regular basis in all other public contexts.

At first sight it may seem problematic for our project that several of the women no longer considered themselves niqabis. In research on conversion to new religious movements, defector accounts have been considered problematic because they often explicitly distance themselves from their former group (Beckford 1985; Robbins 1988). The three former niqabis may be considered defectors, and they might have had ideologically negative biases against the wearing of niqab.

We believe, however, that it can be an advantage to include former niqabis in the study. It has been suggested by researchers working with hidden groups such as new religious movements that defectors often have access to insider knowledge which they, in contrast to current members of these groups, do not have the same vested interest in hiding (Carter 1998). In addition, even though it is necessary to critically evaluate the accounts of defectors, it is equally necessary to scrutinize the account of the adherents, because everybody speaks from a certain position and thereby from a particular interest in the topic. Including different kinds of informants can actually provide valuable knowledge about demarcations, modes of legitimization and conflict lines within the field of study.

It is, however, important to distinguish between different defector positions. Some defectors may become opponents of their former groups, whereas others merely move from the centre to the periphery of the group or become passive members (Barker 1998; Bromley 1998), but are nonetheless still associated with the group.

In our study, the women who could be considered defectors have not taken a final exit from their groups. Two of the women (Khadija and Zeinab) still wished to wear the niqab again in the future, but for practical reasons they had chosen to remove it. In the case of the third woman (Hakima) there was a connection between the cessation of the practice of veiling the face and a change in her perception of Islam, but she still attended Salafi-oriented communities to cultivate relationships with other Somalis. She did, however, feel that she had to hide her new position so as to not be considered an apostate.

Thus, we succeeded in getting access to women differently positioned in regard to the wearing of niqab. We also found that including former niqabis provides an insight into both the processes of choosing and wearing the niqab and what it implies to take it off again. It also sheds light on the fact that wearing a niqab is not necessarily something static, but may change over time and according to changing life circumstances.

5. ETHNIC BACKGROUNDS

The interviewees in this study have Somali, Danish and Arab ethnic backgrounds, which is consistent with other assessments from the researchers and key informants in Muslim communities in Denmark whom we interviewed about the ethnic backgrounds of niqabis. These ethnic backgrounds do not correspond with the demographic composition of the Muslim community in Denmark and appear to differ from the ethnic background of niqabis in other countries.

It should be pointed out that the Muslim community in Denmark is not, as in many other countries, dominated by single ethnicity but is rather characterized by a high degree of ethnic diversity.[6] The Turkish community is the largest and represents about one-quarter of the Muslim population of more than 200,000 individuals. Arabs from different national backgrounds, primarily from Iraq, North Africa and Lebanon (primarily Palestinians) represent close to one-third (not including Somalia).[7] Other significant groups are Pakistanis and Somalis, both representing 10 and 9 per cent. Ethnic Danes represent less than 2 per cent of the Muslim population (Jensen and Østergaard 2007a). The Turks and the Pakistanis are among the oldest Muslim immigrant communities in Denmark; they established their communities in Denmark in the 1960s and 1970s. These communities are mainly organized along ethnic lines. Key informants, both outsiders and insiders, did not know of niqabis in these long-established communities and it seems plausible that niqabis are insignificant in both cases. The Turks are mainly organized in communities with imams from the Diyanet (Turkish ministry of religious matters), which does not support the niqab. The Pakistani group in Denmark is in contrast to the UK, dominated by the spiritual Barelwi movement, which also does not value niqab.[8] We therefore chose to concentrate on identifying and reaching niqabis in the Somali, Arab and convert communities.

---

[6] In the following the number of different groups are from Jacobsen (2007).

[7] Even though Somalia is part of the Arab League, Arabic is not widely spoken and among Danish Muslims it is common to distinguish between Somalis and Arabs.

[8] The Barelwi movement is a revivalist and spiritual movement from South Asia. In South Asian Islam there is a main split and confrontation between the Barelwi movement and the more conservative and strict Deobandi movement. This split is often an important controversy in Pakistani immigrant communities such as in the UK.

The Arab community is a very diverse community which is split between the Sunni and Shia branches of Islam as well being diverse in terms of the nationalities represented. The Iraqi Arabs are mainly Shia, who do not, according to key informants, practise the wearing of niqab in Denmark. On the contrary, at least in some Shia communities, the niqab is regarded as extremist and anti-Shia. This perspective will be elaborated on below. The Arab Sunni mosques often attract congregation members extensively from among Palestinians, North Africans and Somalis and these environments furthermore include most of the converts (Jensen and Østergaard 2007b). This is probably because these environments are more culturally diverse, and Danish is often, together with Arabic, the language of communication. In the main Arab Sunni mosques it is, however, very unusual to observe niqabis even though it is possible to identify one or two at big gatherings.

We have, however, observed the existence of a number of niqabis in certain small study circles and loose private networks. These circles and networks consist of a new generation of relatively young Muslims who cultivate a kind of cross-ethnic Islam. These networks are seldom organized and it was therefore important to not rely entirely on gate-keepers from the established Muslim organizations to reach niqabis, but rather to use personal networks. The niqabis in Denmark are generally relatively young (often in their twenties or thirties) according to our observations as well as assessments from key informants. The niqabis in Denmark generally seem to engage in communities and associations which refrain from cultivating an ethnic identity related to a specific homeland.

This tendency is reflected in marriage patterns among the interviewees. Among the eight women interviewed only one, Amina, has had a marriage partner belonging to the same ethnic and cultural community as she did. The woman in question was also the only woman from the sample over 40 years old, and the only one who started to wear the niqab in a country outside Europe. Six of the women were married to partners with an ethnicity other than their own, whereas the last one had not yet married. The three Danish converts, Hanna, Halima and Busra, were all married to Arabs, and this was also the case for one of the Somali women, Zeinab. The other two Somali women, Hakima and Iman, were married to converts of Danish and American origins.

In the public debates on the niqab, it has largely been portrayed as an issue of integration (or lack of integration) and as an insistence on the continuation of 'un-Danish' customs from a Muslim country of origin.[9] Such an interpretation of Islamic symbols within a national matrix, where the explicitly Muslim comes to signify the foreignness of the migrant, is not exceptional (Johansen and Spielhaus 2012). However, it does not seem to fit our findings: niqabis do not seem to be women with a traditional diaspora identity in the sense of being strongly connected to practices in a Muslim country of origin. The women are either Danish converts or Muslims with a cross-ethnic orientation. Furthermore, for the women in our sample the niqab does not seem to be a matter of a practice brought from their country of origin, since they all explained that they were the first to wear the niqab in their families. Hakima for instance remembered her childhood in Somalia as a time where people were more Somali than Muslim. 'The women covered with a *bandana* in the village where I grow up. You could see their neck. They covered in an African way.'

Thus, the wearing of niqab seems not to express the continuation of practices from a country of origin. Rather, it seems to be connected with an affiliation with Salafism[10] and an admiration for and cultivation of dress codes from the Arab Peninsula where the niqab is widespread. There is therefore reason to scrutinize in more detail the apparent connection between niqab and Salafism, also in a Danish context. The question of religious affiliation was furthermore part of what was required to be addressed in the mapping of niqabis. We will give this question some attention, since it turned out to be a rather complex issue with various methodological implications. Salafi groupings are in themselves rare and elusive since their activities and socializing often take place in private homes and through decentralized personal area networks. They are also hidden in the sense that they, for ideological reasons, often avoid too much interaction with outsiders in order not to dilute their religion (Wictorowicz 2006).

6. RELIGIOUS AFFILIATIONS: A SALAFI CONNECTION?

The eight women interviewed were all Sunni Muslims; one of them, Khadija, was, however, a former Shia who had later turned to Sunni,

---

[9] For example the Conservative People's Party explicitly mentions the wearing of the burka as a problem area for integration and migration policies, www.konservative.dk/Politik/Integrationspolitik/Udspil

[10] A possible Salafi affiliation is often mentioned by Ali (2010), Patel (2012), Roald (2001) and Skovgaard-Petersen (1997, 2009).

more specifically Sufism (see Table 3.1). Seven of the eight women are, or have been, affiliated with what could be termed Salafi environments, even though they seldom identify themselves as such. Through our own observations in Muslim communities and through key informants (researchers as well as community members), it was confirmed that the niqab is not used significantly in established, formal Muslim organizations, but only in the looser and more informally organized networks which cultivate a Salafi-inspired form of Islam. As mentioned above, the majority of informants were recruited through informal networks while only two were recruited through gatekeepers to larger Muslim organizations.

Salafi communities in Denmark are usually loosely organized and cover a wide spectrum of different views and ideologies. Salafi ideas are prevalent in many Muslim environments and so is literature promoting Salafi ideas; much of the Islamic literature which has been translated into Danish and English and sold at Islamic bookshops or distributed at mosques is, in fact, Salafi literature of Saudi origin (Jensen and Østergaard 2007b). In these environments the niqab is admired, encouraged and sometimes regarded as an obligation (*fard*). In some study circles the niqab is obligatory for participants.

Explicitly Salafi-oriented groupings with specific activities such as teaching have been quite limited in the scope of their activities and public profile outside the Muslim community in Denmark. The Salafi groupings often take the form of small study circles centred around an individual sheik who has offered training for his supporters. These study circles usually consist of loose networks without formal membership or organization, and the networks are often temporary and constantly changing. In addition, they are often expelled from the mosques where they conduct lessons and thus frequently move from place to place.[11] They are usually not activists in the sense of taking direct public and political action, but rather they seem to focus on education and the reform of individual practice. There is usually very limited access to such circles for outsiders since participation is conditional on the sheikh's acceptance and dialogue with non-Muslims, and he will generally perceive an outsider to be a risk to the cultivation of, what they consider, pure Islam.

---

[11] They are often expelled because the mosque leadership is not interested in being associated with Salafi ideas.

In 2008 a group of young Muslims in Copenhagen, some of them former students of the known Salafi sheikhs, established themselves around a centre for *dawa* (call to Islam). The Dawa centre distinguished itself from former Salafi circles since they had, for a time, a permanent venue for their events and became independent of any particular sheikh. The founders of the Dawa centre had an ambivalent relationship with all the sheikhs in Copenhagen, as they disagreed with them on authority and strategy.

The Dawa centre was more activist and tried to attract supporters by *dawa*, missions in the form of street and internet missions and public speeches and meetings at their venue. Later, they attempted to have a higher profile and promoted themselves through public demonstrations and happenings such as public campaigns against Muslim participation in elections and attempts to establish sharia zones in certain neighbourhoods.[12]

Women are often encouraged by Salafi sheikhs to participate in study circles but not to participate in Friday prayers. Nor did women from this centre participate in street activities but rather in public lessons at the centre and in women-only activities such as charity events, or they form entirely informal networks which meet in private homes to study or socialize. The communities which support and encourage the use of niqab are thus typically hidden in the sense of being very closed and private.

A means of gaining access to interviewees affiliated with the Dawa centre was through an informant from an earlier study on converts to Islam. He facilitated contact to a Somali woman, Hakima, who was a former niqabi but still socialized with other Somali niqabis. Through her it was possible to make the said location sampling at the centre since she facilitated access to the *Eid* charity party at the centre. Since there was, as mentioned, a reluctance regarding women's participation in Friday prayers in such environments, the charity event, which we attended, is one of the few kinds of public local activities where we had the best opportunity of getting access to these women.

A representative from another loosely Salafi-oriented affiliation of niqabis is the ethnic Danish Hanna from Aarhus, with whom we came into contact through a non-Muslim journalist. In Aarhus there is a mosque which is known to be Salafi oriented. Hanna did, however, not attend this mosque, but did not oppose it either. She explained that

---

[12] The information on the Dawa centre is based on own observations.

she did not prioritize going to mosques since she had small children and she preferred meeting with other women in private homes. A considerable part of her social network consisted of other niqabi women. She explained that she 'tries to follow the original, the authentic Islam'. It was important for her that everything should be proved to be from the Quran and hadith. When asked directly whether she considered herself a Salafi she explained that she 'does not like to put herself in a group'.

Only Hakima, who was in the process of leaving the network, considered the women Salafi and herself a former Salafi. There thus seems to be a discrepancy between outsider and insider views on appropriate terms. The insiders' reluctance to the term Salafi has several reasons.

First of all, Salafism has been a stigmatized term for a number of years, especially after 9/11, since most terrorist attacks by Muslims have been related to Salafism of the jihadist type. Second, there is an ideological aversion to the Salafi designation among the Salafis themselves. This has to do with their view that there cannot be various legitimate forms of Islam. The Salafis regard themselves as those who follow the Prophet Muhammad and the first Muslims and they consider the Salafi form of Islam as the only authentic form, all others are unacceptable deviations. Consequently, people attending these circles will often be reluctant to call themselves anything other than Muslim, because to do otherwise can be interpreted as pluralism, which goes against their tenets. The last reason is that these circles do not usually consist of enduring and formal groups. The types of membership found in these groups could perhaps best be described as a client rather than supporter kind of membership (Beckford 1985: 76–9) because the women's participation in activities are often characterized by instrumental purposes. Some of the women for instance participate because of a specific cause such as the situation in Iraq or in order to meet friends even though they do not agree with the ideology. Furthermore, most of the women do not frequent certain mosques or teaching circles, but can shop around between different choices, including some which are not influenced by Salafism. In many cases the women do not even attend teaching circles but rather form loose private networks based on friendship and common experiences. It is thus important to note that statements about religious affiliation should not necessarily be taken at face value.

We also tried to reach niqabis through established Muslim organizations. In this way we managed to make contact with two women, as mentioned earlier. One was Amina from one of the largest Arab Sunni mosques in Copenhagen. The mosque has no stated religious affiliation, but can be characterized as predominantly inspired by the Muslim Brotherhood. There is, however, a tolerance for a variety of other positions including both Muslims occupied by reformulating Islam in a Danish context and Salafis. While the leadership has mostly consisted of people with an Arabic background, the congregation also consists of Somalis and people with other ethnic backgrounds, and it also attracts many converts. The small number of niqabis in this congregation (the mosque represents about 200 families) is an indication that niqabis are a rare and elusive group.[13]

Amina, who attended this mosque, was the only informant over 40 years old in the survey and the only one who wore the niqab before she came to Denmark. She had used it in her home country of Egypt and in Saudi Arabia and Pakistan where she lived before she emigrated to Denmark. She did not use the term Salafi to describe herself, but did show us different books about the niqab which are connected to that tradition. This woman knew of only a few other niqabis in her social network. This is consistent with the assumption that niqabis are not common in the established congregations. At the same time her participation in that congregation suggests that the niqab, even if not promoted, is accepted outside the more closed and predominantly Salafi environments.

The second organization that provided contact with a niqabi is one of the largest Muslim youth organizations in Denmark which cultivates a spiritual, cross-ethnic form of Islam, and which facilitates dialogue with Danish society. We have never observed niqabis during fieldwork at their activities, but one of the leaders, with whom we have established a relationship of trust during previous studies, was able to identify a member who had previously been niqabi. This woman, Khadija, has not been affiliated with any Salafi circles but began wearing the niqab as a result of her conversion from Shia to Sunni Islam, when she simultaneously became a member of a Sufi order. In her case, the niqab can be seen as a kind of opposition to Shia Islam. This interpretation was confirmed by the fact that her parents were perhaps even more shocked by her new veiling than her conversion since they asked her to, at least, stop wearing it, because they and their Muslim family and friends connected it to Salafism and extremism and thus with being anti-Shia.

---

[13] The number is based on personal communication with the imam. The 200 families are members but the mosque's congregation is larger since there can be up to 800–1,000 attendees at Friday prayer.

The Sufi order is a branch of the traditional *Shadhili* order guided by the US convert Sheikh Nuh Ha Mim Keller. The interviewee is still a member of this Sufi order and has not changed her religious affiliation as a result of the decision to cease veiling her face. According to the interviewee, the niqab is not a part of this order's general practice in Denmark since Nuh Ha Mim Keller does not recommend it in a Western minority context, although he does not entirely reject it either. The interviewee had, however, seen the Sheikh's closest female supporters wearing the niqab in Jordan where he lives. Amina's and Khadija's use of niqab illustrate that the niqab cannot unequivocally be associated with Salafi trends, although it seems to be more prevalent there. The example of Khadija also illustrates how the niqab functions as a marker of transition in the process of conversion, in this case from Shia to Sunni.

7. MOTIVATIONS FOR WEARING A NIQAB

Let us now turn our attention from the religious affiliation and the formation of social networks, and towards the reasons given by the women themselves for wearing the niqab. The women interviewed gave a number of explanations and justifications for why they had chosen to cover their faces, and these reasons were repeated with great consistency. First and foremost, all the women highlighted that they wore the niqab because it was an expression of their love for God. The veiling was seen as something beautiful and glorious, and several of the women added that you should take the Prophet's wives as an ideal, and form your own behaviour after their model. There was broad agreement that it is not obligatory to cover the face, but it is in Islamic legal terms considered a good thing to do because it brings one closer to God.

Iman, a 36-year-old woman with a Somali background, emphasized that it is a good deed that will be rewarded, but it is not a requirement, although she was aware that some Islamic scholars consider it obligatory.

Khadijah, aged 25, who had an Iraqi background and was a former niqabi with a Sufi affiliation further explained:

> It's about your spiritual journey. In order to achieve success and move forward in your spiritual journey, there are some frames that ought to be set. It is the everyday practice of Islam, including one's clothing. But it is by no means mandatory that you have to wear it.

earing a niqab also lives up to an ideal of Muslim female behaviour, which, among other things, is to hide her beauty to the outsider and avoid attention and inappropriate glances. Hanna, who was 23 years old and a convert, said:

> The attention I get has nothing to do with my appearance; it's a matter of what I say. People listen to what I say and not to my body. No one makes passes at you and so you are free from that.

The motive for covering the face to prevent sexual attention may seem paradoxical since this piece of clothing actually attracts a lot of attention in the Danish context. Addressing this, several of the women claim that it is a different kind of attention, which is probably uncomfortable, but not problematic in the same way as the sexually charged attention they would otherwise get if they were not covered.

When asked what attracted the women to the niqab, several made the point that they looked at other women covering their face and found it appealing. They saw them as strong, honourable and self-confident women with respect for themselves. Since covering the face often seems provocative in the Danish context and creates some practical problems, it requires strength and sincere faith to choose this option. The convert Hanna, aged 23, stated:

> It [to cover the face] is something good to do in Islam, and especially now when there is so much opposition to it, it's something where we can show that we are strong – that we do not succumb to pressure.

In this way the wearing of the niqab becomes a sign of strength of your belief and that you keep your faith in God and the Prophet, even at times when you experience resistance. Some of the women, furthermore, pointed out that it was the reward in the hereafter that was the important thing and that it was what made it possible to keep going on in the present, despite the fact that it was difficult.

It is worth stressing that none of the women themselves connected the covering of the face with oppression or an unequal relationship between man and woman. Rather, they saw it as an expression of strength and courage. All the women emphasized that it was their own choice and their own decision to wear the niqab. None of them use explanations such as 'we are used to it' or 'it is tradition.' On the contrary, the women pointed out that it was only after careful consideration, and sometimes in spite of the wishes of their close relations, that they chose to veil their face.

Some of the women said that they discussed it with their husband or friends before they made their decision; others stated that it was an individual decision, and that it surprised their immediate relations. Khadija, of Iraqi background, made the decision in connection with her conversion from Shia to Sunni Islam. Her choice can thus be seen as a rebellion against the standards of her parents and family. Other examples of this can be seen in the choices of the 36-year-old Iman from Somalia and 46-year-old Amina from Egypt, who both point out that neither of their families have a tradition of wearing the niqab. In Iman's case, her family actually asked her to stop wearing it because people in Europe do not understand it, and therefore they were worried about her safety.

It is worth noting that several women themselves referred to the common assumption that they had been asked to cover their faces by their husbands. Thus, they were well aware of the prevailing explanation that points to male requirements and possible coercion as the primary cause of women wearing the niqab. They rejected these explanations outright. One of the women even pointed out that she made her future husband's acceptance of the niqab a prerequisite of marriage. Another said that she thought it was mandatory, while her husband thought it was not. However, he supported her in her choice.

When the choice involved the husband it was, according to the women, because it is not possible to get an education or a job in Denmark as long as you cover your face. They were therefore dependent on the will of their husband to support them. Being a housewife supported by a husband was a consequence of their choice, not the other way around. This is contrary to the public view where the opposite argument is often made, i.e. that the covering is a symbol of the male oppression of women, which also prevents them from working.

Some of the women emphasized the admiration received from other women as a result of their veiling, but they rejected it as a motivation for wearing the veil. According to them, it was all about the joy of obeying God. It can, however, not be excluded that the social prestige that the niqab gives in some circles could also play a role.

8. A CRITICAL EVALUATION OF THE ACCOUNTS

A source of bias from getting access to interviewees through gatekeepers belonging to the religious environment is that the persons designated are likely to be especially devout in their reflections on the subject under discussion (Beckford 1985). In our study, however, only three out of the eight women were directly appointed by gatekeepers with a likely vested interest in how these women would present themselves in interviews. A possible bias rather stems from the fact that it is probably only the most steadfast and strong personalities among the niqabis who are willing to engage in an interview, considering how stigmatized the group is.

It is, indeed, striking that the women in our study seemed very reflective of their choice and that they all basically told the same story about the niqab as an individual choice with an emphasis on niqabis as independent and courageous. It is, furthermore, remarkable that exactly the same themes recur in studies of niqabis in other European countries such as Belgium, France and the Netherlands (see Chapters 2, 4 and 5 in this volume).

The accounts seem to function as counter-stories to discourses in the tense political and public debate around the niqab which frame niqabs as against European values and as a matter of coercion and oppression of women (Moors 2009b; Bakht 2012). Their stories can be perceived as converging towards a collective pattern that occurs when the women discuss their experiences and through retellings readjust their individual accounts. This is analogous to what Beckford has proposed was happening to accounts of converts to Jehovah's Witnesses after he discovered their striking similarity (Beckford 1978).

This does not mean that the women speak falsely about their motives, but rather that they start to form their memories and frame their stories in certain recognizable ways, mostly through narratives that combines personal piety and individual choice. This makes using their accounts as evidence of what actually happened in the process of choosing the niqab highly problematic. However, in several cases we can use the accounts to exclude the explanation of coercion by husbands because these women either chose to wear the niqab before they met their husbands or continued wearing it after they became widows. Furthermore, traditions and pressure from Muslim home countries or families seem to be unlikely reasons for wearing the veil, since all but one of the women were either converts or chose the niqab while living in Europe. It should also be mentioned that only one of the women, the 46-year-old Amina of Egyptian background, began to use the niqab in her homeland, when she was 21. She was however the only niqabi in her family.

The most relevant context for understanding the niqab accounts seems instead to be a quest for religious identity either as part of a process of converting or of religious revivalism. In both cases the religious identity is not self-evident but has to be created. And here the niqab can function as a powerful marker.

The various accounts seemed to express typical features of modern forms of identity, which was characterized by actively created biographies and choice, which were reflexively justified (Giddens 1999). Likewise, the stories are consistent with tendencies in what is described as deterritorialized Islam (Roy 2004). Typical of this form of Islam is a Muslim identity which is not directed towards a specific country and culture but rather is something to be reinvented as freed from culture. The niqab becomes here an outer characteristic that can be added to highlight a certain devout female identity.

In some cases the choice of niqab may be seen as part of an eclectic selection with a strong focus on personal experience, which perhaps could be considered as a kind of spirituality (Bellah *et al.* 1996; Heelas and Woodhead 2005). An example of this is Khadija who has an Iraqi background. As previously mentioned, she converted from Shia to Sunni Islam and at the same time she became a member of a contemporary Sufi order founded by the US convert Nuh Mim Keller. He lives in Jordan, where his female disciples, according to Khadija, wear the niqab. In Denmark the order has only a handful of active adherents and Khadija is the only one among them to cover her face. Khadija's Shia family not only view her conversion but also her wearing of the niqab as fiercely provocative and a form of fanaticism, despite the fact that there are also Shia Muslim women in Iraq who use the niqab. Khadija explained that the niqab in Denmark is often seen as a sign that one is Salafi and thus anti-Shia. Khadija's own emphasis, on the other hand, was on the spiritual experience of wearing the niqab, and she pointed out that she wanted to practise it as long as it provided her with spiritual strength. She was, however, also pragmatic and had decided to put aside the niqab both because it became impractical in relation to her education and because she experienced negative aspects such as feelings of irritation caused by the reactions from the surroundings.

In other cases, the choice of the niqab can be seen as a quest for an identity with firm rules and limits. The niqab seems to be most widespread in Salafi groupings, where external features such as an 'Islamic dress code' are an important part of identity. The Salafi project is to return to what they consider as the true Islam dating from the Prophet's time. They define Islam as being entirely free of what is regarded as culture. Instead their identity is oriented towards a global umma with the same practices everywhere (Roy 2004). In both the case of Khadija and the wider Salafi circles, there seems to be a quest for origin and authenticity involved (Hervieu-Léger 2000). Our methodological point here is that the common pattern that seems to shape the stories means that such testimonies are primarily a source of the women's religious self-understanding.

9. CONSEQUENCES, USES AND DISUSES OF NIQAB

All the interviewees reported experiences of discrimination as a consequence of their niqab. They encountered comments that they saw as contemptuous or condescending and they found that both Muslims and non-Muslims behaved in an aggressive manner towards them.[14] They were for example, scolded by others, both Muslims and non-Muslims, on the street or in public transportation. One had heard that a bomb was likely to blow up as she entered the subway. Another woman had even been expelled from a bank because they feared her being a robber. The biggest problem faced by these women was their limited access to public services, jobs and education. In both Aarhus and Copenhagen several of the women personally experienced that they could not receive public benefits on the grounds that they were deemed to be unsuitable for work in the labour market. It is especially in relation to education and employment that the niqabis experience a serious dilemma. The women explained that in educational institutions and in work situations, even at, for instance, Muslim private schools, they had been ordered to take off the niqab. Four out of the eight interviewees, three converts and a Somali, prioritized their niqab over educational and employment opportunities. One of them studied through an on-line course, and the Somali woman considered moving away from her husband to another country where she could lead a more active life.

One of the women, Amina, who had worn the niqab for twenty-five years, had accepted to discard her niqab in order to study. Her husband suggested this when they moved to Denmark seventeen years ago, but she decided to continue wearing it. After her husband died she was left as the only supporter of her six children and she wished to start teaching again as she used to do in Egypt, from where she had obtained a degree in chemistry. However, she needed to be more proficient in Danish in order to be able to teach so she needed further training. She had been asked to remove the niqab while at school but she explained that she felt naked

---

[14] This seems to be the experience of other countries as well (Shirazi and Mishra 2010; Tissot 2011).

every time she had to remove the niqab and often cried after returning home. She felt very depressed and divided between her two wishes: the wish to keep the niqab and the wish to pursue further education. She explained, however, that it is an obligation (*fard*) to search knowledge and since she did not consider niqab an obligation, she had to choose the way she did. Thus, she had to negotiate between different principles of what she considered proper Islamic behaviour.

The other Arab woman, Khadija, also prioritized education over the niqab. She had, like Amina, tried to keep wearing the niqab in all other public places other than school and work. She began, however, to feel a kind of 'schizophrenia' because she did not wear it constantly and tried to hide it from family members and schoolmates. In addition, the often harsh reactions from both other Muslims and non-Muslims started to make her feel depressed, and her view of the niqab began to disturb her spirituality. In the kind of Sufi ideology followed by Khadija the niqab is a means to the end and not the end itself. As a result, she no longer wears the niqab. This does not, however, mean that she never uses it. She explained that she wore it in situations when she found it appropriate, such as on trips to Arab countries or if an important sheikh from abroad came to give a lecture. In those situations she wore it out of respect and also because she liked to sit on the first row. However, she did not regard herself as a niqabi anymore because she did not wear it on a regular basis.

One of the Somali women, Zeinab, had ceased using the niqab because she had an eye disease and felt that the niqab disturbed her orientation. In addition to this she had also become a mother and she needed to be able to take care of her children in public places, which was difficult if the niqab disturbed her orientation. She had also moved to another town with very few other Muslims and so she thought it was better not to frighten the neighbours.

The last woman, Hakima, ceased to use the niqab for religious reasons. However, she used it in order to attend events in Salafi circles in order to keep in contact with some of her Somali friends. She hid from these friends the fact that she did not share their beliefs anymore by avoiding topics related to Salafism and she also hid the fact that she did not use that kind of clothing style elsewhere. She explained that they would regard her as an apostate from Islam if they knew that she had started to wear a hat or a cap to cover her hair instead of a veil.

These different uses and disuses of wearing the niqab show that there are great varieties in how the women practised the wearing of niqab and that it could change over time and vary in different situations and circumstances. Wearing the niqab has severe consequences for the women in question even though there is not a general ban in Denmark. The women considered it a dilemma to be excluded from educational institutions and work places and so they had to decide which were the more important Islamic principles for them. Therefore the niqab could, at least for the women in question, be considered a very reflective choice. There was an emphasis on the niqab being chosen for the right reasons to give merit and also that it was an either/or situation. One of the women, Hanna, stated that it should be chosen: 'after the necessary considerations and not just for fun. It should not just be something you do occasionally.' The other women seemed to agree. It seemed that half of the women did not wear the niqab regularly, but the inconsistency in use made them depressed or 'schizophrenic' or gave them a feeling of faking. The women in this study thus seemed to count proper niqabis as women who wear the niqab on a regular basis in public places. This qualification of the term is important to note in connection with the quantitative aspects.

The qualitative part of our research has thus revealed some additional complexities of the delimitation of the group of niqabis. For example, that some women only wore a niqab on certain festive occasions, and some only did it periodically. This observation is supported by a later French study (Bouteldja 2011).

The fact that some women may be 'full-time niqabis' and other women only 'part-time niqabis' may add an extra source of uncertainty to the quantitative part of the study and this represents a challenge for researchers when it comes to whom to include as informants. There is, however, a strong tendency among our informants, and in Muslim milieus, to reserve the term niqabis for women who always, or at least regularly, wear the niqab in public spaces. This indicates that reports from informants on the number of niqabis in general would not include those women who only wear the niqab in the mosque or at special religious occasions, and we have also chosen to include as informants only women who wear the niqab, or did wear it, on a regular basis.

10. THE QUANTITATIVE MAPPING: EXISTING ESTIMATES AND DATA ACQUISITION

The quantitative analysis is already given in detail elsewhere and the following is therefore a very brief summary of it (Warburg *et al.* 2013).

It is necessary to have an estimate of the size of the group to be studied beforehand, because the sampling strategy will depend on it. Existing estimates from the Netherlands indicated that about 0.1 per cent of the Muslim women in the Netherlands are niqabis, and half of them were converts of ethnic Dutch background (Moors 2009a, 2009b). A similar frequency seems to be the case in France (Ambassade de France au Pakistan 2010).

Most of our fresh quantitative data were obtained from different informants assumed to have a special knowledge of the number of niqabis, either generally or in a specific stratum.

The quantitative data were acquired from several different strata and types of key informants: researchers, Muslim leaders, a journalist with good contacts in a Salafi-oriented environment in Aarhus and niqabis themselves. We also used location sampling in connection with a big *Eid* festival in Copenhagen (not the same as the *Eid* charity party).

We succeeded in building up trust among different key informants and gatekeepers in the different strata to get access to estimates on the number of niqabis they knew about.

In order to have a prior estimate of the number of niqabis in Denmark we asked three Danish researchers working with Muslim immigrants to give their estimates. They all indicated this to be around 100, and this corresponds to about 0.1 per cent of the approximately 90,000 Muslim women in Denmark who are old enough to wear a niqab.[15]

We also asked different Muslim key informants about the number of niqabis either in Denmark totally or in one of the two largest provincial cities, Odense and Aarhus. The reported figures from these informants are set out below.

Denmark proper:

Spokesman Imran Shah, Islamic Society: 30–40
Imam Abdul Wahid Pedersen, Danish Islamic Centre: max. 100
Spokesman Zubair Butt Hussain, Joint Council of Muslims: 50–150

---

[15] This includes the fewer than 2,000 female converts of ethnic Danish background (Jensen and Østergaard 2007b: 31). The estimated figure of 90,000 women is expounded in Warburg *et al.* (2013).

Odense:

Imam Mohamad El-Khalid, Islamic Society and three other informants: 5–7

Aarhus:

Journalist Pernille Ammitzbøll: 10–20
Niqabi informant: 10–15
Niqabi informant to Lene Kühle, Aarhus University: 18 (including
12 converts)

The different key informants represent different strata and different
geographical regions. Of the three figures for Denmark proper, the first
by Imran Shah is likely to be an underestimate, considering that he
seems to have overlooked or not thought of ethnic Danish converts.[16]
The next two figures of about 100 are in line with those of previous
estimates given by other researchers.

For both Odense and Aarhus we knew that the milieu is so narrow
that the informants practically knew everybody, so that the under-
coverage bias is negligible. Further, the close correspondence between
the estimates given by different key informants in the two cities indicate
that the numbers are reliable and without any appreciable under-
coverage bias.

In Copenhagen, however, there is no single network that allows access
to the majority of niqabis, and we therefore pursued other avenues.

We contacted sixteen major Muslim schools in Denmark for
telephone interviews. Thirteen of them are located in Copenhagen.
The telephone interviews indicated a total number of six niqabis,
which are between 0.3 and 0.6 per cent of all the Muslim mothers
to the pupils in these sixteen schools. This relatively low percentage
indicates that even among the religiously active and engaged
Muslims who put their children in Muslim schools, niqabis are a small
minority.

We reached yet another stratum by interviewing the leading visiting
nurses in three Copenhagen districts and in the city of Elsinore north of
Copenhagen. These interviews gave what we find are reliable *minimum*

---

[16] He agrees with other informants that niqabis are predominantly found among immigrant women
from Morocco and Somalia. He may not know any niqabis of ethnic Danish background. When
one of us (Østergaard) carried out field studies in this mosque in 2004–5, no niqabis were
observed among the converts.

figures for the number of niqabis in these districts, namely twenty-four niqabis for all three Copenhagen districts together and one more in Elsinore.

A location sampling by participation observation at an *Eid* feast on 20 September 2009 in Copenhagen yielded 12 niqabis out of 3,500 adult women. These figures can be used to reach an estimate of the total number of niqabis after making corrections for known effects of ethnic bias in this sample. This particular *Eid* feast was frequented mainly by Muslims of Arab and Somali backgrounds and a few converts.[17] We estimated that perhaps 60 per cent of this group of Muslims in Denmark might participate in such an event.[18] Sixty per cent corresponds to 31,000 women. The 3,500 women at the *Eid* feast can therefore be regarded as a representative sample of these 31,000 women. A proportional projection gives $12/3500 \times 31,000 = 106$ niqabis in Denmark in total.[19]

The last stratum is converts. Four out of 90 converts of Danish ethnic background were reported in an earlier study to wear a niqab (Jensen and Østergaard 2007b: 141). Projections from these figures to the total number of estimated female converts give at least 60 niqabis and rather about 70, but the projection is subjected to a rather high statistical uncertainty.[20] Taken together with the information that in Aarhus 12 out of 18 specified niqabis were converts, it seems well substantiated that a considerable proportion of the niqabis in Denmark are native

---

[17] Turks and Pakistanis hold, for example their own Eid feasts (Østergaard 2006: 157). Turks, Pakistanis and Bosnians account for 42 per cent of all Muslims in Denmark. Few if any niqabis are found among these nationalities, and we can assume that niqabis are concentrated among the other 58 per cent. As mentioned, the total number of Muslim women old enough to wear a niqab is about 90,000. This includes the fewer than 2,000 female converts of ethnic Danish background (Jensen and Østergaard 2007b: 31); 58 per cent of 90,000 is 52,000.

[18] A study covering participation in religious services at festivals showed that 33.3 per cent of Muslim pupils in Danish upper-secondary schools participate in religious services at minimum once a month, 19.4 per cent a couple of times every year, 11.1 only at festivals and 16.7 per cent less than once a year while 16.7 per cent reported never (Jensen 2002). On the basis of these figures, between 67 and 83 per cent of the pupils would participate in an *Eid* feast. The study is, however, mainly based on Muslim pupils with a Pakistani background, a group which according to other studies tends to be more practising than most other Muslims (Gundelach and Nørregård-Nielsen 2007: 51–3). Therefore, we have estimated the percentage to 60.

[19] If we increased the percentage from 60 to 75 (which is clearly an overestimate), the projection would only give 134 niqabis.

[20] Note: 65 per cent of 2,100 converts is 1,365; 65 per cent of 2,800 converts is 1,820; 4/90 of these numbers are 61 niqabis and 81 niqabis, respectively. The 95 per cent confidence interval is from 24 to 196 niqabis among the female Muslim converts in Denmark.

Danish women who have converted to Islam. Also in this respect Denmark resembles the Netherlands and other European countries.

11. TRIANGULATION OF ESTIMATED NUMBERS

In summary we have positively identified at least twenty niqabis in Aarhus, six in Odense, one in Elsinore, six among the parents in the Muslim schools (mostly from Copenhagen), and about twenty-four among mothers in three Copenhagen districts, according to the interviews with visiting nurses. The sum of these numbers is fifty-seven.[21]

These strata are different samples of the population of Muslim women; however, in total they do not represent a complete coverage. The two main factors contributing to the under-coverage bias are: (1) unidentified niqabis in provincial Denmark apart from Aarhus and Odense; and (2) unidentified niqabis in Greater Copenhagen.

The possible contribution from these two factors is summarized here.[22]

We estimate a maximum of ten to fifteen niqabis in provincial Denmark apart from Aarhus and Odense. Of these, we have identified one (in Elsinore).

The under-coverage bias of the Greater Copenhagen data stems from two factors: (1) leading visiting nurses in other districts than the three mentioned were not interviewed; and (2) visiting nurses would not have contact with other niqabis than those with small children and perhaps female relatives to the mothers. Correcting for this under-coverage bias gives an estimated range of 66 to 88 niqabis in Greater Copenhagen.

Summing up these estimates, Aarhus (20), Odense (6), rest of provincial Denmark (10–15), Greater Copenhagen (66–88), gives 102 to 129 niqabis in total. The 57 positively identified niqabis make up between 44 and 56 per cent of this total estimate. This calculation indicates that we have positively identified a fair proportion of the niqabis in Denmark. For comparison, the location sampling at the *Eid* feast gave an estimated total number of 106 niqabis.

These numbers are based on fresh empirical data acquired by interviews and location sampling, and they are thus independent of the three other estimates of the total numbers given by Muslim informants. The

---

[21] There may of course be one or two of the niqabis in the Muslim school stratum which are also reported in the number from the leading visiting nurses.

[22] Details are given in Warburg *et al.* (2013).

two most reliable estimates from these informants are 100 and 50–150, respectively.

Considering that our estimated numbers in the above are over 100, and that the corrections for under-coverage are rather crude, we reached the conclusion that a number of 150 niqabis seems to be the most reliable and with a range of 100–200. The number of 150 niqabis is further corroborated by the separate estimate of about 70 niqabi converts of ethnic Danish background. The probability of a relatively high proportion of converts among niqabis is strengthened by a report from the Netherlands (Moors 2009b).

12. CONCLUSION

In this chapter we have presented an overview of the main findings from this first study of niqabis in Denmark and of the methodological challenges involved when studying rare and hidden groups, in particular when the context is highly politicized. In such a situation, trust is a crucial factor in getting access to informants – and trust takes time. Time was scarce, however, and we therefore chose to emphasize reliability rather than precision in both the quantitative and qualitative analyses. As with all data collection, compromises must be made out of concern of available time and resources (Miles and Huberman 1994: 16–18). What was important was to give an academically sound and robust estimate of the order of magnitude of the number of niqabis in Denmark: are there around 100 or are there around 500? That is the pertinent question, not if there are 130 or 170 niqabis. Regarding the qualitative study, it was important to give a display which was reliable and as bias free as possible of some of the possible positions, narratives and modes of identification that are currently used among Danish niqabis. Basically, for all the women interviewed, wearing a niqab is a personal, voluntary choice motivated by personal piety in the relationship with God. Their accounts are testimonies of the development of their own religious self-understanding. Furthermore, it seems that the niqabis are often associated with cross-ethnic and Salafi-oriented environments.

Having made the above reservations regarding our empirical findings, it is worth noticing that our results cohere remarkably well with findings from other European countries, both in terms of numbers and narratives. They point towards some more general tendencies regarding the use of face veils in Europe, which adds to the reliability of the results. First of all, it is clear that niqabis make up only a very small proportion of the total of Muslim women. These women have become a target for European identity politics that focuses on certain forms of Islam as their 'significant other'. The women seek to avoid this othering, and instead emphasize their personal choice and personal piety in the relationship with God as the primary context for their practices. When they experience critique and sometimes even hostility, these difficulties are just another proof that they are doing something extraordinary for God. In this way, the women articulate themselves along lines that are well known regarding religious identities. Taking on the face veil is a token of a substantial religious change, not only for those who convert to Islam from a non-Muslim background, but also for those women who were born Muslims.

The political interest in the topic also meant that the conclusions of the study did have an effect. After we submitted the report to the Ministry of Interior, the report was classified not to be released before the committee had concluded its work. However, after about two months, rumours about the results began to circulate, the pressure grew for a release of the report, and we were pressured into giving interviews to the press and radio/TV. For a few days we came under political attack by politicians advocating a ban on the burqas, but apparently our message eventually came through. So after this initial political stir the politicians and the public quickly lost interest in the issue of niqabis, mainly because there were so few of them and that half of them were ethnic Danish converts. The Danish government declared that they were satisfied with the outcome of the commissioned work, and they announced two minor modifications of existing law.[23] The idea of a general ban on face-covering clothes seems no longer to be part of current politics in Denmark.

Looking back on the events and the hectic days around the release of the 'Burqa report', we have several times asked ourselves whether it was worth the effort to engage our academic capacities into investigating such a controversial topic as the wearing of face veils. It would have evidently been more convenient to lie low and let others do the job. However, as university researchers we felt the obligation to provide the public with material which allows political decisions to be taken on a

---

[23] The two proposed amendments were in the penal law section concerning illegal coercion, where the maximum sentence was increased from two to four years, and in the Administration of Justice Act, and by which witnesses were explicitly forbidden to hide their faces (www.berlin gske.dk/politik/laes-regeringens-burka-papir).

well-founded basis within the given time-frame and allocated resources. The final outcome of the burqa affair in Denmark is positive confirmation of such a principle, which is vital for a democracy.

REFERENCES

Abell, Peter 1990. 'Methodological Achievements in Sociology over the Past Few Decades with Special Reference to the Interplay of Quantitative and Qualitative Methods', in Christopher, G. A. Bryant and Becker, Henk A. (eds.), *What Has Sociology Achieved?* Basingstoke: Macmillan, pp. 94–116.

Ali, Shaheen Sardar 2010. 'Cyberspace as Emerging Muslim Discursive Space? Online Fatawa on Women and Gender Relations and Its Impact on Muslim Family Law Norms', *International Journal of Law, Policy and the Family*, 24(3): 338–60.

Ambassade de France au Pakistan 2010. 'The Burqa Debate in France' www. ambafrancepk.org/france_pakistan/spip.php?article1679

Bakht, Natasha 2012. 'Veiled Objections: Facing Public Opposition to the Niqab', in Beaman, L. (ed.), *Defining Reasonable Accommodation: Managing Religious Diversity*. Vancouver: University of British Colombia Press, pp. 70–108.

Barker, E. 1998. 'Standing at the Cross-Roads: The Politics of Marginality in "Subversive Organizations"', in Bromley, D. G. (ed.), *The Politics of Religious Apostasy*. Westport, CT: Praeger, pp. 75–93.

Beckford, J. 1978. 'Accounting for Conversion', *British Journal of Sociology*, 29(2): 249–62.

1985. *Cult Controversies: The Societal Response to New Religious Movements*. London: Tavistock.

Bellah, R., Madsen, R., Sullivan, W. M., Swidler, A. and Tipton, S. M. 1996. *Habits of the Heart: Individualism and Commitment in American Life*. Berkeley, CA: University of California Press.

Bouteldja, Naima 2011. *Unveiling the Truth: Why 32 Muslim Women Wear the Full-Face Veil in France*, Open Society Foundation. www.soros.org/initiatives.home/articles_publications/unveiling-the-truth-20110411.

Brems, Eva, Yaiza Janssens, Kim Lecoyer, Saïla Ouald Chaib and Vandersteen, Victoria 2012. '*Wearing the face veil in Belgium*'. Preliminary manuscript for International Seminar: Empirical Face Veil Research, Ghent University, 9 May 2012.

Bromley, D. G. 1998. 'Sociological Perspectives on Apostasy: An Overview' in Bromley, D. G. (ed.), *The Politics of Religious Apostasy*. Westport, CT: Praeger, pp. 3–16.

Byng, Michelle 2013. 'Symbolically Muslim: Media, Hijab and the West', *Critical Sociology*, 36(1): 109–29.

Carter, L. F. 1998. 'Carriers of Tales: On Assessing Credibility of Apostate and Other Outsider Accounts of Religious Practices', in Bromley, D. G. (ed.), *The Politics of Religious Apostasy*. Westport, CT: Praeger, pp. 221–37.

Deding, Mette, Fridberg, Torben and Jakobsen, Vibeke 2008. 'Non-response in a Survey among Immigrants in Denmark', *Survey Research Methods*, 2(3): 107–21.

Chesler, Phyllis 2010. 'Ban the Burqa? The Argument in Favor', *Middle East Quarterly*, 17(4): 33–45.

Erickson, Bonnie H. 1979. 'Some Problems of Inference from Chain Data', *Sociological Methodology*, 10: 276–302.

Faugier, Jean and Sargeant, Mary 1997. 'Sampling Hard to Reach Populations', *Journal of Advanced Nursing*, 26: 790–7.

Feskens, Remco, Hox, Joop, Gerty, Lensvelt-Mulder and Schmeets, Hans 2006. 'Collecting Data among Ethnic Minorities in an International Perspective', *Field Methods*, 18: 284–304.

Forum. Fact book 2008. *The Position of Muslims in the Netherlands: Facts and Figures.* Utrecht: FORUM, Institute for Multicultural Development.

Giddens, A. 1999. *Runaway World: How Globalization Is Reshaping Our Lives.* London: Profile.

Gjersten, M. N. 2009. 'Kejserens nye Burka', *Information*, 21/08, www.infor mation.dk/200934

Grim, Brian J. and Mehtab, S. Karim, 2011. *The Future of the Global Muslim Population: Projections for 2010–2030.* Washington, DC: Pew Research Center.

Groves, Robert M., and Couper, Mick P. 1998. *Nonresponse in Household Interview Surveys.* New York: Wiley.

Gundelach, Peter and Nørregård-Nielsen, Esther 2007. *Etniske gruppers værdier–Baggrundsrapport.* Copenhagen: Tænketanken om udfordringer for integrationsindsatsen i Danmark. Copenhagen: Ministry of Refugees, Immigration and Integration Affairs.

Heckathorn, Douglas D. 1997. 'Respondent-Driven Sampling: A New Approach to the Study of Hidden Populations', *Social Problems*, 44: 174–99.

   2002. 'Respondent-Driven Sampling II: Deriving Valid Population Estimates from Chain-Referral Samples of Hidden Populations', *Social Problems*, 49: 11–34.

Heelas, P. and Woodhead, L. 2005. *The Spiritual Revolution: Why Religion is Giving Way to Spirituality.* Malden: Blackwell.

Hervieu-Léger, D. 2000. *Religion as a Chain of Memory.* Cambridge: Polity.

Holaday, Bonnie, Wang, Ru-Hwa and Turner-Henson, Anne 1991. 'Sampling Rare Populations: Strategies for Finding Subgroups for Health Surveys', *Journal of Medical Science*, 11: 253–61.

Jacobsen, Brian 2007. 'Muslimer i Danmark – en kritisk vurdering af antalsopgørelser', in Warburg, Margit and Jacobsen, Brian (eds.), *Tørre tal om troen. Religionsdemografi i Danmark i det 21.århundrede*, Højbjerg: Forlaget Univers, pp. 143–65.

Jensen, Tim 2002. 'The Religiousness of Muslim Pupils in Danish Upper-Secondary Schools', in Shadid, W. A. R. and van Koningsveld, P. S. (eds.), *Intercultural Relations and Religious Authorities: Muslims in the European Union*. Leuven: Peeters, pp. 123–37.

Jensen, Tina Gudrun and Østergaard, Kate 2007a. 'Omvendelse til islam i Danmark–gætterier og Realiteter' in Warburg, Margit and Jacobsen, Brian (eds.), *Tørre tal om troen. Religionsdemografi i det 21. århundrede*. Højbjerg: Univers, pp. 166–88.

2007b. *Nye muslimer i Danmark. Møder og omvendelser*. Højbjerg: Univers.

2011. *Ekstremistiske miljøer med salafi-grupperinger i fokus*. Copenhagen: Ministry of Social Affairs (www.sm.dk/data/Lists/Publikationer/Attachments/686/ekstremistiske_salafigrupperinger.pdf)

Johansen, Birgitte and Riem Spielhaus 2012. 'Counting Deviance: Revisiting a Decade's Production of Quantitative Surveys among Muslims in Europe', *Journal of Muslims in Europe*, 1(1): 81–112.

Kalton, Graham 2001. 'Practical Methods for sampling Rare and Mobile Populations', *Proceedings of the Annual Meeting of the American Statistical Association*, August 5–9, St Louis: Mira Digital.

Kiliç, Sevgi, Saharso, Sawitri and Sauer, Birgit 2008. 'Introduction: The Veil: Debating Citizenship, Gender and Religious Diversity', *Social Politics*, 15(4): 397–410.

Konservative 2011. Demokratisk *Integration-Udspil*, www.konservative.dk/Politik/Integrationspolitik/Udspil

Lambert, Elizabeth 1990. *The Collection and Interpretation of Data from Hidden Populations*, NIDA Research Monograph 98, US Department of Health and Human Services.

Lettinga, Doutje and Saharso, Sawitri 2012. 'The political debates on the veil in France and the Netherlands: Reflecting national integration models?', *Comparative European Politics*, 10(3): 319–36.

Miles, Matthew B., and Huberman, A. Michael 1994. *Qualitative Data Analysis: An Expanded Sourcebook*. Thousand Oaks, CA: Sage.

Moors, Annelies 2009a. 'The Dutch and the Face-Veil: The Politics of Discomfort', *Social Anthropology*, 17: 393–408.

2009b. *Gezichtsshluiers Draagster en Debatten*. Amsterdam: International Institute for the Study of Islam in the Modern World, University of Amsterdam.

Østergaard, Kate 2006. *Danske verdensreligioner: Islam*. Copenhagen: Gyldendal.

Patel, David, S. 2012. 'Concealing to Reveal: The Informational Role of Islamic Dress', *Rationality and Society*, 24(3): 295–323.

Rapport om brugen af niqab og burka 2009. Copenhagen: Institute of Cross-Cultural and Regional Studies, University of Copenhagen. www.e-pages. dk/ku/322

Roald, Anne Sofie 2001. *Women in Islam*. London: Routledge.

Robbins, T. 1988. *Cults, Converts and Charisma: The Sociology of New Religious Movements*. London: Sage.

Roy, O. 2004. *Globalized Islam: The Search for a New Ummah*. New York: Columbia University Press.

Saharso, Sawitri and Lettinga, Doutje 2008. 'Contentious Citizenship: Policies and Debates on the Veil in the Netherlands', *Social Politics: International Studies in Gender, State and Society*, 15(4): 455–80.

Shirazi, F. and Mishra, S. 2010. 'Young Muslim Women on the Face Veil (niqab): A Tool of Resistance in Europe But Rejected in the United States', *International Journal of Cultural Studies*, 13(1): 43–62.

Skovgaard-Petersen, Jakob 1997. *Defining Islam for the Egyptian State*. Leiden: Brill.

2009. 'Islamic Fundamentalism in Arab Television: Islamism and Salafism in Competition', in Martensson *et al.* (eds.), *Fundamentalism in the Modern World*, vol. *II: Fundamentalism and Communication*, London: I.B. Tauris, pp. 264–91.

Sudman, Seymour, Sirken, Monroe G. and Cowan, Charles D. 1988. 'Sampling Rare and Elusive Populations', *Science*, 240: 991–6.

Tissot, Sylvie 2011. 'Excluding Muslim Women: From Hijab to Niqab, from School to Public Space', *Public Culture*, 23(1): 39–46.

Warburg, Margit, Birgitte Schepelern Johansen and Kate Østergaard 2013. 'Counting Niqabs and Burqas in Denmark: Methodological Aspects of Quantifying Rare and Elusive Religious Subcultures', *Journal of Contemporary Religion*, 28(1): 33–48.

Wictorowicz, Q. 2006. 'Anatomy of the Salafi Movement', *Studies in Conflict and Terrorism*, 29: 207–39.

4

THE BELGIAN 'BURQA BAN' CONFRONTED WITH INSIDER REALITIES

*Eva Brems, Yaiza Janssens, Kim Lecoyer, Saïla Ouald Chaib,
Victoria Vandersteen and Jogchum Vrielink*

This chapter confronts the stated motives of the Belgian legislator who banned face covering in public with the experiences and views of women who wear the face veil in Belgium. Contrasting the insider experiences of the women concerned with the assumptions of the Belgian legislator, it argues that on account of its relying on erroneous assumptions, the Belgian ban does not actually serve its stated purpose, that it is disproportionate and that it denies procedural justice.

1. BELGIUM'S FACE VEIL BAN

Belgium would have been the first country to ban the wearing of face veils in public on its entire territory, if a political crisis hadn't caused the early dissolution of Parliament in May 2010, at a time when the Chamber of Representatives had already voted the ban, and the Senate, which 'evoked' the bill, was due to vote it in a matter of weeks.[1] After elections the political crisis continued, and Belgium was ruled by a caretaker government for over a year. It was during that time that several 'burqa ban' bills were tabled again, as parliamentary initiatives, and that one of them was adopted after brief discussion by a near-unanimous Chamber. A request for expert hearings did not receive sufficient

---

[1] The majority of legislative proposals in Belgium are 'optionally bicameral'. Regarding such proposals, the governing principle is that the Chamber of Representatives has the authority to approve a bill autonomously but the Senate has the right to 'evoke' the approved bill and discuss it. This so-called 'right of evocation' must be invoked within a certain term and it requires a minimum number of members. In this case, evocation had taken place.

support to be granted, and the same fate befell a request for the advice of the Legislative Division of Council of State, a body that advises on the legality and constitutionality of proposed legislation. Moreover, this time the Senate opted against evocation. The 'Act of 1 June 2011 to institute a prohibition on wearing clothing that covers the face, or a large part of it', was published in the *Belgian Official Journal* on 13 July 2011 and entered into force ten days later. This means that, following France – which had adopted its 'burqa ban' in the summer of 2010 – Belgium is the second European country banning the Islamic face veil in public.

In practical terms and 'subject to legal provisions to the contrary', the new Article 563*bis* of the Belgian Criminal Code punishes persons 'who appear in places accessible to the public with their faces covered or concealed, in whole or in part, in such a manner that they are not recognizable' with a monetary fine of €15 to €25 and/or a prison sentence of one to seven days.[2] The only exceptions are 'labour regulations or municipal ordinances due to festivities'. While the terms of the ban do not specifically target Islamic face veils, the political discourse, parliamentary discussions and media coverage accompanying its adoption, do not leave any room for doubt in this respect: the target of the ban are the 200 to 300 women in this country of 11 million inhabitants, who wore the face veil in public.[3]

2. COLLECTING OUTSIDER AND INSIDER VIEWS

Analysing the *travaux préparatoires* of the Belgian 'burqa ban',[4] we identified the Belgian legislator's most important motives for banning the face veil. These consist of three clusters of arguments: protecting women's rights, guaranteeing communication and social

[2] Increased with the legal surcharge factor (i.e. multiplied by 5.5).
[3] There are no official figures on the number of women wearing face veils at any time in Belgium. The Belgian Centre for Equal Opportunities estimates their number at around 200 (De Wit 2010). Representatives of the Centre d'Action Laïque mentioned the figure of 270 during hearings on 13 November 2009 of the Gérin extraordinary parliamentary commission that examined the French legislative proposal (Gérin 2010). This is less than 0.5 per cent of the Muslim population in Belgium.
[4] In addition to an analysis of the parliamentary documents from the legislature that commenced in 2010, and during which the Act of 1 June 2011 was introduced, documents from the 2007–10 legislature were examined as well. Various members of Parliament emphasized that the arguments raised at that time remained relevant.

cohesion, and improving (subjective and objective) safety. In this chapter, we will present the results of our empirical research into women who wear the face veil in such a manner that it talks directly to each of these motives.[5]

The empirical research[6] consisted of semi-structured in-depth interviews, and two focus group discussions[7] aimed at getting insights in the lived realities of the interviewees. We interviewed twenty-seven women between September 2010 and September 2011. As the work of the legislator 'caught up' with the research, fourteen women were interviewed before the adoption of the legal ban, thirteen after its adoption. It is to be noted however, that before the adoption of the nationwide ban, local bans were already in place in most municipalities where women wearing the face veil resided. Twelve women we interviewed were wearing the face veil at that time;[8] ten were former wearers;[9] two wore it occasionally (one of whom had worn it full-time in the past), and three were considering starting to wear it.[10] The interviewees are relatively young,[11] and the majority are married.[12] Most of the current and former wearers we interviewed are second-generation immigrants of Moroccan origin, who speak French or Dutch. A few are first-generation immigrants, only one of which did not speak Dutch or French.[13] Five are women without a migration background who converted to Islam. Of the three potential wearers, two are converted Belgians and one is of Moroccan origin.

This is qualitative research. It has not attempted to count the number of women wearing the face veil in Belgium. Nor does it make any claims

---

[5] For an analysis of these motives from the perspective of human rights law, see Vrielink et al. (2013).

[6] See research report at www.ugent.be/re/publiekrecht/en/research/human-rights/faceveil.pdf

[7] These took place in April and May 2012 – one in Brussels in French and one in Antwerp in Dutch. Nine women participated, two of whom had not been previously interviewed for this study.

[8] Among the women who were wearing the face veil at the time of the interview, eight wore it for more than ten years, two between five and ten years, and two minors had started to wear it recently.

[9] Among the former face veil wearers, one woman wore it more than ten years, six wore it between five and ten years, and two women wore it for less than one year.

[10] All three had already experimented with the face veil, either in Belgium or abroad.

[11] Ten are in their thirties (31–40); seven 25–30; four 18–24; two are minors; two are women in their forties and two are over 50.

[12] It is to be noted that (at least) five of the interviewees are married to a convert (three Belgians, two men of African origin).

[13] This interview was conducted with the help of an interpreter.

to representativeness, even though a significant percentage of the relevant group was reached.[14]

3. THE FACE VEIL IN BELGIUM AND WOMEN'S RIGHTS

3.1. Outsider arguments

Discourse emphasizing women's rights and women's dignity abounds in the *travaux préparatoires*. Strong language is used, branding the face veil as a 'mobile jail', a 'textile prison' or the 'shroud of freedom'. The underlying assumption of this argumentation is that women wearing a face veil are (mostly or always) forced to do so. This assumption clearly emerges from various interventions. The hypothesis that women wear face veils out of their own free will was not or hardly considered. Parallels were drawn with the situation of women in places such as Afghanistan and Iran, alleging that strong disapproval of the obligation imposed on women in these countries to cover themselves[15] logically entails the need to ban face veils in Belgium. In that respect it is noteworthy that the term 'burqa' is generally used in the debates, even though it is not clear whether that specifically Afghan garment has even been spotted in Belgium.[16] In addition, some MPs regard face veils as merely the tip of the iceberg, i.e. an indicator of 'other violent violations of human rights, such as the right to education, the right to control one's own body, the right to free movement in public, freedom of speech and of opinion'.[17]

Similarly, Members of Parliament also regarded the face veil as a symbol of female oppression. From that perspective, some regarded face veils as an offence to the human dignity of *all* women and an inherently reprehensible symbol that by definition entails a 'debasement of the concepts of humanity and women'.[18]

---

[14] To underline this and to resist readers' tendency to 'quantify' the qualitative results, the current report avoids talking in numbers and uses instead terms such as 'most', 'many', 'several' or 'some' (in declining order).

[15] Members failed to observe that, in Iran, this does not (as a general rule) concern clothing covering the face.

[16] Women wearing an Islamic face veil in Belgium generally wear either a 'niqab' that leaves the eyes free, or a 'sitar', covering the eyes.

[17] *Parliamentary report*, Chamber 2010–11, no. 53-219/4, 7.

[18] *Parliamentary proceedings*, Chamber 2010–11, 28 April 2011, no. 53-30, 38. See also: *Parliamentary report*, Chamber 2010–11, no. 53-219/4, 19.

3.2. Insider views

Given the crucial role, in the discourse of the proponents of the ban, of the assumption that the face veil is generally worn under pressure, a first focus in the analysis of the interviews is on women's narrations of how and why they came to start wearing a face veil, and in particular on their agency in this respect. Next, we will zoom in on the interviewees' gender views and practices, as these may throw light both on the assumed link between the face veil and other types of women's oppression on the one hand, and on the other hand on the face veil as a symbol promoting unequal gender relations.

3.2.1. Agency

Starting to wear the face veil   Though some women started to wear the face veil only in their thirties, the large majority of the interviewees started in their teens or early twenties.

All interviewees describe the decision to start wearing the face veil as a well-considered and free decision. They consider it a crucial matter that the wearing of a face veil should be an autonomous personal choice. Several emphasize that from a religious perspective, this has to be an autonomous decision, as Islam explicitly prohibits pressure in religious matters.

> Well as I said in religion one cannot force a person to do something. There is a quranic verse that says 'no constraint in religion'. So religion is a personal choice, one cannot force or oblige a person to practise religion or to wear something she does not want to wear, so I say to myself, one cannot oblige it, I don't think that any good practising Muslim could oblige a person to wear a niqab or anything else.
>
> (interview 8)

The decision to wear the face veil is not described as a moment of revelation or as a break with their previous lives, yet as a personal trajectory of deepening and perfecting one's faith. For the large majority of interviewees, starting to wear the face veil was the result of a process of some length. This involved in many cases the study of religion through books, television, tapes or discussions with fellow believers. Some women went through a phase of experimentation in which they wore the face veil occasionally, or in which they wore it only abroad.

For some interviewees, wearing the face veil was a wish they had cherished for some time before taking the step. Several women narrated that before they wore the face veil, when they saw a woman wearing it, they felt a strong attraction for its 'serenity' and 'beauty'.

> If you just look at someone who wears the niqab, I think that is very beautiful, I think she really has '*nur*' (light) ... Before, I was also very modern, I was really very modern on the street. But when I saw a woman who wore the niqab I just kept watching, I just kept following her with my eyes. Really the whole time, sometimes that was really an hour. But then I got such a beautiful feeling, she looks so beautiful.
>
> (interview 11)

Some women take a face veil wearer in their close environment as a model, and one interviewee reports that her first face veil was a gift from a friend. Yet others did not know anyone personally who wore the face veil before they started wearing it, and none report efforts of persuasion by other women. Similarly, none of the interviewees see their veil as a message to the outside world – it is something they do for themselves and for God. Proselytism is far from their minds. When asked, none of the interviewees want to encourage other women to wear the face veil, even though some say they would be available to help women who have taken the step or who have a strong desire to do so.

Reasons for wearing the face veil   The main driver to start wearing the face veil appears to be a desire to excel in piety. Several women mention the wives of the Prophet as an inspiration. Some interviewees interpret the wearing of the face veil as a religious obligation. Yet the large majority does not see it as an obligation, but rather as a voluntary commitment to a higher level of Islamic practice. All interviewees state that they do not follow any particular school or tendency in Islam. They want to be as pious a Muslim as possible, by applying not only mandatory religious rules, but also the rules that are 'recommended'.

> We believe that you get good points from Allah. Hassanat we call that. Indeed when you do it, you're in a higher rank with Allah.
>
> (former face veil wearer during Antwerp focus group discussion)

In that sense, wearing the face veil does not stand alone. It is part of a life project that considers Islam as 'a lifestyle'.

> K: for me, my religion is my life code ... I mean to say I wouldn't do anything that is not in relation to religion.
>
> S: And it is not only in the part you see on the outside, it can also be in behaviour. For example, we will not insult anyone ...

K: I wore my veil first on the inside before I wore it on the outside. For me, the veil on the inside is the first thing. My veil is my chastity, it is my behaviour, it is my politeness, it is my respect. That's my veil.

(excerpt from Brussels focus group discussion)

In addition, several interviewees emphasize chastity as a motive for wearing the face veil: the wish to protect oneself from the gaze of men, and to reserve one's beauty only for one's (actual or future) husband.

We apply make-up, we do our hair, so it actually changed absolutely nothing, we just made a choice to preserve our body and our beauty only for our husband.

(interview 25)

Well I don't know, there are people who need when they go out in the street to not feel the gaze of men, because to them they feel dirty.

(interview 26)

For some women this is more a 'practical' matter of avoiding unwelcome male attention, which they say they experience from Muslim men in the public space if they go around uncovered.

I have put it on to have peace, being Belgian, having blue eyes etcetera, it was a bit difficult for me ... automatically when I went in the Arab-Muslim neighbourhoods of the capital, I got comments by men: 'are you a Muslim, are you a Muslim ... ?'. Second question was: 'are you married?' ... So at a certain moment that really troubled me.

(interview 3)

Other women however reject the harassment motive:

S: More men touch me with the niqab than without niqab.
Z: In England I experienced the opposite ... it excites the imagination of some people.
N: Also it's really boosting the ego of a man, to think that a woman would wear the niqab for that.
S: and of the woman too, I think.

(excerpt from Brussels focus group discussion)

Three interviewees state that they started to wear the face veil because their fiancé or husband asked them to and they agreed voluntarily with this request.

Well first of all I wanted to get married. So I met a person who was converted to Islam. And one of his conditions was that I had to wear the niqab. A thing I had not thought about ... It was for me a good thing you see, there was nothing bad in it, it was a way of protecting his wife, so I really took it that way. And I put it on immediately to please him.

(interview 18)

Husbands When asked, none of the interviewees knew of any case in which a woman was obliged – by her husband or anyone else – to wear a face veil.[19] One woman said that she knows women whose husbands tried to make them wear it, but they refused and did not wear it. However, several interviewees knew women who would like to wear a face veil, but refrain from doing so because their husband does not want them to.

Several women negotiated with their future husband the right to start or continue to wear a face veil after marriage.

> In fact I always had such a dream to wear a niqab, but it was always difficult at home because it was not allowed. Because they are always worried, because there is a lot of racism, maybe they will do something to you or whatever. And so, I had in fact nobody's support. So when I got married *elhamdulilah* I got the support I needed from my husband and then I took the step to wear it. Yes that is something I really wanted purely for myself so I had really told my husband 'Look if I want to marry you I intend to wear a burqa or niqab, do you agree?' My husband said at first 'yes that is your choice if you want that, in fact you choose it yourself'. But *elhamdulilah* he supported me a little bit.

(interview 12)

Most women report that their husbands supported them in their choice to wear the face veil. For some women, the idea that this would please their husbands a lot seems to have played a role in their decision making, without there being an actual request on his part.

> I got married, we were first married in the Islamic way, that is to say I lived with my parents, while my husband lived also in the house of his parents, and it was something my husband really held very dear. While at the time, it did not interest me at all, and I did not see myself at all wearing the veil. So my husband respected my choice. And step by step in our spiritual advancement together, I started to think about it and to really think about it very, very strongly, and so, even before I lived with my husband, the month of Ramadan, or a few days like that, just like that, to

---

[19] During the search for interviewees, we did interview a social worker who stated that she knew a woman who had been forced to wear the face veil. That same woman had been interviewed by a Belgian newspaper. However, despite many efforts we were not able to interview that woman.

try it, I put it on. And I really felt good with it. First it was at the exit of mosques, from time to time, or when I went to a conference, so it really started like that, little by little. And I really felt a very great well-being. My husband never wanted to pressure me, for him it was something that he held dearly, that he loved a lot, but . . . the wife in the wearing of the face veil has to feel really very well in what she does . . . And so, when we started living together, I presented the matter a little bit as a surprise. The first time we went out together, I was ready, prepared to go out, and arriving at the ground floor, I took out my sitar and I put it on. So my husband was pleased and I was also very pleased.

(interview 19)

Even if they had not sent such signals, some husbands were happy with their wives' decision:

My husband was surprised, but he said 'If you wear that, you can do that if you want it yourself, but don't think you have to do it for me. If you want that, it is a nice extra, but don't think it is mandatory.'

(interview 14)

Some other husbands seemed to consider the matter as something that did not concern them very much.

It was not that he was in favour and it was not that he was against it either; it had to remain my choice in fact. So he accepted and that's it. And afterwards he also accepted that I took it off.

(interview 27)

Several women report that their husbands initially opposed the idea yet they managed to persuade them.

Well you see I got married at 19. So when I wore it, my husband was not too much in favour that I wear it, but I explained him. I told him, you see, you took me with the niqab and so it's OK. And I even showed him some books, so he read them, he understood why I wore it, and afterwards he took it well.

(interview 8)

In some cases, the reason behind the husband's attitude appears to be that he is worried about the hardship life with a face veil would cause to his wife, in others the reason seems to be related to his own interests.[20]

---

[20] For example, in one case a woman who had abandoned the veil wanted to wear it again, but did not do so because her Algerian husband feared that he would be considered a terrorist if his wife wore a face veil.

Similarly, the women who stopped wearing the face veil described this as an autonomous decision, even though in most cases it was made under pressure from street aggression or fear of police enforcement of the (local or nationwide) ban (see below). In most such cases, it was the woman's husband who first suggested that she stop wearing the face veil.

> It was not so hard for me, except of course some days when I felt less strong but I was not afraid, it did not hinder me to go out . . . The concern was rather my husband who found it difficult to cope with all that.
>
> (former face veil wearer during Brussels focus group discussion)

Family On the side of their parents and in-laws, some interviewees report positive reactions to the fact that they started to wear the face veil.

> Yes, in my family they are very much practising . . . My sister-in-law . . . she is a Belgian convert. She also wears the niqab until today . . . And even with the mother-in-law, the mom of my husband, they accepted that, the family of my husband as it is a Belgian family and we explained her and all, they accept that with pleasure. Yes I go shopping with her and she was pleased.
>
> (interview 2)

Yet most interviewees experienced negative reactions from their close family to their decision to wear a face veil.[21] Three interviewees state that their family never knew that they used to wear a face veil.

> For my family that was very difficult for them, they really had a hard time accepting it because they took it as a breach with society, with the evolution of women.
>
> (interview 25)

Summing up Overall, in the women's narrations of how they started to wear the face veil, their agency appears as a strong and determining factor.

Several women show a remarkable degree of individualism and single-mindedness.

> So there, I had to impose myself. I am the way I am, they have to accept me with it or else they do not accept me at all.
>
> (interview 9)

---

[21] In some cases, the negative relationship with family members preceded the decision to wear the face veil and was based on their religious lifestyle in general.

> If I now want to start wearing the niqab, that is really something I want for myself. For me.
>
> (interview 11)

This should not come as a surprise. While for some women the anticipation of a positive reaction from their (prospective) husband is one of the key motives for their decision, all women who take the decision to wear a face veil in Belgium know that they are likely to encounter negative reactions from their loved ones and/or the broader public. This context may be expected to lead to a certain self-selection among potential wearers.

3.2.2. Gender views and patterns

Autonomy and strength The large majority of the interviewees came across as very autonomous women, who made a personal choice and went to great lengths to pursue it. Several women indicated that it takes a strong woman to wear a face veil in Belgium.

> Well, I can tell you that all the sisters I know who wear the niqab and those I knew in Brussels before, they were rather women who feel good about themselves. To the contrary, who have a reply ready when they get a comment in the street, who will not be trampled upon.
>
> (interview 3)

> In contradiction to the idea that a Muslim woman who wears the face veil would be a submitted woman who has not much to say in the couple, who only obeys blindly what her husband tells her ... to the contrary, I find that a woman who is completely veiled ... for me it is a woman with strength, it is a woman who has an enormous self-confidence ... You need it enormously, to be able to live the fact of wearing the face veil, to be able to live it well, to feel complete, to be up to the society in which you live.
>
> (interview 19)

As their ambitious path is a religious one, these women value submission to God, yet reject submission to other human beings.

> For me, it is purely out of submission to God. Because I don't think I would be ready for such difficult efforts for anyone other than God.
>
> (interview 21)

Directly as well as indirectly, many women show annoyance at the fact that outsiders assume that they are being suppressed or dominated by their husbands, and in particular that they are assumed to be forced to wear the face veil.

> It's really, really humiliating, and degrading for the personality of a Muslim girl – I know what I'm talking about – to hear say morning and evening 'it's the men who submit you, it's the men who oblige you, it's the men . . . ' it needs to be said, there is a moment when it needs to stop. We are girls, we are born in Europe, we grew up, we went out, we lived, we have a critical mind, we can judge, we can . . . Why would we be more apt to be dominated by a man?
>
> (interview 23)

> After my first interception by the police, I phoned an organization that defends the rights of persons, and they told me 'Listen, Madam, given that you are stuck, that you have been controlled etc., if you want, we can talk to your husband.' I told them: 'Why do you want to talk to my husband?' 'So that he would let you take off your veil' 'Excuse me? You want to talk to my husband, but it is not him who wears the veil, and it is not him who tells me whether to wear it or not, I am the one you should talk to.'
>
> (Brussels focus group discussion)

In addition, several interviewees took offence with reactions suggesting that they were stupid or in need of enlightenment or education. Their own image of face veil wearers is very different and partly based on countries where women wearing a face veil work in important functions.

> Behind a veil, there can be a teacher, behind a veil there can be a nurse, behind a veil there can be a doctor, behind a veil there is always a great personality. And that's it, you know, people don't look at that.
>
> (interview 27)

Role patterns: practice and views   The large majority of interviewees are housewives. Yet what transpires in some of the interviews is that in a couple in which the wife wears a face veil, there is likely to be a relatively high burden on the husband with respect to domestic errands outside the house. This may be because the wife considers that she should limit interaction with men as much as possible, or because she wants to limit her journeys out of the home on account of the negative reactions of people or the risk of being stopped by the police. In addition, some women link a husband's sharing in household chores to Islamic piety.

N: If they are sincere, they are supposed to follow the message sent by the prophet Muhammed.

S: and the assorted behaviour.

N: and he was at the service of his family; he took care of his own clothes, he did household chores, he swept the room ...

Z: He helped his wives.

(Brussels focus group discussion)

Talking about their own household as well as relating their views on relations within the couple, some women expressed emancipated views.

> I don't have to ask for every step I take to my husband, is it allowed, is it not allowed. I think if you have a normal relationship with your husband ... there is trust and if you say as a woman, 'I go there', that is logical and the same when the man says, 'I go somewhere'. It's not that you have to stay constantly together, but just that it is logical, you have your life together and you also still have your own friends, you also have your family and those things.
>
> (interview 14)

> At my house, we are two to vacuum, two to prepare meals, two to bathe the children, two to change the diapers, two to do the shopping, two to babysit.
>
> (Brussels focus group discussion)

> I don't believe in the traditional thing that the woman should take care of the household and man not. I'm against that. In traditional families that are not Islamic, at my home for example, it is like that. If my brother expects me to cook for him, to iron for him ... no!
>
> (current face veil wearer during Antwerp focus group discussion)

For some interviewees, the life of a housewife is not their first choice, but rather something they have accepted as a result of their wish to wear the face veil. These women dream however of a society in which they would not have to choose between their professional ambitions and their veil.

> I think it is them who are busy to close doors for us, for our future, you know, so it's not us who have chosen that ... It's clear that I will not exercise the same profession that I wanted two years ago ... I wanted to start a company in fact ... It will not be as I wanted it. If it was not that, I would have liked to be an accountant. But, now ... well, it will be religious studies ... Well, I don't see what else I could do, you know ... Studies with which I could keep my veil.
>
> (interview 21)

In the past I also had the notion they have now here in Belgium: the woman who is veiled, is just a stupid house wife . . . I went to Egypt for a year and then I met women with a burqa: she's a lawyer, she's a doctor . . . So I think by myself: actually what she wears does not determine anything . . . And then I started to think, I also want to be like that I want to be who I am. But I also want to achieve something more . . . As a woman I can do all that: I can study, I can work, I can do the same things as any other woman or man. Exactly the same.

(current face veil wearer during Antwerp focus group discussion)

Yet some other women – or occasionally even the same women at a different point in the conversation – express a commitment to traditional gendered role patterns in their discourse.

I never needed to work, *elhamdulilah.*

(interview 23)

A woman stays a woman, she makes the children, she bears them, it is she who is the mom, she is not dad, so I don't agree with the fact of saying 'a man should be equal to a woman' or that a woman should be equal to a man. I personally do not agree, I do not want to be equal to a man, I want to remain a woman, I don't want to do the work of a woman and a mother and do the work of a man on top of that. No, I am not interested in that personally, no. I want to remain a complete woman.

(interview 5)

Women's rights and feminism   None of the women expressed approval of male dominance. Several women pointed out that 'in Belgium' or 'these days', men cannot oblige their wives to do anything against their will, and that in case a husband would seriously try this, divorce is easily accessible.

We are in 2011. And I don't think that a woman would stay with her husband while she does not want to wear something which her husband makes her wear it. I really don't think so. No really not, you know. Because I know many women whose husband only starts talking a little, saying 'you should dress, you should wear a headscarf', just a headscarf and she already said 'no, attorney, I want a divorce'.

(interview 11)

Several women also showed an awareness of some of the current struggles of the women's movement, such as the wage gap, the unequal division of domestic work and violence against women. They bring these topics up either while dismissing the idea that the ban on the face veil would serve to promote gender equality, stating that the Belgian government should have other priorities for gender equality, or as they place their own struggle in the context of the broader struggle for women's rights.

> Let's work for the women who really experience discrimination because they are women. So all those who suffer because they are beaten, and there are many, there are women who die because they are beaten by a partner ... women are harassed on the street simply because they are women, because it is the weak sex.
>
> (interview 1)

However, this does not necessarily imply that they align themselves with 'Western' views on women's rights. Several interviewees took up the defence of Islamic views on gender equality, albeit in different manners. Some argue that Islamic views, when correctly understood, are not so far from 'Western views'.

> I think, if it is 100 per cent Islam, then the woman is already free. It is just that, unfortunately, there is still a big mix between culture and Islam. And it is that culture that actually keeps the woman imprisoned. For example, as you mention forced marriage, or for example, the father decides that the daughter cannot continue her studies, those things. I mean only, that has nothing to do with Islam ... In the end, in Islam, women have freedom, but it is because of cultural influence that it is now like this.
>
> (interview 14)

Others defend Islamic views that are rather different from contemporary 'Western' views, such as the woman as a gem or a queen, and 'different but equal rights'.

> I think why should a woman and a man be equal? A man is created of something completely different and a woman is completely something different. A woman has her rights and duties and a man has to have his rights and duties.
>
> (interview 12)

> My father he took my mother to the hamam, then he went home, he cooked and then he went to pick her up. She was a treasure for him, my mother never went out to work and all that.
>
> (interview 6)

Moreover, many of these women oppose gender mixing. They express the view that – with or without the face veil, but specifically without it – the company of men is to be avoided as much as possible.

> Even if we don't wear the niqab we cannot possibly come among men to
> talk, you understand? That is out of the question.
>
> (interview 11)

It is to be noted that without specifically being asked, some women
expressed disagreement with unequal gender practices in the Muslim
community:[22]

> Women who marry young, who do not continue their studies, to whom
> they impose a lot of things they don't particularly like ... All that is
> completely cultural. I mean to say it is proper to Maghreb countries
> etcetera, to do that. It is a bit up to the women I would say to revolt,
> like in '68 the women revolted here, so I think it is a process that every
> country must do.
>
> (interview 25)

Yet some women also criticize 'Western' gender views or practices.[23]

> They say that women in Islam have no value, but it is precisely in
> Western society that women have no value. Why? If you see a woman
> exposed in all advertisements, for example a car, an almost naked
> woman is put on it, I think why is an almost naked woman needed for
> a car? ... I think in Western society, in fact, women are just used to sell.
> Yes and then I wonder ... the West says that women have no value in
> Islam, but I think the opposite in the West. That women actually have
> no value because they are in fact used as sex objects and as publicity and
> they are literally mocked ... Here in Belgium women are also oppressed,
> they have to work, they have to raise children, it is like it's all mandatory.
>
> (interview 14)

Many references were made to the revealing dress style of other women.
Most of these were made in a tolerant, neutral way – 'they are allowed to
uncover, but we are not allowed to cover'; 'we tolerate them, why can't
they tolerate us'. Yet some women criticized revealing dress styles, with
one woman stating that women should have more self-respect, one
woman saying that there would be less adultery and 'bad disease' if
women covered more, and another saying that men rape women because
they dress this way.

Some women abhor a tendency in society to focus on looks and
appearances, in particular when women are concerned. They say that

---

[22] See also the above quote from interview 14.
[23] It is to be noted that many 'Western' feminists would in fact agree with the criticism expressed
here.

an advantage of wearing a face veil is that in contacts with others, one is not judged by one's good looks.

N: I know that I will not be appreciated because I am pretty or disliked because I am not.
S: I think it is a collateral benefit indeed, as you say, they will rather look to what you have to say instead.

(excerpt from Brussels focus group discussion)

When asked how they related to 'feminism', the respondents distinguished between a type of feminism they like and a type they didn't like.

S: In the name of feminism, some are against us; I think that is why there are more women than men who react against us in the street.
H: But excuse me, S, that is not real feminism . . .
S: Exactly, it is what I tell them: 'you fought for this, so that we could do what we want'.
N: It's not real feminism.
H: There are real feminist ladies.
S: Right, who support us . . .
H: Who support us and say 'we fought so that you could have the choice to wear it or not'.
B: . . . know that you are supported.
C: That is what being a feminist is about, it is giving women the freedom to choose, not imposing on them.

(excerpt Brussels focus group discussion)

Several interviewees accused the proponents of a face veil ban of hypocrisy when it comes to women's rights, as in their interpretation, the ban violates their freedom as women.

Under the pretext of wanting to defend women, they attack them.

(interview 1)

4. CONCLUDING COMMENTS ON THE ARGUMENT FROM WOMEN'S RIGHTS

The research findings show that a central assumption of the Belgian legislator when banning the face veil – i.e. that all or most women who wear the face veil are forced or pressured to do so – is erroneous. While the empirical research does not allow us to conclude whether or not (and if so, how many) women in Belgium are being forced to wear a face veil, it clearly shows that for a significant number of face veil wearers, the face veil is the result of an autonomous choice. Those women experience the ban as a denial of their autonomy with respect to a matter of crucial importance to them, and hence as anti-emancipatory.

Moreover, to the extent that some women may be forced to wear a face veil – a situation we would characterize as one of domestic violence – it may be doubted whether the criminalization of those women (!) would end their predicament. Indeed, as the reaction to the ban of several of the women who choose to wear the face veil is not to abandon it, but rather to stay in as much as possible (see below), there is a real risk that women wearing the face veil against their will would be made to stay in against their will as a result of the ban.

Moreover, the gender analysis of the interviews shows a broad array of different gender views and practices among women wearing the face veil, ranging from very conservative to quite progressive. Islamic characteristics are prominent in their discourse and practice, yet these include progressive interpretations of Islamic rules on women as well as criticism of unequal practices in their own communities. Moreover, the interviews show that these women do not reject women's rights discourse; in fact many appropriate women's rights language to contest the face veil ban. Clearly, the face veil is not an indicator of 'other' violations of women's rights, not a sign that its wearer approves of such violations. The face veil wearers themselves do not consider the face veil as a symbol of women's submission.

5. THE FACE VEIL IN BELGIUM AND SOCIAL COHESION

5.1. Outsider arguments

A second cluster of arguments involves the alleged antisocial character of wearing a face veil. Several Members of Parliament characterized face veils as a 'break from "living in a community" (*le vivre-ensemble*), from public responsibility and citizenship, and from communal ties'.[24] The face veil would disrupt the social environment, since members of the general population indicate 'that they do not wish to encounter something like that in the street'. It is stated that 'Everyone has his own reasons for this, but it concerns a permanent value in any event'.[25] In this respect, one of the legislative proposals refers to work done by the

---

[24] *Parliamentary report*, Chamber 2010–11, no. 53-219/4, 6.
[25] *Parliamentary proceedings*, Chamber 2010–11, 28 April 2011, no. 53-30, 35.

French sociologist, Elisabeth Badinter, who states that women who wear face veils breach soci(et)al norms in an unacceptable way, since they can look at others without being seen themselves; a situation from which these women – according to Badinter – can derive pleasure and a sense of superiority. Badinter argues that this is at odds with our social model, which is based on reciprocity and equality. On a less philosophical level, it is presumed throughout the *travaux préparatoires* that covering the face hinders communication, and that a person who covers her face isolates herself from others and from the community. This is considered to be intolerable: the possibility of having interaction between individuals in public life in order to bring about and reinforce social ties in the community is deemed essential. Members of Parliament argued that it would be impossible for a person, of whom only the eyes are visible, to participate in these dynamics of 'living in a community' because wearing 'face-covering garments largely precludes verbal and non-verbal communication'.[26] The interference with communication arising in this regard would 'consequently be liable to prejudice public order, and lead to social disruption'.[27]

Some Members of Parliament also identify face veils with a rejection of 'Western civilization' or 'our way of living' by fundamentalist Islam. The ban, as such, is allegedly a step to combat Islamism or Islamization in general, and so safeguard Western society and its modes of coexistence.

5.2. Insider views

The argument based on social cohesion and 'living together' merges practical concerns about the ability to communicate with a person covering her face, and normative statements about the need for all members of a society to socially interact with others in public. In the analysis of the interviews, we consider first what they reveal about the degree of social integration of the interviewees through activities in the public sphere in the broad sense, i.e. social interaction in functional settings and contacts with anonymous others as well as neighbours and the like (not including their family and friends). Next we focus on the more specific issue of communication. We conclude this section with stories of positive interactions between women wearing the face

---

[26] Parliamentary documents, Chamber 2010–11, no. 53-85/1, 3.

[27] *Ibid.*, 4. Elsewhere there was mention of a 'social bomb at the foundations of shared values' (*Parliamentary report*, Chamber 2010–11, no. 53-219/4, 22).

veil and other citizens, a type of information many interviewees spontaneously shared.

5.2.1. Social interaction

Some women indicate that their choice to wear the niqab implied
a choice to withdraw from a number of activities. This appears to be
part of a choice for a rigorous Islamic lifestyle overall.

> I organized my life in function of that wearing of the niqab, and so that
> face veil created barriers to all activities I had before ... Because
> I considered that a woman who wears the face veil could not just go to
> a curio market ... from time to time, I liked to go bargain hunting a
> little. Well it was ... I thought it was not possible.
>
> (interview 19)

Yet many state that they live a normal life, with some women saying
that they would in fact live a *less* social life if they could not wear
the face veil, because they would not feel at ease in a number of
circumstances.

> Also for contact outside, I saw it as easier to wear my niqab. If I did not
> wear the niqab I would have found it difficult to go out and address the
> teacher, doctor, cashier or others.
>
> (interview 7)

However, many women also report avoiding certain activities outside
the house or avoiding as much as possible to go out on their own,
because of fear of aggressive reactions of others, or of confrontation
with the police (see below).

Some of the interviewees attended school when they started to
wear the face veil. Some interviewees report taking off the face veil
right before entering the school premises. Some interviewees
changed to home schooling after starting to wear the face veil and
obtained their secondary school diploma in that manner. Some of the
interviewees had a job while they were wearing the face veil. They took
off the veil at work. A few others were involved in voluntary work
within their communities: lectures and support to Muslim women,
and childcare.

Yet overall, the types of social activities the interviewees mention,
mostly relate to their roles of mothers and housewives: accompanying
the children to and from school, taking the children to the park, shopping and errands, talking to neighbours, going to the market, going to

the post office or other administrative offices, going to the hospital and so on. Several women mention the use of public transport, driving a car, day trips and foreign travel.

> I am outside a lot because I have activities outside. I take the kids to their diverse activities they have in the week, they have several.
>
> (interview 1)

> So we took a week in the Ardennes, we went to France, we went everywhere, I mean to say we were never embarrassed to go where we wanted and I wore my face veil.
>
> (interview 24)

> It does not hinder me to do anything. I mean to say, if I want to go shopping, to take my children to an amusement park – well it is true, there one is the little black animal, the little attraction of everybody, but for me that does not hinder me to do anything.
>
> (interview 9)

> Yes, some people were laughing then, 'hey a woman in niqab on a motorcycle', but I do not think it stops you, the other people in fact stop you from doing certain things, but not yourself . . . so I think you can integrate completely in society and you can do everything when you wear that.
>
> (interview 14)

> At the time I lived in a neighbourhood of old people . . . And these people recognized me without any problem and they acted toward me as if they saw whoever else in the street . . . We were good neighbours, and I remember that when we moved, the old people were even sad because they told us: 'Oh, we knew you so well and we knew that we could count on you, that we could ask you something.' There was even an old lady, who lived upstairs where I lived, and whose children did not visit her. And she told me, 'it is so good of you, that you come and visit the elderly', because I visited her from time to time with my children. So it does not stand in the way of anything at all. It is enough to want to accept the difference and to understand that behind that face veil, there is a person who is completely normal.
>
> (interview 25)

5.2.2. Communication

Several interviewees expressed a self-image as very open or sociable persons. Many women state that from their perspective, communication is perfectly possible.

As I am so in the habit of wearing it, I do not especially feel the fact that I have it on, so I talk to a person as I would without it. So when I am in a shop, when I need anything, I go and ask it, I mean to say, in fact I don't feel that I have it on.

(interview 4)

Me, as I told you, I talk to everybody, everybody sees me laugh; they answer me in the same tone if they want. When they don't want, that's another matter.

(interview 9)

But my voice they can still hear, does it matter whether it is behind a veil or a wall ... I am very social and here, the environment where I live, everybody knows me. I talk to them with the niqab and I am very social with the people, even with non-Muslims and with the Jews. I can interact with everybody, you can hear me, it is only my face that is covered. But we can still have a good contact and get along well.

(interview 12)

Yet several interviewees also indicated that there appears to be a communication barrier on the side of others. Some women show understanding for this reaction.

It's true that it is us who have to go to the others, that is true ... It is us who have to take the step; it is true that the people don't make the effort to come to us.

(interview 7)

Yes, I think also, now, thinking back, I think there is actually an image – closed, sectarian – when covering completely the face, because the people in general ... Well, when you smile to the people, they immediately have more sympathy and all that. And there, I could be smiling, but they did not see me, it was a bit bizarre, you know, I mean I think I must have transmitted an image a bit closed.

(interview 10)

And I think that the human being ... the fact of not seeing the person, it is something scary, I can understand ... In fact it limits from the other side of the barrier, but not from us.

(interview 18)

The face veil, I would say, creates this ... visual barrier at the level of the people, so one wants to say to the people, that we stay human beings behind that piece of cloth. We can stay equally charming, polite, cool, we understand, we can make jokes, no problem. And you come to, I remember, to make big smiles under my niqab so that my eyes would smile, so that the person in front of me would see that in the end I was not a monster, or that I was a human being. I am a person behind it . . . I made a social effort yes, I mean often I did. Often I squeezed my eyes really tight so that they would see that I was laughing.

(interview 24)

Several women relate stories of situations in which people addressed an accompanying man, rather than talking to them. They express frustration at being ignored.

I remember being in the emergency wing with my small baby, and that the doctor at the time talked only to my husband. Absolutely only to him, and despite that he addressed himself only to him, it was me who knew everything concerning my child, his state, his fever, and so it was me who answered, but despite that, when she talked, she talked only to my husband.

(interview 19)

Some interviewees have experienced that they engender a sense of fear in some other people. They link this to the negative image of the face veil that is projected by the media. Several women state that this fear disappears when they can establish contact.

I understand completely that people are scared . . . I understand completely, it is normal, it is covered, it is hidden, you don't know what is underneath. At first sight, it's shocking . . . yes I understand because this is what they have been shown in the media.

(interview 5)

In the shops I have not often come across difficulties with the cashiers or similar things, I just had once with a client . . . she jumped when she saw me . . . And to relax the atmosphere a bit, I told this lady, 'Please excuse me, I did not want to frighten you.' She tells me: 'Oh, you are kind', in fact . . . it is sufficient to have good behaviour to show to others that our difference is not an obstacle for a relationship.

(interview 26)

A few women have the habit of lowering their veil in some circumstances to facilitate face-to-face communication.

I know to hide my eyes when I need to hide them and when I want to show my eyes, when I am in front of a person where I can talk to her, and that I estimate that it is the moment to lift it a little bit, so that they see my look, I do it . . . When I am in an office and there are only women, no worry, I take it off automatically ... so when I arrive in a public office where there are men, well I still try, toward the lady who is in front of me, to show my look, because well, if you smile or you react with the eyes, well, she can see that I have understood or that I have smiled at her or that I have answered her smile.

(interview 5)

5.2.3. Stories of positive interactions

Many women reported positive contacts with anonymous other people. Sometimes these are simply stories of being treated like any other person.

Yes yes, that still exists. It's true, when I am with the little one in his buggy and someone holds the door for me, or someone plays with him, small things like that, yes ... Sometimes they look at me but when I start a discussion for example in a waiting room, well, they see in the end that I am not the monster they thought.

(interview 9)

Making claims to specific arrangements for the accommodation of their face veil is far from the women's minds. Yet some interviewees experienced such accommodation in some contexts, which made them very happy.

Once at the forum, we were in an office where there were several offices, and I had to come back another time, and when I come back the next time, I find an office for me alone, they had prepared an office only for me. And then I explained to the lady, I told her she need not have done that. She told me 'No, I prefer to be with you like that, so you can take of your niqab.' And I thanked her for that gesture, I was really pleased.

(interview 8)

Also, several women told stories of how a conversation with an initially suspicious stranger turned into a positive exchange, an actual encounter.

I met people in a supermarket ... who told me: madam, we don't know why you wear that, why you cover entirely. I came closer to a gentleman, I explain to him what the religion says. It is not mandatory but if it you do it by yourself ... He told me 'maybe it is your husband who forced you'. 'You see, I do my shopping all alone, and I drive all alone, there is nobody with me.' And he was satisfied. I explained Islam to him a little bit, I explained to him a little why and all ... You can arrive at a point where you will be satisfied.

(interview 2)

Once even I was near a shop and there is a man who comes really close to me and says: 'I really want to take off your niqab'. And I say to him: 'Yes, and why?' He: 'Ah, madam, do you talk?' 'Yes of course I talk.' 'Let's say your husband passes here now and sees you talking to me?' I tell him: 'But there is no problem, I have my mobile phone in my pocket, if you want I can even call him.' He says: 'That is great, I never knew that a veiled woman could talk to a man and that she could defend herself.' I say: 'I can defend myself, I can talk, I can even explain to you.' By the way, the conversation lasted more than half an hour and in the end he tells me: 'it is one of my best days'.

(interview 8)

A few women show a sense of humour in their interactions with other people who show their discomfort.

Yes, it happened to me [that she frightened people], but I used to make it into a joke. I said 'don't worry, I don't bite, I never swallowed little kids all raw', in fact they were persons with kids . . . Well, the children, with them you can quickly de-dramatize, because there are masks, there is carnival . . . With children sometimes in the subway, I lifted 'peekaboo!' [laughs]

(interview 3)

5.3. Concluding comments on the argument from social cohesion

The empirical findings reveal the erroneous character of one of the assumptions of the Belgian legislator banning the face veil – i.e. that women who wear the face veil are not able to and do not wish to interact with others in society. Instead it appears that – at least before the ban – women wearing a face veil were in fact interacting in numerous ordinary ways with society at large.

Moreover, it appears that the ban is not likely to achieve its stated purpose of increasing the social interactions by these women, and risks instead being counterproductive. This is the case because many women who choose to wear a face veil are strongly attached to it, and continue to wear it despite the ban, yet avoid going out (see below). Hence, instead of increased social interaction, the effect for these women is a serious deterioration of their social life, their interactions with society at large, and their mobility.

To the extent that women take off the face veil and that this results in their being more easily approached by others in the public sphere, the ban realizes part of its objective. Yet the research findings suggest that a ban is a disproportionate measure to achieve that effect. Practice shows that women can and do communicate with their face veil on. As the women's narratives of positive exchanges show, this is a matter of goodwill on both sides, which is likely to be better realized by other than repressive means. Nevertheless there seem to be specific contexts in which social interaction is unreasonably hampered by the covering of a person's face. To the extent that face-covering bans are motivated by concerns of communication and social interaction, they may be justified when they are limited in time and space to those contexts.

6. THE FACE VEIL IN BELGIUM AND THE ISSUE OF SAFETY

6.1. Outsider arguments

The argument on safety entails that one must be recognizable and identifiable in public places for various safety reasons. In this respect, one can distinguish between arguments on objective safety, and those regarding subjective safety.

To start with the former issue: several Members of Parliament linked face covering to criminal activities. For example, reference was made to a robbery at a post office in France, allegedly committed by two men wearing burqas. There was also mention of a terrorist attack in Pakistan where a person had used a face veil as a disguise. Some members further argued that weapons can be hidden under the clothing targeted by the prohibition.[28] Moreover, there are frequent references to the situation of mothers covered in a face veil fetching their children from school. It was argued that uncovering is required because one must be sure that the person who collects the child is indeed the mother.

In addition reference was also made in the proposals and in Parliament to a subjective feeling of unsafety, generated by the confrontation with persons who conceal their face: 'It is a plain fact that people who intentionally withdraw from social interaction instil mistrust amongst their fellow citizens.'[29] Therefore, it was stated that 'avoiding clothing that conceals the face … [would have] a positive influence on people's feelings of safety'.[30] In this respect, instituting a prohibition on such clothing was compared to placing street lamps

---

[28] This argument overlooks the fact that the ban only targets the face veil, not the wide garments that usually accompany it.

[29] *Parliamentary proceedings*, Chamber 2010–11, 28 April 2011, no. 53-30, 23.

[30] *Ibid.*

in a dark alley, in order to reduce fear of crime and provide a feeling of security to the public.

6.2. Insider views

The interviews do not provide much information that might substantiate the safety risk women wearing the face veil might constitute to others. Yet they reveal a manifest and serious safety risk for the women who wear a face veil, as they are confronted with regular aggression from anonymous others in the public sphere.

6.2.1. Veiled women as a safety risk

From the information in section 5, it is clear that veiled women confirm experiences in which they engender feelings of unease or fear in others. At the same time, the women's stories also show that it is possible to overcome these feelings and establish a normal type of contact. Such normal contacts appear to exist in particular with persons with whom there is regular interaction, and who may therefore be assumed to be 'used to' the veil, such as neighbours, teachers or shopkeepers. In addition, first-time meetings occasionally allow to transform an initially negative reaction into a positive contact, when both the face veil wearer and the other person are able and willing to talk to each other.

As far as objective safety is concerned, it is noteworthy that among the interviewees, there is a general willingness to identify themselves to the police or other authorities by lowering their veil. Many state explicitly that they are willing to identify to a male official as well as a female. Only a small minority is prepared to unveil only for a female official.

6.2.2. Veiled women's safety

One of the most striking findings of this study are the numerous reports of aggression the women confront from anonymous people in shops and public places. Most of this is verbal abuse with occasional physical abuse. For many women, these were not isolated incidents, but a fact of daily life, engendering a strong sense of unsafety.

> I felt harassed all the time, as soon as I went outside ... people making signs of throat cutting or a rifle, things like that.
>
> (interview 10)

> When I am alone I never feel safe, because I am called 'Al Qaeda' or 'wife of Osama bin Laden', or things like that or threats ... Really racist remarks you get ... In any case you don't feel comfortable, because

they say also really ugly expressions . . . Like 'go, go back to your country', or 'what's that, people running around in curtains'.

(interview 12)

There are nasty ones. There are some when I pass like that and they see me, they do not even talk to me, they spit. Yes, with the niqab. They see me like that and they say 'ooooiiiihhhh' and they spit in front of me.

(interview 2)

Some incidents in particular made a deep impression on the interviewees, because of a specific sense of injustice, because of their intensity, or because of the presence of their children. Several interviewees relate that they defended themselves against such abuse. Sometimes a certain pride in their reaction appears to be the reason for remembering a particular incident.

There are specific cases like the time when I was harassed by a rather big man . . . I am not very tall, I measure less than 1 metre 60 – who did not hesitate to come and harass me while I was with my children . . . in fact I passed with my children, they came from their sport activity, I went to fetch them, and I went to the stop of the bus I had to take, and that man was already at the bus stop. And he simply said, 'here we are in a democracy, you do not have the right to hide like that'. I did not answer; I went to take a seat, so I asked my children to sit down. And when I passed . . . he came, he tore my veil away. So he tore with his two hands. I know that my children were crying, so he scared my children . . . and there was a lady who defended me, and I defended myself . . . because he came back, to continue to harass me.

(interview 1)

Once, I recall until today, I had gone to the Colruyt with my daughter who was still a baby, in her buggy. And when I was in the Colruyt there was a man who followed me, he followed me until I arrived at the cashier. So there was a man on one side and a woman on the other and they were really nasty you know, I cried . . . I really don't see why they harassed me while I had done nothing to them, I was with my baby and it really hurt me you know, until today.

(interview 27)

Several women emphasize that they are particularly worried about the impact of such public incidents on their children, as well as by the fact that some aggressors address themselves directly to the children.

What has always been the most difficult thing for me, is when they managed to touch my children. I have four children and when I visit

my mother, at her building there are these elderly Belgian ladies who, when I arrive, on purpose close the door ... they block the elevator ... you could film that, it's funny because they run like that ... But the problem started when she started to address my children ... It was the day of Eid ... my daughter was dressed in traditional Moroccan dress. And she said to my daughter ... 'why are you dressed like a monkey?'
(Brussels focus group discussion)

Some women reported that when they reacted to an instance of aggression, some of the bystanders seemed to treat them as the aggressors. This was the case for a woman who hit a man after the latter had torn off her niqab, as well as for a woman who turned around to talk back to an old man who had pushed and insulted her.

Even without the occurrence of incidents, some women reported a feeling of unsafety, related to a tense atmosphere in their environment. The following exchange took place in the Brussels focus group:

κ: As soon as I was alone, it could be simply in a waiting room in a hospital, I felt harassed ...
s: ... oppressed.
H: Strangely enough you feel at the mercy of people in fact. Despite the fact that ... we have a personality that is ...
N: extrovert. Yes, you're open to others, sociable.
H: Approaching people, no problem. And there, strangely, how one feels ... diminished.
s: You feel weakened in fact.
H: It's an unbearable feeling, really unbearable.

Some women stated that they experienced more verbal aggression from women than from men. Several stated that they experienced aggressive reactions also from Muslims.

Yes, I have had comments from women who wear a headscarf.
(interview 4)

They were two women who were immigrants, which I am not. It was a totally surrealist painting, when they told me in Arabic 'we did not come from Morocco to see that here'. Well, go back to Morocco, I was born here, where do I go?
(woman with Moroccan roots during Brussels focus group discussion)

Many women report that they experience fewer or less serious aggressions when they are accompanied by their husbands than when they go about by themselves.

It was often when I was alone. People are less scared to harass a woman alone than one in company, simply.

(interview 10)

Several women experienced an increase in aggressive reactions. Some talked about an increase since the 9/11 attacks, which they linked to the association that is made in public opinion between Islam and terrorism. Others point to the introduction of local bans or to the national 'burqa ban' debate and its mediatization as the time when abuse started to increase. They think that the negative image of Islam in general and of the face veil in particular that is projected in the media seems to give people permission to react in an aggressive manner. The following excerpt is from the Brussels focus group discussion:

H: Then came 9/11.
K: Ah yes, that played a big role.
H: It really played a very big role ... Suddenly everyone had legitimacy to do whatever they wanted toward us.
K: There was also the police rule.[31]
H: Yes ... that is when I started to wear it only part-time, not only because I was concerned about the police; it was more a feeling of insecurity in relation to the people ... I know myself and I am not big and strong enough to face the racism of the people.

Moreover, it appears that many people now refer to the ban in their interventions vis-à-vis women who wear the face veil, acting as a kind of vigilante police.

For me, the concern with this law is that it has a double punishment ... The first punishment is that it hinders us ... to have a real active social life, to drive, to go out, to work ... And the second punishment is that all the citizens feel invested with a heroic mission ... to make sure the law is respected.

(current face veil wearer during Brussels focus group discussion)

In addition to the stories of aggression, several interviewees told stories of discrimination on account of their wearing the face veil. These related among others to refusal of treatment of a veiled woman by hospital staff, refusal of vendors at a curio market to sell their goods to a veiled woman, and refusal by a school director to let a mother pick up her child from school when wearing her face veil.

---

[31] Reference is made here to the local ban that was introduced several years before the nationwide ban.

Fear of aggression, caused by accumulated experiences of aggression, causes some women to avoid going out by themselves, while others shift to part-time wearing of the face veil or abandon it altogether. The latter category – who abandoned the face veil because they could no longer bear the aggression – are left frustrated about this.

6.3. Concluding comments on the argument from safety

The research findings show that feelings of subjective unsafety do not necessarily accompany contacts with veiled women, and that they can be overcome. Hence, to the extent that subjective safety is the ground for intervention, this might be better achieved by other than repressive means.

Moreover, in light of the general willingness among face veil wearers to identify themselves by showing their face to persons in authority, the risk for objective safety in the general public sphere appears exaggerated, if not unfounded. Instead, there appears to be a real safety risk for the women who wear the face veil, on account of aggressive behaviour by the public. To the extent that aggression against women who wear the face veil increased as a result of the bans, the bans' impact on objective safety has therefore been a negative one.

7. AFTER THE BAN

In the sections above, it became clear that the way women wearing the face veil in Belgium experience the wearing of that veil in their daily life, is significantly influenced by the existence of local bans and the adoption of a nationwide ban. In this section, we explore this theme some more. First, we briefly zoom in on the reactions to the adoption of the nationwide ban, and continue with the interviewees' experiences with police enforcing the (local or nationwide) ban.

7.1. Reactions to the adoption of the ban

The feelings shown by interviewees about the ban include indignation, frustration, humiliation and worries about how to live their lives from now on. Talking about the reasons behind the ban, many state that they do not understand the arguments, or that these are ridiculous. Strong statements abound.

> They are really . . . ruining our lives.

(interview 8)

Many interviewees express a feeling that Muslims or Islam are being targeted.

> For me it is simply Islamophobia.
>
> (interview 19)

Yet it does not seem that this results in alienating the women from Belgian society. Throughout their discourse, a sense of citizenship emerges, in which for instance they identify themselves as Belgian citizens, and Belgian politicians as 'our politicians' – notwithstanding several women expressing a wish for emigration to a Muslim-majority country. Consider the following excerpt from the Brussels focus group discussion:

z: They talk to us a lot about respect and all that; I want to respect the law of the country in which I live, but also think we should be respected as individuals.

n: as citizens.

z: yes, as a citizen.

n: who is active in society, knowing you pay your taxes, you participate in society.

z: exactly.

Many women implicitly express the idea that the criminal law should not deal with an issue like this, referring to the – in their view – harmless nature of the incriminated behaviour. During the Brussels focus group discussion, this was addressed as follows:

c: So when they ask you 'why were you arrested?', it is 'because I cover my face'. That is completely ridiculous. We did not harass anyone . . .

n: We have become guilty persons.

k: We are outlaws.

n: Outlaws, indeed, while . . . I don't steal, I don't harass people, I comply with my duties as a citizen.

h: It's frustrating . . . we are all born here, we always moved around freely, when from one day to the next, I saw myself [mimics looking around in fear].

n: Right, as if you are wanted by the law.

h: I really had the feeling that I had escaped from prison . . . watch out, watch out, a police car.

k: I had that feeling for a very long time.

h: But it's not normal. In the end . . . we are Belgians you know. That's the most bizarre thing, that we are Belgians.

(excerpt from Brussels focus group discussion)

During both focus group discussions – which took place a few months after the end of the interviews, when the reality of the ban being in force had fully sunk in – participants expressed a real worry about 'the next step', fearing in particular that after the face veil, also the headscarf might be banned in public space. The following exchange during the Brussels focus group discussion illustrates this point:

C: So they attacked us on the niqab now, what will it be in a few years?
K: It will be the hijab.
C: And I can tell you that one day we will not be able to wear our headscarf, we will not be able to wear our jilbab, we will not be able to celebrate our festivities.

A prominent finding is the interviewees' frustration that this political intervention in their lives took place without any knowledge of their lives and without consulting them or researching into their situation.

They don't know us or they don't want to know us simply.

(interview 9)

I think it's a real pity ... that in a democratic country they vote such a law, without taking the advice of the persons concerned.

(interview 25)

Some interviewees try to get into the minds of the proponents of a ban and imagine that a compromise might have been found if only there could have been a dialogue.

If we need to be identified more than the norm ... if they need to give us a badge that we have been identified or a booklet with a stamp, well I don't know, something that might maybe help the police to say, OK this person was already identified ... no problem, we are ready for any dialogue, we are ready for every proposal.

(interview 5)

It was one of the solutions I had proposed, to change the colour if black was shocking, wear more lively colours, because they say, all in black, we were being stigmatized with that colour. That is to say it is not an obligation that it should be black ... So one of the proposals I also made is to be able to go out with someone identifiable if for example we need to be identifiable at every moment ... If I was beside my husband, at that time, there they know, it is the wife of that person.

(interview 7)

7.2. Confrontations with the police

The majority of women report having been stopped once or several times by the police. In the majority of cases this was for the purpose of identification after which they were let go or received a warning. Six of these women had been fined, four of these were fined several times. Most of these appear to be applications of local bans, as they took place before the entry into force of the legal ban. Several women who have not been stopped or fined, knew other women who did.

Several women report that the police regularly did not interfere when they saw them walk veiled on the street, despite the existence of a local ban.

Some women report that the police intercepted them because they had been alerted by citizens.

Most women who had had a confrontation with the police over their face veil, stated that the police treated them correctly. Some mentioned specifically that the police were polite or that they explained why they intervened. In several cases, they related that the police were uncomfortable with the situation or apologized to them.

> He came to me and said 'I'm sorry, I would have preferred not to do it, but my boss gave me the order.'
>
> (Brussels focus group discussion)

Yet some women reported that the police insulted or ridiculed them.

> And once I had been identified … they started to mock me … I had my son with a small puppet in his hand, they said, 'Ah well, if it is an obligation for you, why is that puppet of your son not wearing a face veil too?'
>
> (interview 25)

At the same time, some other women reported reacting in an assertive manner, engaging in discussion with the police.

> And I tell him 'no, there is no ban'. 'But yes yes yes, there is a ban, in all of Europe it is prohibited'. Apparently the guy did not know his file too well. I told him 'no, listen, it is not banned in all of Europe'. And I started in fact … to discuss a bit with him … He said 'no, but in any case, we are in Belgium, and Belgium forbids it'. I say 'OK, do you want to identify me?' he says 'No, I don't want to identify you, I want you to take off that veil.' I say 'in fact it is just for fun or what?'. He said 'You call it what you want, I ask you to take off that veil.' … I did it, of course. I took

off my veil. I say: 'but you know that I will put it back on at the corner of the street'. He says: 'well, if I see you again at the corner of the street, I'll stop you again'. I said 'OK, fair enough'. [laughs]

(interview 23)

Police interceptions have an impact on many interviewees. Two women say they had cried. Some interviewees declared that they minded the public embarrassment most of all: the fact of being seen to be intercepted by the police. Several women reported experiencing a police confrontation as traumatizing.

Yes, it was on the street, and certainly when everybody was looking, I minded that very much ... yes it was as if I had just come out of a shop and the people would think I had stolen something or something like that.

(interview 17)

Several strategies appear to be adopted for avoiding such confrontations: some play hide and seek with the police, some avoid going out as much as possible, others decided to only go out by car.

Since that happened that day, so twenty-one days ago, I have not been out on foot. Only by car with my husband.

(interview 17)

[We] were so frightened ... of being arrested, they were watching every movement, we did not go out to the park anymore, we did not go out shopping. When I needed to go anywhere, it was mandatorily by car. I had a dentist 200 metres from my home, I had a friend who came from Laken to pick me up by car to drive me to the dentist who was 200 metres.

(interview 25)

One woman said that a shop owner had offered refuge to veiled women from the police.

They have even been called by a shop manager who said 'If there is police who enters, when you are followed etc., come into the shop and knock at the office, you can go in there.' Because they know that these women are not dangerous, they know them and they recognize them.

(interview 3)

And one woman said that she had replaced the face veil with a hygienic face mask after the local police told her on the phone that they do not react against such masks.

A: So I call them back and I say 'what about a mask? Can someone wear a mask?' He says 'we have no problem with a mask'. So I thought by myself, when I need to go to the city administration or something like that, I'll wear a mask.

EB: And have you gone out yet with such a mask?

A: Yes, very often ... I went to the mutuality, and when I had to arrange papers at the [name of city administration building]; and to the hospital, when I go for my pregnancy, I wear it always.

(excerpt from Antwerp focus group discussion)

Several women stopped wearing the face veil out of fear of police enforcement of the (local or nationwide) ban, often in combination with fear of street aggression.

Gradually as the law was voted,[32] I was arrested several times by the police, I had no life anymore, because my husband ... worked a lot at the time, he left at 7 a.m. and came home at 10 p.m., I did not go out, I had no life, my children were at home all the time, to do my shopping I needed to wait until someone could drive me in a car, same thing to see a doctor, it was hell ... It was not feasible. It's either the unsafety vis-à-vis the outside word that totally lacks respect for us, or vis-à-vis the authorities, who have no respect either.

(former face veil wearer during Brussels focus group discussion).

7.3. Concluding comments on impact of the ban

When discussing the immediate impact of the face veil ban, it is not possible to distinguish between the impact of local bans and that of the nationwide ban.[33] Moreover, in its impact on the women's behaviour, police enforcement of the ban is closely linked to the reactions of the public at large. This is so because police may intervene after being alerted by a member of the public, and because members of the public tend to interpret the ban as a justification for intervening themselves with veiled women. It is also so, because the fear that dominates the lives of many veiled women is caused by the combination of both: whenever they go out on the street, they have to be ready for both expressions of public aggression, and confrontation with the police. This fear makes

---

[32] Later corrected in the sense that it was a local ban that was adopted.

[33] In fact the Act on the nationwide ban leaves local bans intact, and as these are more simple from an administrative point of view, it may be assumed that the police in most localities continue to impose administrative fines for violations of local bans rather than criminal fines for violation of the nationwide ban. To what extent the introduction of the nationwide ban has led to increased enforcement of 'dormant' local bans is not known.

some women abandon the face veil, while others avoid going out except by car. Police enforcement of the ban has a strong negative impact for many women, even when the police are friendly and correct.

In a broader perspective, the hasty adoption of the ban, without any effort to enter into contact with the women concerned, is experienced as a breach of democratic principles. Contrary to the stereotypes of women wearing the face veil that permeate the parliamentary discourse, the interviews show an openness to discuss the problems society may have with the face veil. The general and self-evident willingness to identify themselves when needed, is a prominent expression of this constructive attitude, that is shown moreover in the compromise suggestions made by some women (see 7.1.).

8. OVERALL CONCLUSION

The Belgian Parliament banned the face veil without bothering to obtain information about the lives and experiences of the persons wearing it. As a result, all three motives for the ban are at least in part based on erroneous assumptions. A crucial assumption is that all – or nearly all – women who wear the face veil are forced or pressured to do so. The finding of this study that this assumption is wrong, undermines not only the argument from women's rights, but also has a strong impact on the other motives. This is so, because women who have a strong personal attachment to their face veil – a situation the Belgian legislator did not anticipate – do not consider abandoning the veil as a first choice when confronted with the ban. Many prefer instead to continue wearing the veil yet avoid going out in public except by car. As a result, the ban has counterproductive effects vis-à-vis two of its stated goals: it denies women's autonomy and therefore restricts women's rights instead of furthering them; and it reduces social interaction for a number of the women concerned. In addition, the research suggests that social interaction involving those women can be improved without resorting to repressive means. Moreover, the women's general willingness to identify themselves throws doubt on the objective safety risk caused by the face veil. As for the subjective safety risk, the research suggests that it may be overcome by non-repressive means. The contrast reveals on the other hand a serious safety risk for women wearing the face veil, which has increased by the introduction of the ban. Hence from the perspective of the women concerned, the effects of the ban are negative on all three fronts: women's rights, social interaction and safety.

Yet, as is by now abundantly clear, the Belgian legislature considered in the first place the perspective of others – outsiders – who are confronted with women wearing the face veil. For those others, the sight of a face veil is an affront to women's dignity. Similarly, those others do not want to interact with women wearing a face veil in shops or on the street, and feel unsafe when they come across a face veil because they associate it with terrorism and fundamentalist Islam. For outsiders then, the fact that fewer face veils are around after the ban, is an improvement on all three fronts: women's rights, social interaction and safety. As the research has shown, solutions promoting women's rights, social interaction and safety for all without resorting to repressive means, are possible. They require real human contact, in which people get to know each other's concerns, and generate tolerance through mutual understanding – values that cannot be voted into existence as a ban can.

REFERENCES

De Wit, J. 2010. 'Kamer keurt boerkaverbod goed', *Gazet van Antwerpen*, 2 April.

Gérin, A. 2010. *Rapport d'information fait en application de l'article 145 du règlement au nom de la mission d'information sur la pratique du port du voile intégral sur le territoire national*, 26 January 2010, 74.

Vrielink, J., Ouald Chaib, S. and Brems, E. 2013. 'The Belgian "Burqa Ban"': Legal Aspects of Local and General Prohibitions on Covering and Concealing One's Face in Belgium', in Alessandro Ferrari and Sabrina Pastorelli (eds.), *The Burqa Affair across Europe: Between Private and Public*, Farnham: Ashgate.

5

FRANCE VS. ENGLAND

Naima Bouteldja

> *I can remember the first time I wore a niqab on a public train. It's a very funny story actually because I was a little bit nervous of going into London and I was wearing my niqab and I was going to be on my own ... I sat down on the train and the lady opposite me was a punk. So she looked at me like, 'What a weirdo!' and I looked at her like, 'You're such a weirdo, because you have the coloured hair, the earrings and eye makeup'... and she just looked at me very strange, but then suddenly she was OK. She spent a few seconds examining me and I spent a few seconds examining her but then I just relaxed. We just felt comfort in the fact that we were both just expressing different ways of life. She smiled at me, like a warm smile ... It's a very clear memory. I can even remember nodding my head at her to show her that I'm smiling and we went on our own ways.*
>
> (Naweeda, 31, High Wycombe, UK)[1]

> *Now they speak about the values of gender equality, but do women receive equal pay in France? They haven't even been able to pass a law on this issue. Are there as many women as men in the National Assembly? They are talking to us as if the French Republic had always defended gender equality! It's false! It's recent and has not even been fully achieved. Besides, one must understand that as a woman who wears the niqab, I totally refute the argument which claims that wearing the niqab is a submission to man.*
>
> (Eliza, 31, Paris)

1. FRENCH AND UK POLITICAL CONTEXTS BEHIND THE VEIL DEBATES

In mid 2010, I was approached by the Open Society Foundations to conduct research into the ongoing debate over the full-face veil in France. While the controversy had been raging for more than a year, the voices of French niqabi remained largely absent from print and broadcast media outlets covering the issue. But this was hardly a surprise, as ever since the first public outcry over Muslim women's dress code in 1989, the sidelining of the people at the heart of these debates has been a recurrent motif in France. The French cross-party Parliamentary Commission to Study the Wearing of the Full Veil, established in June

---

[1] All the names have been changed and the ages stated are those at the time of the interview.

2009 and tasked with exploring the impact of the veil on 'women's freedom and dignity', deemed it sufficient, after having heard the testimonies of more than 200 'experts', to interview just one niqabi.[2] In a context where empirical data on the practice of full-face veiling was non-existent, André Gérin, a communist MP and the commission's president, was not even able to sense the air of general contempt when he boasted to journalists that 'to perfect our judgement, we absolutely wanted to listen to at least one woman who wears the full veil'.[3] But the extent of the marginalization of French niqabi was only to become fully apparent to the team during our fieldwork in Paris and other French cities, between October 2010 and January 2011.

The primary objective of the Open Society research was to create a space in which the stories of the women we met could be related as accurately as possible, while attempting to understand their religious practices and backgrounds as well as their motivations for adopting the full-face veil. Another goal of the research was to assess the impact of the media discourse and the proposed legislation on the women's daily experiences, as well as on their sense of belonging and identity. Despite the saturated coverage, the potential repercussions of a hostile media and political onslaught on the physical and moral well-being of those who wore the veil seemed never to have been a source of concern for French legislators. The outcome of our research, *Unveiling the Truth: Why 32 Women Wear the Full-Face Veil in France*, was published in April 2011, on the day of the enactment of the veil ban in France.[4]

A couple of months later, I undertook another study on the full-face veil, but this time in the UK.[5] Although both projects shared similar objectives, the experiences gained from the French report as well as the contrasting attitudes of the French and British elites towards the

---

[2] Kenza Drider, a young woman from Avignon, was the sole niqabi called before the Commission and was requested to appear with her face uncovered. The Parliamentary Commission's report – *Rapport d'information au nom de la mission d'information sur la pratique du port du voile intégral sur le territoire national* – can be accessed at www.assemblee-nationale.fr/13/pdf/rap-info/i2262.pdf

[3] 'Une femme portant le niqab auditionnee', *AFP*, 9 December 2009.

[4] Loi no. 2010-1192 du 11 octobre 2010 interdisant la dissimulation du visage dans l'espace public [Act prohibiting the concealment of the face in public]. The law states that the concealment of the face is prohibited in all public places with penalties for non-compliance of up to €150, which can be accompanied or replaced by compulsory citizenship classes. Article 4 of the law also states that any person forcing a woman to wear the full veil faces a year's imprisonment and a fine of €30,000. If the woman concerned is under 18 the punishment increases to €60,000 and up to two years' imprisonment.

[5] At the time of writing this chapter, the publication date for the UK report had not been set by the Open Society Foundations.

expression of religious manifestations by their Muslim populations meant that certain issues briefly touched upon in the French study could be more fully explored in the UK study. In France, the impending ban on the full-face veil, its widespread public condemnation and the demonization of those who wore it, combined with their exclusion from the public debate, induced a sense of urgency that was not prevalent in the UK. However, this is not to say that Britain was a stranger to the veil mania. In fact, Britain even tasted its first national debate on the full-face veil before France. In October 2006, more than two years before André Gérin's open letter[6] demanding the creation of a parliamentary commission on the 'burqa', former British Foreign Secretary Jack Straw had also felt the urge to share, with readers of his local newspaper, his uneasiness when talking to Muslim women whose faces he couldn't see.[7] In both countries the interventions by the two politicians were to unleash an avalanche of reaction that transcended their national political and media circles. But a closer look at the content and tone of the politicians' respective comments, as well as the responses they elicited, testify to two very different political momentums.

While official figures provided by French intelligence sources a few months later were to indicate that the niqab is a marginal phenomenon in France,[8] André Gérin the initiator of the full-face veil debate in France makes, in his open letter, an extremely alarmist assessment of what he called the 'burning topic' of the 'burqa' which, he claims, is a source of concern for 'thousands of citizens'.[9] Without citing any concrete examples or incidents relating to the full-face veil, his letter conflates several issues and at times borders on hysteria: 'must we give allegiance to a doctrine of radical fundamentalism, Salafism, which is leading an anti-French and anti-white struggle? Can we in the twenty-first century accept that a woman is subdued to a man's will, [can we accept] the repudiation of women considered as impure according to an

---

[6] Gérin's open letter was addressed to the conservative Prime Minister François Fillon.

[7] Jack Straw, 'I want to unveil my views on an important issue', *Lancashire Evening Telegraph*, 5 October 2006, and republished by the *Daily Telegraph* and the *Guardian* on 6 October 2006. See www.telegraph.co.uk/news/1530718/I-want-to-unveil-my-views-on-an-important-issue.html and www.guardian.co.uk/commentisfree/2006/oct/06/politics.uk

[8] In July 2009, an article published in *Le Monde* reported that according to intelligence sources, 367 women wear the full veil in France, while another article published by *Le Figaro* two months later put the number at fewer than 2000. See, 'Selon les services de la police nationale 367 femmes portent la burqa en France', *Le Monde*, 30 July 2009; Cécilia Gabizon, 'Deux mille femmes portent la burqa en France', *Le Figaro*, 9 September 2009.

[9] The full letter can be accessed at http://reveilcommuniste.over-blog.fr/article-30144822.html

archaically and misogynistic conception of sexual morality?'[10] The communist MP further describes the burqa as 'a rejection of integration, gender equality' and the undermining of 'femininity'. By contrast, Jack Straw's article opens with his recollection of an encounter a year earlier, in his constituency advice bureau, with a niqab-wearer whom he describes as 'a pleasant lady' who spoke 'in a broad Lancashire accent'. Although this was not his first meeting with a niqabi, Straw alleges that this particular interview prompted him to decide that in future he would ask all veiled women who came to his surgery to unveil their faces. Towards the end of his article Straw assesses that 'wearing the full veil was bound to make better, positive relations between the two communities more difficult', equating the veil to a 'visible statement of separation and of difference'.[11] Beyond this criticism – relatively mild in comparison to Gérin's ramblings – Straw doesn't stoop to further generalizations to stigmatize the wearing of the full-face veil with a procession of negative associations, and even admits to reconsidering one misconception he had held after discussing the issue with a veiled constituent.

It took no time, however, for Straw's intervention to trigger a stream of violent anti-veil reactions across the British media spectrum, with respective headlines from the tabloids, the *Daily Express* and *Daily Star*, demanding 'Ban the veil' and 'Get 'em off!' and interactive readers' polls asking whether the burqa should be banned.[12] In the broadsheets, *Sunday Times* columnist Simon Jenkins wrote that it was 'reasonable to ask' veiled women who were unable to understand Jack Straw's discomfort why they would 'want to live in Britain'.[13] And like many of their counterparts in France, some British columnists rallied against the veil under the banner of women's liberation. In the *Daily Mail*, Allison Pearson argued that the full-face veil 'implies a submission that is upsetting when women here fought so hard to be free'.[14] Joan Smith in the *Independent* claimed that she couldn't 'think of a more dramatic visual symbol of oppression, the inescapable fact being that the vast majority of women who cover their hair, faces and bodies do so because they have no choice', associating the plight of the niqabi in the

[10] *Ibid.*   [11] *Ibid.*
[12] 'Veil should be banned say 98%', *Daily Express*, 17 October 2006 www.express.co.uk/news/uk/1350/Veil-should-be-banned-say-98-37
[13] Simon Jenkins, 'Political fancy footwork under Straw's veil of moderation', *Sunday Times*, 8 October 2006.
[14] Allison Pearson, 'Here's why the veil offends me', *Daily Mail*, 10 October 2006.

UK with those in Afghanistan and Iraq.[15] In the political arena Straw also received the support of several Labour Party heavyweights including Gordon Brown[16] and Harriet Harman,[17] who asserted that 'the veil is an obstacle to women's participation on equal terms', as well as from Tony Blair who deemed that the veil was 'a mark of separation', but added, 'no one wants to say that people don't have the right to do it. That is to take it too far.'[18]

But while Gérin managed to rapidly build an anti-veil consensus among the mainstream political forces in his country and the French intelligentsia, it was far from uncommon in the UK to hear mainstream voices condemning Jack Straw's article and his approach to the issue. 'That a powerful man can say to a completely powerless woman, I think you should take your veil off, I think is completely and utterly wrong and insensitive' commented the then Mayor of London, Ken Livingstone.[19] Recalling the events that preceded the race riots in Oldham during the summer of 2001, another Labour politician, MP John Denham, considered that the 'anti-Muslim stories' Jack Straw's intervention prompted demonstrated that, 'however genuine Straw ... may be, recent history suggests this is not the way to go'.[20] Interestingly, the feminist argument was also deployed by commentators opposed to Jack Straw's comments. In the *Times*, India Knight accused 'old "feminists"' of being prejudiced against Islam, pointing out that a piece of fabric could not be an indicator of unhappiness and that veiled women had 'every right to their modesty, just as their detractors have every right to wear push-up bras'.[21] In the *Guardian* Madeleine Bunting considered that 'one of the impulses for women who choose to take the niqab is how highly

[15] Joan Smith, 'The veil is a feminist issue', *Independent on Sunday*, 8 October 2006.
[16] Graham Wilson, 'Brown breaks ranks to back Straw over lifting Muslim veils', *Daily Telegraph*, 11 October 2006, www.telegraph.co.uk/news/uknews/1531106/Brown-breaks-ranks-to-back-Straw-over-lifting-Muslim-veils.html
[17] 'Veils harm equal rights – Harman', 11 October 2006. http://news.bbc.co.uk/1/hi/uk_politics/6040016.stm
[18] 'Blair's concerns over face veils', 17 October 2006 http://news.bbc.co.uk/1/hi/uk_politics/6058672.stm
[19] 'Salman says: the veil sucks', *Evening Standard*, 10 October 2006. The article can be viewed here: www.islamophobia-watch.com/islamophobia-watch/2006/10/10/rushdie-says-the-veil-sucks.html
[20] John Denham, 'How not to have a debate', Comment is Free section, *Guardian*, 9 October 2006. www.guardian.co.uk/commentisfree/2006/oct/09/comment.politics2
[21] India Knight, 'Muslims are the new Jews', *Sunday Times*, 15 October 2006 http://z13.invisionfree.com/julyseventh/ar/t851.htm

sexualised public space in this country has become'.[22] And even in the right-wing newspaper, the *Daily Mail*, Peter Oborne accused Jack Straw of political opportunism, commenting, 'it is quite the nastiest and most irresponsible politics I have seen from a mainstream political party in my life'.[23] Oborne supported claims that Jack Straw's comments had led 'to a number of assaults on British mosques . . . [and] a sharp rise of physical assaults on Muslims'.[24] Britain also provided an astonishing example of inclusivity of veiled women's voices when Channel 4 announced, in the same year as Jack Straw's veil article and the Danish cartoons uproar,[25] that a woman wearing the niqab would be delivering its Alternative Queen's message at Christmas.[26] Khadijah, a British convert, whose great-grandmother had been a suffragette, explained that although it might be hard for people to understand, she felt liberated when wearing the niqab. She also considered Britain to be the best country possible in which to freely practise her religion, a claim that would be echoed by many of the veiled women we interviewed in the UK.

During the French debate on the full-face veil, not only was the idea of a niqabi appearing in a neutral – let alone positive – light on prime-time French TV outside the realms of possibility, but it is also impossible to provide an example where a French politician or established journalist has defied attacks on women who wear the full-face veil, or supported their right to wear what they wanted. The handful of French politicians who went against the grain belonged to the smaller Communist or Green parties. These politicians argued more generally against the political opportunism of a government in desperate need of distracting the electorate, or against the general atmosphere of anti-Muslim racism, but in many cases doing so while also condemning the wearing of the

[22] Madeleine Bunting, 'Jack Straw has unleashed a storm of prejudice and intensified division', *Guardian*, 9 October 2006 www.guardian.co.uk/commentisfree/2006/oct/09/comment.politics

[23] Peter Oborne, 'Blair. The veil. And a new low in politics', *Daily Mail*, 21 October 2006. www.dailymail.co.uk/news/article-411783/Peter-Oborne-Blair-The-veil-And-new-low-politics.html #ixzz2QrBqY9gD

[24] *Ibid.*

[25] In 2006 we also saw the high-profile employment tribunal case of *Aishah Azmi v. Kirklees MBC*, involving the suspension of a teaching assistant for refusing to remove her niqab before male teaching colleagues. The case drew public comments from newspaper commentators and a number of government ministers including the Prime Minister, Tony Blair, in support of the local authority. See http://news.bbc.co.uk/1/hi/uk/6068408.stm, www.guardian.co.uk/politics/2006/oct/17/immigrationpolicy.schools

[26] Video can be watched at www.youtube.com/watch?v=Xlszdcd3Kck

full-face veil. For instance, Noël Mamère, a Green MP, considered that the 'burqa debate' and the law had 'stigmatize[d] the second religion of France' and made Muslims 'ultimately unwanted'. But Mamère was opposed to the wearing of the full-face veil, arguing that the existing laws were sufficient to 'restrict the presence of these women in burqas in public places'.[27] On 13 July 2010, when the French Assembly adopted the law banning the concealment of the face veil in public places, most Socialist MPs, alongside Green and Communist MPs,[28] refused to take part in the vote. Benoît Hamon, the spokesperson for the Socialist Party explained that while his party was 'totally opposed to the burqa', as it represented a 'prison for women', he feared that a law banning it in public places would be hard to implement.[29] Another Socialist MP, Jean Glavany summed up the stance of the Socialist Party by explaining that the risk of the law eventually being overturned by the French Council of State and/or the European Court of Human Rights would represent 'a priceless gift for the fundamentalist'.[30]

The attempts to ban the full-face veil in France and Belgium were to reignite the debates in the UK. However, similar calls to ban the niqab in 2010 made by the Europhobic UK Independence Party,[31] and by the Conservative Party backbench MP Philip Hollobone,[32] who introduced a private member's bill to outlaw the covering of the face in public places, met with no political backing. The day after Hollobone stated that he would not speak to any veiled constituent who refused to uncover her face, former Tory immigration minister Damian Green, declared that a ban would be 'unBritish'.[33]

---

[27] 'Voile intégral: un parfum de Vichysme', ATP, 4 May 2010. The article appears on Le Figaro: www.lefigaro.fr/flash-actu/2010/05/04/97001-20100504FILWWW00311-voile-integral-un-parfum-de-vichysme.php

[28] With the exception of Communist MP Andre Gérin who was the instigator of the French debate on the full-face veil.

[29] RTL, 6 January 2010. www.rtl.fr/actualites/politique/article/benoit-hamon-non-a-une-loi-de-circonstance-sur-le-port-du-voile-integral-video-5931800560

[30] Marwan Chahine, 'Le voile intégral se glisse dans un hémicycle échauffé', Libération, 7 July 2010.

[31] 'UKIP vows to ban the burka to win over working class voters', Daily Mail, 16 January 2010 www.dailymail.co.uk/news/article-1243513/UKIP-vows-ban-burka-win-working-class.html

[32] On 30 June 2010, Philip Hollobone's Face Coverings (Regulation) Bill was presented in the House of Commons. The bill can be viewed at www.publications.Parliament.uk/pa/cm201011/cmbills/020/2011020.pdf

[33] Andrew Grice, 'Champion of UK burka ban declares war on veil wearing constituents', Independent, 17 July 2010, www.independent.co.uk/news/uk/politics/champion-of-uk-burka-ban-declares-war-on-veilwearing-constituents-2028669.html; Allegra Stratton, 'Copying

2. UK AND FRENCH SAMPLE GROUPS

The Open Society Foundations' research project on the face veil in France started a few weeks before the ratification of the veil ban by the Council of State in October 2010.[34] During a three-month period, we conducted thirty-two interviews, mainly in Paris, Lyon, Avignon and Marseille. The research in the UK benefited from a longer time-span: the fieldwork took place between July and November 2011, during which time we were able to interview a total of 122 women, mostly in London, Birmingham, Glasgow, Luton and High Wycombe. The contrast in the number of interviews conducted in each country was not simply the result of the difference in time dedicated to each project. Although no reliable figures exist, it was evident that even before the ban's enactment in France niqab-wearers in the UK far outweighed those in France. Therefore it was easier to find 122 veiled women willing to participate in the UK research than thirty-two in the French one.

Both studies are qualitative researches. In France, the interviews were initially secured through pre-existing contacts, and thereafter through the recommendations of the first women we interviewed. In the UK, the interviews were obtained through several channels: grass-roots activists; Islamic organizations; mosques and Islamic events. We also randomly stopped and interviewed nine veiled women in the streets and shops of London.

Reflecting the ethnic composition of Muslim communities in the two countries, the majority of our respondents in France were of North African (Algerian and Moroccan) backgrounds, while in the UK the women were mainly of Asian descent (Pakistani, Bangladeshi and Indian). Eight of the women in France were 'converts' – those who grew up in non-Muslim households, later embracing Islam – compared with fifteen in the UK. In the two samples the great majority of interviewees were respectively French (30 respondents out of 32 with 29 born

French ban on burqa would be un-British, says minister', *Guardian*, 18 July 2010, www.guardian.co.uk/uk/2010/jul/18/burqa-ban-unbritish-immigration-minister. In response to the passing of the French law banning the veil, the then Environment Secretary Caroline Spelman declared that wearing the niqab was 'empowering' to some women. See Rosa Prince, 'Caroline Spelman: wearing burka can be "empowering"', *Sunday Telegraph*, 18 July 2010, www.telegraph.co.uk/news/7897148/Caroline-Spelman-wearing-burka-can-be-empowering.html
[34] The French National Assembly adopted the bill to ban face covering on 13 July 2010. On 14 September 2010 the bill also sailed through the Senate and on 7 October the Council of State ratified the law.

TABLE 5.1   French and British interviewees: demographics

	French sample		British sample	
Age group	18–30 years old	22	14–17 years old	5
	31–44 years old	6	18–24 years old	34
	Over 45 years old	4	25–34 years old	61
			35–45 years old	17
			46–60 years old	5
Marital status	Married	21	Married	82
	Single	7	Single	36
	Divorced	4	Divorced	4

in France) and British (103 out of 122 with 77 being born in the UK) citizens and in both countries the women we talked to were overwhelmingly young and a majority of them were married (see Table 5.1).

Data on the respondents' employment status and educational qualifications provide some of the most interesting reading, particularly in the UK. In both countries the information collected on qualifications and employment status overwhelmingly depicts the women as educated and desirous of a professional career.

In France, nearly one-third of the women interviewed were, at the time of the research, in paid work: three were self-employed (a hairdresser and two clothes designers); two worked in the same call centre, which allowed them to wear their niqab and the remaining five (three nannies, a youth worker and a call-centre worker) had to remove their full-face veil at work.

Another eight French respondents told us they were job hunting and a further two were on maternity leave. When asked, most interviewees told us that, given the opportunity, they would have liked to work. Only two French respondents stated that they were specifically not job-seeking, believing that women should stay at home. One of them, a 19-year-old housewife from Avignon commented: 'I really don't have my place outside, whether it is in a Muslim country or in France. I believe the place for the Muslim woman is in the home, I think that it is inside her home that she will blossom.'

In the UK, forty of the women (33 per cent of the sample group) held either a full- or part-time job at the time of our study. This is significant when compared to the 28 per cent of the entire female Muslim population of England and Wales in paid work, according to the

TABLE 5.2   British sample: employment

British sample	Housewife	47
Social status	Employed and self-employed	40
	Student	32
	Jobseeker	3
Work environment	Work in a Muslim environment	19
	Work in a mixed-faith environment	13
	Work in both Muslim and mixed-faith environments	1
	Work from home	7

2001 Census.[35] Nearly half of the UK respondents in paid work were employed in the education sector as teachers or teaching assistants, many but not all, in Muslim-faith schools. We also interviewed two call-centre workers, a childminder, a nurse, a freelance journalist, a graphic designer, a political campaigner, an interpreter, an NHS employee, a counsellor and a dentist.

Thus respondents in the UK generally occupied more qualified positions than their French counterparts and only three of them removed their niqab while at work. A 30-year-old teacher and counsellor from Glasgow, explained that she took the decision to remove her niqab when she counselled couples believing the veil could undermine the quality of her work:

> The reason I don't wear it in a counselling session is because to actually benefit that couple's marriage I have to interact and I have to use my face and I have to use expressions. You have to build rapport and the only way you can build rapport is if you actually don't have that barrier in place because it's seen as a barrier then. And for that reason I take it off because there's more benefit in me helping them with their marriage than there is for me to establish a connection with Allah personally.'

Only one UK-based respondent told us that her employer – the NHS – refused to allow her to wear the niqab (see Table 5.2).

In the field of education, in France, fourteen interviewees had achieved at least the equivalent of A-level qualifications (baccalaureate), ten had gained vocational qualifications, and eight women had

---

[35] Female (women aged 16–59) economic activity status: by religion (April 2001) in England and Wales, in percentages (Census 2001, Office for National Statistics 2001).

TABLE 5.3   French sample: education

French sample	No qualification	8
Level of	Vocational qualification	10
Qualification	Baccalaureate	9
	Undergraduate degree	2
	Postgraduate degree	3

not obtained any academic qualifications. The 2004 headscarf ban in state schools had a direct impact on a few of the French respondents with at least three foregoing school knowing that they would inevitably be expelled. Additionally, Eliza, a clothes designer from Paris said that as a result of wearing the hijab at the age of 14 she was (unlawfully) expelled from school in 1994[36] and had to study by correspondence until success-fully taking her baccalaureate a few years later. The experience of study-ing in isolation, missing friends as well as teachers to explain things, drained her desire to pursue her studies at university. Another 19-year-old Parisian respondent, who worked as a nanny related that she started wearing the jelbab during her baccalaureate examination year and despite obeying the ban, by removing her headscarf in front of the school gates each morning, she alleged being harassed by the school authorities who couldn't fathom what had happened to the former, 'trendiest girl in the school'. Teachers would make disparaging comments on her full-length outfits, which affected her decision to leave school: 'I could no longer stay. It's impossible to bear constant criticism.'[37] (See Table 5.3.)

By contrast, the level of qualification achieved by British respondents is remarkably high when compared to national statistics, especially if we consider that at the time of the interviews over a quarter of the respond-ents were still in education. Seventy-seven of the respondents in the UK (63 per cent) had attained at least A-levels or, in the case of a couple of interviewees, its equivalent abroad. Twenty-eight interviewees held at least a Bachelor's degree and 16 had a postgraduate qualification. Only twelve women (10 per cent) had no qualifications, which compares favourably to 36 per cent of the total female Muslim population with

[36] The law banning religious signs at school was voted through Parliament some ten years later, in March 2004.
[37] Testimonies like these are echoed in CCIF (Coalition against Islamophobia in France) reports documenting many cases – post the 2004 headscarf ban – of harassment of Muslim students for wearing dresses and skirts deemed too long by the school authorities.

TABLE 5.4   British sample: education

British sample	None	12
Level of	O-levels or GCSEs	12
Qualification	Vocational qualifications	9
	Diploma (14–19 years old)	7
	A-levels	33
	Bachelor degree	28
	Postgraduate qualifications	16
	Other	5

no qualifications, according to a 2004 ONS annual population survey.[38] (See Table 5.4.)

A majority of our respondents were second-generation migrants which might help to explain why the niqabi women in the UK case study are better educated and with a superior employment rate than the wider female Muslim population in the UK. What can be established from the responses, however, is that at least in certain sectors, the wearing of the veil in the UK doesn't seem to be an insurmountable hindrance to gaining educational qualifications in academic institutions and securing a qualified job later on in life.

In France, with the exception of Eliza (prior to her expulsion), no other interviewee reported attending school dressed in a headscarf, let alone a full-face veil. In the UK, our respondents' stories testify to noticeable variations in the school uniform policy of (non-Muslim) state schools regarding the niqab and even the hijab.[39] While the headscarf is generally accepted in British state schools, one interviewee reported that she was advised by her school not to wear it and a couple of women were forbidden to wear the jelbab. However, a number of respondents also reported that they hadn't encountered any issues while wearing the niqab at their local state school. Fareena, an 18-year-old from East

[38] Annual population survey, January 2004 to December 2004 (Highest qualification: by sex and religion – Great Britain), Office for National Statistics.

[39] Department of Education guidelines say that: 'It is for the governing body of a school to decide whether there should be a school uniform and other rules relating to appearance, and if so what they should be.' However, school governors must to adhere to a number of acts including the Human Rights Act (1998) and the Race Relations Act (1976) when formulating school uniform policy. Although the Department of Education has laid out guidelines these are not obligatory and need to take into consideration religious freedom, health, security and learning issues. See http://media.education.gov.uk/assets/files/pdf/s/school%20uniform%20guidance.pdf

TABLE 5.5   British and French interviewees: face veil wearers

British sample		French sample	
Between 1991 and 1995	4	Between 1994 and 1999	3
Between 1996 and 2000	17	Between 2000 and 2004	2
Between 2001 and 2005	41	Between 2005 and 2010	27
Between 2006 and 2010	44		
In 2011	16		

London, told us she couldn't wear the jelbab at her secondary school as the authorities argued, 'it wasn't part of the school uniform'. However, when we met her she was attending a local state-run college where she was allowed to don the full-face veil. In Birmingham, Karima, 24, was encouraged to remove her headscarf when she was attending a Catholic secondary school in Rockingham: 'They said that they would prefer it if I don't put the hijab [on]. The head of year said that to me. And the reasons the head of year gave us, is that I may be subject to some racism while at the school.' A few years later Karima went to college in Birmingham and wore the niqab unchallenged.

3. THE FULL-FACE VEIL: A GROWING CONTEMPORARY PHENOMENON?

The information and data collected during our research suggest that prior to the late 1980s/early 1990s the wearing of the full-face veil was at best a marginal practice in the UK and that since then it has significantly increased. Although the sample was too small to be conclusive, we could observe a similar trend in France. The overwhelming majority of French respondents started wearing the niqab after 2004, with only three (or four) women adopting it between the mid to late 1990s.[40] Similarly we were unable to find one single respondent in the UK who had begun donning the full-face veil pre-1990. Most of the women we spoke to in the UK started wearing it after 2000 (see Table 5.5).

It could be argued that as over 80 per cent of our UK interviewees were under 18 in 1995 the likelihood of encountering any women who wore the niqab pre-1990 was always going to be remote. But during the

---

[40] One respondent who had been wearing the niqab for 'about ten years' couldn't remember the precise year of adoption – either 1999 or 2000.

in-depth interviews, some of the British and French women who had adopted the niqab in the 1990s recalled that at the time the wearing of the full-face veil was an uncommon practice. For example Aicha, a housewife in her early forties, who grew up in London and adopted the veil in 1992, while she attended university, commented that her relatives found her decision to wear the veil, 'really strange because nobody wore niqab in those days. It was really quite hard to buy them as well – you just had to make them. I remember . . . me and my friend just making them . . . If somebody went to Saudi you'd ask them, "Bring me a niqab back!" But you couldn't really find them here.' By contrast, when asked how they had come across the niqab, many women who adopted it in the 2000s responded that the full-face veil was a part of their surroundings. Karima, a 24-year-old student from Birmingham who adopted the niqab in 2003 observed the full-face veil as being, 'everywhere in Birmingham. Since I was 14, I was exposed to it everywhere.' Other statistics in the UK, such as the number of friends and/or family relatives who had worn the niqab prior to the respondent, also indicate a sharp rise in the number of niqab-wearers since the early 2000s.

Our respondents were generally very young when they first wore the full-face veil. Our figures show that in both countries, the great majority of the women first adopted the niqab either as teenagers or young adults. Out of 122 UK respondents, 98 women were aged between 16 and 25 years old when they first took up the niqab compared to 23 out of 32 women in France.

4. ISLAMIC EDUCATION RECEIVED DURING FORMATIVE YEARS

Since the niqab is a practice, which has been adopted at a predominantly young age, it was essential to examine the religious background of the respondents' families and the kinds of Islamic education our respondents received during their childhood. Leaving converts aside, the majority of interviewees, both in France and the UK, were born into what can be described as traditional Muslim households, where parents wanted their children to grow up knowledgeable about Islam, while often conflating religion with certain local cultures/traditions. There were, of course, great disparities in the religious practises of the different families, but during the in-depth interviews most interviewees related a familiar story of parents who instilled in them the basic tenets of Islam (the belief in God and his Prophet Mohammed; the practice of fasting during Ramadan; and for the most observant families – in particular in the UK – the performing of the five daily prayers). Only a small minority of women described their parents as being non-religious/practising. Out of the twenty-four respondents who grew up in a Muslim household in France two described either one or both of their parents as being non-religious (cultural Muslims), compared to nine out of 105 in the UK.[41]

Seventy-five per cent of UK respondents who grew up in Muslim families received some form of 'extra' Islamic education – at their local mosque or through personal tutoring[42] – beyond that provided by their parents.[43] Although the French respondents were not questioned about it, the practice of sending one's kids either to the mosque or an Islamic tutor seemed, at the time, more widespread among Muslim families in the UK than in France. In the UK, even the respondents who qualified their parents as not very observant in their childhood said that they nonetheless sent them to the mosque or engaged an Islamic tutor as these were common practices among Muslims households. The parents of Farida, a 33-year-old South London housewife, neither prayed nor fasted when she was a child, but used to send her and her siblings to the mosque every Saturday and Sunday. When we pointed out the apparent contradiction, Farida commented that her parents' decision to send their children to the mosque was more cultural than religious, adding: 'I think it was all about growing up, being respectful towards your elders and your parents, not having boyfriends, getting a good education and just being respectable.'

---

[41] In the UK, fifteen respondents were converts (thirteen from a Christian background, while two had atheist parents) and a further two respondents (who are sisters) were raised in the UK by their Kenyan Christian mother. Their Muslim father, who lived abroad, asked their mother to raise them as Muslims. She took them to church but also encouraged them from an early age to broaden their knowledge of Islam by asking their Algerian Muslim neighbours to teach them the Islamic tenets. They also had a close aunt, living in the UK, who was a Muslim. So despite growing up in a non-Muslim household their experiences differed significantly from converts who either had no relationship, or a very distant one with Islam, in their formative years.

[42] Islamic tutoring was generally provided by a neighbour, family acquaintance or relative who would either visit the respondents' home or would receive the respondent at his/her home and teach them how to read the Quran and/or impart general knowledge about Islam.

[43] This figure could be higher if we only take into consideration the respondents who grew up in the UK. Indeed more than half of the respondents who neither attended the mosque nor had an Islamic tutor in their childhood were born abroad. Many women who grew up in majority Muslim countries (Pakistan, Somalia, Saudi Arabia and Algeria) told us that they were generally provided with some form of religious education at their local schools. The figure of 75 per cent also hides important disparities between the children who were exposed to regular Islamic education outside their home (for example, some of the women attended the mosque every evening during school term over a period of many years during their childhood) and those who only received it sporadically.

Many respondents also pointed out how their parents' Islamic beliefs and practices were infused with local traditions from the societies where they were born. A teacher at an Islamic school in East London, believes that her parents' prohibition on cutting her hair when she was a child was the result of their former proximity to Sikh communities:

> Islamically, now I know there's no reason why you can't cut your hair. It's totally allowed! You're supposed to cover your hair but I think the reason why that happens in Pakistani culture is because obviously Pakistan and India were together. Lots of Hindus and Muslims were mixed and Hindus, sorry Sikhs, are not allowed to cut their hair. So I think our traditions are very wound up.

And in general respondents in both countries highlighted the differences between their own current understanding and practice of Islam and what was passed on to them by their parents in their formative years. Chayma, a student at an East London Islamic institute, considered that her knowledge of Islam is more grounded on *proper* Islamic knowledge than that of the previous generation:

> They did the basics: my mum and dad and my uncles never missed their prayers. They told us the basics: we were told not to lie; to eat haram and those kinds of things. The way we do it now, we do specific research and specific knowledge-based stuff; we read up on aqīdah[44] etc. Theirs was quite simple – it was more practice based.

During the in-depth interviews many respondents spoke about a watershed moment when they took the initiative to deepen their knowledge of Islam either by enrolling on classes or by conducting their own research through books and the internet. Nadjet, a 20-year-old from a small town in France, is a classic example:

> As my parents are 'Muslims' in inverted commas, I already had some notion of Islam within my family. But I decided to start taking classes in the Koran and Arabic. Therefore I tried to deepen [my knowledge of] religion. I sought truth rather than traditions and customs that are mixed with religion.

Like many other interviewees, Rokkiya, a part-time teacher from Hackney, in East London, started to explore her religion more closely when she attended university:

---

[44] Aqīdah refers to all matters related to God, his names, his attributes, the angels, the prophets, the Day of Judgement and predestination (Ramadan 2004: 253).

It wasn't until university that I actually started reading into Islam myself, then I started actually praying properly and looking into it properly and knowing exactly what I'm doing and why I'm doing it.

The information gathered both in the testimonies and quantitative interviews strongly suggest that the Islamic knowledge received in childhood through parents, mosques or personal tutoring, in most cases in the UK and all cases in France, was not directly conducive to the adoption of the full-face veil in our respondents' later life. For all respondents in France and a majority in the UK, the decision to wear the niqab, rather than being a logical outcome of early Islamic education, represents a point of departure from the past.

4.1. Family's role in the adoption of the full-face veil

The niqab is often perceived as reflecting and reproducing hierarchical power structures privileging male over female, parent over child by coercion or outright force. These assumptions are undermined by our findings, which reveal multidimensional and dynamic relationships in decision making on the niqab. In the UK, the dynamics inside the family units and friends' circles are multiple (female friends encouraging each other, mothers influenced by daughters, an older sister inspired by a younger sibling, etc.). Many of our narratives in both countries unveil a broad range of feelings and perceptions, which are totally absent from the mainstream discourse: from the tension that the wearing of the niqab can trigger inside families in relation to non-mahram[45] relatives, the embarrassment felt by some husbands (or relatives) on tasting the reproving or shocked looks of passers-by, to the awkwardness felt by the unveiled mothers confronted by their daughter's devotion, and the U-turns made by fathers and husbands over their daughters' and wives' veil.

While the image of domineering parents, forcing their daughters to wear the face veil looms large in the mainstream press we found no evidence forthcoming. On the contrary, the in-depth testimonies revealed that when parental pressure had been applied, it was *always* to convince a daughter to remove the veil. One of the most unexpected

---

[45] A mahram is a relative whom a Muslim man or woman cannot marry: one's parents, siblings, children, nephews and nieces are all deemed mahram. A Muslim woman who wears a hijab or niqab doesn't need to cover herself in front of mahram relatives. Many respondents reported that wearing the full-face veil in front of uncles, cousins or brothers-in-law, had triggered tensions within members of the extended families. As a result some women decided not to wear the niqab in front of their non-mahram male relatives to avoid any tension.

outcomes of the French research was the high number of family conflicts triggered by the adoption of the full-face veil. In total, twelve fathers in France either disagreed or strongly disagreed with their daughters' decision to wear the veil compared to five who agreed. The opposition to the full-face veil was even stronger among the respondents' mothers, with a majority of them (twenty) initially disagreeing with their daughter's decision and only four supporting it. Knowing that their parents would oppose it, many young women initially wore the niqab secretly.

Eliza wore her veil secretly for two years and was terrified at the thought of being caught by her father:

> He had sworn that if he caught me . . . I think he would have cut my head off! . . . Even when I was wearing the jelbab, the long headscarf, [he didn't like it] . . . especially because on top of everything my father is designer by profession; he would take them and he would slash them with his scissors . . . So we played cat and mouse for a long time! And finally, it was me who wore him down and not the opposite. And I can tell you today that . . . the feeling of fear I had at the time for my father was greater than for their law.

Another 19-year-old Parisian student adopted the niqab without her parents' knowledge, but neighbours saw her with it and reported her to her family. She recalled that her parents believed that she was going through a stage and kept pressuring her with disparaging comments:

> 'You're not normal', 'You've got psychological problems', and 'You're unstable' . . . And it's even more hurtful coming from your close relatives and your family.

Far from being an isolated case, many other parents in France questioned their daughter's sanity when they adopted the full-face veil. Shafia's parents feared that she would 'become a terrorist' and were convinced that she had joined 'a sect'. A 19-year-old from Avignon remembered how she was mocked by her family: 'My mother said that I was crazy, that it was nonsense and that it had no place in religion. My father said more or less the same thing; that it was only the extremists who were doing this.'

Many other French interviewees struggled to make their family accept their choice. One respondent was (temporarily) expelled from her house and another one was given the ultimatum to remove her veil or be kicked out. In fact, many of our respondents' parents held views that were in line with those spread by the mainstream media, with daughters commonly labelled by their parents as 'extremist', 'Salafist' or 'Islamist'.

The role of the husband, another family figure often publicly portrayed as wielding undue influence over niqabi women, was also examined in the surveys. In France nine out of twenty-one married respondents adopted the full-face veil only after getting married and of those we determined that only one of the women had been directly encouraged by her husband to wear it.

Barta lives in Marseille and was on maternity leave when we met her. An energetic woman in her late twenties she recalled that before meeting her husband, a local imam, she was not wearing the headscarf. She admits her involvement in religion occurred because he was practising and she wanted to explore Islam. As with many other interviewees, her path to the niqab was progressive: the adoption of the headscarf led (two years later) to the jelbab and then to the full-face veil after four years of marriage. She explained

> For my husband it's an obligation, but he never forced me to wear it. He has always been very patient with me. But through time, in fact, it became automatic to wear it.

Barta was adamant that her husband never obliged her to wear the full-face veil but it was clear that he had played a role in her decision:

> He has always been advocating it . . . It's true that it was him who showed me that it was an obligation, but he never told me that I had to wear it.

There was no evidence that the other husbands encouraged or coerced their wives to adopt the full-face veil. On the contrary some women wore it despite the reservations of their husbands, as in the case of a hairdresser from Paris who was married to an Algerian resident. Despite having one son together, he had received several deportation orders and she was frightened he would get deported. Having already thought about the niqab after reading that the wives of the Prophet had worn it, the anxiety over her husband's situation led her to pray to God promising that if He granted her husband French nationality she would start wearing the niqab.

> I did my udu [ablution] correctly, I did the salat [prayer] correctly, I prostrated myself for a long time before God and I said: 'If you want me to wear the niqab, then give my husband his papers immediately.'

One week later her husband obtained French citizenship. But when she related the prayer to him, he was unsupportive and as a result she decided to wait until he relented.

> I was really annoyed so I made duas [supplication to Allah] asking Allah to change the heart of my husband because I didn't want to do it without his consent ... For us it's easy to live hidden but with him he has to face all the stares that fall on his face. It's not easy to walk side by side with us. I didn't want to impose it on him so I waited until he was ready. Then finally he said okay.

Other testimonies reveal that husbands were not necessarily opposed to the niqab but were fearful of the hostile reception their wives would be exposed to in the streets.

By contrast in the UK, parents were generally more supportive or indifferent towards their daughter's niqab than their counterparts in France. In total, thirty-seven fathers supported their daughters' decision with twenty-six opposed (the rest of them being indifferent or not aware their daughter wore a niqab). Fifty-seven mothers agreed with their daughters' choice, outweighing the thirty-three who disagreed. But even when parents didn't see the full-face veil in a good light, serious conflicts were seldom.

The respondents' testimonies reveal a broad range of unexpected initial reactions. For example a 41-year-old from Luton who donned the niqab in her early twenties told us about both the pride her father felt and the quiet embarrassment of her mother, and believed that in the back of their minds her parents might have wondered who would want to marry their daughter now that she was wearing a full-face veil.

None of the fathers of the converts agreed with their daughters' niqab. Djamila, a 25-year-old former model from Brixton said that her father had a hard time coming to terms with his daughter's transformation:

> My dad has always raised me up and said to me, 'If you're going to do something, do it properly! Otherwise don't do it at all.' And I always used to use that when I used to talk to him. 'That's what you taught me, and that's what I'm doing!' And he was like, 'You've gone from one extreme to the other! You've gone from wearing no clothes to being fully covered.' And he just couldn't get it ... He said, 'Why couldn't you cover your hair like normal people? Why do you have to always go to the extremes?'

However, the attitude of many fathers was not set in stone. Some who had initially strongly opposed their daughter's decision in time resigned themselves to it while others even grew to take pride in their daughter's niqab, as in the case of Farida's father whose perception of the veil changed as he became more practising himself:

> I think it was a bit too much for him at the time . . . He would say, 'Why is your abaya dragging on the ground?' He didn't like that . . . Now if you were to take your niqab off he wouldn't be very happy . . . So he was very opposed to the idea at first. I think as he became more and more spiritual he came more and more into Islam. He gradually took some pride about it.

As with the French case studies, the only instance when pressure was applied by parents in the UK was when a father ordered his daughter to remove her veil. Aleema, a former teacher from East London reported being hit by her father when she first started wearing the headscarf at the age of 13. She adopted the headscarf after hearing a lecture on the hijab by an American Imam:

> I put it on straight away after listening to his lecture. But I think that's because I had a rebel inside me. You know at that age you want to rebel, you want to be different . . . So I guess that was my rebellion – I put the hijab on.

As with a few other respondents in the UK survey, the experience of being harassed by a young man who followed her while she was attending college was the initial trigger for wearing the full-face veil. Aleema wore it for a full year but when her father found out he burned it and threatened to burn her with it if he ever caught her again. By the time she started attending university, Aleema's family were growing increasingly worried over her behaviour, and to keep her in check decided that the best course of action was to marry her off. But, in an ironic twist of faith, her marriage enabled her to start wearing the full-face veil again. Her recollection of her arranged marriage is worth quoting

> My family as a whole . . . were all involved in this: 'What is wrong with her?' 'There's something wrong with her!' . . . 'She's going to run off to Afghanistan. She's going to become the wife of a Mujahideen and have lots of Mujahideens. Get her married! Stop her university!' . . . So they took me to Pakistan against my will and then they got me married *hamdulillah* for the best . . . I had offers from outside of the family: brothers who were in Medina who were studying there. And I know some sisters were like, 'Run away from home'. 'We'll help you'. And I said, 'No, no. I can't do that to my parents' . . . So I put my trust in Allah . . . I went to

Pakistan and got married ... Pleasant surprise, he was practising ... It was a big shock for my dad because my dad said to him at the walima the following day ... 'You know you have to shave this off. No more beard.' And my husband said, 'I'll leave your daughter but I'm not going to leave my beard.' So my dad sat and held his head and said, 'Oh what have I done? I've got an extremist daughter and I've got an extremist son-in-law.'

We twice met Aleema at her home. She is an articulate and confident woman who is home-schooling her two young daughters. Despite her ordeal, she told her story with no apparent resentment or sadness, possibly because her father's attitude, as in the case of other respondents, had also evolved through time. Another interesting aspect of Aleema's testimony lies in the fact that she wears the niqab on a full-time basis except in front of her non-mahram male relatives to avert any conflict with her father.

While none of the French interviewees raised this issue, many women who wore the niqab on a full-time basis in the UK reported having to uncover their faces in front of their male cousins or brothers-in-law to avoid tensions with their in-laws or extended family. Over a third of the UK respondents who wore the niqab permanently told us that they went unveiled in front of non-mahram relatives. These family tensions further testify that the practice of the niqab often introduces an Islamic ethos inside Muslim households which clashes with established cultural practices as illustrated by the comments of a 51-year-old woman from Glasgow:

> If I was to wear my niqab and to go to a relative's house and keep it on some of them would be offended ... They've known us from childhood and they'd [say], 'What's the need now!' Our culture is different. Our culture isn't an Islamic culture. That's what I believe because if it was Islamic we would have been taught from the beginning but we had to find out for ourselves.

In the UK, thirty-nine of the eighty-two married women had adopted the veil after their marriage. Among those only four husbands disagreed with their wife's decision while the overwhelming majority 'strongly agreed'. A diverse picture emerges from the testimonies and data collected on the husbands' behaviour. In one case it was clear that a husband was exerting direct pressure on his wife to wear the niqab on a permanent basis. In a couple of other cases, husbands had also strongly encouraged their wives to wear the niqab. But at the other end of the scale a marginal number of women wore it against their partner's will. Furthermore, as with the fathers, the husbands' attitudes towards the niqab were not always unwavering, with some cases revealing their opinions had either changed or were ambiguous.

Rachida is a young softly spoken woman who, when single, had worn the niqab selectively in places where there were large numbers of Muslim men – in particular when going to the mosque. She had adopted the niqab in her late teens, some years after her eldest sister had done so. To avoid verbal and physical harassment, Rachida used never to don her niqab when visiting 'predominantly white areas' but this changed when she met her husband who wanted her to wear the veil constantly, regardless of wherever she went. Her husband considered the niqab a compulsory religious practice and although she didn't share his view she found herself compelled to obey him: 'I feel like it's a struggle but [wearing] it represents to me being obedient to my husband, and sometimes obedience is something that you don't like to do but you have to do it and I hope Allah accepts it from me.'

In Glasgow we spoke to one respondent whose husband had been studying religion in Saudi Arabia for many years, and wanted her to wear the niqab. But she only decided to wear it three years into her marriage, arguing that she needed to do her own research and that wearing it before she was fully convinced would have meant doing it to please her husband rather than doing it for the sake of God. When we presented the same argument to Rachida, she replied that by pleasing her husband she was also pleasing God.

Rachida argued that her husband doesn't, strictly speaking, force her to wear the niqab but the pressure he was putting her under was undeniable as shown in this extract:

> I've had this conversation with my husband so many times and he says, 'It's your choice to wear it but I've asked you to wear it . . . It's your choice whether you want to wear it or not.' But I know that it would upset him if I was to take it off . . . I say to my husband, 'Can't I just wear it in the places where there is a need to wear it. For example this morning I had a hospital appointment and it was [early] in the morning . . . Now there's nobody there and I was going for my scan and it's a woman's unit' . . . and he still said, 'No'. That made me upset because I think there should be a place where a woman can lift up her niqab.

The original decision for Rachida to wear the niqab was not linked to her husband, as she started wearing it before she met him, but under his

22222222222222

pressure she was reluctantly wearing the veil on a full-time basis. The situation with her husband was all the more regrettable considering that she reported having suffered from frequent abuse.

The story of Rachida, like that of Aleema, narrated earlier, was the most extreme example of coercion we came across. A few husbands had also played a significant role in their wives' decision to wear the full-face veil, but without coercing them. The most obvious example is provided by a 29-year-old student from Birmingham. She started wearing the niqab only to go to the mosque to perform her Taraweeh[46] prayers during the month of Ramadan. As with a number of other respondents, the presence of Muslim men congregating outside the mosque prompted her to wear it. When Ramadan ended, she stopped wearing it but put it on again while her husband was away because she knew it would make him happy.

> My husband went to hajj, and I was behind, and I think just missing him so much, and wanting to be closer to him, pleasing him that I wore it; because I knew that he would be pleased with it. Not that he had anything to do with my decision. But it was just to please him really.

The attitudes of the husbands, like the fathers, were not unyielding. For example, one respondent related that her husband who was initially delighted when she adopted the niqab now would rather have her not wearing it:

> Because of all the media and I think he just feels that I'm more . . . I don't know, when I go out he may fear that I'm the focus of attention . . . He jokes: 'Oh why don't you take it off!' Just jokingly, but I know he's serious as well.

Some women also pointed out that their husbands were either deeply self-conscious or even embarrassed when they were going out together. With a great degree of contempt Chayma described the embarrassment felt by her husband when they were together in predominantly white areas:

> I notice the difference in him . . . I'm like, 'You know what. If you can't take it I don't need to be out with you because my sisters are girls and they handle it better than you do' . . . We went to the Aquarium and the London Eye and he's very aware. If I talk in my normal voice he'll get embarrassed, like I'm drawing attention. And I'm like, 'You're

[46] Additional prayers performed by Muslims specific to the month of Ramadan.

embarrassed because of the way I'm dressed. When the bus comes up to East London you're not embarrassed anymore because everyone's Muslim and they know what you're like' ... We do have tensions and we do have arguments when we go somewhere else. It's better for us not to go to white areas.

One of the most striking contrasts between the UK and French surveys, when studying the respondents' social networks, was the number of niqabis known to the interviewee before she herself adopted the niqab. In France, the great majority of the interviewees were the first both in their own household and among their friends to wear the full-face veil. In the UK, forty-seven interviewees had relatives who were already wearing the niqab before they wore it themselves,[47] and a majority had at least one close friend who was wearing the niqab before they did. In other words, the niqab was a visible part of the environment inhabited by most of our respondents in the UK even before they adopted it, while it was considered an oddity in the surroundings of the French interviewees. Only a quarter of UK respondents knew of no friends or relatives who were wearing the niqab prior to them. It appears obvious – at least in the short term – that an environment where the niqab is highly visible is conducive to the increasing uptake of the full-face veil among the UK Muslim female population, as friends and relatives influence or inspire one another.

The sister of one London respondent started conducting some on-line research when she heard that some relatives who lived abroad were wearing the full-face veil. She soon discovered Islamic literature endorsing face covering and decided to wear it as well. This in turn triggered our respondent to follow in her sister's footsteps:

> I felt like I actually liked it when my sister was wearing niqab. It felt like she was very comfortable: she felt very protected and had a new kind of freedom. So I started looking into it as well and she said don't wear it until you are convinced and then you can wear it. And so I started looking into it and when I looked at the evidences I just thought I had to ... But my mother doesn't wear niqab. She never has worn niqab.

Another 29-year-old interviewee from High Wycombe, said that some 'sisters' she knew introduced her to the niqab, but she waited until being convinced before wearing it:

---

[47] Fifteen mothers, fourteen sisters, six cousins, four sisters-in-law, and another eight respondents had more than one relative who was wearing the niqab before them.

I had sisters around me that would always explain and say that to please Allah we should cover ourselves up, etc. And *mashaAllah*, they weren't very forceful, they didn't force the niqab on me, they would just advise me: this is what you should do. So I wanted my intentions to be purely to please Allah. And not do it because everyone else is doing it.

A US respondent who has been living in London for a few years might have summed up properly the influence exercised by the surroundings when she commented that Muslims in the UK were probably more supportive of the niqab than in other European countries because the practice was fairly widespread within the Muslim population in the UK:

Here there's no one single household that is not touched by the niqab in some way. And there's no Muslim household where a friend of a friend, or the sister or the mother or the in-laws – somebody – wears niqab in that family, in that household. So [Muslims] can't really be discriminatory towards it. They have to support it because it's a part of who they are: a part of the family, a part of their outer circle, so there's a lot more support for the niqab from the Muslim community here than there would be in any other European country or even in the States.

4.2. Islamic references?

In both France and the UK, a majority of respondents wore the niqab each time they left their homes (23 out of 32 in France and 93 out of 122 in the UK).[48] The frequency of wearing the niqab among the other respondents varied from, 'most of the time' to 'rarely'. In general the reasons for not wearing the veil on a permanent basis were related to work, family opposition and the fear of being abused. Besides, interviewees who didn't always wear the niqab usually considered it as a noncompulsory religious practice and therefore had a pragmatic attitude towards it. In France ten women believed the niqab was compulsory contrasting with fourteen who thought the opposite. In the UK, thirty-nine women considered it obligatory against sixty-five who didn't. But in all cases, all the women we spoke to considered the full-face veil as a highly commendable religious practice. Assia, a 21-year-old from Rennes, wore the veil permanently, despite believing that she was not obliged to do so but like many other respondents she wanted to emulate the Prophet's wives:

---

[48] As mentioned earlier in the UK we distinguish between those who wore it even in front of their cousins and brother-in-laws (sixty) and those who didn't (thirty-three).

Given the proof from each scholar, I think that for a woman it's not compulsory. But for me the best examples are the wives of the Prophet. I know they were dressed in this manner and I try to follow them *insha Allah*, in their clothes or in whatever they do.

What is the opinion of Muslim scholars on the veil? Even in secular France, politicians couldn't elude this issue when seeking to ban the niqab and sought the backing of the (perceived) sources of authority on the subject. When asked, alongside other Muslim representatives, to offer his organization's expertise before a parliamentary commission, Mohammed Moussaoui, the President of the CFCM (French Council of the Muslim Faith) argued that the face veil was not a 'Quranic prescription but a religious practice based on a minority opinion'.[49] A majority of French Muslim representatives concurred that while the wives of the Prophet Mohammed were instructed to cover their faces this did not refer to the wider Muslim community, as the injunction's sole purpose was to protect the Prophet from indirect attacks which targeted his wives. The Prophet's wives became the 'mothers of the believers', a unique status granted to them, which meant that unlike other Muslim widows, they couldn't remarry after the Prophet's death.

However, when surveying Islamic literature and pronouncements on the subject little effort is needed to find opinions stating otherwise. Sheikh Haitham al-Haddad,[50] a London-based scholar who holds positions on a number of advisory boards of Islamic organizations, was mentioned by a few of our UK respondents as one of their sources of authority. Sheikh Haitham's position is that the practice of the niqab is based on 'an orthodox Islamic opinion'. During an Islamic lecture al-Haddad argued that on the basis of the interpretation of two Quranic verses 'some scholars say that women should cover all of their bodies, and some scholars say that women should cover all of their bodies and they are allowed to uncover their faces and their hands'.[51] In defence of the obligatory face-veil option Sheikh Haitham points out that despite the difference of opinion no scholars have ever stated 'that [women] must uncover their faces'[52] or claimed that 'the [first]

---

[49] See *Rapport d'information no. 2262, Voile intégral: le refus de la République*, p 391 (see n. 2).

[50] Sheikh Haitham was born in Saudi Arabia and studied under Sheikh Bin Baz. See www.sabeel.org.uk/index.php?option=com_content&view=article&id=105&catid=29&Itemid=65

[51] www.youtube.com/watch?v=oZD4Tst-a8U&list=PL0B68C599EED95259&index=2&feature=plpp_video

[52] *Ibid.*

interpretation [was] wrong'. Although he does not state that the niqab is an obligation, Al-Haddad claims that there is a consensus among Muslim scholars on at least three points: under certain circumstances a woman's face has to be covered; the 'niqab is an Islamic dress'; and no Muslim scholars deny that the niqab is 'a better Islamic dress' for Muslim women.[53]

Additionally, even among the scholars who do not consider the full-face veil compulsory there are differences as to the various degrees of importance ascribed to wearing it. The niqab can be deemed 'highly recommended', 'recommended' or just 'permissible', depending sometimes on specific circumstances. Because there is no single source of authority within Sunni Islam,[54] the various opinions which prevail among the Muslim communities on a range of non-consensual issues rely on a series of intertwined factors: from the networks and channels of transmission of Islamic literature in a language accessible to the majority, the international and national contexts, to the mindset and personal situation of every single Muslim.

One of the central themes of the public controversy on the full-face veil in France was the alleged grip Salafist and radical groups had on the niqabis. Given both the controversial nature of the matter and the demonization that they were experiencing it was impossible to directly ask French respondents whether they associated themselves with any specific Muslim schools of thought, or if they labelled themselves Salafi. A series of questions however did reveal that only one respondent had ever been a member of a Muslim organization[55] and that a majority of interviewees (eighteen) attended the mosque only sporadically.

In fact, many French respondents were dismissive of their local imams and more generally of French Muslim 'representatives' whom they perceived as unsupportive as most Islamic institutions in France adopted a conciliatory tone with the French political elites – on one hand opposing the ban while on the other criticizing the practice of wearing the full-face veil. A young woman even told us that she boycotted mosques because she generally disagreed with the sermons.

---

[53] www.youtube.com/watch?v=-eevSabe-
do&feature=autoplay&list=PL0B68C599EED95259&playnext=1
[54] All respondents we interviewed in the UK were Sunni. Although we were unable to verify this in France, it's unlikely – although of course not impossible – that any of the French respondents would have been Shi'ite.
[55] One respondent in Marseille was a board member of her local mosque. We interviewed the local imam's wife who was encouraged by her husband to wear it.

Additionally only a few interviewees in France could provide specific names when asked about the scholars who had influenced them: a couple citing Saudi Islamic scholars such as Ibn Baz[56] and Al-Albani.[57] Some respondents said that it was while reading about the life of the Prophet that they realized they should be wearing the veil, and a couple of women also told us that they had actually started researching and reading about the full-face veil only after adopting it. For example Eliza explained that the practical aspect of the niqab rather than its religious dimension is what initially attracted her to it:

> What it brought home to me was that you can go out in the street, someone can stare at you as much as they want, but nobody knows whether you are cute or not. In certain circumstances this can be worth all the gold in the world. The process of knowing, of discovering people who were wearing it, of discovering scholars who were advocating the niqab, it happened after I started wearing it. It was more to reinforce the fact that I was doing it.

In France, the overwhelming majority of the women interviewed are highly unlikely to have adopted the full-face veil as a result of any direct encounter or involvement with a Muslim organization/group, local Imam or through the teaching of a Muslim scholar based in the country.[58] Most French respondents we spoke to journeyed to the niqab by themselves and seem to have based their decision on Islamic literature they found on the internet and in books (often without necessarily remembering the authors' names) but outside any structure, institution or group. In some marginal cases, the full-face veil was even adopted without the respondent being fully aware of its religious significance.

By contrast, taken together, the UK respondents' testimonies depicted an environment where Islamic literature promoting the full-

---

[56] Abdul Aziz Bin Abdullah Bin Abdul Rahman Bin Muhammad Bin Abdullah Al-Baz (1910–99) was one of the main Salafi scholars of the twentieth century alongside Sheikh al-Albani and Sheikh al-Uthaymeen. Sheikh Bin Baz scaled the religious hierarchy in Saudi Arabia over the course of the twentieth century and the support for his fatwas, on a wide range of contemporary issues, illustrated the influence he wielded throughout the Saudi kingdom.

[57] Sheikh Muhammad Nasiruddin al-Albani (1914–99) was also an influential Salafi scholar. Sheikh al-Albani's differences with the Saudi religious elite surfaced on the issue of the niqab when he authored a book, *Hijjab ul Maraatil Muslima* in which he concluded that women should not cover their faces – a decision that was at odds with a number of other scholars inside Saudi Arabia.

[58] To the exception of Barta from Marseille who was mentioned earlier.

face veil in English was much more accessible, not only through books, pamphlets and websites as in France but also through local and international Muslim speakers and scholars who delivered talks and lectures in mosques or at Islamic conferences and through a variety of other channels such as Islamic institutions based in the UK and abroad.

Karima a teacher from Birmingham started wearing the niqab after attending seminars in a masjid. One session was dedicated to the full-face veil, providing her with the different, yet mostly favourable, opinions of Muslim scholars on the issue:

> I started wearing it is because when I was 16, I went to a series of seminars in the masjid, and it was just for women. And in there, there was a question and answer session about niqab. And that made me think: 'I think I would like to do that, that seems really good.'

A 41-year-old housewife who is one of the few respondents who adopted the niqab in the early 1990s, did so after listening to talks by prominent Salafi scholars organized by Jimas[59] when she was at university: 'I'd go to conferences with scholars there who would say that it's not obligatory but it's something highly recommended.' Many other respondents related that they went on consultation websites such as IslamQA[60] to find out about the niqab.

Several interviewees started wearing the niqab while attending Islamic institutions. The most striking example was provided by two respondents who went to a Muslim boarding school in the north of England when they were younger. We conducted qualitative interviews with them and can conclude that the Islamic teaching they received at the school played a central role in their decision to wear the full-face veil. Salia from Glasgow is the eldest of seven siblings (including six sisters). In the late 1990s, aged around 13, she was sent to a Muslim boarding school in Lancashire. Her mother had come across a leaflet promoting a new Muslim boarding school and decided to enrol her, wanting a thorough Islamic education for her daughter. Salia would subsequently spend six years in the institution that she described as

---

[59] A Salafi organization set up in the UK. Also known as Jamiyyat Ihya Minhaj as Sunnah (JIMAS), the Society for the Revival of the Prophetic Way.

[60] See www.islamqa.com/en, IslamQA, which was launched in 1997, and provides authoritative responses to Muslim-related questions. The site's founder and supervisor is Salafi Saudi scholar Sheikh Muhammed Salih Al-Munajjid who studied under Bin Baz. http://islamopediaonline. org/profile/muhammad-saalih-al-munajjid

subscribing to the 'hanafi deobandi' tradition.[61] While, according to the school authorities, the niqab is not strictly speaking part of the school uniform, it is strongly encouraged and widely worn by the pupils who attend the school.[62] Salia recalled being taught that the full-face veil 'was fard [compulsory]. That's what they taught. Obviously the people that want to do it do it, the ones that don't, don't.' Salia's mother didn't welcome her daughter's decision to wear it.

> [The school] encouraged it and [my daughter] accepted it wholeheart-edly. I wasn't for it at first. She was very young and she insisted on wearing the full jilbab and the niqab ... For a 13-year-old I wouldn't have thought she was mature, but she was very set in her ways. We did have a lot of ups and downs about it at the very beginning: me saying, 'No!' and she saying, 'Yes!'.

Her mother's opposition meant that Salia had to wait a few more years before being able to wear it full-time. None of her five younger sisters wear the niqab, including one who attended the same school a few years later, but who chose to leave after six months. During the course of the interview, Salia explained that she had been drawn towards religion from a very early age: 'Some kids want to play with their toys. I wasn't like that. I liked to pray ... I can't remember when I started.' She had come across the full-face veil a few years before attending the Islamic boarding school through one of her mum's friends and had hoped to wear it one day:

> When I was a very young girl at primary school there was a mother that used to wear niqab. That was the first time I came across niqab and I always thought to myself, 'When I grow up I want to do that' because she was so different from everybody else ... She was my friend's mum and I really liked her, I really looked up to her and I thought, 'I'm definitely going to do that and Alhamdulillah I got into the field where I was able to do that. So that was the first ... she inspired me.'

[61] Hanafi-Deobandi refers to the adherents of the Indo-Pakistani reformist movement (centred in the Dār al'Ulum in the district of Deoband) which was founded in 1867. The goal of the school was to preserve the teachings of the faith in a period of non-Muslim rule and considerable social change by promoting Muslims to a standard of correct practice; central to that goal was the creation of a class of formally trained and popularly supported ulama. The school follows the Hanafi school of jurisprudence, named after Abu Hanifa an-Nu'man ibn Thābi which is adhered to in many parts of South Asia including Pakistan, Bangladesh, India and Afghanistan (Esposito, 2008).
[62] Phone interview with author on 15 May 2012.

The school environment and the teaching she received in the Muslim boarding school unquestionably played a significant role in Salia's adoption of the niqab, but her decision should probably not be reduced to it. Salia, like her other siblings, was first initiated into Islam by her grandfather who tutored them on a regular basis. Without any prompting she described herself as a child who was more interested in religion than her peers (presumably her siblings and cousins). When asked what had ultimately convinced her to wear it, Salia replied: 'It was something in me already'. We also asked her whether she had tried to convince her other sisters to wear it: 'I always did tell them but I'm not forcing anybody because it's up to you to do it when you are ready.' It is impossible to predict what would have happened if Salia had not attended the Muslim boarding school, but given that her interest in the niqab manifested itself before enrolling at the school it is conceivable that she would have worn it regardless of her schooling at some stage in her life.

Although no official statistics exist, the niqab forms part of the dress code of a marginal number of Muslim day schools and boarding schools in the UK. One hostile article published in the *Daily Telegraph* identified three schools.[63] We contacted two of them and were told that the niqab was recommended but not an obligatory dress code. Both institutions, however, taught their students that the niqab is a compulsory (*fard* or *wajib*) religious practice for Muslim women. It's reasonable to assume that these institutions have contributed to the uptake of the niqab among the UK Muslim female population, albeit marginally. It is, however, difficult to argue that these institutions are fuelling a recent surge, as one of these schools (whose school uniform policy hasn't changed since its inception) was established in the mid 1990s.

A couple of British respondents started wearing the niqab after enrolling at Islamic institutions in Pakistan. Sometimes it was not the teaching they received in those institutions that directly contributed to them wearing the niqab but external factors. A Scottish respondent from Glasgow started donning the veil after enrolling at the Al Huda Islamic Centre[64] in Islamabad because of the attention she was getting

---

[63] See David Barrett, 'British schools where girls must wear the Islamic veil', *Daily Telegraph*, 2 October 2010; Laura Clark, 'The British Muslim schools where EVERY pupil is forced to wear the veil – and Ofsted inspectors have approved them', 4 October 2010, www.dailymail.co.uk/news/article-1317393/The-British-Muslim-schools-EVERY-pupil-forced-to-wear-veil.html

[64] Al Huda International Welfare Foundation is an educational establishment (that also undertakes social welfare programmes), which was founded in Pakistan in 1994 and has branches in the USA and Canada. www.alhudainstitute.ca

from males. A US respondent adopted the niqab after learning about it when she attended an Islamic school in the outskirts of Chicago; not directly while studying the school curriculum but through another student who was wearing it:

> I asked her 'Why are you wearing this?' and 'What does it mean to you?' 'Is it a part of Islam or is it what Asians do?' And she explained to me everything about the niqab and she gave me some books about the veil . . . and they explained what classical scholars thought of the veil.

As in France, one of the most striking aspects when encountering niqabis and listening to their testimonies is the centrality of religious practices in their daily lives and the amount of time many of them dedicate to deepening their knowledge of Islam. In the UK over half of the respondents attended the mosque at least once a week and most women attended either sisters' circles[65] or Islamic lectures on a regular basis. Many women had also enrolled in Islamic courses, either by attending classes or through on-line distance learning.

Chayma from East London was at the time of the interview following on-line courses in Islamic studies. She also studied at a local Islamic institution and she related that she occasionally attended intensive courses during weekends or the summer period:

> Basically I'm doing on-line studies with a Saudi university because it's comprehensive and discusses all the viewpoints and then I go for Ebrahim College. I go there for Arabic and stuff. And then there are other institutes if they have spare courses . . . I do intensive weekends. So generally what's available I'll go along to it.

A relatively more relaxed political context in the UK allowed us to draw an accurate picture in relation to the respondents' religious affiliations. While all the interviewees explicitly or implicitly reported that they were Sunni Muslims, seventy women provided further information. Although their answers are varied, the two main Islamic traditions,

---

[65] Sisters' circles consist of informal gatherings of Muslim women, very often hosted by one of the participants, to discuss specific Islamic issues, sometimes through the study of a particular book. In general, one of the women, deemed knowledgeable by her peers, will lead the discussion. The testimonies provided by respondents all highlighted the fact that the women who attended sisters' circles held different positions on the niqab: while some would don it, other participants would not even be wearing a hijab (headscarf). Sisters' circles seem to generally gather Muslim women from the same geographic area along relatively non-sectarian lines, i.e. regardless of the level or nature of their Islamic practice.

147

which emerged from our sample, are the Hanafi Deobandi tradition and the Salafi tradition.[66] The most commonly cited source of authorities by the women in our sample were classical scholars of the early generations and those usually linked to the Salafi tradition such as Sheikh Bin Baz, Sheikh Albani, Sheikh Uthaymeen[67] and Ibn Taymiyya.[68]

A 24-year-old from Birmingham we spoke to had no issue with calling herself a Salafi and told us that she followed the Hanbali fiqh (jurisprudence):

> Since I was 14, I was exposed a lot to the Salafi daw'ah. So it was a lot of the time influences from older scholars: Ibn Al Qayyim,[69] Ibn Taymiyya, Ahmad ibn Hanbal,[70] these scholars, books from Imam Abu Hanifa[71] ... I would be more comfortable in taking knowledge from the older scholars of our time ... than from the scholars who are alive today.

But as expected many women also rejected the Salafi label because of the negative connotations associated with it or because they consider this type of association as sectarian. Many women insisted on simply referring to themselves as Muslims without using any denominational adjectives.

[66] Although the Deobandi and Salafi movements have been described as revivalist movements, formed during eras of waning Muslim empires and expansionist Western ones, as pointed out by many researchers neither the Deobandi nor the Salafi traditions represent easily identifiable monolithic movements. See Wiktorowicz 2006; 'Traditionalist' Islamic Activism: Deoband, Tablighis, and Talibs, Barbara D. Metcalf, Social Science Research Council. http://essays.ssrc.org/sept11/essays/metcalf.htm

[67] Sheikh Abu 'Abd Allah Muhammad ibn Saalih ibn Muhammad ibn al-Uthaymeen at-Tamimi (1925–2001) was a contemporary of Bin Baz. He was a member of the Saudi Board of Senior Ulema. www.fatwa-online.com/scholarsbiographies/15thcentury/ibnuthaymeen_whatthep aperssay.htm#2

[68] Born in 1263 Taqī al-Dīn Abū al-'Abbās Ahmad ibn 'Abd al-Salām ibn 'Abd Allāh ibn Muhammad ibn Taymiyyah is a precursor to Muhammad ibn 'Abd al-Wahhāb, who was reportedly influenced by the writings of Taymiyyah. www.britannica.com/EBchecked/topic/280847/Ibn-Taymiyyah

[69] Ibn Qayyim al-Jawziyah, Shams al-Din Abu Bakr was a Hanbali jurist from Baghdad and a disciple of Ibn Taymiyyah and compiler of his works (Esposito, 2003).

[70] Ahmad Ibn Hanbal was an Eighth Century Muslim theologian, jurist and a collector of the traditions of the Prophet Muhammad. The Hanbali school that spread after Hanbal's death was a jurisprudence seated in traditionalist thinking, opposed to rationalist innovations. Followers of the Hanbali school included ibn Taymiyyah. www.britannica.com/EBchecked/topic/10121/Ahmad-ibn-Hanbal

[71] Abu Hanifa an-Nu'man ibn Thābi (eighth century) was known for his systematization of Islam legal doctrine that lay the foundations for the Hanafi school of jurisprudence. The school is widely followed in India, Pakistan, Turkey, Central Asia, and Arab countries. Hanifa's work was as a response to growing attempts to assert Islamic principles to legal issues using authentic Islamic texts. www.britannica.com/EBchecked/topic/2209/Abu-Hanifah

A respondent from London was adamant in her rejection of any label arguing that 'people who name themselves, label themselves, ostracize others and it becomes like a clan, like a cult, like a clique and I don't wanna become a part of that because then it means I'm this and anybody who's not this is outside of my circle and this is not what the Prophet [was preaching].'

A 22-year-old student from East London also refused people labelling her a Salafi but said that she could define herself as such if Salafism was defined in a way commonly understood by Muslims:

> I've had this from a lot of people who ask, 'Are you Salafi?'. . . I wouldn't say that. Salafi has a few different meanings nowadays and I would say I wouldn't call myself a Salafi as such. I would just call myself Muslim. If somebody were to understand Salafi as meaning people who take from what the Prophet did, the early three generations, the pious companions and what they did, and the scholars of this ummah like the four Imams . . . I would say, 'Yes, then I do take from what they do . . . '. And in that context I would say that I am a Salafi. But generally because of the negative connotations it sometimes has . . . I would stay away from calling myself Salafi, I just call myself Muslim. I think labels are not so important.

While for many French respondents the full-face veil was the result of a personal and individualistic journey, in the UK cities we visited, most interviewees were connected to a dynamic religious network of fellow Muslims. The growing number of niqabi in the UK is undoubtedly linked to the proliferation of books, pamphlets, Islamic lectures, on-line Islamic courses and specialist websites as well as local and international Islamic institutions, which promote or encourage, in the English language, the wearing of the full-face veil.

4.3. Why wear the full-face veil?
Respondents in France and the UK, when asked to explain in their own words why they had been drawn to the veil provided a variety of answers which testified to there being no one single path that led to the niqab. In most cases the adoption of the full-face veil is the by-product of a spiritual journey with many interviewees relating their desire to deepen their relationship with God: their desire to be in perpetual contact with Him, their search for perfection, and their willingness to imitate the example of the Prophet's wives. But while motives of a spiritual nature were paramount, a plethora of other factors played a role in the *initial* decision to adopt the full-face veil. In some exceptional cases these

factors overshadowed the religious dimension of the veil, albeit temporarily, as the quest for greater piety ultimately motivated the respondents to keep it on.

Djamila from Brixton, London, started wearing the niqab after a man who she had known before converting to Islam made an obtrusive comment about her physical appearance while seeing her exiting a local mosque with a hijab. She had previously seen other women at the mosque wearing it but was unaware of its religious significance: 'I didn't do it because Allah says to do that. I didn't do it for those reasons at first; it was more to get through the day.'

A teacher from East London initially wore the niqab to attend a wedding after being warned by a female relative not to walk in the streets wearing make-up while her face was uncovered. At the time she knew little of the niqab's significance:

> I'd seen people wearing them. I didn't really know it was anything to do with Islam to tell you the truth ... I thought maybe it was to do with culture. I thought maybe it's to do with Islam. I wasn't sure what it was but I thought it was something good.

But the motives of these two respondents evolved over time. After learning more about the niqab they became convinced it was a religious necessity and kept it on. In Paris, Barbara a young youth worker adopted the niqab when she went to convert to Islam in a local mosque to avoid being recognized by her parents in the streets. Instead of wearing a hijab, which would have made her easily identifiable, she adopted the veil. The initial driver for wearing the veil was not of a religious nature but like other respondents, Barbara considered the full-face veil as 'a religious obligation' and wears it whenever she has the opportunity.

In a number of instances the casual harassment of interviewees by male passers-by led to the adoption of the niqab as in the case of Liz from High Wycombe:

> I was walking to take my son to school. I [was] ... wearing these clothes and covering my hair and this dirty man, he is a non-Muslim ... you know like a man who is breaking his neck to see this woman. This is exactly how this man was looking at me ... I felt so violated, I felt disgusted, I was so upset; and I am thinking I am covering myself, because I don't want be harassed ... and yet this man is still looking at me ... And I said, 'you know what, that is it! I am covering up. This is my body ... I should be able to choose who can look at me and who can't.

But even when the wearing of the niqab was triggered by an incident of this nature the religious dimension remained of primary importance in the medium and long term. We spoke earlier about Aleema who ended up adopting the veil after a young man had followed her all the way to her school, where he confronted her. We asked her why she carried on wearing it and like many respondents Aleema replied that she wanted to emulate the Prophet's wives:

> I always used to look at the companions and they used to be ... they are my heroes and my role models. So I wanted to be as much as I could like them. That's why I wore it afterwards.

Respondents mentioned many other factors: Eliza in Paris cited the onset of puberty as playing a role in her decision to wear the niqab. In Luton, a young respondent (Interviewee 52) mentioned the birth of her first child as a source of inspiration for wearing it:

> When you have a child inside you ... emotionally it moved me and made me look into how babies are created and how they are born and all the blessings Allah has given us. And that is when your eyes are opened: the light comes on. So it was with conviction around that time that I started wearing it. I thought, 'You need to be a good role model'.

For many respondents particularly in the UK, the local environment was also a major contributing factor. Many women moved in circles where Muslim women, be it friends, relatives, fellow students or just acquaintances, were wearing the niqab and felt inspired or encouraged by it. In France, ten of the women surveyed started wearing the veil after the beginning of the national debate (April 2009), and among them some confirmed that rather than the public controversy scaring them off it had instead made them consider the pertinence of the niqab. Shafia, a young Parisian who was not even wearing the hijab in April 2009, commented that it was the heated discussions 'which put a flea in my ear' and motivated her to look more into her religion.

> I asked myself, 'why?' ... And then I tried to understand what it represented, where it was really coming from ... Then I read the Qur'an and I bought books. And afterwards I told myself, 'I'm a Muslim, and if I'm a Muslim and one attacks a part of my religion, then as a Muslim I must be part of the struggle. I'm not killing anyone. The minimum that I can do as a Muslim woman is to wear the niqab, given that they are attacking this little bit of my religion.'

Ultimately further interviews would have undoubtedly offered a wider range of motivations for adopting the niqab. But in both countries, the spiritual motivation remained the driver surpassing all other considerations if not initially then at least in the long run. Many women recalled the immense feelings of happiness they felt the first time they wore the niqab. A 29-year-old student from Paris felt as if a 'huge weight had been lifted' from her shoulders recalling: 'I won't say ecstasy but, anyway, I honestly felt great'. Another Parisian said that she felt 'as if she was floating on a little cloud' and one respondent in Birmingham commented that she felt like 'the most beautiful woman in the world'.

Interestingly in the UK, the value most commonly associated with the niqab by our respondents was 'freedom'. Djamila, the 25-year-old convert and mother of two daughters from Brixton, who at one point, was considering a modelling career decided shortly after converting to Islam to cover her entire body and face behind a black veil. Having 'displayed' her body in two radically contrasting ways, she was in no doubt which one had left her with a greater sense of liberty. Djamila even alluded to her previous life as a form of 'imprisonment' and in doing so reversed one of the most potent stereotypes of niqabi-wearers:

> Before I was Muslim I went into modelling. When we'd go out . . . [my father] used to show me off to his friends. Or we'd go to an event sometimes with rich people and people would come up to me and say, 'You should be the one modelling up there' and he'd be so proud . . . That kind of shaped why I do wear [the niqab] . . . because I have freedom to be judged for who I am. People can deal with me for me and not for what I look like, and I like that type of freedom.

The feeling of liberation from the dominance of physical appearances described by Djamila was echoed by many other respondents. A young respondent from London argued that the niqab was liberating from a 'Western' perspective,

> because now I don't have to worry about which people are looking at me and what they are thinking of me. They can't judge me on how I look, and it's all about what I am saying and doing.

Liz, who is of mixed-race descent, felt that the niqab gave her confidence and freed her from the prison of racial stereotypes, as she felt she was no longer defined by her skin colour but instead was being judged on her actions and words:

[B]eing black all my life, my skin is quite dark, I have always been picked on. I had a lot of racism because I was dark. I was always called crocodile skin: 'your skin is very dark and it's tough . . . ' And I was called 'darky', 'blacky', 'nigger this, nigger that' . . . They wouldn't see me as a person. So when I wore the niqab I wasn't seen as a 'black' sister. They didn't judge me according to my skin colour, according to how I looked underneath. They judged me according to how I treated them. They saw me as a person. And this gave me the confidence, I was like: 'you know what, I am judged according to what I think and say, and how I treat people and not to what I look like'.[72]

5. THE EXPERIENCE OF ABUSE

The stream of violent insults many respondents were regularly subjected to in public places was undoubtedly one of the most disturbing outcomes of the research in France. Our first field trip in Paris gave us an acute sense of their experiences when just a few minutes after meeting two young niqabi in Gare du Nord, a middle-aged woman taunted them that shortly they would no longer be able to wear their veil. Niqab-wearers in the UK were significantly less exposed to harassment from non-state actors as demonstrated in the statistics we collected. Out of 30 French interviewees, 19 related that they were abused 'often' or 'every time they left their house'[73] compared to 10 respondents out of 118 in the UK.[74]

> In France, the insults ranged from fictional characters like Batman, Darth Vader and Fantomas to ruder words like whore or slut. Remarks made by members of the public also referred to women's rights, the ban of the full-face veil ('but this is forbidden!' 'it's a €150 penalty' . . .) to the respondents' right to live in France and denial of citizenship ('go back to your country' 'we are in France here!' . . .)

Echoing the experiences of many other interviewees a 19-year-old from Paris recalled one such incident while waiting for a bus with another niqabi friend:

---

[72] In most cases, it is almost impossible to define the age, appearance and sometimes even ethnicity of a woman who wears a niqab, particularly when the niqab is worn with an additional thin layer over the eyes.

[73] The question was not relevant for two women who only wore the full-face veil on rare occasions.

[74] The question was not relevant for four UK respondents who had just adopted the veil. We received no response about the frequency of verbal abuse from four UK-based respondents.

On another day I was at the bus stop and a woman called us bitches and [said] that her mother had fought precisely for women, for equality and blah blah blah . . . and that some women who wore the burqa, the niqab were suffering.

When we asked Fatima, another young Parisian, to tell us what comments people were making to her when they were being abusive she hesitated before reeling off a list of insults: 'Bitch, scarecrow, dirty whore, carnival, Mardi Gras, sex object, things like that'. And yet it was not the profanities uttered by people that shocked her the most but the experience of having her picture taken by a complete stranger in the Métro:

One day I was on the train. A man came and sat just in front of me. He got his phone out and he took a photo. It shocked me . . . He remained in front of me: he took a picture and laughed as if I was a monument or a circus freak.

Four other French respondents reported incidents of a similar nature where commuters or passers-by took unsolicited photographs of them in an insulting manner.

A couple of women reported being refused service in shops. A young woman who was ill was denied medicine by a pharmacist on the pretext that he had been robbed by someone dressed as a niqabi:

I was Porte de la Villette (in Paris). I had to buy some medicine as I was not feeling well . . . There was a little old man there, and as I came in I said: 'Good morning'. He replied, 'Can you turn around so that I can see your face?' I don't know whether it was a joke but he was very happy, very proud of himself [laughter]! I responded, 'But sir I can't turn around, my face is in front of you.' . . . He told me, 'Yes what do you want?' I told him, 'Since you are a pharmacist . . . ' He [interrupted], 'No! You get out of my pharmacy! The last time someone like you came in, I was burgled! Get out! You think you are in your own country! You are not in your own country!' And many other nasty things like that followed. And since I couldn't insult him back, as it would have been pointless me wearing this dress – if you can't bear it it's pointless to keep it on, so I cried! He didn't hear it, but under my seetar tears were pouring down.

Many women observed that they were never bothered in public places when accompanied by a male relative and like others Nadjet a 21-year-old from Rennes, couldn't understand how she could be perceived as an oppressed victim and yet at the same time be constantly treated to verbal assaults in public places:

You have some people who sigh loudly [saying], 'we are in France here!' and 'oh a fine!' . . . It's true that it happens every day, as soon as I leave the house. Now unfortunately, I can't always go out. But the few times when I do go out it happens . . . They tell us that we are submissive to our husband and all of that, but I say to myself that if we are really oppressed women then it's sadness that you should have for us. But in the end it's pure rage that they have for us. It's spite, while they should pity us if they think we are being beaten!

While the vast majority of French respondents reported suffering from verbal abuse, more than 60 per cent of UK respondents told us that they had 'never' or 'rarely' been verbally harassed in public places. Another main difference between the two countries resides in the greater diversity of experiences reported in the UK. In France, the first couple of interviews provided a fairly accurate indication of the levels of abuse experienced by most niqabis living in other cities and towns. By contrast, the frequency of the abuse experienced in the UK varied greatly from city to city, and sometimes even within the same area, from one individual to another.

In Luton, among the five women interviewed, three had never been exposed to any type of abuse, while two respondents reported being verbally abused 'often' and 'sometimes' respectively. One woman who said she was 'often' subjected to abuse described an incident when she was walking along a road early in the morning:

This person looked like a very educated woman in her car with a man sitting next to her in a suit and everything . . . And she actually rolled her car [window] down in the middle of all the traffic to tell me to 'eff off' and 'go back home'. And the people behind her were laughing at me just because this woman told me to 'go home'. I was more British than some of these people. At least I've got better manners.

Chayma who lives in East London but has grown up in a small city in Yorkshire said that she was 'never' harassed in London but 'often' abused when she visited her mum in the north of England. A few women who also lived in East London told us that they had 'often' been confronted by passers-by who would make offensive comments, as testified by Wassila a 25-year-old who lives in Forest Gate:

'Go back to your country!' They'll call you a 'black bitch'. They'll say, 'You effing nigger', 'You Batman'. They're very nasty, they've got dirty language.

A number of factors seem to have influenced the frequency of the harassment in the UK: the ethnic, religious and class composition of a location, the respondent's daily routine and, as in France, variations that happened over time were mainly explained by national and international events centring on 'Muslim issues' and their related media coverage.

In both countries respondents reported that the culprits were predominantly white people but in France another striking outcome of the research was the high number of respondents, who without even being prompted, complained that they had on several occasions been abused, sometimes violently, by people of Arab descent and/or Muslims. Beyond informing us of the unlikely profiles of some of the abusers, these narratives were also telling in that they provided an indication of the (low) levels of cultural and religious assertiveness of the French Arab and/or Muslim populations and highlighted the extreme marginalization of French-based niqabi-wearers.

A number of French interviewees expressed astonishment at what they perceived as a blatant lack of solidarity from fellow Muslims. Although responses on this issue were varied and often subtle, the great majority of interviewees were adamant that they were not receiving any support from Muslims, and particularly Muslim representatives.

The first interviewee we met in Paris couldn't conceal her deep bitterness towards her 'community':

> What hurts me the most . . . it's the community. Because . . . when an unbeliever looks at you weirdly you can understand as you can tell yourself 'he doesn't know; he may never have even heard of it. It's not his religion and at least he doesn't claim to be Muslim. Or maybe it was just an inquisitive look' . . . The community hurts us more than the others . . . an Arab guy with a Muslim name . . . I asked him if it would be possible to pray on time [at work] . . . and he answered in an arrogant and pompous tone, 'No way. There is no praying here; it's a workplace and blah blah blah . . . ' and subhanAllah it has to be the one who is neither Arab nor Muslim who tells me, 'don't worry, I'll see what I can do for you!' It's our umma [Muslim community] who is frankly rotten . . . frankly it's an ignorant, pompous and stupid umma!

While she was shopping with her 17-year-old son, a respondent from Lyon was violently confronted by an Arab man who was then hit by her son. As a result the police were called to the scene.

I was near the till in Carrefour. I was with one of my sons – I was close to the till while my son was slightly behind me, but he could see what was going on. The man was ranting at me and my son approached him telling him: 'Are you mad or what?' The man told him: 'Fuck you!' Then he turned towards me and he said 'w-h-o-r-e' which is when my son hit him.

Several other interviewees were insulted and a couple were even spat on by people of Arab descent. Some women were also confronted by Muslims who hinted that their niqab was evil. A middle-aged woman from Paris told us that sometimes Muslims when they'd see her would pronounce Islamic invocations of protection:

'a'uzubileh min el cheytan el rajim' [I seek refuge with God from Satan, the accursed] ... Or else when they see me, they would say: 'AstakhfAllah [God forgives me], astakhfAllah!' ... I don't respond because there is nothing to say.

Eliza in Paris believed that the feeling of shame felt by some Arabs and/ or fellow Muslims over the full-face veil was reflective of an inferiority complex:

There is also the verbal violence of the Arabs. Well this one is the expression of complete insecurity vis-à-vis the way I choose to express my Islam ... It's not necessarily marginal but it's something else; for them it's similar to, 'Oh you are shaming us!' It's really [this feeling]. Once when I was in the supermarket doing my shopping, ... someone came behind me and told me in Arabic: 'It's your fault that we live so badly in France' ... and I laughed. I didn't want to be aggressive but I felt like asking her whether she had her identity card [laugher]!'

Like a couple of other interviewees, she also considered that it was a generational issue with elders and community leaders more likely to feel embarrassed over the veil than younger generations who even when not necessarily religious 'recognize what racism is'.

The attitude of Muslims was clearly not a source of great concern for UK-based respondents as none of them spontaneously criticized British Muslim representatives or reported any incidents. When asked if they had been abused by Muslims some women replied positively but in all cases the occurrence of abuse was rare, and its nature never serious. A few women also mentioned that the harassment came from family members in the form of negative or hurtful comments.

6. HOW CONTEXT SHAPES ABUSE

In both countries, physical assaults were not a common occurrence. Only two interviewees in France and fifteen in the UK said that they had been subjected to physical harassment. Generally this included being spat on, shoved, hit by objects (eggs, a plastic bottle, a ball) or having one's niqab torn off. The most serious incident involved a respondent in Avignon who while she was leaving school with her children was threatened by a man holding a long knife.[75]

But the description of physical assaults by French and UK-based respondents highlighted another major difference between France and the UK; namely that of interpreting the types of behaviour which fall inside and outside the parameters of 'physical abuse'. In France, the majority of the women who were violently pushed, spat on, or whose veils were pulled didn't qualify such actions as physical assault. In the UK, all of the respondents who were treated similarly classified such acts as physical abuse. This difference also extended to the definition of verbal abuse. For example, in the UK one respondent from London reported (during a survey questionnaire) that she had been verbally abused. On further questioning she said that she was once called a 'ninja'. In comparison, one respondent in the south of France, who had a passer-by taunt her, 'Is it carnival today?' did not consider the comment to be abusive. The specific context (the different tone and demeanour of abusers) may have contrasted markedly in both cases, but it is still apparent, from a number of other testimonies gathered, that the level of 'acceptance/internalization' of both physical and verbal abuse was far greater in France, while the intolerance shown towards any form of verbal/physical abuse was noticeably greater among respondents in the UK.

During the in-depth interview Shafia from Paris reported being aggressively pushed on the Tube but when we later conducted the survey questionnaire she reported 'never' having been physically harassed. A young respondent from East London who described a similar incident when she was commuting considered it as a physical assault:

> Once I remember I was on a tube. It was at Stratford station and I was walking. There were lots of people and this man barged me very hard on my shoulder as he was walking past and he did it on purpose because there was plenty of space for him to walk by himself and there was plenty of

[75] The interviewee told us that he was later arrested and charged.

space for me to walk. And I felt very, very upset because I thought, 'He's a man, how can he do that to a lady!''

Another respondent from West London who reported physical harassment described the incident when a middle-aged woman tried to pulled down her veil while she was on the bus:

She came and sat next to me and she turned around and she says to me 'are you gonna blow up?' I said to her, 'What?' 'Are you gonna blow up?' I said, 'Course I'm not! Leave me alone!' And then she turns around and says 'Are you a terrorist?' I said, 'I'm not a terrorist. I don't have time for you, please leave me alone'. She turns around, she goes 'Take that off your face, take that off', and she grabbed my niqab and she tried to pull it down. Alhamdulillah it got half way down and I stopped her, cos my niqab was quite tight, and I said to her, 'How dare you!' As I stood up to say, 'How dare you!' she pulled it down again and I pulled it up [again].[76]

By contrast Eliza described a similar incident the day after Nicolas Sarkozy's high-profile speech on the niqab and yet she didn't report it as physical assault:

At one station, a woman came up close to me. I was very near the door, and she said, 'Sorry, are you getting off?' I thought she wanted me to move to let her pass by, but I wasn't completely blocking the door . . . But I kind of moved back a bit and she said, 'all right, because in any case I'm going to tear that thing off you!' and just then I had the instinctive reaction to push her back and to try to protect myself as I wasn't expecting it at all . . . There were three [people] trying to move her away, and she was coming back and they were pulling her away. She came back and a man managed to push her off the train, but she came back on board and was screaming exactly what Sarkozy had said! That it was in the name of the woman's dignity; that it was not in the Quran . . . She was screaming while I was not even responding to her. It was not as if the conversation had become heated, that there were insults being hurled back and forth. Not at all! She was screaming all by herself.

While acknowledging that variations existed in the perception of abuse *within* each national sample group, the main differences in the way interviewees define abuse, when comparing both countries, provides a useful insight into how each national context has shaped the respondents' understanding and levels of tolerance towards abuse.

---

[76] The respondent called the police and her aggressor was charged and sentenced to community service.

In France the widespread rejection of the niqab created a climate in which abuse was more frequent than in the UK. French politicians and commentators debating the full-face veil showed no concern for the welfare of niqabi women caught in the whirlwind of debates which, given their intensity, were likely to trigger negative reactions against niqabis. For example, the six-month parliamentary commission tasked with enquiring into the practice of the full-face veil – mobilizing significant resources and the participation of all mainstream French political parties – never investigated the abuse experienced by niqab-wearers at the hands of passers-by and commuters. The only violence worthy of interest was that suffered by female victims who had allegedly been forced into wearing the full-face veil by male relatives or Salafi groups. Yet overwhelming evidence published in our report revealed that the only violence recorded was being carried out by those who opposed the niqab. In the UK, a more rooted and robust tradition of monitoring hate crimes from the work of anti-racist organizations, research centres and governmental agencies,[77] as well as with the introduction of recent laws, redefining and extending 'racially aggravated offences' and outlawing 'stirring up hatred' on religious grounds,[78] also imply that violence experienced by ethnic and religious minorities is less likely than in France to be brushed aside and go completely unreported in the mainstream press. These two different contexts have had a direct bearing on the climate of impunity, clearly more widespread in France, and have crucially shaped the perceptions of victims of religiously motivated abuse in both countries.

REFERENCES

Esposito, J. L. (ed.) 2003. *Oxford Reference Online*. Oxford University Press, Northern Ireland Public Libraries.
(ed.) 2008. *The Oxford Dictionary of Islam* (on-line edition). Oxford: Oxford University Press.
Ramadan, Tariq 2004. *Western Muslims and The Future of Islam*. Oxford University Press.
Wiktorowicz, Quintan 2006. 'Anatomy of the Salafi Movement', *Studies in Conflict & Terrorism*, 29: 207–239.

[77] This refers to community-based grass-roots organizations such as the network of Asian Youth Movements, the Newham Monitoring Project, the Institute of Race Relations, the Commission for Racial Equality and the anti-racist initiatives of the now defunct Greater London Council.
[78] The Crime and Disorder Act 1998 www.legislation.gov.uk/ukpga/1998/37/part/II/crossheading/raciallyaggravated-offences-england-and-wales; the Racial and Religious Hatred Act 2006, www.legislation.gov.uk/ukpga/2006/1/introduction

PART II

DEBATING THE FACE VEIL

6

INSIDER PERSPECTIVES AND THE HUMAN RIGHTS DEBATE ON FACE VEIL BANS

Emmanuelle Bribosia and Isabelle Rorive

SUMMARY

The 'burqa bans' adopted in Belgium and France and contemplated elsewhere in Europe, have mobilized human rights activists and scholars, who are nearly unanimous in accusing governments and public authorities banning face veiling of violations of religious freedom and discrimination on grounds of religion as well as gender. Yet like the governments banning the face veil, the human rights activists did not have much information at their disposal concerning the experiences of women wearing it. In this chapter, the human rights debate about the face veil is revisited, taking into account the insider perspectives of those women.

1. A HARD CASE ENTANGLED IN A POOR DEMOCRATIC PROCESS

For years now, the practice of the Muslim faith has been at the heart of several globally debated polemics, for instance the 2009 referendum in

This contribution was presented in a preliminary version at the Workshop on Illegal Covering: Comparative Perspectives on Legal and Social Discourses on Religious Diversity, held at the International Institute for the Sociology of Law (Onati, Spain), 17–18 May 2012. We are grateful to all the participants for their very fruitful comments on the previous version of this chapter and we are especially indebted to Prof. Pascale Fournier and Prof. Valérie Amiraux who directed the workshop. The contribution is part of the IUAP project P7/27 on the Global Integration of Human Rights. Towards a User's Perspective, coordinated by Prof. Eva Brems and financed by Belspo.

Switzerland banning the construction of minarets and vehement reactions against a mosque to be built two blocks away from Ground Zero in New York. One of the latest controversies concerns the full facial veil, which led several European countries to adopt regulations or legislation commonly known as 'burqa bans'. Terminology is not without significance here. The burqa refers to a specific type of dress worn in Afghanistan[1] which is intrinsically linked to the tyrannical Taliban regime in the Western imaginary world. The face veil commonly present in the West is black, leaves the eyes free and is named the niqab by the women wearing it. The latter generally oppose the term burqa not only because it is inappropriate, but also because its use is perceived as a way to link them to negative and violent images of Islam.[2]

Striking in the nationwide or local bans in place or in discussion in France,[3] Belgium,[4] the Netherlands,[5] Italy (Möschel 2014), Germany[6] and Spain[7] is the very strong support those bans have received from politicians of mainstream democratic parties while they were often initiated by far-right-wing or populist parties. It contrasts sharply with the small amount of persons wearing the integral veil in those countries as illustrated by the empirical findings presented in the first part of this book. Only Denmark (see Chapter 3 in this volume) and Switzerland[8] refrained from legislating on the issue partly because

---

[1] Loose garment, often of light-blue colour, which covers the body from head to toe with only a net in front of the eyes.

[2] See research report (p. 4) at www.ugent.be/re/publiekrecht/en/research/human-rights/faceveil.pdf

[3] Law no. 2010-1192 of 11 October 2010 prohibiting the wearing of clothing covering one's face in public spaces (*loi interdisant la dissimulation du visage dans l'espace public*), JORF no. 0237, 12 October 2010.

[4] Law of 1 June 2011 prohibiting the wearing of any clothing totally, or principally, hiding the face (*Loi du 1er juin 2011 visant à interdire le port de tout vêtement cachant totalement ou de manière principale le visage*), Moniteur belge, 13 July 2011.

[5] Bill to introduce a general prohibition to wear face-covering clothing (*Voorstel van wet tot instelling van een algemeen verbod op het dragen van gelaatsbedekkende kleding*), 6 February 2012, Kamerstukken II, 2011/12, 33165, no. 1–2, and the critical opinion of the Council of State (28 November 2011) which very much doubts whether there are compelling reasons to introduce such a prohibition.

[6] In Germany, the Government of the Land Hessen has adopted an act prohibiting the wearing of the burka in the public service (M. Mahlmann, 'Flash-report – Prohibition of the burka in the Land Hessen', available at www.non-discrimination.net/content/media/DE-29-2011%20Burqa.pdf).

[7] Amnesty International, *Choice and Prejudice: Discriminations against Muslims in Europe*, 24 April 2012, available on-line www.amnesty.org/fr/library/info/EUR01/002/2012/en, 98–101.

[8] In September 2012, the Swiss Senate rejected by 93 votes to 87 an initiative aiming at banning full-face veiling from public spaces. Speaking in the name of the majority, one leader of the centre-right radical party stated that 'banning the burqa would be excessive and would encourage

of the low numbers of persons concerned. In addition, although human rights activists and many scholars are accusing parliaments and public authorities banning face veiling of human rights violations and of being populist their voices remained often entirely unheard, when not confidently rejected as disconnected from reality.

In this respect, the Belgian case is bewildering. Despite an ongoing political crisis which left Belgium without a federal government for eighteen months between June 2010 and December 2011, the federal Parliament passed the so-called 'anti-burqa Bill' through the urgency procedure and with almost unanimous approval. Only Eva Brems, professor of human rights at Ghent University and MP for the Flemish Green party, voted against the Bill. Two other MPs linked to the Green parties abstained. All other members of the House of Representatives supported the bill, which was considered a matter of principle to be handled urgently. Such a 'Stalinist vote' (Delgrange 2013) followed a parliamentary procedure where traditional parties blended their draft bills with the draft of the extreme-right party. No expert or NGO were consulted, no role was assigned to the equality body, i.e. the Centre for Equal Opportunities and Opposition to Racism. Moreover, the Council of State was deprived of its mission to give its opinion as to the respect of fundamental freedoms, and no reliable figures on the phenomenon of the wearing of the burqa – actually, the niqab in Belgium – were available. Criticisms coming from Amnesty International,[9] Human Rights Watch,[10] the Human Rights League[11] or the former Commissioner for Human Rights of the Council of Europe[12] were received with indifference. Double standards were applied: on the one hand, the hearings which took place before

---

tourists from Muslims countries to have negative opinions of the country'. He added that 'Today in Switzerland wearing this type of clothing for religious reasons doesn't pose any problems in daily life and is a rare practice in the Swiss Muslim community' (Swissinfo.ch Swiss news World Wide, 28 September 2012).

[9] 'Amnesty et la loi interdisant le voile intégral en Belgique', press release, 5 May 2010, www.amnestyinternational.be

[10] 'Questions–réponses sur les restrictions relatives aux symboles religieux en Europe. Contribution au débat sur le rôle de l'Etat en matière de religion et de pratiques traditionnelles', 21 December 2010, www.hrw.org

[11] 'Interdiction du port du voile intégral: une mauvaise solution à un vrai problème', 28 March 2010, www.liguedh.be

[12] Viewpoint published on the website of the Council of Europe: www.coe.int/t/commissioner/Viewpoints/100308_en.asp

the French National Assembly[13] justified the fact that none had to be organized before the Belgian House of Representatives; on the other hand, the opinion of the French Council of State was put aside in the name of the sovereignty of the Belgian state.[14]

Our position is certainly not to advocate in favour of the burqa, the niqab or any integral veil, which dehumanize women and lead to self-exclusion. On the one hand, women who are forced to cover themselves deserve strong support and protection. On paper, this has been achieved in Europe: illegal coercion and detention of women are well entrenched in criminal law and they certainly give right to divorce. This is not the main problem. In countries where gender equality is legally implemented, one may ask whether fighting efficiently against violence against women is best achieved through more criminal law. On the other hand, women who authentically choose to veil their face and body endorse a radical posture, often grounded on religion or decency, which might be viewed as a paradox: they conceal themselves but become very visible.[15] Their choice disturbs women's rights defenders and might even be unbearable for those who are struggling in Islamic countries for more freedom and equality. Today, one cannot ignore that universities in new democracies like Tunisia are facing huge pressures from ultra-conservative Salafists demanding the right for women to wear the niqab and segregated classes.[16]

This is, however, not the standpoint of this chapter in which we try not to be entangled in a genuine feeling of discomfort towards any kind of face veil. We do not deny that tackling the wearing of the face veil in Western societies is a 'hard case'. The question of how one should address what can be seen as regressive behaviour without

---

[13] The French information mission only interviewed one face-veiled woman after she agreed to put off her veil (National Assembly, 'Information Report on the fact-finding mission on the practice of wearing the full veil on national territory' (hereafter, Information Report), 44–5 and 158).

[14] Report of the House of Representatives' Commission for Interior, *Parliamentary Documents of the House of Representatives*, session 2009–10, doc. no. 52-2289/5, 22, 26 and 29.

[15] French Human Rights League, 'Prise de position de la LDH dans le débat sur le voile integral', 21 March 2010 (www.ldh-france.org/Prise-de-position-de-la-LDH-dans). See also D. Bouzar, 'La burqa, un signe sectaire et non religieux', *Le Monde*, 22 June 2009, www.lemonde.fr/idees/article/2009/06/22/la-burqa-un-signe-sectaire-et-non-religieux-par-dounia-bouzar_1209923_3232.html

[16] Media coverage of the occupation of the Faculty of Literature, Arts and Humanities at the University of Manouba (Tunis) in 2011 is troublesome. See, for instance: Coline Tison, Pierre Creisson and Pierre Tailliez for Camicas Production, 'Tunisie: étudiantes contre Salafistes', in *66minutes*, 22 January 2011 (available on YouTube).

compromising individual freedoms is challenging. As law professors attached to the democratic process, the rule of law and the respect of fundamental freedoms, we thought that our duty was to look at it dispassionately and to denounce the process at the end of which new offences or administrative sanctions are being enshrined in the law of European countries. We claim that the political process failed to produce an accurate expression of the different interests that should be taken into account (at least in Belgium) and that democratic debates are full of snap judgements (in all countries concerned). This could be seen as anecdotal. Official figures of women wearing the niqab in European countries are very low.[17] Their backgrounds are diverse: diplomats' wives and tourists, recent immigrants who sometimes start to wear the face veil after their arrival on European territory, nationals who come from a Muslim background or who are converted.[18] However, there is much more at stake, namely the rest of the Muslim population who, to a large extent, is experiencing discrimination due to stereotypes and negative views.

Against this background, we intend to revisit the legal debate about the face veil taking into account the insider perspectives of those women, as presented in Part I of this volume. On the whole, it is surprising that neither public authorities banning the face veil nor human activists advocating against such a process had much information at their disposal relating the experiences of the women concerned.

2. A CHALLENGE TO HUMAN RIGHTS

Burqa ban debates are stuffed with human rights rhetoric. Both proponents and opponents of such bans have relied upon the language

---

[17] Amnesty International, *Choice and Prejudice: Discrimination Against Muslims in Europe*, 92, n. 255. There are only scarce official figures on the number of women wearing face veils in Europe. In Belgium, the figure most often presented is between 200 and 300 women, which is less than 0.5 per cent of the Muslim population (see Chapter 3 in this volume). In France, the figures go from 400 to 1900 women (0.1 per cent of the Muslim women) wearing the face veil (see Open Society Foundations 2011. In the Netherlands, the number is estimated to a maximum of 400 women (0.1 per cent of the Muslim women) (Moors 2009) and in Denmark the population of niqabis would amount to a maximum of 100 women corresponding also to about 0.1 per cent of the Muslim women in Denmark (see Chapter 3 in this volume).

[18] Open Society Foundations 2011: 37–45.

of human rights to the extent that equally important rights or principles conflict (or seem to conflict) with each other (Tourkochoriti 2012):[19]

> On the one hand, such laws and regulations have been justified on the grounds that they protect the dignity and equal rights of women, help preserve public security and reflect national values, such as official secularism [or living together]. On the other hand, such laws have been attacked on the basis that they undermine women's rights to equal treatment, freedoms of expression and of religion and are counter-productive to their purported aims of promoting integration.[20]

Belgium and France are key case studies. These are so far the only countries to have national legislation banning the full veil. The French one is currently being reviewed by the European Court of Human Rights (ECtHR).[21] On 6 December 2013, the Belgian Constitutional Court backed the federal law.[22] Its ruling is fraught with petitions of principle as the Court held that individualization by means of facial recognition is linked to the very 'essence' of any individual and that forbidding any cloth, even a religious cloth, preventing such an individualization responds to a pressing social need.[23] The purpose of this paper is not to scrutinize the Belgian ruling as such (Christians et al. 2013; Chapter 7 in this volume) but to assess the human rights arguments altogether against the backdrop of the Council of Europe protection system. The legal arguments used to challenge the burqa bans in the light of human rights go far beyond freedom of religion (Barton 2012; Hunter-Henin 2012). The criminalization of the covering of the face when being in areas open to the public could be held in violation of the

---

[19] Report of Asma Jahangir, Special Rapporteur on Freedom of religion or belief, (E/CN.4/2006/5, 9 January 2006, §52).
[20] Article 19, 'Legal Comment. Bans on the full face veils and Human Rights. A Freedom of expression perspective', December 2010 (www.article19.org/data/files/pdfs/publications/bans-on-the-full-face-veil-and-human-rights.pdf) (hereafter Legal Comment).
[21] Application filed by a Muslim woman before the European Court of Human Rights against the French burqa ban, SAS v. France, req. 4383/11, 11 April 2011. See also the written submission by the Human Rights Centre of Ghent University.
[22] Belgian Constitutional Court, ruling on annulment no. 145/2012. Samia Belkacemi and Yamina Oussar, two Muslim women wearing a headscarf totally or principally hiding their face, filed a claim for annulment and suspension of the so-called 'anti-burqa' Act before the Constitutional Court, on 27 July 2011 (appeal no. 5191). Another action in suspension and annulment was brought by a Belgian atheist woman in September 2011 (appeal no. 5204) and a third action in annulment was brought by the NGO 'Justice and Democracy' in November 2011 (appeal no. 5244).
[23] Belgian Constitutional Court, 6 December 2012, case no. 145/2012, §B.21.

right to privacy,[24] the freedom of religion and the freedom of (and even the freedom to) peaceful assembly. Furthermore, the bans from public facilities, the refusal of service and the risk to be fined and imprisoned could be seen as degrading treatments. And finally, this general ban could be challenged as discriminatory because of its adverse impact on Muslim women.

In the limited scope of this chapter, we focus on the two prominent arguments which are freedom of religion and freedom of expression, on the one hand (section 2.1.) and non-discrimination, on the other hand (section 2.2.).

2.1. Freedom of religion and freedom of expression

Until now, the international and European case law related to the wearing of religious dresses or symbols have overwhelmingly focused on freedom of religion and belief. In our view, bans of full face veils should be assessed through a more comprehensive framework taking into account freedom of expression (see Chapter 7 in this volume).[25] This is all the more justified as wearing the full veil does not have one single meaning. As it results from the empirical findings, women who choose to wear the niqab do so for a wide range of different motives and hold it as an expression of their religious, cultural, political or personal identity or beliefs (Bribosia and Rorive 2004: 961–2).[26] And applying a different scrutiny on face veil bans depending on its particular meaning in individual cases is unworkable.

In international human rights law, it is generally acknowledged that freedom of expression protects all forms of expression including non-verbal expression such as clothes or symbols.[27] Regarding freedom of religion, the UN Human Rights Committee stressed that 'the observance and practice of religion or belief may include not only ceremonial acts but also such customs as . . . the wearing of distinctive

---

[24] Full-veiled women would be affected by the ban in their possibility to establish a social life, to develop relationships with others outside home, which could impair their autonomy and dignity (ECtHR, *SAS* v. *France*, application no. 43835/11, written submissions on behalf of Liberty, 7 May 2012, point 18).

[25] Article 19, 'Legal Comment', §42.

[26] Open Society Foundations 2011. Regarding the difficulty of assigning one meaning to the wearing of the hidjab, see the dissenting opinion of Judge F. Tulkens in the *Leyla Sahin* case (ECtHR (GC), *Leyla Sahin* v. *Turkey*, 10 November 2005, §11).

[27] Human Rights Committee, General Comment no. 34, 'Freedom of Opinion and Expression', 2011, §12.

clothing or head coverings'.[28] In the *Ahmet Arslan* case, the ECtHR held that the conviction of members of a religious group – Aczimendi tarikatÿ– who were wearing distinctive clothing (made up of a turban, baggy trousers, a tunic and a stick) in public areas fell within the ambit of freedom of religion as guaranteed by Article 9 ECtHR.[29] According to the ECtHR, the subjective feeling is the relevant factor here. In other words, freedom of religion is at stake when the wearing of a particular garment is inspired by a religion or belief, independently of determining 'whether such decisions are in every case taken to fulfil a religious duty'.[30]

2.1.1. The role of the margin of appreciation before the European Court of Human Rights
Traditionally, the Court underlines the lack of European consensus to yield a wide margin of appreciation to the states 'where questions concerning the relationship between State and religions are at stake' and especially when dealing with issues of religious symbols in educational institutions (Rorive 2009).[31] One could wonder whether this loose scrutiny test should apply to a dress that can either be religious or political depending on the intent of the woman wearing it.[32] In any case, even in issues concerning religious symbols, the national margin of appreciation has been narrowed down on some occasions (Brems *et al.* 2012).[33] In the *Ahmet Arslan* case, the Court stressed that a general ban on religious dresses applicable to public areas open to all should be distinguished from regulations on religious symbols in public institutions (schools, universities, etc.) where religious neutrality might take precedence over the right to manifest one's religion. Such an approach should tighten the margin of appreciation of national authorities banning the face veil in public.[34]

---

[28] General Comment no. 22, §4. This statement was shared by the Special Rapporteur on Freedom of religion or belief, Asma Jahangir (Report, E/CN 4/2006/5, 9 January 2006, §40). See also Human Rights Committee, *Hudoyberganova* v. *Uzbekistan*, Communication No. 931/2000, UN doc. CCPR/C/82/D/931/2000 (2004).

[29] ECtHR, *Ahmet Arslan* v. *Turkey*, 23 February 2010.

[30] ECtHR (GC), *Leyla Sahin* v. *Turkey*, 10 November 2005, §78. For a similar reasoning in relation to the wearing of the niqab, see Tribunal of police of Brussels (Etterbeek), 26 January 2011, *Jurisprudence de Liège, Mons et Bruxelles*, 2011/12, 1066–74.

[31] See, for instance, ECtHR (GC) *Leyla Sahin* v. *Turkey*, 10 November 2005, §109.

[32] Article 19, 'Legal Comment', §69.

[33] In this line, see Human Rights Committee, *Singh* v. *France*, no. 1852/2008, 4 December 2012 (CCPR/C/106/D/1852/2008).

[34] See ECtHR, *Vajnai* v. *Hungary*, 8 July 2008: 'when freedom of expression is exercised as political speech [. . .] limitations are justified only in so far as there exists a clear, pressing and specific

2.1.2. Justification of the restriction to freedom of religion and expression

During the Belgian and French parliamentary debates, many aims were put forward to sustain the criminal bills: protection of public security, safety and public order, gender equality, human dignity, sociability (*communication*), the 'living together' (*vivre-ensemble*), secularism, protection of Muslim women forced to wear the burqa, fight against Islamization and intolerance towards the Western world, etc. (Barton 2012: 11; Delgrange 2013). Among these, only public security and public order, protection of human dignity and gender equality (under the heading of 'protection of rights and freedoms of others') equate to one of the legitimate aims listed in Articles 9 and 10 ECHR.[35]

Undoubtedly, the legitimacy of some of the aims pursued in criminalizing the face veil is questionable. Can considerations of sociability justifiably circumvent our freedom of religion or our freedom of expression in any public places? To which slippery slope could the 'living together' (supposedly 'pleasant') argument bring us when applied to justify human rights interference? However, the core of the legal debate is not here. The judicial control of the legitimacy of the aim(s) pursued when limiting freedom of religion or freedom of expression is usually not very strict. The contentious issue relates to the assessment of the 'necessity in a democratic society' assessment and the proportionality test.

2.1.3. Are the 'burqa bans' necessary and proportionate to achieve public security or public order?

The argument of public security is based on the fact that concealment of one's face in public could disturb prevention and immediate repression of infractions. During the parliamentary debates in France and Belgium, the threat to public security was exemplified with the risk of the integral veil being used to commit crimes and to hide weapons.[36] The amalgam

social need. Consequently, utmost care must be observed in applying any restrictions, especially when the case involves symbols [red star in a post-communist country] which have multiple meanings. In such situations, the Court perceives a risk that a blanket ban on such symbols may also restrict their use in contexts in which no restriction would be justified' (§51).

[35] 'Living together' could potentially be subsumed in a non-substantial conception of 'public order'. For a discussion on this issue, see French Council of State, '*Study of possible legal grounds for banning the full veil*', report adopted by the Plenary General Assembly of the Conseil d'Etat, 25 March 2010, 26–9 (hereafter *Study for Banning the Full Veil*).

[36] National Assembly, 'Information Report', 178; *Parliamentary Documents of the House of Representatives*, Session 2009–10, Report, 9 April 2010, doc. no. 52 2289/005, 8 and 16. See also *Parliamentary Documents of the House of Representatives*, Session 2010–11, Report, 18 April 2011, doc. no. 53 0219/004, 7.

between Islamism, violence and the full veil was debated as an obvious fact without relying on any single instance.

Of course, public security may justify specific human rights interferences, in particular in situations such as identity controls or airport security checks. Conversely, the requirement of a general ban of the full veil in all public spaces is highly doubtful. In the *Ahmet* case, the ECtHR found a violation of the freedom of religion and belief, holding in particular that there was no evidence that the applicants had represented a threat to the public order or that they had been involved in inappropriate proselytism during their gathering. This evidence-based approach seems the only one able to prevent a curtailment of human rights based on fear.[37] Under national and European human rights standards, forbidding the full veil could be justified neither by a virtual or unproven risk for public security nor on mere speculation or presumption. The suitable test relates to 'an actual threat to public [security] or the sufficiently strong likelihood of one'.[38] This is in line with the jurisprudence of the ECtHR. In the *Vajnai* case, a criminal offence for the display of a red star that was considered as a totalitarian symbol under Hungarian criminal law was at stake. While assessing the restriction to the freedom of expression, the European Court held that '[a]s regards the aim of preventing disorder ... the Government has not referred to any instance where an actual or even remote danger of disorder triggered by the public display of the red star had arisen in Hungary. In the Court's view, the containment of a mere speculative danger, as a preventive measure for the protection of democracy, cannot be seen as a "pressing social need".'[39]

No evidence of any actual threat is supporting the French or the Belgian legislation. First, the parliamentary debates focused on the integral veil as being a danger for public security. Other ways of covering one's face (motorcycle helmet, hood, etc.) found only anecdotal reference. This could shed some doubts as to whether the pressing need of identifying people was the real concern of the legislator.

---

[37] In this sense, see the dissenting opinion of Judge Françoise Tulkens in the *Leyla Sahin* case (2005) in which she underlined that only 'indisputable facts and reasons whose legitimacy is beyond doubt – not mere worries or fears – are capable of satisfying th[e] requirement [of a pressing social need] and justifying interference with a right guaranteed by the Convention'.

[38] French Council of State, *Study for banning the Full Veil*, 33–4. See also Article 19, 'Legal Comment', §59.

[39] ECtHR, *Vajnai v. Hungary*, 8 July 2008, §55.

Furthermore, it is absolutely not demonstrated that being able to identify someone circulating in any public area at any time is indispensable to guarantee public order or public security. As the French Council of State put it, no link between criminality and the wearing of the integral veil has ever been evidenced: 'A general prohibition would therefore be based on artificial preventive considerations, which have never been accepted as such in case law.'[40] The empirical findings confirm this line of reasoning as they show a general willingness of the face veil wearers to identify themselves by showing their faces to persons in authority reducing the relevance of presenting face-veiled women as a safety risk (Brems *et al.* 2014).[41]

Second, even if they could be held necessary to maintain public security, the French and the Belgian Acts do not pass the proportionality test. In the French Council of State's words, '[m]easures [infringing upon rights and freedoms] should not be excessive in terms of their geographical, personal and substantive fields of application or in their effects'.[42] Accordingly, 'public safety cannot … be relied upon as a justification for requiring everybody to have their faces uncovered at all times and in all places'.[43] Yet, the French ban (public space, except from places of worship) and the Belgian ban (places accessible to the public) have a particularly broad geographical scope and do not rely on any specific risk to public policy assessment. Actually, such an assessment would better be made at the municipal level.[44] Moreover, in the light of the case law of the ECtHR, the use of criminal law to sanction the prohibited conduct could also be seen as an aggravating factor.[45] In this respect, the Belgian criminal Act is even less likely to meet the proportionality test because it allows the judge to impose not only a fine, but also a prison sentence for concealing one's face in public.

It is worth stressing that during the Belgian parliamentary debates, the Flemish Christian Democrats put forward another conception of

---

[40] French Council of State, *Study for Banning the Full Veil*, 36.
[41] Nevertheless, one must admit that in some cases Muslim women may be reluctant to identify themselves when asked by the police as illustrated by an incident that occurred in Molenbeek (Brussels) in May 2012. Here, a Muslim woman was arrested and brought to the police station by two policewomen after she refused to remove her integral veil during an identity check. 'Le contrôle d'une femme portant le niqab provoque des tensions à Molenbeek', *Lalibre.be*, 1 June 2012, 12h53.
[42] French Council of State, *Study for banning the Full Veil*, 35.   [43] *Ibid.*   [44] *Ibid.*, 37.
[45] ECtHR, *Vajnai* v. *Hungary*, 8 July 2008, §58.

public security based on the feeling of the general population when encountering a person wearing the full veil.[46] Such feelings of insecurity would validate a general ban. This is close to the concept of non-material public order or morality referred to by some French academics or parliamentarians[47] before the fact-finding mission, discarded altogether by the French Council of State.[48] If the inquiries led in Belgium and France confirm the fact that many people in Belgium and France feel uneasy in front of women wearing the niqab, this does not mean that this uneasiness could be a legitimate ground to prohibit it. In the *Vajnai* case, the ECtHR clearly denied that a subjective conception of security or public order could justify restrictions to freedom of expression. The Court accepted 'that the display of a symbol [the red star] which was ubiquitous during the reign of [the communist] regimes may create uneasiness amongst past victims and their relatives, who may rightly find such displays disrespectful'.[49] However, it ruled 'that such sentiments, however understandable, cannot alone set the limits of freedom of expression'.[50] In very strong words, the Court went on to state that 'a legal system which applies restrictions on human rights in order to satisfy the dictates of public feeling – real or imaginary – cannot be regarded as meeting the pressing social needs recognized in a democratic society, since that society must remain reasonable in its judgment. To hold otherwise would mean that freedom of speech and opinion is subjected to the heckler's veto'.[51]

2.1.4. Are the burqa bans necessary and proportionate to achieve human dignity and gender equality?

Human dignity and gender equality, which were extensively alluded to during parliamentary debates in France and Belgium, could only be legitimate aims regarding the prohibition of the facial veil. Those aims are absolutely irrelevant to legitimize the general ban of the conceal-ment of one's face in public. Indeed, the wearing of a helmet or large sunglasses has nothing to do with women's dignity. Further evidence that those Acts are hardly neutral.

---

[46] *Parliamentary Documents of the House of Representatives*, Session 2010–11, Plenary Assembly, CRIV 53 PLEN 030, 55.
[47] National Assembly, 'Information Report', 179–80 and 554–9.
[48] French Council of State, *Study for Banning the Full Veil*, 28–9.
[49] ECtHR, *Vajnai v. Hungary*, 8 July 2008, §57.   [50] *Ibid.*   [51] *Ibid.*

The issue of human dignity and gender equality partly depends on whether women are compelled to wear the integral veil or not.[52] The empirical studies available so far[53] show that the vast majority of face-veiled women claim to wear it out of a personal and autonomous choice, without alleging any family or social pressure to do so and even sometimes against the will of their relatives (Brems *et al.* 2014). Actually, the issue of consent, choice and pressure is a tricky one (Ford 2012; Fournier and Jacques 2013) and empirical studies also show that the relationship women develop towards their veil is context specific. The dichotomy on which legal categories are built (women wearing the facial veil vs. women not wearing it, full veiled women with total free will vs. women forced to wear the full veil) cannot capture the complexity of daily life.

Forcing women to veil themselves is undoubtedly contrary to their dignity and to equality between men and women. According to the Parliamentary Assembly of the Council of Europe, '[n]o woman should be compelled to wear religious apparel by her community or family. Any act of oppression, sequestration or violence constitutes a crime that must be punished by law. Women victims of these crimes, whatever their status, must be protected by member states and benefit from support and rehabilitation measures.'[54] In this respect, it might be argued that the ban of the face veil is aimed at protecting the dignity of those women forced to wear it. Whether a criminally sanctioned blanket ban is likely to achieve this aim remains to be seen. The former Commissioner for Human Rights, Thomas Hammarberg, the Belgian Human Rights League and Human Rights Watch stressed that 'rather than help women who are coerced into wearing the veil, a ban would limit, if not eliminate, their ability to seek advice and support. Indeed, the primary impact of legislation of this kind would be to confine these women to their homes, rather than to liberate them'.[55] Testimonies of

---

[52] *Parliamentary Documents of the House of Representatives*, Session 2009–10, Report, 9 April 2010, doc. no. 52 2289/005, 27 and 30. See also *Parliamentary Documents of the House of Representatives*, Session 2010–11, report, 18 April 2011, doc. no. 0219/004, 12.

[53] Mainly the one conducted by the University of Ghent, on a sample of 27 women wearing or having worn the full-face veil in Belgium (out of approximately 200 to 300 on the Belgian territory) (the results of this study are commented on in this book) and the one conducted by the Open Society Institute on a sample of 32 Muslim women wearing the full-face veil in France (2011).

[54] Parliamentary Assembly of the Council of Europe (PACE), Resolution 1743 (2010), Islam, Islamism and Islamophobia in Europe, §15.

[55] Human Rights Watch, 'Belgium: Muslim Veil Ban Would Violate Rights. Parliament Should Reject Bill for Nationwide Restrictions', 21 April 2010, www.hrw.org; Thomas Hammarberg,

some women wearing the full veil in Belgium and France show that one of the adverse effects of the legislative bans is that these women avoid, from now on, going out in order to escape from verbal or physical aggressions or from confrontation with the police (see Chapter 4 in this volume). The 'anti burqa' Acts seem to have missed their target and to be counterproductive to the promotion of dignity and gender equality.[56]

During parliamentary debates, several French or Belgian MPs underlined the profound incompatibility of women's full veiling with human dignity (Delgrange 2013).[57] As the Parliamentary Assembly of the Council of Europe put it, 'the veiling of women, especially full veiling through the burqa or the niqab, is often perceived as a symbol of the subjugation of women to men, restricting the role of women within society, limiting their professional life and impeding their social and economic activities [and . . .] that this tradition could be a threat to women's dignity and freedom'.[58] The idea that Western values are going to save these women, assumed to be of foreign background, is never far away. Again, the issue is much less straightforward in Europe where the empirical findings reported in the first part of the book show that a significant number of full veiled women are converted and do not come from a Muslim background. Known as the Zeal of the Convert phenomenon, such findings led Denmark to renounce to legislate on the matter. Although, the burqa ban was part of an integration initiative approved by the Conservatives' parliamentary group in 2009, the project of such a ban was abandoned after the publication of a report commissioned by the Ministry for Social Affairs and written by a research team from the University of Copenhagen. The issue of human dignity and integration could hardly be a crucial one anymore after academics had found that among the approximately 150 women wearing the niqab in Denmark about seventy were converts from a Danish background (see Chapter 3 in this volume).

'Rulings anywhere that women must wear the burqa should be condemned – but banning such dresses here would be wrong', www.commissioner.coe.int; Human Rights League (Ligue des droits de l'homme), 'Interdiction du port du voile intégral: une mauvaise solution à un vrai problème', 28 April 2010, http://liguedh.be

[56] See the declaration of Eva Brems, Representative of the Flemish Green Party (Groen), *Parliamentary Documents of the House of Representative*, Session 2010–11, Report, 18 April 2011, doc. no. 53 0219/004, 16; see also Article 19, 'Legal Comment', §64.
[57] French National Assembly, 'Information Report', 113–15.
[58] PACE, Resolution 1743 (2010), §15.

The legal question to be addressed is whether, in the name of human dignity and/or gender equality, the state could and/or should act against women who choose to fully veil themselves, so as to protect them against themselves? The issue was not discussed as such in Belgium (Delgrange 2013). One Flemish liberal MP argued in this sense: 'The full face veil must be prohibited even if it is worn voluntarily. This is indeed an infringement of the person's dignity but also of dignity as a matter of principle, generally speaking. This is an insult to the conception of the human person and the woman.'[59] Another French-speaking liberal MP drew a parallel between the burqa ban and the French ban on 'dwarf tossing',[60] judged in conformity with human rights requirements by both the French Council of State[61] and the United Nations Human Rights Committee.[62] In their reasoning, dwarf tossing was contrary to human dignity as such and, respect for human dignity being part of public order, the public authorities were allowed to ban it to guarantee public order.

Conversely, in France the issue led to heated and controversial debates. The Report of the National Assembly stated: 'it is very difficult to draw from the constitutional principle of dignity that the State could judge of the dignity of the persons and protect them against themselves'. Furthermore, the French Council of State clearly stressed that fundamental principles of protection of human dignity and equality of men and women are not appropriate to justify a general ban of the face veil as they 'cannot be applied to persons who have deliberately chosen to wear the full veil'.[63] The main arguments underlying this statement may be wrapped up into two main points.[64]

First, as to the principle of protecting the human dignity, the French Council of State underlines the subjective interpretation of what is contrary to the dignity of one's person, referring to 'the different perceptions of the image society projects of the (often naked) female

---

[59] *Parliamentary Documents of the House of Representatives*, Session 2010–11, Report, 18 April 2011, doc. no. 53 0219/004, 19. Our translation ('Le vêtement qui couvre le visage doit également être interdit si certains le portent volontairement. C'est en effet une atteinte non seulement à la dignité de la personne, mais également à la dignité de principe, de manière générale. Cela reste une insulte à la conception de la personne humaine et de la femme').

[60] *Parliamentary Documents of the House of Representative*, Session 2009–10, Report, 9 April 2010, doc. no. 52 2289/005, 30.

[61] French Council of State, 27 October 1995, 'Commune de Morsang-sur-Orge, Ville d'Aix-en-Provence', *Revue trimestrielle des droits de l'homme*, 1996, 657–93.

[62] Human Rights Committee, *Wackenheim v. France*, CCPR/C/75/D/854/1999, 26 July 2002.

[63] French Council of State, *Study for banning the Full Veil*, 23.   [64] *Ibid.*, 21–2.

body'.[65] It then recalls the two existing conceptions of dignity 'that may contradict or limit each other: that of the collective moral requirement to protect human dignity, perhaps at the expense of freedom of self-determination ... and that of the protection of freedom of self-determination, as a consubstantial aspect of the human person'.[66] This last interpretation clearly prevails in the European Court of Human Rights case law in which a principle of personal autonomy is deduced from the right to respect for private life and implies 'that we should all be able to live according to our convictions and personal choices, even if it means putting ourselves at moral or physical risk, provided we do not harm anybody else'.[67] This conception renders the motive of protecting human dignity to ground a general ban of the full veil highly debatable in the cases of women who have wilfully chosen to wear it.

Second, the principle of equality between women and men, which was at the core of the debates before the French National Assembly, was presented as manifold: the full-face veil amounted to a mark of 'sexual apartheid', an instrument reducing women to mere objects or a way to remove women from the public space altogether (Barton 2012: 15–18).[68] Legally speaking, the French Council of State points out that '[w]hile [the gender equality principle] is applicable to others, it is not intended to be applicable to the individual person, i.e. to the person's exercise of personal freedom, which may in some cases lead to the adoption of a form of behaviour that could be interpreted as sanctioning an inferior situation, in the public space like anywhere else, provided there is no violation of physical integrity'.[69]

In cases where people have to be protected against their own will or clearly assumed decision, it is hard to see how criminal sanction may either be appropriate or proportionate. Is it not paradoxical, or even cynical, to pretend freeing women from what some MPs named a

---

[65] Ibid., 22.   [66] Ibid., 21.

[67] ECtHR, KA and AD v. Belgium, 17 February 2005 (no. 42758/98). In this case related to sadomasochist practices, the Court held that '[t]he right to engage in sexual relations derived from the right of autonomy over one's own body, an integral part of the notion of personal autonomy, which could be construed in the sense of the right to make choices about one's own body. It followed that the criminal law could not in principle be applied in the case of consensual sexual practices, which were a matter of individual free will. Accordingly, there had to be "particularly serious reasons" for an interference by the public authorities in matters of sexuality to be justified for the purposes of Article 8 §2 of the Convention' (§83).

[68] French National Assembly, 'Information Report', 109–13.

[69] French Council of State, Study for banning the Full Veil, 22–3.

'moving prison' by sending them to jail (in the Belgian case)?[70] Moreover, again in the Belgian context, it is astonishing to see that only women are the targets of the new criminal provisions. Contrary to France,[71] no offence was provided for to sanction those who force them to veil themselves.

2.2. Non-discrimination

Even if the French and Belgian 'burqa bans' are neutral on their face, they could be held indirectly discriminatory on the ground of gender, religion and even race or ethnic origin. The dividing line between religion and race is often blurred and, in the burqa debates around the adoption of the bans, Islamophobic and racist statements were not rare (Amiraux 2011).[72] The parliamentary works of both the French and the Belgian 'anti burqa' Acts show that Muslim women wearing the full-face veil were the main targets.[73] The major parts of the debates were devoted to discussing the incompatibility of the wearing of the full veil with the Belgian and French values and identities. In addition, both Acts have been until now exclusively enforced against Muslim women.[74] This would amount to establishing a prima facie case of differential treatment.

The bans could be challenged because of their potential multiple or intersectional disparate impact on Muslim women – as women, as Muslims and as members of a minority ethnic group. Such an impact is well documented in the empirical studies in Belgium and France. In both countries, the full veil controversy, its large media coverage and the adoption of local or national bans have increased the risk for those women to be exposed to 'overt forms of discrimination, but

---

[70] F. Dubuisson and A. Lagerwall, 'Les dangers de la loi "anti-burqa"', *La Libre Belgique*, 12 April 2011.

[71] Article 4 of the Law no. 2010-1192 of 11 October 2010 prohibiting the wearing of clothing covering one's face in public spaces.

[72] Amnesty International (2012: 17).

[73] In Italy, the burqa bans are even not neutral on their face (Möschel 2013).

[74] Data on enforcement patterns in France is sparse, but the Ministry of the Interior announced that one year after the law came into force, 354 checks had been conducted, resulting in 299 condemnations. 'Loi sur le voile intégral: près de 300 femmes verbalisées en un an', *Le Monde* (4 April 2012, 19:55), www.lemonde.fr/societe/article/2012/04/10/loi-sur-le-voileintegral-pres-de-300-femmes-verbalisees-en-un-an_1683364_3224.html. 'There were no explicit indications as the proportion of those enforcement actions conducted against women wearing burqas. However, an independent organization, Touche Pas à Ma Constitution, reported that 367 women had been cited and interrogated (*ibid.*), suggesting that the vast majority of enforcement actions have been against veiled women' (Pei 2013: n. 68).

also threats or actual physical attacks from individuals outside their community who view the state's apparent sanctioning of the veil as justification for their behaviour' (see Chapter 4 in this volume).[75] As the Report of the Open Society Foundations (2011) put it, 'Interviewees who wore the niqab before and after the controversy were adamant that they had noticed a shift in people's attitudes illustrated by an increase in the level of abuse the women had received since the full-face veil became a matter for national debate.'[76]

Discrimination on the ground of gender, religion and race – being direct or indirect – is clearly prohibited under the European Convention on Human Rights.[77] The prohibition, enshrined in Article 14 ECHR, must be combined with another provision of the Convention, which could be Article 8 (private life), Article 9 (freedom of religion) and/or Article 10 (freedom of expression). One should bear in mind that gender, religion and race are 'suspect' grounds in the ECtHR anti-discrimination case law, which means that 'very weighty reasons' are required to justify differences of treatment based on those grounds and that the Court will apply a very strict scrutiny test. Furthermore, the recent case law of the ECtHR focuses on stereotypes, prejudice and history of discrimination to determine the intensity of its control (Gerards 2007: 33–9; Gerards 2012). Stereotypes and prejudice are not far away in the issue of Muslim women wearing the full veil,[78] as the debates surrounding the adoption of the burqa bans have shown. As a matter of legal principle, the non-discrimination route through a combination of Article 14 with freedom of religion or expression is the most suitable one to challenge the French and the Belgian Acts (Pei 2013).

While we have seen that some of the aims sought to be realized by the burqa bans could be held legitimate, both bans appear highly disproportionate to those aims because either they could be reached through less intrusive means[79] or they lead to counterproductive results. In this regard, empirical findings show that a significant proportion

---

[75] 'Article 19, 'Legal Comment', §65.   [76] Open Society Foundations (2011: 17).

[77] ECtHR (GC), *Thlimmenos* v. *Greece*, 6 April 2000; ECtHR (GC), *DH and others* v. *Czech Republic*, 13 November 2007. European Union Agency for Fundamental Rights and European Court of Human Rights, *European Handbook on Anti-Discrimination Law*, 2010, 19–21.

[78] Thomas Hammarberg, 'Human rights' comment "European Muslims are stigmatized by populist rhetoric"', October 2010, http://commissioner.cws.coe.int/tiki-view_blog_post.php?postId=99; Amnesty International (2012: 4–7.

[79] ECtHR, *SAS* v. *France*, application no. 43835/11, written submissions on behalf of Liberty, 7 May 2012, point 32.

of women wearing the full veil will not abandon this practice but rather will avoid going out in public except by car. Can we truly pretend that social cohesion and gender equality are better served (Brems et al., 2013)? Moreover, veiled women report being subjected to an increase of verbal – or occasionally physical – aggressions in shops and public spaces since the adoption of local or national burqa bans. In the name of safety, could it be that those Acts put veiled women's safety at risk (*ibid.*)?

3. CONCLUSION

In this chapter, we argued that a general ban on face veils in all public spaces fails to meet human rights law standards and that the empirical findings presented in Part I of this volume are unravelling many parts of the public discourse upon which state intervention was based. Beyond France and Belgium, it is striking to note how the full veil becomes the 'common enemy' of politicians in countries such as the Netherlands, Italy, Spain and even some parts of Germany. Politicians are waving national as well as European identities and values. They forget that human rights are at the core of these values and that being forced to be free is not part of the game. With the rise of extreme-right-wing parties in Europe and the financial and economic crisis in the background, the burqa bans *appear to take on a symbolic significance*: politicians are showing to their electorate that they are doing 'something' about immigration, integration and the Muslim question. The fact that a substantial amount of fully veiled women are converted is totally overlooked. In Denmark, however, this was enough to stop a national ban. This is obviously not to say that sectoral bans which present a tailored response to a specific situation should be rejected altogether. All kinds of legal norms are already regulating the wearing of the face veil in European countries (school and public services regulations, hospital policies, anti-discrimination law). One could say that the impact of a general ban is therefore marginal. The final point we want to make here is that it actually goes far beyond the issue of the face veil and has a detrimental effect on the whole Muslim community in Europe. It would probably reinforce racism and prejudice and might make some Muslim women more dependent on the patriarchal sectors of their community. In the end, it might just produce more burqas.

As the French Human Rights League put it: 'Wearing the full veil' could be a 'voluntary thraldom, as many testimonies attest. In this case, freedom may not be imposed through coercion but rather result from education, social conditions and personal choice: one cannot emancipate people against their own free will; one might only provide them with the conditions for their emancipation.'[80] The issue of consent is a complex one. Muslim women who veil themselves (most of the time, occasionally, in specific situations) have to navigate through their community, family and personal relationships, which are ridden with power relations. To tackle such a tricky issue, public authorities have to rely on scientific data, not on common sense or prejudice, and take human rights and the democratic process seriously.

REFERENCES

Amiraux, V. 2011. 'Burqa bashing: does religion stand for race in the EU?', paper presented at the Russell Sage Conference, New York, 9–10 December.
Amnesty International 2012. 'Europe: Choice and Prejudice: Discrimination against Muslims in Europe', 24 April, on-line at: www.amnesty.org/en/library/info/EUR01/001/2012
Barton, D. 2012. 'Is the French Burka Ban Compatible with International Human Rights Law Standards?', *Essex Human Rights Review*, 9: 1–27.
Brems, E., Bribosia, E., Rorive, I. and Van Drooghenbroeck, S. 2012. 'Le port de signes religieux dans l'espace public: Vérité à Strasbourg, erreur à Genève?', *Journal des tribunaux*, 602–3.
Bribosia, E. and Rorive, I. 2004. 'Le voile à l'école: une Europe divisée', *Revue trimestrielle des droits de l'homme*, 951–83.
Christians, L. L., Minette, S. and Wattier, S. 2013. 'Le visage du sujet de droit: la burqa entre religion et sécurité', *Journal des tribunaux*, 242–45.
Delgrange, X. 2013. 'Quand la burqa passe à l'Ouest, la Belgique perd-elle le Nord?', in O. Roy, and D. Koussens (eds.), *Quand la burqa passe à l'Ouest. Enjeux éthiques, politiques et juridiques*, Presses universitaires de Rennes, coll. Sciences religieuses, in press.
Ford, R. F. 2012. 'Headscarves, hairstyles and culture as a civil right: a critique', text published as a part of the 2010–11 guest professor programme organized by Sciences-Po and the French–American Foundation on the theme of 'Equal Opportunity', and discussed at the Workshop on Illegal Covering: Comparative Perspectives on Legal and Social Discourses on Religious Diversity, held at the International Institute for the Sociology of Law (Onati, Spain).

[80] French Human Rights League, 'Prise de position de la Ligue des droits de l'homme dans le débat sur le voile intégral', www.ldh-france.org/IMG/pdf/Voile_integral.pdf

Fournier, P., and Jacques, E. 2013. 'Voiles/Voiler', in E. Bribosia and I. Rorive (eds.), *L'accommodement de la diversité religieuse. Regards croisés – Canada/Europe/Belgique*, Bruxelles, PIE Peter Lang, in press.

Gerards, J. 2007. 'Discrimination Grounds', in M. Bell, D. Schieck and L. Waddington (eds.), *Non-Discrimination Law*, Oxford and Portland, OR: Hart, pp. 33–184.

2013. 'The Discrimination Grounds of Article 14 of the European Convention on Human Rights', *Human Rights Law Review*, 13(1): 99–124.

Hunter-Henin, M. 2012. 'Why the French Don't Like the Burqa: Laïcité, National Identity and Religious Freedom', *International and Comparative Law Quarterly*, 61: 613–39.

Moors, A. 2009. *Gezichtssluiers. Draagsters en Debatten*. Amsterdam School for Social Science Research.

Möschel, M. 2014. 'La burqa en Italie: d'une politique locale à une législation nationale', in O. Roy and D. Koussens (eds.), *Quand la burqa passe à l'Ouest. Enjeux éthiques, politiques et juridiques*, Presses universitaires de Rennes, coll. Sciences religieuses, pp. 237–50.

Open Society Foundations 2011 'Unveiling the Truth. Why 32 Muslim Women Wear The Full-Face Veil in France', available on-line: www.opensocietyfoundations.org/sites/default/files/a-unveiling-the-truth-20100510_0.pdf

Pei, S. 2013. 'Unveiling Inequality: Burqa Bans and Nondiscrimination Jurisprudence at the European Court of Human Rights', *Yale Law Journal*, 122: 1089–102.

Rorive, I. 2009. 'Religious Symbols in the Public Space: In Search of a European answer', *Cardozo Law Review*, 30: 2669–98.

Tourkochoriti, I. 2012. 'The Burqa Ban: Divergent Approaches to Freedom of Religion in France and in the USA', *William and Mary Bill of Rights Journal*, 20: 791–852.

Vrielink, J. 2013. 'De Grondwet aan het gezicht onttrokken. Het Grondwettelijk Hof en het "boerkaverbod"', *Tijdschrift voor Bestuurswetenschappen en Publiekrecht*, 250–60.

7

SYMPTOMATIC SYMBOLISM: BANNING THE FACE VEIL 'AS A SYMBOL'

Jogchum Vrielink

'The burqa is a symbol of women's oppression . . . It is worse than the swastika'.[1] A Belgian public intellectual made this statement, as part of his arguments in favour of the country's 'burqa ban'. Similar reasons for banning the face veil have been advanced in both the French and Belgian parliaments, and elsewhere.

Proponents of a ban have claimed, for instance, that face veils (or the practice of wearing them) cannot be regarded as anything other than a symbol that entails a 'debasement of the concepts of humanity and women'.[2] Relatedly, the face veil is often regarded as an emblem or sign that is inextricably associated with misogynist and otherwise anti-democratic regimes such as that of the Taliban in Afghanistan,[3] and

---

Part of this chapter is based on a text co-authored with Eva Brems and Saïla Ouald Chaib (Brems et al. 2013).

[1] Moral philosopher Etienne Vermeersch quoted in Verschelden (2012). After having been called to account on this statement by the editor of a Jewish magazine, Vermeersch apologized for his statement. He did maintain 'the burqa is a symbol of the oppression of women, and of a whole range of fundamentalist ideas'.

[2] *Parliamentary proceedings*, Belgian Chamber 2010–11, 28 April 2011: 38. See also *Parliamentary report*, Belgian Chamber 2010–11, no. 53–219/4: 19. For France, see e.g. French Parliament, Assemblée nationale, *Rapport d'information fait au nom de la delegation aux droits des femmes et à l'égalité des chances entre les homes et les femmes sur le projet de loi interdisant la dissimulation du visage*: 15; French Parliament, Assemblée nationale, *Discussion en séance publique, première séance du mercredi 7 juillet 2010*. The theme was also developed by the Gérin commission (France), which described the face veil as a symbol of sexual apartheid: Gérin (2010: 43 and 109–11).

[3] See e.g. *Parliamentary proceedings*, Belgian Chamber 2010–11, 28 April 2011, no. 53–30: 37 and 46; *Parliamentary report*, Belgian Chamber 2010–11, no. 53–219/4: 5.

184

more generally with a form of Islam(ism) that is fundamentally at odds with democracy and the rule of law.[4]

Though there are several aspects to these arguments, one resultant claim is that the face veil should be prohibited on account of its being an inherently reprehensible or 'undemocratic' symbol, in and of itself.[5] On this view, the face veil coincides with or embodies worldviews that are incompatible with a democratic society, necessitating or at least justifying the garment's prohibition.

This ground for banning the face veil is investigated in this comment, taking into account the empirical findings presented in this volume. In doing so I will first take a look at banning symbols more generally, identifying some common problems plaguing such prohibitions (section 1). Subsequently, a number of issues specific to banning the face veil 'as a symbol' will be discussed (section 2).

1. BANNING SYMBOLS?

In considering whether one can or should ban the face veil because the garment (allegedly) constitutes an undemocratic or otherwise objectionable symbol, comparable to the swastika or other totalitarian emblems, it is useful to first turn to these latter 'comparators'.

In this regard it can be pointed out that bans on symbols, qua symbols, are not very common to begin with. Most countries consider the practice of prohibiting symbols to be at odds with their conceptions of freedom of speech. Illustrative of this is that Germany, during its 2007 EU presidency, unsuccessfully proposed an EU-wide ban on symbols associated with Nazism, as part of efforts to harmonize rules throughout the member states for dealing with racism.[6] When Germany set out its final plans in this regard, it had already withdrawn the prohibition of symbols such as swastikas. During preliminary

---

[4] *Parliamentary report*, Belgian Chamber 2010–11, no. 53–219/4: 5, 6 and 11; *Parliamentary proceedings*, Belgian Chamber 2010–11, 28 April 2011, no. 53–30: 33, 34, 40 and 43.

[5] *Parliamentary proceedings*, Belgian Chamber 2010–11, 28 April 2011, no. 53–30: 38. See also *Parliamentary report*, Belgian Chamber 2010–11, no. 53–219/4: 19.

[6] Efforts that eventually resulted in Council Framework Decision 2008/913/JHA of 28 November 2008 on combating certain forms and expressions of racism and xenophobia by means of criminal law. Earlier attempts to come to an EU-wide ban failed as well. In 2005, for instance, a coalition of German Conservatives, Liberals and Social Democrats in the European Parliament called for a ban on all Nazi symbols. These plans were dropped as well, due to strong opposition from those concerned with civil liberties on the one hand and since it proved impossible for member states to agree on *which* symbols should be banned on the other hand.

discussions, other European countries had proved too wary of such legislation for a Community-wide ban to be achievable. The proposal, when initially launched in the media, also sparked strong opposition from groups and organizations that use the symbol for cultural or religious reasons.

Only in rare cases have European countries introduced general[7] bans on certain symbols. That is the case, most notably, in Germany[8] and Austria[9] for symbols associated with National Socialism, such as the swastika. The post-war criminal codes of both countries render it unlawful to publicly use or display the swastika, other Nazi symbols, and even symbols that can be mistaken as such; thereby establishing – in the words of the German Constitutional Court (Bundesverfassungsgericht) 'a communicative "taboo"'.[10] Furthermore, and more recently, in some Eastern European countries Communist symbols have been banned, often in combination with symbols associated with National Socialism. Accordingly, in Hungary it is prohibited to publicly display 'symbols of despotism', which (expressly) include the swastika, the SS sign, the arrow-cross, the hammer and sickle and the five-pointed

[7] A number of other countries have bans that are limited to specific contexts. For instance, in Latvia 'racist symbols' are banned in the context of demonstrations and pickets, whereas in Spain, Portugal and Belgium similar symbols are forbidden in the context of sports events. In Moldova, a ban was enacted in October 2012 prohibiting communist(-era) symbols for political (party) purposes. Additionally, while most countries lack regulation banning symbols, case law has sometimes brought the public display of fascist or other totalitarian symbols under general criminal or anti-racist provisions. See EU Network of Independent Experts on Fundamental Rights (2005: 87–89) (this text is partially outdated, however, due to developments since 2005).
[8] §86a German Criminal Code (*Strafgesetzbuch*) prohibits the use, distribution, production, stocking, importing, etc. of symbols of unconstitutional organizations (or symbols which are so similar as to be mistaken for such symbols). These organizations are, *inter alia*, parties which have been declared to be unconstitutional by the Federal Constitutional Court or parties or organizations of which it has been legally determined – in a manner no longer subject to appeal – that they are substitute organizations of such parties; organizations which have been banned – in a manner no longer subject to appeal – because they are directed against the constitutional order or against the idea of international understanding, or as to which it has been determined – in a manner no longer subject to appeal – that it is a substitute organization of such a banned organization; former National Socialist organizations.
[9] Sections 1 and 3 Insignia Act (Law 84/1960, as amended by Law 117/1980) prohibit the public wearing, displaying, depicting or disseminating of insignia of an organization that is prohibited in Austria, such as (neo-)Nazi organizations, particularly under Section 12 §1 Association Act (*Vereinsgesetz*). The latter provision prohibits associations if their purpose, name or form of organization is illicit.
[10] See *inter alia* Bundesverfassungsgericht 1 June 2006, 1 BvR 150/03, §18; Bundesverfassungsgericht 18 May 2009, 2 BvR 2202/08, 2805 (2806) §16: 'Die Norm errichtet ... so ein kommunikatives "Tabu"'.

red star.[11] Likewise, in Lithuania,[12] and Poland[13] public display of symbols of Nazism and Communism is a criminal offence.

However, as the examples show, such bans tend to be, first, linked to a history within which the relevant symbols are intimately associated with the actual abolition of democracy in the respective regions,[14] and with crimes against humanity and genocide. In this respect, such prohibitions have a very particular history and historicity, and cannot simply be compared to or equated with banning face veils on 'symbolic' grounds.

Moreover, the case-law of the European Court of Human Rights (ECtHR) – which is not particularly known for its protective attitude towards extremist or 'undemocratic' (symbolic or pure) speech[15] – demonstrates that prohibiting symbols is everything but self-evident *even* in such situations. In *Vajnai* v. *Hungary*, the Court ruled, for example, that the application of the Hungarian ban on communist symbols to someone wearing a red star during a demonstration amounted to a violation of Article 10 of the European Convention on Human Rights (right to freedom of expression). The ECtHR was mindful of the fact that, for many people in Hungary, communist symbols were associated with painful memories of mass violations of human rights committed under the totalitarian Soviet regime, but according to the Court the red star did not *exclusively* represent totalitarian rule. It had and has multiple meanings.[16] Nor had Hungary shown that the use of

---

[11] Article 269b Hungarian Criminal Code. Display for academic, educational, artistic or journalistic reasons is allowed. See also Decision no. 14/2000 (V.12) of the Constitutional Court, dealing with the constitutionality of Section 269b.

[12] The ban was introduced in June 2008. When it led to a court ruling in September 2008 that fined a woman in Vilnius 500 litas (€145) for selling souvenirs containing Soviet symbols, Parliament amended the law (in March 2009), in order to prevent other salesmen from incurring such fines. Moreover, courts have been reticent to apply the ban. Most notably, an administrative court in Klaipeda ruled in favour of four (radical right-wing) individuals who, at the national independence parade, displayed posters with photographs of swastikas recovered at ancient archaeological sites. The court concluded that such swastikas should properly be regarded as historical heritage rather than as Nazi symbols (Administrative Court of Klaipeda, 18 May 2010).

[13] Article 256, §2 Polish Criminal Code.

[14] Outside of Europe, the manufacture, use or distribution of the swastika or any Nazi symbol is prohibited in Brazil, since 1989, but only if it is done with the intent to propagate Nazism (art. 20, §1, Federal Statute 7.716/89; as altered by Federal Statute 9.459/97).

[15] See Hare (2009: 78–9); Vrielink (2014: n. 24).

[16] ECtHR, 8 July 2008, *Vajnai* v. *Hungary*, §52 (arguing that 'this star also still symbolises the international workers' movement, struggling for a fairer society, as well certain lawful political parties active in different Member States'). *Mutatis mutandis*, the same holds true for face veils, of course; arguably even more so (see section 2 below on the views of the wearers). See also, generally e.g. Hussein (2009: 81–9); Williamson and Khiabany (2010: 89–91).

the star had generated any danger of violence or disorder. Therefore, there was no 'pressing social need' for the interference with free speech.[17] In its conclusion, the Court warned against banning symbols, per se, in an unequivocal way:

> The Court is of course aware that the systematic terror applied to consolidate Communist rule in several countries, including Hungary, remains a serious scar in the mind and heart of Europe. It accepts that the display of a symbol that was ubiquitous during the reign of those regimes may create uneasiness among past victims and their relatives, who may rightly find such displays disrespectful. It nevertheless considers that such sentiments, however understandable, cannot alone set the limits of freedom of expression.[18]

Furthermore, even if one were to accept the (faulty) premise that someone who uses or wears a symbol necessarily supports the ideology (allegedly) associated with it, such a form of association seems too weak an affiliation to be legitimately penalized. A symbol does not, in itself, imply further action: it tends to be a passive display of affiliation at most. In the same way that a gang member cannot be punished for gang crimes, merely on account of his having a gang tattoo, carrying or wearing a(n alleged) 'symbol' would generally not seem to imply a strong enough form of responsibility to hold someone legally accountable for the regime perceived to underlie such a symbol. As such, when and where such symbols are banned from public life in general, this comes close to sanctioning people for the mere fact of having opinions,[19] thereby threatening the very core of the right to freedom of opinion and expression.

Moreover, bans on symbols tend to raise suspicions of discrimination, both directly (e.g. as to the specific viewpoints they curtail), and indirectly (e.g. as regards the groups that are disparately impacted by such bans). Regarding the latter, Hindu and Falun Gong groups for instance

---

[17] ECtHR, 8 July 2008, *Vajnai v. Hungary*, §55. See also: Buyse (2011: 133–8).

[18] ECtHR, 8 July 2008, *Vajnai v. Hungary*, §57.

[19] Of course bans on symbols such as the swastika often also have the goal of averting social habituation to them. However, in order for this argument to be relevant or convincing, it would still seem to require that the symbols should pose some direct or indirect danger to public order in and of themselves, and it is hard to see how this is necessarily the case in *every* instance in which a symbol is publicly displayed. Compare: Hörnle (2001: 255) (the author argues that the penalization of behaviour that does not result in any tangible harm (or concrete risks thereof), like the prohibition of symbols, is difficult to reconcile with the general principles underpinning the German criminal law system).

have successfully argued that a general ban on the swastika would discriminate against them as a religious community and interfere with their freedom of religion.[20] Even in Germany, case law has determined that 'religious swastikas' (e.g. on websites and temples) do not therefore fall under the general ban.[21] The relation between face veils as a symbol and a particular (religious) group, i.e. Muslims, is more direct still, which would again seem to render a ban thereof – on 'symbolic' grounds – even more problematic.

Finally, one can point to the undesirable and counterproductive practical effects that prohibitions of symbols usually have. First, due to their far-reaching nature, general bans on symbols leave little room for (restrictive) interpretations, which tends to yield all kinds of absurd effects. In Germany, the use of Hitler's picture on a postcard was ruled to be unlawful,[22] as was the use of swastikas on a displayed vintage model aeroplane.[23] Even producing and selling *anti*-fascist clothing and buttons, making use of the swastika in order to impugn Nazism (e.g. crossed-out swastikas and swastikas being put into trash cans), initially led to convictions,[24] before being reluctantly reversed by the Federal Supreme Court (Bundesgerichtshof).[25]

A second issue having to do with practical effects, is that the prohibition of symbols often seems to *encourage* rather than discourage the movements associated with these symbols. Criminalization instils resentment and greater determination on the part of those sharing its underlying ideology, as well as rendering that ideology more attractive to (some) outsiders (e.g. since it bestows the wearers of the symbol with an

---

[20] They likened banning the swastika, on account of its associations with Nazism, to banning the cross simply because the Ku Klux Klan uses burning crosses.

[21] In 2002, for instance, a Falun Gong association received a notice from the Mannheim district court for displaying the Falun emblem on its website. This emblem contains a swastika (as well as several additional swastika-like symbols), although it has a different colour and points in a different direction than the Nazi swastika. In November 2003, the Mannheim district court rendered a verdict of not guilty and declared the display of the Falun emblem legal under German law (Amtsgericht Weinheim, 1 Ds Js 33613/02, 13 November 2003). The public prosecutor appealed the ruling, but in March 2004 the original judgment was upheld (Landgericht Mannheim, 4 Qs 3/04, 1 March 2004).

[22] Oberlandesgericht München, 4 StRR 142/06, 7 August 2006.

[23] Oberlandesgericht München, NStZ-RR 371, 14 July 2005.

[24] See Landesgericht Stuttgart decision 18 KLs 4 Js 63331/05, 29 September 2006; Oberlandesgericht Stuttgart, decision 1 Ws 120/06, 18 May 2006.

[25] Bundesgerichtshof, 3 StR 486/06, 15 March 2007. The court stated that it was 'convinced of the fact that members of extreme-right organizations would never make use of items that make a mockery of their "sacred" symbols'. The court did add, however, that for the use of these symbols to be legal, the anti-Nazi meaning has to be 'immediately apparent'.

aura of martyrdom, and by turning the associated ideology into 'forbidden fruit', by the legal taboo attached to it).[26] Likewise, the empirical research regarding the face veil shows that the introduction of a ban, if anything, *increased* the commitment by the (former) wearers to the garment's underlying values.[27] Furthermore, there are indications that the wider Muslim community feels stigmatized and singled out by the ban.

2. THE FACE VEIL AS A 'SYMBOL'?

The previous section demonstrates that it is generally problematic to ban symbols, regardless of what type of symbol it concerns. However, it is important to note a number of crucial differences between examples such as swastikas and communist symbols on the one hand and the face veil on the other hand, which make it even more problematic to prohibit the latter as a 'symbol'.

To begin with, it is *outsiders* who regard and label the face veil as a symbol, and attribute a specific (negative) meaning to it. For the women wearing the veil, it is, in the first place, a religious practice, and a positive one at that. The empirical chapters in this book make abundantly clear that respondents wearing the face veil[28] do not regard it either as a means of proselytism or as a symbol of oppression. Interviewees across all studies describe the decision to start wearing the face veil as a well-considered and free decision in which their personal agency plays a central role. Wearers cover themselves for a variety of motives such as their personal relationship with God; a desire to excel in piety and perfect one's faith; considerations of chastity and modesty; deflecting sexual attention; and connecting with and maintaining their identity as Muslims in day-to-day life. Many regard it as a form of liberation (e.g. from the pressures of fashion and appearance, from the male gaze, etc.).

Furthermore, the fact that wearing the face veil is a religious practice, implies that wearing the Islamic face veil is not only protected by the freedom of speech, but by the freedom of religion as well, and that – in turn – obliges authorities to exercise restraint in advancing or imposing

---

[26] See e.g. Newman and Rackow (2011: 144–5).
[27] Even though this does not seem to involve the (negative) values that the French and Belgium legislators discern behind the face veil (see section 2 below).
[28] Or those that used to wear it previously.

their own (negative) interpretations of this practice or 'symbol'.[29] This interpretive restraint entails that governments and courts must – whenever possible – refrain from imposing their own interpretation of religious rules and practices. By labelling a certain religious practice a 'symbol', attributing a negative meaning to it (that is not shared by its practitioners), and subsequently *prohibiting* the practice on the grounds of that meaning, one would seem to violate this core element of freedom of religion. At least, in the absence of there being larger interests or decisive arguments that objectively override or discredit the views advanced by practitioners.[30] If not, then by the same token that the burqa is interpreted (and prohibited) as a symbol of oppression, the crucifix could – viewed with the detachment of an uninformed outsider – be taken (and prohibited) as a sign of veneration of or even incitement to torture and inhumane treatment (compare Roedig 2010).

Of course, one could counter – as some proponents of a ban have done – that the views of the wearers are unrepresentative, misleading or misguided. The former could, to some extent, be the case. One may expect a certain degree of self-selection among the participants in the empirical studies, in the sense that liberated women are more likely (to be able to choose) to participate. However, at the same time, the interviewees in several countries (particularly in the Netherlands, Belgium and Denmark) make up a considerable percentage of the small target group. Furthermore, the researchers have tried, by various means, to ascertain whether certain groups were missing from the population of respondents they managed to reach, but were unable to identify relevant hiatuses. In Belgium, for instance, after inquiring with several NGOs and professionals, the research team was able to learn only of one single woman that, according to a social worker, had been forced to wear the face veil. Despite numerous efforts it turned out to be impossible to interview this woman,[31] but the case seems to stand as a lonely 'exception that proves the rule', in the sense that it draws attention to the apparent rarity of such cases; reinforcing rather than discrediting the established findings.

---

[29] In that regard it is useful to reiterate that even in Germany, 'religious swastikas' are – in practice – exempt from the general ban (see section 1 above).

[30] Interpretive restraint does not, of course, imply that 'anything goes' in the name of religion; practices that are clearly contrary to objective public order and general welfare (e.g. human sacrifice) can naturally be prohibited, positive support of practitioners for these practices notwithstanding.

[31] The woman had been interviewed by a Flemish newspaper (Gijs 2011).

A second reason for not taking the views of veil wearers, as revealed by the empirical research, seriously, has to do with the claim that the research results may be consciously misleading on the part of the respondents. While this is a critique that can be levelled against all interview-based research, it is no doubt true that, in recent years, respondents will have been especially aware of the political relevance of research concerning the face veil, making it quite possible that some of them may have responded accordingly. However, the earliest interviews, by Moors, pre-date the period in which the ban truly became a political issue, and these interviews nonetheless yielded the same results as later research. What can be granted to the critics is that the studies in this volume – like all qualitative small-scale interview studies – do not allow for drawing far-reaching conclusions. No one seems to be doing that though. The only claim, if any, being made is that the findings should be taken on their merits, given the absence both of genuine indications of fraud, and of research results contradicting the findings. In any case, the mere fact that there can be doubts about the motives of respondents cannot reasonably be used in support of a ban.

Finally, some proponents of a ban argue that respondents – while perhaps not consciously trying to mislead the researchers – are nonetheless misguided in that they themselves have internalized their own subjugation, and are suffering from 'false consciousness'. This issue is dealt with extensively elsewhere in this volume.[32] Here it may suffice to raise the question of whether such an assumption, that fails to seriously engage with the expressed opinions and beliefs of those directly involved, can constitute a credible and legitimate basis for a general ban. In the end, the paternalistic argument – like the 'symbolic' argument – seems to have more to do with cultural biases than with rationally informed legislative decision making.

REFERENCES

Brems, Eva, Vrielink, Jogchum and Ouald Chaib, Saila 2013. 'Uncovering French and Belgian Face Covering Bans', Journal of Law, Religion and the State, 2(1): 69–99.
Buyse, Antoine 2011. 'The Truth, the Past and the Present', in Antoine Buyse and Michael Hamilton (eds.), Transitional Jurisprudence and the European Convention on Human Rights. Cambridge University Press, pp. 133–8.

[32] Additionally, see Brems et al. (2013: 85–6 and 94–5).

EU Network of Independent Experts on Fundamental Rights 2005. *Combating Racism and Xenophobia through Criminal Legislation: the Situation in the EU Member States*. Brussels: European Commission.

Gérin, André 2010. *Rapport d'information fait en application de l'article 145 du règlement au nom de la mission d'information sur la pratique du port du voile intégral sur le territoire national*. Assemblée Nationale.

Gyo, Inge 2011. 'Taboe wordt langzaam doorbroken. Antwerpse moslima's: gevangen in hun eigen huis', *De Standaard*, 25 January: 18–19.

Hare, Ivan 2009. 'Extreme speech under international and regional human rights standards', in I. Hare and J. Weinstein (eds.), *Extreme Speech and Democracy*. Oxford University Press, pp. 62–80.

Hörnle, Tatjana 2001. 'Offensive Behaviour and German Penal Law', *Buffalo Criminal Law Review*, 5(1): 255–78.

Hussein, Shakira 2009. 'Looking in or Looking out? Stories on the Multiple Meanings of Veiling', in T. Dreher and C. Ho (eds.), *Beyond the Hijab Debates: New Conversations on Gender, Race and Religion*. Cambridge Scholars Publishing, pp. 81–89.

Newman, Christopher J., and Rackow, Peter 2011. 'Undesirable Posters and Dubious Symbols: Anglo-German Legal Solutions to the Display of Rightwing Symbolism and Propaganda', *Journal of Criminal Law* 75(2): 142–55.

Roedig, Andrea 2010. 'Burqa, the cross we must bear', *Presseurop* 21 July.

Verschelden, Wouter 2012. 'Als symbool is de boerka erger dan de swastika', *De Morgen* 2 June.

Vrielink, Jogchum 2014. '"Islamophobia" and the Law: Belgian Hate Speech, Legislation Speech and the Wilful Destruction of the Koran', *International Journal of Discrimination and the Law* 14(1): 54–65.

Williamson, Milly and Khiabany, Gholam 2010. 'UK: The Veil and the Politics of Racism', *Race & Class*, 52(2): 85–96.

8

BAS LES MASQUES! UNVEILING MUSLIM WOMEN ON BEHALF OF THE PROTECTION OF PUBLIC ORDER: REFLECTIONS ON THE LEGAL CONTROVERSIES AROUND A NOVEL DEFINITION OF 'PUBLIC ORDER' USED TO BAN FULL-FACE COVERING IN FRANCE

Rim-Sarah Alouane

1. INTRODUCTION

> [The veil is] like a second skin to me. It is supple as a living membrane and moves and flows with me. There is beauty and dignity in its fall and sweep. It is my crown and my mantle, my vestments of grace. Its pleasures are known to me, if not to you.
>
> (Kahf 2008: 27)

In his speech in Cairo on June 4, 2009, President Barack Obama called on Western countries to 'avoid dictating what clothing a Muslim woman should wear' (Obama: 2013) in a clear reference to a French ban on full-face covering,[1] that mainly concerns women wearing this type of clothing for religious reasons. As will become clear in this chapter, President Obama and former President Nicolas Sarkozy have different ways of defending and protecting freedom of religion and are finding no common ground.

France constitutionally recognizes and guarantees the freedom of opinion and religion in Article 10 of the Declaration of the Rights of Man and the Citizen of 1789 (Declaration of 1789) by stating that 'No one may be disturbed on account of his opinions, even religious

---

[1] By the expression 'full-face covering', are principally concerned the wearing of the burqa and the niqab, two different garments worn mainly by women in the Middle East. The burqa is 'a full-body garment, including head covering, with typically a grid or eye-holes allowing vision' and 'the niqab is a body and head-encompassing dress with the face below the eyes covered by a veil' (Grillo, Shah 2012).

ones.' But this recognition is guaranteed only as long as 'the expression of such opinions does not cause a breach of the peace as established by law'. Freedom of religion in France must coexist with the principle of neutrality of the state and of *laïcité*, resulting from the Law on Separation of the Churches and State of 9 December 1905 (Law of 1905), also proclaimed in the first Article of the French Constitution of 1958, that implies a strict separation between church and state.[2] This separation 'prohibits churches to use law to impose obedience and their creeds, and the State forbids itself to promote a specific Church' (Bauer 1999: 27). But banning the wearing of the full-face covering in all public places goes much further than this. Indeed, the issue concerning the wearing of religious symbols within the public space has led to a heated debate on the scope and limits of freedom of religion and neutrality of the state. The burqa hysteria was raised in a context of controversial biased debates on *laïcité* and especially on the public visibility of Islam in France. Former President Sarkozy and his government, supported by politicians both from the right and the left wing and also by women's rights groups, considered the burqa and the niqab as a symbol of an archaic vision of the role of women and a sign of their oppression[3] incompatible with France's republican values of liberty and gender equality (see Chapter 5 in this volume).

At the request of the former French Prime Minister François Fillon, the Conseil d'Etat wrote a report (2010) on this sensitive issue, which strongly condemned the adoption of a law that would prohibit the wearing of the burqa and the niqab. Even though the Conseil d'Etat's judges held that a legislative ban was possible in a few specific cases (public safety, fight against fraud), it nevertheless remained opposed to a total ban. This highlights the great fragility of the legal foundations of

[2] Despite its constitutional nature, the implementation of the principle of *laïcité* is not without exceptions. The Law of 1905 does not apply in overseas territories, such as Saint Pierre and Miquelon, French Polynesia, Wallis and Futuna and New Caledonia. In Guiana, the Royal ruling of 1828 which organizes and subsidizes the Catholic religion is still in force as it was recalled by the Conseil d'Etat in its ruling *Beherec* (1981). The Alsace-Moselle is governed by the *Concordat* of 1801. As a result, the state officially recognizes the Roman Catholic Church, Protestant Churches and the Jewish religion, and all of them benefit from state funding. The Constitutional Council recently recognized the Alsace-Moselle's specificity as a fundamental principle recognized by the laws of the Republic and constitutionally protected (Constitutional Council, no. 2011–157 QPC, 5 August 2011, *Société SOMODIA*).

[3] Further discussion: read the hearing of Sihem Habchi, president of women's rights group *Ni putes, ni soumises* at the parliamentary commission on full-face covering in France: www.assemblee-nationale.fr/13/cr-miburqa/08-09/c0809004.asp (accessed: August 2013).

such a law; not only because of its disregard for the concept of human dignity in law, but also because of the major importance of preserving our democracy by trying to reconcile and find a balance between freedom of religion and conscience and the principles of religious neutrality and the preservation of public order. The legal issues that arise from the full-face veiling controversy are numerous.

First, the law was adopted on the ground that such a garment worn by women can be a threat and a disturbance to public order. However, the former government in a confidential report consulted by the French newspaper *Le Figaro* estimated that a maximum of two thousand women[4] – of a population of 65 million – wear the face veil for religious or philosophical reasons. 'Marginal phenomenon in France' (as demonstrated in the analysis on the full-face-covering phenomenon conducted by Bouteldja in Chapter 5 of this volume), the potential threat to public order would be a phantom menace.

Second, the law provides many exceptions to face concealing, such as processions or celebrations, as well as the wearing of a helmet or a mask for doctors. Hence, the question arises how can one legally justify that there is a public disturbance when a woman wears a full-face covering and not when a man wears a wig and a fake moustache, which are included in the exceptions allowed by the law?

Third, concealment of the face had already been banned by a decree of 19 June 2009;[5] its scope was limited to concealment in the context of public demonstrations, since such concealment was considered as a hindrance to the search of perpetrators of crimes committed during such demonstrations. Article R-654-14 of the decree of 2009 only mentions the case of 'unlawful concealment', which suggests that there are lawful cases of concealment. But when the Act of 2010 came into force, the legislature decided to prohibit any kind of concealment, whatever the reason or the circumstance. But behind the cover of this general expression which is 'the concealment of the face in public' in fact, the legislature intended to specifically prohibit the wearing of the burqa and the niqab. However, as noted above – see the dialogue of the deaf between the Conseil d'Etat and the Constitutional Council – the adoption of the law was not without intense legal debates.

---

[4] Gabizon C. 'Deux mille femmes portent la Burqa en France', *Le Figaro*, 9 September 2009.

[5] Décret no. 2009–724 of 19 June 2009 relatif à l'incrimination de dissimulation illicite du visage à l'occasion de manifestations sur la voie publique [Decree on criminalization of illegal concealment of the face on the occasion of events on public roads].

Indeed, the Act of 2010 awoke an old controversial doctrinal debate about the definition of public order and its components under French law, which also had a strong impact on the mobilization of the concept of human dignity to justify the ban.

This chapter will aim to give answers to the questions raised by the adoption of the Act of 2010 especially regarding the controversies and the legal consequences of the definition of public order through a study of the heated arguments between the Conseil d'Etat and the Constitutional Council during the pre-adoption period of the law and the consequences on women wearing the full-face covering.

2. THE REFUSAL OF THE CONSEIL D'ETAT TO VALIDATE THE BAN ON FULL-FACE COVERING: THE NECESSITY OF A (RE)DEFINITION OF PUBLIC ORDER

In its crucial report of 31 March 2010, the Conseil d'Etat considered that:

> Prohibition of the full veil would violate various fundamental rights and freedoms: individual freedom, personal freedom, right to privacy, freedom of expression and freedom to manifest one's convictions, notably religious, and prohibition of any discrimination.

This report (Conseil d'Etat 2010) calls on the government to be cautious and to favour conciliation rather than prohibition and rejected any general prohibition based only on the wearing of the full-face covering and on *laïcité*: indeed, it was established that the use of the principle of *laïcité* can hardly justify a ban extended to all public spaces,[6] which is beyond any reference to religious expression (*ibid.*: 19):

> Secularism cannot provide the basis for a general restriction on the expression of religious convictions in the public space.

Moreover, the Conseil d'Etat also rejected any general ban of the wearing of the full-face covering on the grounds of the protection of human dignity and the principle of gender equality; if both are recognized and protected under French law, their grounds are way too uncertain and could lead not only to a violation of individual freedom but also to a discriminatory prohibition concerning only Muslim women. The

---

[6] See the position of the ECtHR: *Ahmet Arslan v. Turkey* [2010] ECtHR (no. 41135/98) (23 February 2010).

Conseil d'Etat warned the government to not use dignity and under-scored the weakness of the concept of human dignity considering it as

> Legally debatable, given the range of circumstances to be taken into account, and particularly in the event that a person who has reached the age of majority deliberately chooses to wear the full veil.
>
> (*ibid.*: 22)

In its report, the Conseil d'Etat surprisingly reversed its 1995 decision *Commune de Morsang sur Orge*,[7] in which it had subsumed human dignity under public order by validating the prohibition on the practice of dwarf tossing on the grounds that such an activity would violate human dignity[8] and hence public order. However, it seems that the position of the Conseil d'Etat has to be qualified: if it does not recommend a general ban on the full-face covering, it recommends and admits though the possibility of prohibition on any forms of face covering in public space; according to de Béchillon (2010):

> It [the Conseil d'Etat] advises against the adoption of a law of general prohibition, considering the excessive fragility of its possible legal foundation. But it believes it conceivable to prohibit by law the concealment of the face in many places or circumstances for which the requirements of public safety or the imperatives of the fight against fraud brings a serious justification.

The Conseil d'Etat considers that such a prohibition would be more acceptable if it is based on the protection of a redefined notion of public order (2010: 27).

In French law, the traditional 'material' conception of public order [*conception matérielle de l'ordre public*] is a tripartite notion[9] composed of peace, health and public safety (Hauriou 1927: 445). According to the Conseil d'Etat such foundations are a solid legal basis for a prohibition on concealment of the face, but have to be limited to specific conditions and specific locations with a sufficient proven risk of disturbing public order. In other words, the notion of public order cannot justify a ban on face concealing. Thus, a general ban could only be based on what Mathieu (2010) calls an immaterial conception of public order

---

[7] Conseil d'Etat, 27 October 1995, no. 136727 Commune de Morsang sur Orge.

[8] According to the Conseil d'Etat, tossing dwarves – even in an entertainment show – is considered using a human being affected with a physical disability as a projectile.

[9] See article L-2212-2 of the Code Général des Collectivités Territoriales 'Municipal police is to ensure order, safety, security and health'. Our translation: 'La police municipale a pour objet d'assurer le bon ordre, la sûreté, la sécurité et la salubrité publiques'.

[*conception immatérielle de l'ordre public*], a conception also used by Parliament in its report on the examination of the bill on the full-face covering.[10] If public order in the administrative case law is essentially viewed in its traditional definition, it has nevertheless also been extended to morality[11] and human dignity.[12] The Conseil d'Etat still considered those legal grounds as fragile for a general ban of face covering, and exploring what legal foundation might be used as a solid legal ground for such ban, mentioned that this would require 'a completely new legal definition of public policy' (2010: 29) corresponding to a 'minimum requirement for the reciprocal demands and essential guarantees of life in society'. According to the Conseil d'Etat

> These demands and guarantees, like respect for pluralism for example, are of such fundamental importance that they determine the way in which other freedoms are exercised and if necessary require the effects of certain acts of the individual will to be prevented. In our Republic, these fundamental requirements of the social contract, which are both implicit and permanent, could have the following implication: when an individual is in the public space and likely to come across another person quite fortuitously, he may neither renounce his membership of society, nor cause it to be denied by concealing his face from the sight of others to the point of being quite unrecognizable.
>
> (*ibid.*)

By reconfiguring the issue as it did, the Conseil d'Etat raised the central question of the debate: what are the 'minimum requirements of life in society' and do these justify the restriction of certain fundamental rights and freedoms (individual liberty, freedom of religion, freedom of movement), that also form the core of the social pact? Moreover, serious doubts were raised on the constitutionality of the law, which is why a preventive referral to the Constitutional Council was soon considered and was supported by a majority of members of the National Assembly, even if the procedure was certainly more political than legal. The Constitutional Council was seized by the former presidents of the National Assembly (Bernard Accoyer) and the Senate (Gérard Larcher) to undertake a constitutional review of the new law prohibiting the concealment of the face in public.

[10] Projet de Loi Interdisant La Dissimulation du Visage dans l'Espace Public. Rapport no. 699 (2009–10) 8 September 2010.
[11] Conseil d'Etat, 18 December 1959, no. 36385 36428, Société Les Films Lutétia.
[12] Conseil d'Etat, 27 October 1995, no. 136727 Commune de Morsang sur Orge.

3. THE TENUOUS REASONING OF THE CONSTITUTIONAL COUNCIL TO JUSTIFY THE CONSTITUTIONALITY OF THE LAW

With the exception of an interpretative reservation concerning places of worship open to the public,[13] the Constitutional Council simply stated in a concise and very poorly motivated decision that the Act of 2010 did not violate any fundamental freedom.

The Constitutional Council used the ground of proportionality review: this is a classic review of state interference in the exercise of freedoms and regularly used by administrative judges and the European Court of Human Rights (ECtHR). This is to ensure the reconciliation of constitutional principles involved: the fundamental rights and freedoms objects of the state interference and the principles used to justify the interference.

Despite the reservation of interpretation relating to places of worship open to the public previously mentioned, the Constitutional Council does not specify the 'constitutionally protected rights potentially affected' mentioned in the fifth paragraph of the decision:[14] neither freedom of movement, nor the respect of privacy or freedom of expression are evoked by the Council to justify the decision. The provision on which its determination is based emphasizes the legislature's power to control its citizens.[15] Article 4 of the Declaration of 1789 provides that

> The exercise of the natural rights of every man has no bounds other than those that ensure to the other members of society the enjoyment of these same rights.

Article 5 adds:

> The Law has the right to forbid only those actions that are injurious to society. Nothing that is not forbidden by Law may be hindered, and no one may be compelled to do what the Law does not ordain,[16] [and] no

---

[13] Constitutional Council, no. 2010–613 DC of 7 October 2010, §5: 'However, prohibiting the concealing of the face in public cannot, without adversely affecting Article 10 of the Declaration, result in restricting the exercise of religious freedom in places of worship open to the public'.
[14] Ibid.: 'Parliament has enacted provisions which ensure a conciliation which is not disproportionate between safeguarding public order and guaranteeing constitutionally protected rights'.
[15] §3: Article 4 of the Declaration of 1789 proclaims: 'Liberty consists in being able to do anything which does not harm others: thus the exercise of the natural rights of every man has no bounds other than those which ensure to other members of society the enjoyment of these same rights. These bounds shall be determined solely by the law'.
[16] Ibid.

one may be disturbed on account of his opinions, including religious ones, as long as the manifestation of such opinions does not interfere with the established law and order.[17]

By choosing to refer to these standards, the Constitutional Council underlined that the constitution intended to leave the legislature a margin of appreciation that includes a limitation of these freedoms.

Furthermore, the constitutional objective to protect public order[18] is a key element to control constitutional freedoms so it is no surprise that the legislature used the protection of public order to justify the prohibition of concealment of the face in public, even if the state failed to adduce evidence that the full-face covering is a threat to public order.

But the warning made by the Conseil d'Etat against a redefinition of public order has not been completely heard. The Constitutional Council gave no contours to the notion of public order and it implicitly recognized an immaterial conception of public order which tends to protect the 'minimum requirements of life in society' in an 'open-faced Republic' (*République à visage découvert*),[19] a form of social public order which includes a new conception of human dignity linked to freedom and gender equality.[20] The Constitutional Council, by implicitly integrating and recognizing this new kind of human dignity as a legal ground to ban the full-face covering adopted the position of the Conseil d'Etat in the case law *Commune de Morsang-sur-Orge*, a position implicitly reversed by the Conseil d'Etat itself in its report on face veiling, where the highest administrative court underscored 'the principle of human dignity implies by its nature respect for individual freedom' and considered that invoking

> The protection of dignity as grounds for banning the full veil – which would then have to be a general ban in the public space – is fraught with very serious uncertainties ... The fundamental principles of protection of

---

[17] *Ibid.*, Article 10.

[18] Constitutional Council, no. 80–127 DC, 20 January 1981 *Loi renforçant la sécurité et protégeant la liberté des personnes* (Act strengthening security and protecting freedom of individuals) and Constitutional Council, no. 82–141 DC, July 27, 1982, *Loi sur la communication audiovisuelle* (Act on audiovisual communication).

[19] The government created a website called 'La République se vit à visage découvert', which gives information on the prohibition on concealment of the face: www.visage-decouvert.gouv.fr/documents.html (accessed August 2013).

[20] Mathieu, B. 'Peut-on interdire le voile intégral au nom du principe de dignité ?', *Le Monde*, 30 April 2010.

human dignity and equality of men and women are not readily applicable in this area.

(Conseil d'Etat 2010: 21)

By doing so, the Constitutional Council actually goes against the essence of this concept in its original definition, in liberal assumptions of individuals as rational and autonomous agents exercising free will.[21] The consequences resulting from the redefinition of public order will first affect the police, the first authority in charge of the protection of public order, who feared the increase of racial tensions and violence against them during identity controls. A policeman declared:

> We talk about individual freedom, but I do not see how to determine if the husband constrained his wife [to conceal her face]. This is the privacy of homes. It is not for us to determine whether it is coercion, religious choice or provocation.[22]

As for consequences on women, the Act of 2010 establishes the right of the legislature to restore a kind of equality of appearance and dress and of gender equality in the public space on behalf of society towards those who broke this equality. The establishment of this equality requires not only the obligation to uncover one's face in public space but includes also educational measures on gender equality, through for example, the obligation to follow a *stage de citoyenneté*[23] (citizenship course) as a penalty for breaching the ban. The Act not only wants to remove any symbolism of what it considers as oppression, but also seeks liberation from that oppression. Undeniably, the legislature intruded into issues of morals and customs and tries to give content to republican values. The issue here is that the state did not take into account that there are women wearing that kind of religious attire who do it willingly and freely – as the 'result of a personal and individualistic journey' for some, and as a 'religion obligation' for others (see Chapter 5 in this volume) – and the Conseil d'Etat noted (2010: 22):

---

[21] On this point, see the dissenting opinion of Judge Françoise Tulkens in the Leyla Şahin's judgment of the Grand Chamber of ECtHR. *Leyla Şahin v.* Turkey *[2005] ECtHR (NR. 44774/98)* (10 November 2005).

[22] Leprince, C. 'Burqa, les policiers non plus ne veulent pas d'une interdiction', *Rue89*, 11 May 2010. Our translation: 'On parle de liberté individuelle, je ne vois pas comment déterminer que le mari contraint sa femme. C'est l'intimité des foyers. Ce n'est pas à nous de déterminer s'il s'agit de contrainte, de choix religieux ou de provocation.'

[23] Further details available on the website of the French Ministry of Justice: www.justice.gouv.fr (accessed August 2013).

It should also be pointed out that the assessment of what does or does not detract from the dignity of the person is, at least potentially, comparatively subjective, as shown by the fact that the wearing of the full veil is in most cases voluntary.[24]

4. CONCLUSION

'Unenforceable', 'stigmatizing', 'infringing individual liberties': the Act of 2010 has been widely criticized, especially by the Muslim community and women claiming their right to wear the full veil.[25] Since its adoption, three hundred women have been fined,[26] and violence and insults against them increased, leading them to be 'effectively under house arrest'.[27] Bouteldja underscores in this volume (Chapter 5) that 'the stream of violent insults many respondents were regularly subjected to in public places was undoubtedly one of the most disturbing outcomes [of her research] in France'. According to her findings

> In France, the insults ranged from fictional characters like Batman, Darth Vader and Fantomas to ruder words like whore or slut. Remarks made by the members of the public also referred to women's rights, the ban of the full-face veil ... to the respondents' right to live in France and denial of citizenship ('go back to your country' 'we are in France here').[28]

On the legal level, the Conseil d'Etat without rejecting the possibility of prohibiting face concealment in public space, somehow managed to reconcile the protection of fundamental rights and freedoms through a redefinition of public order which excludes human dignity. Yet the Constitutional Council opened Pandora's box by including human dignity within the definition of public order. Undeniably, by using human dignity as an instrument to justify the constitutionality of the Act of 2010, the constitutional judges actually revealed the legal uncertainties surrounding this notion, and also increase the legal instability of such a law, which is a threat to legal certainty. If we follow the reasoning

---

[24] See also the answers of the respondents to the question 'Why wear the full-face veil' in the research conducted by Bouteldja (Chapter 5 of this volume).

[25] See the TV report made by France 24: 'loi sur le voile intégral: près de 300 femmes verbalisées en un an'.

[26] Warren, M., '300 women fined under full-face veil ban', *The Local*, 11 April 2012.

[27] Chrisafis, A. 'France's burqa ban: women are "effectively under house arrest"', *Guardian*, 19 September 2011.

[28] See the interviews Bouteldja conducted for this volume (Chapter 5) with French niqabi women who shared their experiences of wearing the full-face covering after the adoption of its ban.

of the Constitutional Council, all things that 'may be shocking in terms of public values' (Koussens 2009: 327–8) can come under the scope of a prohibition based on the violation of human dignity. Yet in France, pornography is not prohibited, and neither are violent consensual sexual relations, scarification of the body or indecent attires. Therefore, why would the wearing of the full-face covering be treated differently and be considered as a violation of human dignity? More importantly, how to bring the proof that the full-face covering causes a disturbance to public order? How will the redefinition of public order impact on women wearing a full-face covering?

At the same time, the face-covering ban introduced into French law a novel concept of 'immaterial public order'. The question can be raised whether the ECtHR would support such a conception. Faced with inter- ference in a Convention right that is prescribed by law, the ECtHR will probably have to examine if such interference pursues a legitimate goal. Moreover the protection and defence of public order is justified to the extent that there is a proven risk of disturbance,[29] and in that sense, the full-face covering will certainly fail to qualify as a significant threat to public order. While Strasbourg's Court would unlikely reject entirely the decision of the Constitutional Council, we cannot exclude that it would empty most of its scope by limiting its implementation to situations of proven disturbance of 'material' public order.

On 22 September 2011, the Police Court of Meaux[30] condemned two women wearing the niqab to pay a fine of €180 and €82 for violating the Act of 2010. On July 2012, a woman wearing the niqab was stopped by police for an identity control in Marseille. She refused to submit herself to such a control causing an altercation in which two policemen were attacked. She was arrested but eventually released, the police fearing reprisals afterwards.[31] On June 2013, the police proceeded on controlling the identity of a woman wearing the niqab which ended in confronta- tions between the police and passers-by who considered the control as 'illegitimate'.[32] And on July 2013, serious riots started in Trappes after the controlling of the identity of a niqabi (according to Le Monde, a policeman yelled at her that 'we are not in Kabul' and her husband tried

---

[29] See Conseil d'Etat, 19 May 1933, no. 1741317520, Benjamin, Administrative Court of Paris, 22 December 2006, no. 0619140/9/1, Association Solidarité des Français.

[30] Unpublished decisions. Further information: www.courrierinternational.com/article/2011/09/ 22/la-double-peine-des-femmes-en-niqab (accessed August 2013).

[31] 'Marseille, le voile de la discorde', Le Point, 25 July 2012.

[32] 'Argenteuil: affrontement après le contrôle d'une femme en niqab', Libération, 12 June 2013.

to oppose the identity check.[33] By legislating and criminalizing instead of conciliating and accommodating, the legislature and the government probably worsened the situation of those women who are indeed forced to wear such a garment, by forcing them to stay at home and to disappear from public life. They also outcast women, who consider the full-face veil as their 'second skin' (Kahf 2008: 27), or as a part of their spiritual journey, and classify them as a public danger and impose upon them their vision of freedom and dignity on behalf of French republican values and protection of public order. Finally, no concrete proof has been brought about the risk of public order disturbance caused by the full-face covering. The threat to public order more likely comes from the abuse and occasional assault on women wearing the full-face covering exacerbated by the former government when it made the face veil a controversial issue (see Chapter 5 in this volume). All this shows the limits of this law which may be emptied of its substance in the future.

REFERENCES

Bauer, J. 1999. *Politique et Religion*, Presses universitaires de France.
Béchillon (de), D. 2010. 'Voile intégral: éloge du Conseil d'Etat en théoricien des droits fondamentaux', *Revue française de droit administratif*, 26: 467–71.
Conseil d'Etat 2010. *Study of Possible Legal Grounds for Banning the Full Veil*, 25 March: www.conseil-etat.fr/fr/rapports-et-etudes (accessed June 2013).
Grillo, R. D. and Shah P. 2012. *Reasons to Ban? The Anti-Burqa Movement in Western Europe*. MMG Working Paper 12-09. Göttingen: Max Planck Institute for the Study of Religious and Ethnic Diversity.
Hauriou, M. 1927. *Précis de droit administratif et de droit public*, Recueil Sirey.
Kafh, M. 2008. 'From her Royal Body the Robe Was Removed: The Blessings of the Veil and the Trauma of Forced Unveilings in the Middle East', in J. Heath (ed.), *The Veil: Women Writers on Its History, Lore and Politics*, Berkeley, Los Angeles, CA and London: University Press of California.
Koussens, D. 2009 'Sous l'affaire de la burqa … Quel visage de la laïcité française?', *Sociologie et Sociétés*, 41: 327–47.
Mathieu, B. 2010. 'La validation par le Conseil constitutionnel de la loi sur "le voile integral"', *Semaine juridique édition générale*, 42: 1930–2.
Obama, B. 2009. 'Remarks by the President on a new beginning', *Cairo University*, Cairo, 4 June: www.whitehouse.gov/the-press-office/remarks-president-cairo-university-6-04-09 (accessed August 2013).

---

[33] E. Vincent, 'Trappes: radiographie d'une émeute', *Le Monde*, 16 August 2013.

9

ISLAMIC VEIL BANS: THE GENDER EQUALITY JUSTIFICATION AND EMPIRICAL EVIDENCE

Erica Howard

1. BANS ARE NECESSARY TO PROMOTE GENDER EQUALITY

The question whether there should be legislation banning people from wearing religious symbols in public areas is debated in many European countries (Grillo and Shah 2012: 12–13). These debates, both at the political and at the popular level, often focus on whether Muslim women and girls should be prohibited from wearing face coverings (niqabs and burqas) or, although to a lesser extent, headscarves (hijabs) in public. The argument that legislative bans on the wearing of Islamic headscarves and face-covering veils are necessary for the promotion of gender equality[1] is heard time and time again in these political and popular debates to justify imposing such bans.[2] For example, in the debates that have taken place in Holland over the last ten years or so, words like 'oppression or submission of women' and 'obstacle to eman-cipation' recur and the face veil is described as unfriendly or hostile and degrading to women (Moors 2009). Former French President Sarkozy called the niqab 'a sign of subservience, a sign of debasement' (Open

---

[1] For a more extensive theoretical discussion of this argument, see Howard (2012b). This is only one of a number of arguments used in favour of bans. For an analysis of the arguments in favour of bans and the counter-arguments which can be brought forward against these, see Bakht (2012) and Howard (2012a). This chapter focuses on the gender equality argument only.

[2] See, for example, Commission de Réflexion (2003: 57); Human Rights Watch (2009: 9); Conseil d'Etat (2010); Johnson (2010); Gilligan (2011); Vrielink *et al.* (2011: 631); Chambre des Représentants de Belgique (2011: 5, 6, 7, 9, 10, 14); Rijksoverheid (2012); Open Society Foundations (2011: 19–20); Bouteldja (2013: 3–5); Chapter 2 in this volume.

Society Foundations 2011: 30). Similar language has been used in the Belgian debates on the law banning face-covering clothing in public, where the terms 'prison' or 'mobile prison' were used in relation to the burqa (Chambre des Représentants de Belgique 2011: 9, 10, 14; Vrielink *et al.* 2011). But the argument can also be found in the case law of certain courts.[3] Often in these debates, the term burqa is used, although this garment is very seldom worn in Europe. Silvestri suggests that 'mentioning the *burqa* seems to have a more dramatic effect, because everyone has in mind the consequences of the Taliban regime and its abject treatment of women' (2012: 277).

The argument is that Muslim women who wear headscarves or face veils do so because they are made to do so by men, be it spouses, family, communities, religious leaders or the state (McGoldrick 2006: 13–15) and thus these veils are seen as symbols of the oppression of women and as going against a woman's fundamental rights and freedoms. Islam is thus perceived as a paternalistic religion which does not recognize the equality of the sexes and holds that women are inferior to men. Therefore, face-covering veils and headscarves need to be banned to preserve the dignity and rights not only of the women who wear them but also of all women. The public manifestation of inequality between men and women that the face veil represents is, as Mullally (2011: 39) writes of France, seen as 'damaging, not only to the dignity of the veiled woman, but to those who share public spaces with her'. And, in the parliamentary debates in Belgium, the face-covering veil is described as a symbol of the oppression of women and as such an offence to the dignity of all women (Vrielink *et al.* 2011: 631).

Another related concern, frequently raised in case law, is that if some women or girls are allowed to wear certain forms of religious clothing, those who do not want to wear it will be forced to do so as well and this oppression needs to be prevented by bans on these forms of clothing or face covering.[4] Therefore, bans on the wearing of Islamic head scarves

---

[3] It was used, for example, by the ECtHR in *Dahlab* v. *Switzerland* app. no. 42393/98, 15 February 2001, 13 and by both the Chamber and the Grand Chamber of the same Court, in Şahin v. *Turkey* app. no. 44774/98 2005) 41 EHRR 8 (Chamber), paras. 106 and 2007) 44 EHRR 5 (Grand Chamber), para. 115. Both cases concerned Islamic headscarves.

[4] See, for example: *Karaduman* v. *Turkey* app. no. 16278/90 and *Bulut* v. *Turkey* app. no. 18783/91, both (1993) D & R 74, 93, 108 (European Commission of Human Rights), which concerned Islamic headscarves; Şahin v. *Turkey* app. no. 44774/98 2005) 41 EHRR 8 (Chamber), paras. 106 and 2007) 44 EHRR 5 (Grand Chamber), para. 115; for the UK, *R (on the application of SB)* v. *Head Teacher and Governors of Denbigh High School* [2006] UKHL 15 (HL), para. 18 (concerning a

and face veils are seen as necessary to emancipate Muslim women and girls and to free them from oppression.

It has to be noted that, although this argument is used in debates on all forms of Islamic clothing, face-covering veils are most strongly opposed as they are seen as particularly oppressive, but the argument is also used in relation to bans on the wearing of headscarves, particularly in certain settings like education and the civil service. For example, Loenen (2009: 315) writes: 'a major argument put forward to ban head-scarves in public schools derives from the idea that the headscarf is symbolic of the inferior position of women in Islam and that many girls and women are pressured into wearing it'. Some people argue that the headscarves should be banned too as the simple headscarf can be seen as 'but the first step to full fabric incarceration' (Alibhai-Brown 2011). The participants in the Belgian research presented in the first part of this book expressed their concern that a ban on the wearing of the headscarf in public places could well be the next step, after the wearing of face-covering clothing in public places was prohibited in Belgium in 2011 (Brems et al. 2012: 35). The same concern was expressed by some of the French interviewees (Open Society Foundations 2011: 68).

The argument that Islamic face veils (and headscarves) need to be banned to emancipate Muslim women and girls, to free them from the male oppression they are under is, however, based on a very stereotypical view of Muslim women as 'the victim of a gender oppressive religion, needing protection from abusive, violent male relatives, and passive, unable to help herself in the face of a culture of male dominance' (Evans 2006: 15–16).[5]

What is lacking in all the debates are the voices of the women who wear headscarves and face veils. For example, Brems et al. (2012: 2), state that it was striking to find in the political debates about banning the face veil in Belgium, 'a complete lack of knowledge about women who wear the face veil' and 'the complete absence of the voices of women wearing

schoolgirl who wanted to wear a jilbab, a long plain dress covering arms and legs, against the school uniform rules); R (on the application of X) v. Head Teacher and Governors of Y School [2008] 1 All ER 249, para. 64 (concerning a schoolgirl who wanted to wear a niqab against school uniform rules).

[5] Evans distinguishes another stereotype of Muslim women: the aggressor or 'the Muslim woman as fundamentalist who forces values onto the unwilling and undefended'. She points out that these stereotypes are inherently contradictory (2006: 15–16). However, the first stereotype lies behind the gender equality justification for legislative bans on veils. For more on this see ibid.; Bakht (2012: 80); Howard (2012a: 62–3).

the face veil'. This is also true for the Netherlands and France (Bouteldja 2013: 1; Moors 2009: 18; Moors 2013: 1 and 7; Open Society Foundations 2011: 11 and 20–1;) and for Canada (Bakht 2012: 53). This lack has also been pointed out by Judge Tulkens, in her dissenting opinion in Şahin v. Turkey, a case concerning a student wearing a headscarf, who stated: 'what is lacking in this debate is the opinion of women, both those who wear the headscarf and those who choose not to'.[6]

An exception to this appears to be Denmark. As described in Chapter 3 in this volume, the Danish Ministry of the Interior commissioned the research when the issues of women wearing face-covering clothing became part of the political debate. The report of the research did have the effect that politicians and the public quickly lost interest in the issues of women wearing face veils, 'mainly because there were so few of them and that half of them were ethnic Danish converts' and, therefore, 'the idea of a general ban of face-covering clothes seems no longer part of government policy in Denmark' (Warburg et al. 2013: 15).

Therefore, with the exception of Denmark, there appears to be a real lack of attention for and knowledge about the reasons why women wear the face veil or the headscarf. This is why the empirical evidence presented in Part I of this volume concerning women wearing face veils is important, as it gives a voice to the women themselves and it shows a very different picture.

2. WHY DO WOMEN WEAR FACE VEILS?

The empirical research shows that all the women interviewed emphasize that they wear the face veil of their own autonomous personal choice, that it was their own well-considered decision to wear the veil, often in spite of disapproval of parents and other close relatives. They see it as part of an expression of their love for God. Religious considerations are central in their decisions. For most of them it is a 'personal trajectory of deepening and perfecting their faith' (Brems et al. 2012, 5; see also Chapters 3 and 5 in this volume; Moors 2009: 29–30, 39; Open Society Foundations 2011: 13, 14 and 40). This research thus suggests that women who wear face veils often are not forced to do so by men, but make their own personal choice to do so. This is also true for the Islamic headscarf, as the research done by

---

[6] Şahin v. Turkey app. no. 44774/98 2007) 44 EHRR 5 (Grand Chamber), dissenting opinion Judge Tulkens, §11.

Human Rights Watch in Germany on the wearing of the headscarf confirms. Their report states that 'all the cases documented by Human Rights Watch ... have all involved adult women insisting that their decisions were personal, not imposed' (2009: 32).

The research reported on in this volume also shows what many of the women interviewed think about the gender equality argument brought forward in the debates. First of all, many say that they do not know of women who are pressured into wearing the face veil (Brems *et al.* 2012: 8). But in all reports it is clear that the women themselves reject the idea that the face veil is a sign of oppression and gender inequality. For example, one French interviewee stated: 'I totally refute the argument which claims that wearing the niqab is a submission to man' (Chapter 5 in this volume). Moors (2009: 55) writes that, for the women concerned, the face veil is not a symbol of women's oppression. Bouteldja (Chapter 5 in this volume) reports that assumptions that the niqab reflects and reproduces hierarchical power structures privileging male over female by coercion and force, are undermined by the findings. Warburg *et al.* (Chapter 3 in this volume) found that 'none of the women themselves connect the covering of the face with the oppression or an unequal relationship between men and women' and that they reject this explanation for wearing the face veil outright. And, in Belgium, many of the women interviewed showed 'annoyance at the fact that outsiders assume they are being suppressed and dominated by their husbands, and in particular that they are assumed to be forced to wear the face veil' and several interviewees were offended by suggestions that they needed enlightenment or education (Brems *et al.* 2012: 24 and 25).

3. CAVEATS

A number of caveats must be placed on the above. First, the research in the countries concerned is not representative of all women who wear face veils, as the reports make clear. The research reports recognize that there are women who are pressured into wearing face veils or headscarves and that the research possibly did not reach these women. As Alibhai-Brown (2011: point 5) writes: 'there is no evidence that all the women [wearing face veils or headscarves] are making rational, independent decisions'. Therefore, the fact that many of the women interviewed did wear the face veils out of a personal choice and without any coercion does not mean that such coercion does not exist.

Pressure from family appears to play a particular role in relation to the wearing of headscarves by school girls and college students, as both Joppke (2009: 12) and Lister *et al.* (2007: 99) point out. Killian (2003: 572) reports on research which showed that, in France, 'the majority of adolescents and preadolescents who veiled [in this case: wore the headscarf] did so because of family pressure. Many indicated that if they did not veil, their parents would not allow them to attend school' (see also Joppke 2009: 12; Lister *et al.* 2007: 99). On the other hand, not all schoolgirls see this as pressure from parents. For example, Gereluk (2008: 117–18), reports that a number of Muslim girls in London 'were adamant that they had not been forced to wear the hijab'. They 'felt that there was a difference between "parental guid-ance"' and "oppression" and that "their parents" wish to have them wear the hijab was a sign of their guidance and love'. Therefore, it cannot be denied that, in some cases, pressure from family or community elders or religious leaders is applied not only to schoolgirls and college students, but also to other Muslim women, although this is certainly not the case for all women and girls who wear Islamic face veils or headscarves.

Another caveat is that there are many different, overlapping and intersecting, reasons why women and girls wear face veils or headscarves. Based on research across Europe, Lister *et al.* discuss the following reasons why Muslim women wear headscarves: (1) as an ethnic and religious signal; (2) as an affirmation of identity and a means to negotiate one's own identity and as a sign of independence; (3) because of pressure from family; and (4) as a political act or as a sign of a new and radical interpretation of their faith (2007: 99–100). It is suggested that the first two correspond to the reasons found in the empirical research reported on in the first part of this book, that women wear face veils as a sign of their religious piety and as an affirmation of their love of God, doing so out of their own free will. The interviewees appear to freely choose to wear the face veil – and many had worn the headscarf before they adopted the face veil (Open Society Foundations 2011: 13; Brems *et al.* 2012: 4) – because they see it as part of who and what they are as part of their identity (see, for example, Chapter 3 in this volume). The empirical research suggests, as mentioned above, that they make this choice not because they are being told to do so by men, but because they are modern, emancipated women who make up their own minds about what they wear and how they present themselves in public. And, the latter two meanings, given by Lister above – pressure from family and a political act or as a sign of a radical interpretation of their faith – appear to be firmly rejected by the interviewees in the research reported on in this volume.

Another caveat is that the above might suggest that there is a clear distinction between, on the one hand, wearing veils and headscarves out of personal choice and, on the other hand, doing so under direct coercion. In practice, this is often much more complicated and there are a number of subtle ways in which pressure can be or might be exercised.

4. THE GENDER EQUALITY JUSTIFICATION FOR BANS

From the above and from the empirical research, it is clear that women wear headscarves and face veils for a variety of reasons. Many women do not do so because they are pressured into this by men but because they freely choose to do so. The research shows that there may be more women who would like to wear a face veil but that they are not doing so because of pressure from their parents or husband, who are worried about the reactions from the environment if a woman does wear a face veil (Brems et al. 2012: 8; Moors 2009: 52; Open Society Foundations 2011: 35–6; Chapter 2 in this volume). That many women wear a headscarf or face veil because they choose to do so is ignored in political and popular debates where the idea dominates that all women who wear these garments are oppressed and thus need liberating. The justification for enacting bans on the wearing of face veils and headscarves is thus based on a false premise and does not give any attention to the voices of the women involved.

Although the empirical research has shown that many women do not wear the face veil under pressure from other people, it has not shown that such pressure is never brought to bear. Some women and girls are, as mentioned above, pressured into wearing headscarves or face veils. But, even if only a small number of women are under pressure, would that not be sufficient reason for a ban? It is submitted that it is not. Bans in these cases are not only not necessary, but they are also counterproductive for achieving the emancipation of this group. Bans could very well lead to these women not being allowed to go out of the house at all and thus not being permitted to go to school or to work. Rather than hindering their emancipation, allowing this group of women to wear these garments would promote their emancipation because it might be the only way they can go outside the home and study or work. For example, in relation to the pressure on schoolgirls referred to above, Killian (2003: 572)

Lister *et al.* (2007: 99) and Joppke (2009: 12) all point out that wearing a veil or headscarf is the only way some of these girls are allowed to go to school or to take part in school excursions and sports activities (see also Chapter 5 in this volume). And Van Gulik (2009) writes that 'banning the headscarf is the worst possible response to the need to bring people into mainstream society. Our research[7] showed that the ban serves to exclude, rather than include'. She also reports that 'all of the women we spoke to told us they had freely chosen to wear it. But the bans do them harm, leaving them unable to work in the jobs they had chosen, and causing them to lose financial independence.' This is also pointed out by some of the interviewees in the Netherlands, who recognize that there are men who want to restrict their wife's movements severely, for example because they are jealous, but that these women are not helped by a ban on the wearing of a face veil, because the men would not become any less dominant and the women would not go out at all anymore. Moreover, a ban would punish the victims, who are in this way excluded from access to education, public transport, etc. (Moors 2009: 52 and 56; Chapter 2 in this volume). Therefore, allowing women and girls to wear headscarves and face veils, gives them a chance to gain equality in and through work and education.

There is another problem with using gender equality as a justification for bans on the wearing of headscarves and face veils. It is based on the view that Islam is a paternalistic religion where men determine what women should wear. But the accusation of paternalism levelled at Islam can be just as well levelled at the people in these debates, at the politicians who argue for legislation banning headscarves and/or face veils: banning women and girls from wearing them is another form of prescribing what women should wear. Or, as Silvestri writes: 'the patronizing tone about "subjugated women that need saving" becomes itself an expression of patriarchy, another form of oppression' (2012: 288). Both sides ignore a woman's human right to autonomy and to free choice as guaranteed by Article 8 ECHR. Marshall (2006: 460) writes that 'the position may be reached that banning means imposing one set of standards and denies these women freedom as autonomous persons in their own right: seemingly in the name of gender equality'. Or, as Lyon and Spini (2004: 341) write 'the answer to one constraint (the religious obligation to wear the *foulard* [head-scarf]) cannot be another constraint (the obligation not to wear it):

---

[7] For this research, see Human Rights Watch (2009).

an effective process of liberation cannot be based on a prohibition [their emphasis]'. And, Judge Tulkens, in her dissenting opinion in *Şahin v. Turkey*, states that she fails 'to see how the principle of sexual equality can justify prohibiting a woman from following a practice which, in the absence of proof to the contrary, she must be taken to have freely adopted' and that '"paternalism" of this sort runs counter to the case-law of the Court, which has developed a real right to personal autonomy on the basis of Article 8'.[8]

It can thus be said that banning headscarves and other religious symbols is just as paternalistic and oppressive of women as forcing them to wear these. What to wear or what not to wear is imposed on women by, in the one case, their family or community or, in the other case, the state, both without any attention for what the women themselves want or without any respect for their freedom and autonomy to choose for themselves. As Van Gulik (2009), writing about headscarf bans in Germany and the fact that some women are indeed coerced into wearing the headscarf or other religious clothing, sums up rather well: 'however, our experience and research tell us that oppression cannot be uprooted by a state itself coercing the victims, but rather through education, access to justice and economic opportunity. Women's rights are about autonomy. And real autonomy means freedom to make choices whether others like these or not.' Or, as Bakht (2012: 76) sums the above up: 'undoubtedly, there are also multiple and overlapping reasons why women choose to wear the niqab', but 'utilizing coercive and state-sanctioned means of removing this clothing publicly will hardly be effective in promoting autonomy, equality and justice'.

5. CONCLUSION

It is therefore submitted that the gender equality argument for banning headscarves and face veils, prevalent in political and popular discussions on such bans, is false. The empirical research in this book suggests that many women wear face veils out of choice, not because they are pressured by men to do so as is assumed in the debates. A consideration of the opinions of the women themselves is very often totally absent in the deliberations and discussions on proposals for legislation or in

---

[8] *Şahin v. Turkey* app. no. 44774/98 2007) 44 EHRR 5 (Grand Chamber), dissenting opinion Judge Tulkens, para. 12. For the case law on this, see the opinion.

media reports. The gender equality justification is thus grounded in a false premise about the oppression of women. And legislative bans themselves can also be seen as an oppression of women, of their autonomy and free choice, by the state. As one of the French interviewees said about the ban on the full face veil: 'they say it's our husbands who are locking us away but it's actually they who are locking us away' (Open Society Foundations 2011: 74).

There are undoubtedly women and girls who are pressured into wearing face veils or head scarves, but this group will not be helped by bans. On the contrary, this group may well suffer most from a legal ban, because it will stop them from going out, from gaining more emancipation through education and work. As Evans (2006: 13) concludes, 'the reality [of banning religious clothing] is that some women will no longer be able to pursue their education or their careers in public places. If a feminist analysis is to be undertaken, the harm done to these women must be taken into account.' The above clearly shows that gender equality is not a valid argument for the banning of Islamic face veils and headscarves.

REFERENCES

Alibhai-Brown, Y. 2011. 'Sixteen reasons why I object to this dangerous cover-up', The Independent, 4 April, www.independent.co.uk/voices/commentators/yasmin-alibhaibrown/yasmin-alibbaibrown-sixteen-reasons-why-i-object-to-this-dangerous-coverup-2261444.html (accessed 6 August 2013).
Bakht, N. 2012. 'Veiled objections: facing public opposition to the niqab', in L. Beaman (ed.), Defining Reasonable Accommodation, Vancouver: University of British Columbia Press, pp. 70–108.
Brems, E., Janssens, Y., Lecoyer, K., Ouald Chaib, S. and Vandersteen, V. 2012. Wearing the Face Veil in Belgium (Human Rights Centre, Ghent University) www.ugent.be/re/publiekrecht/en/research/human-rights/face veil.pdf (accessed 6 August 2013).
Chambre des Représentants de Belgique 2011. DCO 53 0219/004. Proposition de Loi Visant à Interdire le Port de Tout Vêtement Cachant Totalement ou de Manière Principale le Visage. 18 April, www.dekamer.be/FLWB/PDF/53/0219/53K0219004.pdf (accessed 6 August 2013).
Commission de Reflexion sur L'Application du Principe de Laïcité dans la République 2003. Rapport au Président de la République, December, 57, www.ladocumentationfrancaise.fr/var/storage/rapports-publics/034000725/0000.pdf (accessed 6 August 2013).

Conseil d'Etat 2010. *Study of Possible Legal Grounds for Banning the Full Veil.* 25 March, www.conseil-etat.fr/cde/media/document/RAPPORT% 20ETUDES/etude_voile_integral_anglais.pdf (accessed 6 August 2013).

Evans, C. 2006. 'The "Islamic Scarf" in the European Court of Human Rights', *Melbourne Journal of International Law*, 7(1): 52 www.austlii.edu.au/au/ journals/MelbJIL/2006/4.html (accessed 6 August 2013).

Gereluk, D. 2008. *Symbolic Clothing in Schools: What Should Be Worn and Why.* London: Continuum.

Gilligan, A. 2011. 'Why banning the veil would only cover up the real problems for British Muslims', *Daily Telegraph*, 16 April, www.telegraph.co.uk/jour nalists/andrew-gilligan/8455884/Why-banning-the-veil-would-only-cover-up-the-real-problems-for-British-Muslims.html (accessed 6 August 2013).

Grillo, R. and Shah, P. 2012. *Reasons to Ban? The Anti-Burqa Movement in Western Europe.* MMG Working Paper 12–05, Max Planck Institute for the Study of Religious and Ethnic Diversity. www.mmg.mpg.de/publica tions/working-papers/2012/wp-12-05/ (accessed 6 August 2013).

Howard, E. 2012a. *Law and the Wearing of Religious Symbols: European Bans on the Wearing of Religious Symbols in Education.* London: Routledge.

2012b. 'Banning Islamic veils – Is Gender Equality a Valid Argument?' *International Journal of Discrimination and the Law*, 12(3): 147–65.

Human Rights Watch 2009. *Discrimination in the name of neutrality: headscarf bans for teachers and Civil Servants in Germany*, www.hrw.org/en/reports/ 2009/02/26/discrimination-name-neutrality-0 (accessed 6 August 2013).

Johnson, B. 2010. 'Spanish lawmakers to take up burqa ban', 18 July: http:// worldnews.about.com/b/2010/07/18/spanish-lawmakers-to-take-up-burqa-ban.htm (accessed 6 August 2013).

Joppke, C. 2009. *Veil: Mirror of Identity.* Cambridge: Polity.

Killian, C. 2003. 'The Other Side of the Veil: North African Women in France Respond to the Headscarf Affair', *Gender and Society*, 17, 567–90.

Lister, R., Williams, F., Anttonen, A., Bussemaker, J., Gerhard, U., Heinen, J., Johansson, S., Leira, A., Siim, B., Tobio, C. and Gavanas, A. 2007. *Gendered Citizenship in Western Europe: New Challenges for Citizenship Research in a Cross-National Context.* Bristol: Policy Press.

Loenen, T. 2009. 'The Headscarf Debate: Approaching the Intersection of Sex, Religion and Race under the European Convention on Human Rights and EC Equality Law', in D. Schiek and V. Chege (eds.), *European Union Non-Discrimination Law: Comparative Perspectives on Multidimensional Equality Law.* Abingdon: Routledge-Cavendish, pp. 313–28.

Lyon, D. and Spini, D. 2004. 'Unveiling the Headscarf Debate', *Feminist Legal Studies*, 12: 333–45.

McGoldrick, D. 2006. *Human Rights and Religion: The Islamic Headscarf Debate in Europe.* Oxford: Hart.

Marshall, J. 2006. 'Freedom of Religious Expression and Gender Equality: Şahin v. Turkey', Modern Law Review, 69(3): 452–61.

Moors, A. 2009. Gezichtssluiers draagsters and debatten [Face veils, wearers and debates]: www.cie.ugent.be/documenten/gezichtssluiers_2009.pdf (accessed 6 August 2013).

Mullally, S. 2011. 'Civic Integration, Migrant Women and the Veil: At the Limits of Rights?', Modern Law Review, 74(1): 27–56.

Open Society Foundations 2011. Unveiling the Truth: Why 32 Muslim Women Wear the Full-Face Veil in France: www.soros.org/initiatives/home/ articles_publications/publications/unveiling-the-truth-20110411 (accessed 6 August 2013).

Rijksoverheid 2012. Kabinet akkoord met gelaatsbedekkende kleding [Government agrees with ban on face-covering clothing]: www.rijksover heid.nl/nieuws/2012/01/27/kabinet-akkoord-met-verbod-gelaatsbedek kende-kleding.html (accessed 6 August 2013).

Silvestri, S. 2012. 'Comparing Burqa Debates in Europe: Sartorial Styles, Religions Prescriptions and Political Ideologies', in S. Ferrari and S. Pastorelli (eds.), Religion in Public Spaces: A European Perspective. Farnham: Ashgate, pp. 275–92.

Van Gulik, G. 2009. 'Headscarves: the wrong battle', www.hrw.org/en/news/ 2009/03/14/headscarves-wrong-battle (accessed 6 August 2013).

Vrielink, J., Ouald Chaib, S. and Brems, E. 2011. 'Het "Boerkaverbod" in Belgie [The 'Burqa ban' in Belgium], Nederlands Tijdschrift voor de Mensenrechten, 36(6/7) 623–38.

10

WOMEN'S OPPRESSION AND FACE-VEIL BANS: A FEMINIST ASSESSMENT

Dolores Morondo Taramundi

Whereas the different European 'hijab debates' in the 1990s and early 2000s centred mainly around the principle of secularism and the right to freedom of religion, with rather marginal, perfunctory and inconsistent references to gender equality, in later debates regarding face veils, arguments about sex equality and women's dignity or oppression have acquired a much more central role.

Yet in what terms is sex equality or women's oppression discussed in the debates regarding face veils? In what follows I propose a feminist[1] assessment of two, in my opinion, urgent and rather unexplored questions: first, the issue of women's oppression, as a *feminist* objection to the face veil; and, second, a discussion of the feminist objections to face veil bans.

1. WOMEN'S EQUALITY ISSUES: POLITICAL MANIPULATION AND MISCONSTRUCTION

For the purpose of carrying out a feminist assessment, I think it is important to examine two features of the debate that have had (and still have) an important bearing on the way equality claims are forwarded and understood. The first issue that strikes the eye is the political manipulation of gender equality claims. A second feature, which is less visible perhaps, is the misconstruction of 'women's

---

[1] Feminism comes in all shapes and sizes, not always perfectly compatible among themselves. In what follows, I shall proceed from a position of radical feminism, a form of critical theory originating in the second wave, whose interest lies mainly with social power structures, and in particular, with patriarchy or sex–gender systems.

oppression'. These features do overlap and mingle together in many arguments, but they are also rather complex questions in their own right. In what follows I shall comment on them very briefly, just to gain some clarity regarding the debate in order to move on to the two pressing questions I have mentioned before: the feminist argument on women's oppression regarding face veils, and the feminist objections to the face-veil bans.

1.1. Political manipulation of women's equality issues

A first feature of the debate that we need to clear up is, thus, the political manipulation and the opportunistic/electoral use of gender equality issues by political figures and parties whose sudden 'feminist' faith should have prompted diffidence and scorn. It has not been so, and it is not rare to find scholarly analyses that consider such utterances as the Western feminist standard or conception of sex equality (Mancini 2012:414 ff.). The manipulative character of gender equality claims has long been denounced as 'instrumentalisation' (Benelli et al. 2006: 8; Roux et al. 2007), 'manipulation' (Casalini 2010) or 'sordid political calculations' (Laborde 2012: 398). Yet I would like to pinpoint some issues that might be helpful in confronting the opportunistic context of gender equality objections to face veils, avoiding the trap of simply transferring the falsity of the motives in making equality claims to the falsity of the equality claims themselves.[2]

The use of 'women' (or 'womanhood' or 'femininity') in defining and/or contrasting emerging political groups is well documented in feminist theory: women are very often both the battleground and the exchange objects of political struggles and pacts in patriarchal societies (Abu-Lighod 1998; Armstrong 1987; Oliva Portolés 2007). As we shall discuss later on, the fact that women do take part in these dynamics (that they have 'agency') is not contradictory with these being patriarchal dynamics or women being exchange objects.

Another significant point is the 'ethnicization' of sexism. This is not new, either. The review of the feminist debate around, for example, the

---

[2] In this respect, it is interesting to note the role attributed to those women who are part of the 'Other' but hold an opinion loudly and explicitly dissenting from (the authoritative or legitimized or acknowledged opinion of) their group. The most glaring example is NPNS whose opinion is almost never cited without mentioning (the few times that it is cited) that they are/were financed by such-and-such a party, that they were instrumental to the government, that their discourse has been used or adopted by well-known Islamophobes, etc.

problems of domestic violence and black families in the USA might prove useful. The 'ethnicization' of sexism is accomplished by comparing dominant society's normativity, values or professed ideals (gender equality) with the ethnic/religious group's practices (cases of gender violence, patriarchal interpretation of religious norms or patriarchal traditions of cultural groups), thus presenting generalized and stereo-typed accounts or images of the minority group as deviant from a model that is not the practice of the majority either.

Yet the ways in which the 'ethnicization' of sexism is discussed and confronted might be deleterious for women's freedom. One such move is to respond to xenophobic or racist uses of sexism by entering into a comparison of 'ideals' or by reversing the comparison (majority's practices of subordination vs. minority's ideals). Or by denying that minority discriminatory practices even exist. In any case, women lose.

In order to confront this kind of problem, feminist studies have developed, in the last twenty years or so, the notion of intersectionality (Crenshaw 1989; Grabham et al. 2009). Intersectionality in relation to veiled Muslim women is a rather complex discussion that requires a separate study. Here, I would like to note simply that today, just like twenty years ago, the lack of a clear under-standing on how different systems of oppression interact undermines both feminist and anti-racist struggles. But today, unlike then, intersectional analyses are burdened with theoretical and methodo-logical conundrums, and have been criticized for not having any more to offer to feminist theory or even for impoverishing feminist analytical tools (Conaghan 2009; McCall 2009). Despite a consci-entious effort by a number of authors to approach the regulation of (face) veils as a question of intersectional discrimination (Delphy 2006; Scott 2007), most of the analyses fall short in addressing the *interaction of the systems* of oppression and the doubts about (current understandings of) intersectionality grow.

1.2. Misconstruction of the notion of 'women's oppression'
This second question is clearly related to the first, because the miscon-struction of the notion of women's oppression has been instrumental in rejecting or downplaying women's equality objections to face veils.

Not being really feminist claims, mainstream political usage of 'wom-en's oppression' has mostly consisted in already well-assessed rhetorical devices that associate hijab – burqa/niqab – Taliban regime or FGM, without further interest in women's condition (Muslim or otherwise)

(Benelli *et al.* 2006: 7; Casalini 2010). I shall not spend further argument on them.

My interest here lies with the scholarly accounts of 'women's oppression' that have contrasted those political usages. They are mostly construed around two sets of arguments.

In mainstream political discourse, 'women's oppression' is, first of all, intended as the fact that women are (or are supposed to be) forced to wear niqabs by husbands or other family members (usually male) as part of their religious or moral obligations. This reduction of women's oppression to the coercion of the individual woman is reinforced by the counter-arguments in scientific literature: women forced into wearing niqabs are certainly entitled to be defended and protected by the law. Yet, as the empirical research in Part I of this volume shows there are women who wear the niqab voluntarily and even against the opinion or the will of husbands and/or fathers (see Chapters 2–4 in this volume); these women would be discriminated against by a law prohibiting the mere use of the garment.

As we shall discuss later on, the feminist concept of women's oppression is not about individual women being coerced into anything. I sincerely hope it does not take feminism to oppose women being coerced into wearing any kind of garment; using coercion with women should be simply subsumed under existing legal provisions about coercion and violence, as has already been objected in relation to anti-burqa rules (Laborde 2012: 406).

Contrarily to what might appear, far from being the final point to the debate, it is exactly when women (at least some, or even many, women) wear the niqab voluntarily that the feminist objection regarding women's oppression starts, as we shall see in the next paragraph.

The second set of arguments relates to the meaning of the niqab and the burqa as oppressive or sexist symbols; here the usual rejection is linked to the question of autonomy that we shall discuss later on: niqabs and burqas are polysemic, says the scientific literature opposing this kind of objection (Delphy 2006: 59). Women wearing them have many different motives that cannot be traced to oppression, as manifested by interviewees in Part I of this volume. Here again, the social and structural dimension of oppression is diluted in the atomized selves of individual women performing certain practices. Yet in the feminist argument regarding women's oppression, the link between the individual motives of a gesture and the causes or the meaning of that gesture is much more complex.

2. FEMINIST ARGUMENTS ON WOMEN'S OPPRESSION

Feminist arguments on women's oppression are made within a discourse about power, particularly about power as it is theorized by a significant part of critical thought, that is, in terms of oppression and/or domination. Let us take a classical work on the topic, Iris Marion Young's *Justice and the Politics of Difference*.

> Entering the political discourse in which oppression is a central category involves adopting a general mode of analysing and evaluating social structures and practices which is incommensurate with the language of liberal individualism. (Young 1990: 39)

The concept of women's oppression is thus linked to that of patriarchy or sex–gender systems. In the framework of the sex–gender system, women's oppression is not about individual women (although it certainly has an effect on individual women).[3] It is a collective question, a group condition. It is not about coercion in individualistic, legal terms, but about women's condition in society and their life choices.

> Oppression also refers to systematic constraints on groups that are not necessarily the result of the intentions of a tyrant. Oppression in this sense is structural, rather than the result of a few people's choices or policies. Its causes are embedded in unquestioned norms, habits and symbols, in the assumptions underlying institutional rules and the collective consequences of following those rules. (*ibid.*: 41)

And extremely important for our discussion here, we must note that in the feminist conception, women's oppression does not picture a 'war of the sexes', or a conspiracy of males against women.

> The systemic character of oppression implies that an oppressed group need not have a correlate oppressing group. While structural oppression involves relations among groups, these relations do not always fit the paradigm of conscious and intentional oppression of one group by another. (*ibid.*)

---

[3] Those effects are mediated by many other conditions such as other power systems (racism, class hierarchy, legal status, religious discrimination, heteronormativity, etc.), personal circumstances, social settings, legal mechanisms and so forth. Thus there is no pure 'women's experience' as such that can be recognized independently from all these other issues. This does not mean that categories such as 'women' or 'women's experience' are useless or meaningless. It does not mean either that all systems of oppression or 'power over' are equal or have the same capacity to structure people's lives and life spheres (labour, family, education, politics). That is why most radical feminists continue to give priority to patriarchy as a perspective on social power analysis.

It is in this sense that we said before that the acknowledgement that women wear the face veil voluntarily does not close the discussion on the feminist concept of women's oppression; on the contrary, it opens it. Patriarchy is a regime, an ensemble of practices and institutions that subordinate women: that women *act* within patriarchy is constitutive of, not contradictory with, the fact that it is an oppressive structure of relations between the sexes, and that women are the oppressed. Thus the concept of women's oppression does not deny women's agency, it qualifies women's agency. What characterizes patriarchy, then, is not that women have no voice or no agency, but that their voices and their agency are hetero-designated and serialized.

How does all of this relate to a feminist objection to face veils on grounds of women's oppression?

Many feminists feel torn when having to position themselves in the debate on burqa bans. They know that the legislation is merely intended as xenophobic control and power show over Muslim communities, but they feel that most opposition to the legislation is construed as a defence of the veil (even in terms of a fundamental or a human right). So the context creates a 'with me (the veil) or against me' situation that is for (radical) feminists a dilemma; and, alas, not a false dilemma, as Christine Delphy would suggest (2006).[4] And that is because in the arguments rejecting the bans, feminist concerns about women's oppression are systematically downplayed or not even addressed.

A first problem, that we have already seen, is that scholarly literature considers women's oppression only in relation to women forced to wear face veils. When women give their consent, women's oppression could only be sustained (1) if the meaning of the veil were inherently or objectively oppressive, degrading, humiliating and so on, or (2) if we

---

[4] To put it very shortly, for Delphy the dilemma that has drawn feminists to keep quiet is false because since the law is racist, its racism is directed also against Muslim women so there is no alternative between Muslims or women. While this is a true and discerning account of the bans, I think the dilemma is posed by the opposition to the bans: the manner in which it has been deployed mostly as a defence of the veil itself (sometimes in terms of a fundamental right), the overwhelming silence regarding the gendered nature of this practice, the complexities of its meaning and implications regarding women, femininity and sexuality. These dilemmas are not new to feminism, either. They are now known to depend not so much on the shortcomings in feminist analyses and concepts, as on the awkward position of feminist epistemology in patriarchal settings. Catherine MacKinnon has made clearly the point: 'Feminism affirms women's point of view by revealing, criticizing, and explaining its impossibility. This is not a dialectical paradox. It is a methodological expression of women's situation, in which the struggle for consciousness is a struggle for world' (1983: 637; see also n. 5).

accepted that those women are alienated and that we must deny their autonomous choice in order to protect them from themselves (or from their alienated acceptance of their communities' oppressive practices).

These arguments are then quite easily demolished by critics (Edwards 2012; Laborde 2012; Chapter 6 in this volume) and, thus, women's oppression is no longer an issue. Even more, the opposition to the bans might turn swiftly into a fundamental human right to wear face veils, which are simply 'pieces of fabric', aesthetic choices of dress as devoid of meaning as large sunglasses (although paradoxically claiming the highest protection of fundamental and human rights at the same time).

We shall turn our attention to the second issue, women's autonomy, in the next paragraph and treat now the question of the meaning of the veil and its relation to the feminist concept of women's oppression.[5]

Scholarship seems to agree that veils are polysemic. However, on a closer look, polysemy is hardly ever assessed; rather it is simply used to close the discussion on the meaning of (face) veils in relation to women's oppression. Consider, for example, Cécile Laborde's insightful analysis on paternalism: 'In the republican paternalist view, the hijab[6] is not merely a sign of religious piety: it is an obstacle to free thinking and learning' (2012: 400). I think the idea of the hijab as a *mere* sign of piety (or as a *mere* sartorial choice, or as a *mere* mark of political/ethnic belonging) is no less problematic to argue than the veil as a symbol of subjugation. Polysemy is not introduced to draw our attention to the interaction of different social dynamics (and to the role that patriarchy might play in them), but to deny that the veil has anything to do with women's oppression, as if women could 'choose' among its different meanings.

The polysemy of the veil is, nevertheless, central for a feminist discussion on oppression. Two features of the (face) veil polysemy must be noted. First, polysemy is based on the individual reasons (motives) for veiling. Second, it is almost always and almost only discussed around its semantics.

[5] The question of the meaning of the (face) veil has been sometimes addressed as a 'women's dignity' issue. I would rather continue to speak of women's oppression here, because 'dignity' has become a very undetermined and rhetorical concept in legal and political discourses. It is very often used in order to give an objective or undisputable appearance to highly contested issues (such as women's condition in society or sex equality), and thus would serve more the purpose of hiding than of shedding some light over our present discussion.

[6] Although a good part of her arguments on the meaning of veils are made in relation to hijabs, she explicitly maintains that, phenomenologically, there is not such a relevant difference between wearing the hijab and the niqab (Laborde, 2012: 404).

In current scholarship, the (face) veil has many or various meanings because wearers give many (or rather, some differentiated) reasons for donning it. As pointed out in the empirical research chapters in the first part of the volume (see Chapters 2–4 in this volume), there are no wearers that advance duress or coercion as reasons for wearing it (arguably those women would be the most difficult to reach by research interviews), but even reasons that could be prima facie considered within patriarchal submission models (i.e., wearing the niqab because your husband wants you to, feeling protected, etc.), are reinterpreted as expressions of individual, self-conscious, autonomous choice. At the end of the day, oppressive or patriarchal reasons are not acknowledged, the complex system of relations that creates polysemy is neglected, and the (face) veil presented as having changed meaning.

This position is highly problematic from a feminist perspective, partly due to its methodological individualism that obscures the social and group character of oppression structures (including language or symbols), and partly due to its extreme voluntarism, as far as the linguistic dimension of the argument is concerned. The empirical research chapters of this volume highlight this critical feature, when they emphasize the individualistic, single-minded attitude of face-veil wearers ('I say, let me do my thing, this is the Netherlands', Chapter 2, p. 37; see also Chapters 3 and 4). This seems to be a remarkable difference with UK findings (see Chapter 5, pp. 115–60). However, giving names (or meanings) to things is, and has always been, an exercise of power. And thus feminism tends to be very careful about voluntarism in resignification processes, especially in the case of women (or other subordinated groups).

The polysemy of the veil does not amount to arbitrary voluntarism. Within the polysemy there is a system of relations, meanings are articulated; there is a complexity and not simply a choice of meanings at hand for the individual user. Meanings are conventional, conventions express and reflect power relations, and the capacity of the users to alter them is not reducible to individual motivations.

Women's oppression issues regarding the face veil (or any other female dress code, for that matter) question precisely that point. To do so, they have to put into question a second, related, feature of face veil polysemy, that is, the fact that it is generally construed on semantics alone. In fact, most of the empirical research so far is based on what Annelies Moors calls the 'subjective feelings' (Chapter 2) or in the 'insider views' (see Chapter 3). Moving from semantics to syntax and pragmatics would render the voluntarism of the process of resignification of the veil more difficult, and would make the polysemy of the veil fully explicit. The defenders of the argument that the veil is not an oppressive sign because it is polysemic, do not pose the questions about the relations between the veil and other signs (for example male dress codes) or between the veil and other practices and institutions of its context that contribute to its meaning (Amorós 2009: 81ff.).

This problematical understanding of the polysemy of the face veil is tightly linked to an idea of autonomy that recognizes no context, no power structure, no syntax and no pragmatics: an almighty voluntarism based on extreme individualism, which is not only at odds with feminist accounts of women's oppression, but with any kind of critical social thinking.

3. FEMINIST ARGUMENTS AGAINST THE BANS

In this section I shall concentrate on some feminist arguments against face-veil bans. Feminists, and a radical feminism of the kind I have been following throughout this chapter, might (and do) adhere to many other arguments against the bans.[7] For reasons of space I shall concentrate on what might be called very roughly 'specifically' feminist arguments.

In the mobilization against face-veil bans, there are some arguments that are called 'feminist' or, at least, it is claimed that feminists should recognize them as their own. These are mostly anchored to the notions of women's autonomy and of sex discrimination. I think that there are feminist arguments on both, but that those arguments as currently presented in scholarly literature must be critically reconsidered.

The argument on women's autonomy runs as follows: there are women who want to adopt the face veil for many different reasons, it is their choice, and the face veil constitutes an important element of their identity as Muslim women. If those women have chosen those other 'values that are more important to [them]' (Laborde 2012: 402), voluntarily renouncing the Western understanding of sex equality,[8]

---

[7] Just to mention a few: that criminal law should be the last recourse (*ultima ratio*) in democratic societies; that proportionality should be preserved; that criminal law (and, even more, criminal law on its own) cannot change hegemonic social practices and attitudes; that there is nothing to prove that prohibiting face veils will enhance Muslim women's power within their communities, or protect them from gender violence, or hinder patriarchy.

[8] There is a side argument that (Western) feminism should adapt its standards and definition of women's oppression to fit these women's views. Feminist definitions of patriarchy and of women's oppression that label the face veils as signs or symbols of subordination fail to include all women's

their autonomy and freedom of religion should be respected and given priority.

This argument is seriously flawed. First, it presents the principle of sex equality as a subjective right that individual women can trade off or renounce. Sex equality is not a subjective right, it is a constitutional principle from which rights are derived (right not to be discriminated against on grounds of sex, or right to equal pay, or to equality within marriage, etc.). Denying political recognition or legal protection to the voluntary renunciation/rejection of sex equality by these women is not protecting them against themselves, a form of 'illiberal' paternalism (*ibid.*; but whoever said that feminism is liberalism applied to women? MacKinnon (1987: 21)). It protects sex equality against competing visions of relations between the sexes (theories of complementarity, for example) that are put forward by those women's religious practices. Everyone in society (women in particular, as things go) has a legitimate interest in the principle of sex equality being upheld and protected. Whether this should be done by criminalizing those practices is another set of questions.

Second, it presents a context-free conception of these women's autonomy that would be highly criticized in any other discussion. As we have seen in the discussion on the meaning of the veil, this argument does not care about the setting in which these women's autonomy is expressed. Feminist objections to face veils on grounds of women's oppression question precisely the decision-making modalities currently available to Muslim women to autonomously re-signify the face veil. It is up to research to go on to ask questions about the syntax and the pragmatics of face veils (and not only about their semantics).

In the meantime, feminist objections to face-veil bans might be positioned under the heading of 'autonomy' as follows: for the radical feminism I am defending here, social groups are not essences, they are the expression of group relations in society and as such they change and adjust (also, for our case here, through 'cultural interpellation', Amorós 2006: 233). It is therefore in the interaction with other social groups that the elements and practices that define each group, in our

views on the issue, and thus they are biased, ethnocentric, orientalist and so on and so forth. This position fails to understand what feminism is. Feminism is heterogeneous, plural, not always compatible across its different currents. As a matter of fact, the 'feminist' arguments in favour of the veil could be easily attributed to 'choice feminism' and other currents of 'third-wave' feminism. This would also explain most of the disagreement subsisting between those arguments and the feminist position that I have been defending here.

case face veil-wearing Muslim women, are shaped: depending on how these women interact with other social groups their practices might become reinforced, more rigid and dogmatic, or on the contrary more flexible.

Are criminal bans on the veil likely to make the relations that define veiled Muslim women more dogmatic or more flexible?

Let us consider the history of other garments, equally charged with gendered ethical meanings: only fifty years ago women wearing trousers in Spain would be considered indecent, frowned upon. Though there were some dress codes and regulations, female trouser-wearing was not criminalized. Consider now the very different fate of topless sunbathing which has been heavily regulated as indecent exposure. In fact, it is still today charged with symbolic meanings that trousers have lost: practising topless or not practising it is, still today, wrapped up with notions of value assertion, decency, resistance, rebellion and so on.

Personally, I think that it is unlikely that garments as heavily sexualized as the niqab or the burqa can ever be 'ethically deactivated' (Amelia Valcárcel, quoted in Amorós (2009)) and that they might have to be simply dropped, as corsets were. Yet I think it is for Muslim women, and not for criminal legislation, to try.

A second feminist objection to veil bans is based on sex discrimination. Since the veil is a gendered practice, banning it would discriminate against women in the exercise of their rights to freedom of religion or freedom of expression.

Also in this case, from a (radical) feminist point of view, the argument is flawed and would need to be rendered more complex, particularly as far as intersectionality is concerned.

Let us start by saying that the feminist conception of discrimination, and therefore of anti-discrimination law, is not coincidental with currently hegemonic (liberal) conceptions. Equality law, anti-discrimination provisions and the concept of discrimination are meant 'to eradicate not gender differentiation, but gender hierarchy' (MacKinnon 1987: 22). With this background, to try to consider veil bans as discriminatory against women vis-à-vis Muslim men, who do not have to wear sexed dress marks or bear limiting identity signs, is somewhat paradoxical: can we argue that norms should not target practices that subordinate women because they would not affect equally the men in their groups?

These norms are arguably aimed at excluding the visibility of Muslim communities from the public space of European countries (together with other measures, such as bureaucratic hindrance to build mosques, for example). However, in the cases of female dress codes we must be aware of intersectional issues that are absent in the case of sites of worship.

In as much as women are used both in constructing (by Muslim groups) and in contrasting (by Western societies) emerging political groups, they are particularly hit by the legislation and policies used in the 'battle'. But we should bear in mind that we have here an intersection between the 'overburden of identity' (Le Doeuff 1989) carried by these women within the dynamics of their communities in the attempt to preserve or reinvent their traditions (a burden that is not equally shared by men), and the targeting of these particularly visible elements of collective identity by highly symbolic legislation.[9]

The feminist objection to the bans on grounds of discrimination is not based on sex discrimination but on an intersectional account: these bans target a group of women (a particular subset of Muslim women) who would be by law obliged to adopt higher standards of compliance with the principle of sex equality than any other group of women involved in patriarchal or oppressive practices, from top models to battered women who do not make official complaints, from women that marry for money or to secure a social position to fashion victims and surgery addicts, with the only possible exception of prostitutes, who are still criminalized in certain countries but certainly not for not being emancipated enough.

4. CONCLUSIONS

In this chapter, I have tried to argue against current uses of the argument on 'women's oppression' both in European political discourses against the face veils and in the scientific literature opposing their ban. The argument on 'women's oppression', in its feminist meaning, is not about individual women being forced to do something (as wearing a face veil, for example), but on women's conditions in society to determine their life choices. This perspective leads us to assess critically both the notion of polysemy of the veils, which cannot amount to voluntary choice of meaning, as well as complex issues of

---

[9] That the legislation is symbolic, that is, a gesture practically indifferent to the effects of its implementation, does not mean that it is without costs for our democracies, because of the constitutional values and the legal and political culture that it contributes to altering/creating.

autonomy and discrimination. The chapter acknowledges that there are feminist arguments against the face-veil bans based on women's autonomy and on intersectional accounts of sex discrimination, but they are not as straightforward as usually presented and should be deployed in a manner that does not support or reproduce sex oppressive structures.

REFERENCES

Abu-Lughod, Lila (ed.) 1998. *Remaking Women: Feminism and Modernity in the Middle East*. Princeton University Press.

Amorós, Celia 2006. 'Feminismo y multiculturalismo', in Celia Amorós and Ana de Miguel (coords.), *Teoría feminista: de la Ilustración a la globalización*, vol. III, Madrid: Minerva Ediciones, pp. 217–64.

2009. *Vetas de ilustración. Reflexiones sobre feminismo e Islam*. Madrid: Cátedra.

Armstrong, Nancy 1987. *Desire and Domestic Fiction: A Political History of the Novel*. Oxford University Press.

Benelli, Natalie, Hertz, Ellen, Delphy, Christine, Hamel, Christelle, Roux, Patricia, Falquet and Jules 2006. 'De l'affaire du voile à l'imbrication du sexisme et du racisme. Editorial', *Nouvelles Questions Féministes*, 25(1): 4–11.

Casalini, Brunella 2010. 'Immigrazione, Islamofobia e manipolazione politica della questione di genere', *Cosmopolis*, 5(2): 141–56.

Conaghan, Joanne 2009. 'Intersectionality and the Feminist Project in Law', in E. Grabham *et al.* (eds.), *Intersectionality and beyond: Law, Power and the Politics of Location*, Abingdon, Oxon. and New York: Routledge-Cavendish, pp. 21–48.

Crenshaw, Kimberlé 1989. 'Demarginalizing the Intersection of Race and Sex: A Black Feminist Critique of Antidiscrimination Doctrine, Feminist Theory and Antiracist Politics', *University of Chicago Legal Forum*: 139–67.

Delphy, Christine 2006. 'Antisexisme ou antiracisme? Un faux dilemma', *Nouvelles Questions Féministes*, 25(1): 59–83.

Edwards, Susan S. M. 2012. 'For her own good! Criming the niqab', *International Family Law*, 2: 203–8.

Grabham, Emily, Cooper, Davina, Krishnadas, Jane and Herman, Didi (eds.), 2009. *Intersectionality and beyond: Law, Power and the Politics of Location*. Abingdon, Oxon. and New York: Routledge-Cavendish.

Laborde, Cécile 2012. 'State Paternalism and Religious Dress', *International Journal of Constitutional Law*, 10(2): 398–410.

Le Doeuff, Michèle 1989. *L'Etude et le rouet*, translated as *Hipparchia's Choice: An Essay Concerning Women, Philosophy, etc.* Oxford: Blackwell.

McCall, Leslie 2009. 'The Complexity of Intersectionality', in Grabham *et al.* (eds.), pp. 49–76.

MacKinnon, Catherine 1983. 'Feminism, Marxism, Method, and the State: Toward Feminist Jurisprudence', *Signs*, 8(4): 635–58.

1987. *Feminism Unmodified. Discourses on Life and Law.* Cambridge, MA and London: Harvard University Press.

Mancini, Susanna 2012. 'Patriarchy as the Exclusive Domain of the Other: The Veil Controversy, False Projection and Cultural Racism', *International Journal of Constitutional Law*, 10(2): 411–28.

Oliva Portolés, Asunción 2007. 'Hacia una genealogía del pensamiento crítico feminista en Egipto', in Amorós, Celia and Posada, Luisa (eds.), *Feminismo y multiculturalismo*. Madrid: Instituto de la Mujer, pp. 129–46.

Roux, Patricia, Gianettoni, Lavinia and Perrin, Céline 2007. 'L'instrumentalisation du genre: une nouvelle forme de racisme et de sexisme', *Nouvelles Questions Féministes*, 26: 84–105.

Scott, Joan W. 2007. *The Politics of the Veil.* Princeton University Press.

Young, Iris Marion 1990. *Justice and the Politics of Difference.* Princeton University Press.

11

THE RETURN OF A PERSECUTING SOCIETY? CRIMINALIZING FACIAL VEILS IN EUROPE

Maleiha Malik

> *Nor, and this is the crucial point, does it seem that other civilizations evolved to such perfection the essential mechanism which made this continuous growth possible: the construction of a rhetoric of persecution capable of being turned at will from one category of victim to another, including if necessary those invented for the purpose. This is what made the victims of persecution in the west for all practical purposes freely interchangeable with one another, and persecution itself a permanent and omnipresent feature of the social fabric, continuously expanding the range and scope of its activities.* (Moore 1987: 151–2)

Full facial veils have been criminalized by legislatures in France and Belgium as well as being the focus of constitutional challenges: the national constitutional courts in Belgium[1] and France have upheld the criminal ban as valid but the French law will now be challenged in the European Court of Human Rights.[2] A large volume of academic literature is now emerging about this topic (Bowen 2011; Brems *et al.* 2012; Moors 2009; Open Society Foundations 2011; Tourkochoriti 2012). In this chapter, I want to undertake an exploratory discussion of these very contemporary responses within Europe through an analysis of Europe's past. In particular, I examine whether R. I. Moore's

I am grateful to the Centre for European Law, King's College London, for supporting this project through research grants (2011–13). Drafts of this chapter were presented at: the International Seminar on Empirical Face Veil Research, Human Rights Centre, University of Ghent, 9 May 2012; and the Religion and Diaspora Workshop, University of Oxford, 11–12 July 2012. I thank the organizers and all the participants for their invaluable comments.

[1] The Belgian decision is available in Dutch and French at the following reference: Arrêt no. 145/ 2012 du 6 décembre 2012. For a summary and an analysis of the decision in English, see Saila Ouald Chaib, 'Belgian Constitutional Court says Ban on Face Coverings does not violate Human Rights', 14 December 2012, *Strasbourg Observers*, www.strasbourgobservers.com (accessed 1 September 2013).

[2] The *SAS* v. *France* (application no. 43835/11) case against France has been assigned to the Grand Chamber of the European Court of Human Rights: see press release of the European Court of Human Rights of 30/05/2013, ECHR 165 (2013).

conception that there is a European 'model of persecution' (persecution understood in its wider not legal meaning) which he developed through an analysis of European history between the tenth and thirteenth centuries, is useful in understanding the legal regulation of the full facial veil in the contemporary period.

My main argument is that there are aspects of R. I. Moore's concept of Europe as a 'persecuting society' (or a European model of persecution) that help us to understand the contemporary political and legal responses to the full facial veil in the European public sphere. Moreover, framing the analysis in this way may also be useful because it helps us to distinguish between political and legal responses to the full facial veil that are illegitimate persecution from other forms of legal regulation which are more likely to be a legitimate and justifiable response in a liberal democracy. This chapter is an exploratory discussion of this topic rather than a comprehensive legal or social science analysis of the criminalization of the full facial veil that is now documented in the emerging academic literature on the topic.[3]

1. 'A PERSECUTING SOCIETY'

Moore's main argument in *The Formation of a Persecuting Society* was that the period between the tenth and thirteenth centuries in Europe, which saw substantial change in the nature of the state and the legal system, was also a period in which there was a great rise in the persecution of groups such as lepers, heretics and Jews. It is sometimes assumed that these periods of persecution were ad hoc resorts to violence. Moore challenges this assumption by arguing that persecution, during this crucial period, was an essential feature of what he labels the 'first European revolution'. A range of key religious, political and legal changes during this period laid down the foundations for state formation which included the mechanism for the persecution of vulnerable groups who did not fit into the emerging definitions of what it meant to be Western European (Moore 1987: 9–10). This mechanism for persecution was made possible by changes such as the Fourth Lateran Council in November 1215 that not only promulgated a working definition of the recognized and legitimate Christian community, but that also provided the political and legal mechanism for sanctioning those convicted of

---

[3] See n. 2.

heresy. This mechanism, Moore argues, was not just limited to that historical period but had the potential to be adapted and applied to a much wider range of victims. Crucially, this period also saw changes in the nature of the legal system from a segmented to a state-based society. Moore argues that this wide framework provided a European model for persecution within which persecution could be sustained long after it had served its immediate function of offering either a political or a financial advantage. Moreover, this provided a mechanism of rhetoric and persecution of the 'other' that was capable of being turned at will from one category of victim to another (*ibid.*: 151).

Moore's analysis of the European model of persecution differs in important ways from other accounts that assume that persecution was a response to popular anxieties about those who were different in their beliefs or their way of life such as heretics, Jews or homosexuals. Moore distinguishes between the interests of ecclesiastical/political power who put into place the bureaucrats who prosecuted heretics and the general public. By doing so, he is able to challenge the assumption that persecution always had a widespread origin within the antipathy, passion and hatred of the 'general public', although once violence and prejudice did emerge there were large numbers of people who were prepared to join in, often with great savagery (*ibid.*: 111).

Moore's analysis of the formation of European nation states during the crucial period between the tenth and the thirteenth centuries, and the importance of persecution to these political and legal changes, is of general interest but it also provides some important insights into the way in which law can be used as a mechanism for persecution. Moore identifies the way in which law itself has to take on a different function and form in order to meet the new demands for the identification and sanctioning of those who do not fall within the accepted definition of the Christian community. In the emerging political and legal system in which heresy needed to be identified and sanctions, governing authorities (religious or political rulers) had to develop the mechanisms to seek out and punish those who had committed the new offences of heresy, even if no particular individual in the general public had complained of a harm caused to her.

Moore concludes that

> This is precisely the transition which took place in the attitude to heresy in the second half of the twelfth century, from reacting to dramatic and aggressive expressions of anti-clerical sentiment to actively seeking out those who were disseminating heretical beliefs, on the premises that they

must be there to be found, and that any failure on their part to make their whereabouts and activity obvious only confirmed the insidious cunning with which they concealed themselves.

(*ibid.*: 104).

The response of political and legal institutions to the requirement to actively seek out heretics meant that there had to be a shift in the function and form of the legal apparatus: from a reactive function for the state to one in which the state was actively involved in initiating prosecution (*ibid.*: 158). These changes also provided the context in which political and ecclesiastical authority was able to extend its power: it had to develop a more sophisticated system of professional bureaucrats who were their agents to oversee these new prosecutions for heresy; it was able to extend its reach deeper into the private lives of individuals and communities and this process was also an opportunity which, in turn, provided the context for consolidating the power and identity of an increasingly centralized form of political and legal system.

2. LEGAL REGULATION OF THE FACIAL VEIL: BELGIUM AND FRANCE

Full facial veils in the public space have now been criminalized in France and Belgium. They have also been subject to legal regulation in a number of other European states such as Italy, Spain, Denmark and the UK. A number of common themes emerge in the political and legal developments that led to not only the regulation in specific spheres which is a common feature of many jurisdictions but the criminalization of full facial veils through a general ban in the public sphere which is a feature of legislation in countries such as France and Belgium.

One interesting aspect is that in both France and Belgium, the call for a general criminal ban emerged after 'concern' was voiced by some sections of the political class rather than from a widespread social or political movement that was insisting that legislation was an urgent priority. Of course there is general anxiety about Islam, Muslims and the veil among the general populations in both France and Belgium, as demonstrated by the electoral success of far-right political parties such as Front National or Vlaams Belang. Nevertheless, as I argue below, general anxiety and the far right alone could not have secured the criminalization of the full facial veil without the intervention and support of mainstream political elites in France and Belgium. In Denmark, a general criminal ban was resisted by mainstream political forces despite the popularity of the far-right Danish People's Party. In France and Belgium, unlike Denmark, mainstream politicians preferred a very different strategy: they accommodated rather than challenged common anxieties about the full facial veil thereby appeasing rather than challenging the far right.

In France, the criminalization of the full facial veil came into effect on 11 April 2011. The legislation has its immediate origin in the political intervention of André Gerin, a Communist Party deputy from Vénissieux, who voiced concern about full facial veils after a high-profile legal decision and subsequent discussions in the French media to deny French citizenship to a woman (Faiza M.) because her choice to wear a full facial veil was indicative of her failure to adopt the Republican value of gender equality (Bowen 2011). Gerin's political initiative led to the establishment of the cross-party Parliamentary Commission to Study the Wearing of the Full Facial Veil in France. The Parliamentary Commission heard from a wide range of people (approximately 211 testimonies) including feminists, human rights activists, politicians, secularists, academics, journalists and Muslim organizations. Gerin, the Commission's President, stated 'to perfect our judgement, we absolutely wanted to listen to at least one woman who wears the full facial veil'. Only one French Muslim woman, Kenza Drider, was heard by the Commission after she agreed to the Parliamentary Commission's condition that she give evidence without wearing a full facial veil.[4]

In Belgium, despite a serious political crisis in which there was no federal government in Belgium for nearly eighteen months between June 2010 and December 2011, the politicians chose to focus on the criminalization of the full facial veil as a matter of the most urgent priority. The legislative proposal to prohibit clothing that covers the face, or a large part of it, entered into force in July 2011, making Belgium the second European country to criminalize the full facial veil. No Muslim women who wore the full facial veil were consulted. No human rights bodies, NGOs or other organizations were invited to submit evidence. Most significantly, unlike France, the Belgium Conseil d'Etat was not invited to give its opinion about the compatibility of the legislation with fundamental freedoms despite the conclusions of a

---

[4] See analysis by Stuart Weir, 'We must let Muslim women who wear the veil speak for themselves', *Open Democracy*, 12 April 2011.

range of leading human rights experts (Amnesty International, Human Rights Watch and the Commissioner for Human Rights of the Council of Europe).[5]

Before moving on to an analysis of general criminal bans against the veil, it is worth noting the example of Denmark as a contrast to France and Belgian. It is an example of a European state that has a popular far-right anti-Islam party (the Danish People's Party), which was a part of the ruling coalition before 2011. There was also considerable popular pressure, especially since the politicizing of Islam and Muslims since the Danish cartoons controversy, to regulate Muslim religious practices, especially highly visible practices such as the facial veil. In Denmark, the Conservative Party announced in 2009 that it would 'work for a ban against burqas'. Unlike countries such as France or Belgium, the issue was transferred to the Ministry of the Interior that, in turn, asked the University of Copenhagen to investigate and report on the fact relating to the use of the burqa in Denmark. The use of the burqa was a minority practice among Danish Muslim women. Despite a very public and heated debate, the Danish government announced that rather than a general blanket ban using the criminal law, they would use two modifications to address the issue: first, sentence enhancement against those individuals who coerced a woman to wear a full facial veil; and, second, provisions to regulate the wearing of the full facial veil by witnesses in court proceedings (see Chapter 3 in this volume).

3. CREATING FALSE KNOWLEDGE ABOUT MUSLIM WOMEN: THE COMPLICITY OF POLITICAL ELITES

> For all those who were to be persecuted, we have seen, it was necessary first to create an identity.
>
> (Moore 1987: 143)

How does the contemporary use of the criminal law to ban the full facial veil echo the tropes of an earlier persecuting society? One key recurring trope is the role of the political elite who are involved in creating and

---

[5] Emmanuel Bribosia and Isabelle Rorive, 'Illegal coverings and legal discourse: the case of Belgium', paper presented to Seminar on Illegal Covering in Europe, Onati, May 2012, copy on file with the author.

sustaining false knowledge about the victims. Moore's analysis of the rhetoric of persecution breaks down the term 'popular' and separates the actions, responsibilities and interest of different groups in society. Moore also helps us to understand that the production of knowledge (or rather false knowledge) about the victims of persecution, as well as the destruction of their actual identity, was a crucial feature of Moore's European model of persecution (*ibid.*: 140–3).

These insights are useful in an analysis of the contemporary representation of Muslim women who wear the full facial veil because it allows a differentiation between popular anxieties (the discomfort of those who live side by side with Muslim women who wear the full facial veil) from the representations that are created by powerful elites and the political class such as politicians and the media. This distinction is important because it allows us to note that political elites have been the major originators of the rhetoric of persecution against Muslim women who wear the facial veil, even if popular far-right movements have been the main actors in the political mobilizing on this topic and against Muslims in Western Europe.

Post 9/11 and 7/7 discussions of Islam and Muslims in Europe have led to a rapid process of racialization that represents Muslim religious practice as pathological and barbaric (Malik 2008). The resulting cultural racism has hardened into an anti-Islam ideology that has now been adopted by far-right political parties throughout Europe (although in the UK this politics is limited to street movements such as English Defence League rather than political parties). This emerging anti-Islam far-right politics now covers a vast expanse throughout the European Union: from the Danish People's party and Geert Wilders's Freedom Party that were until recently part of the ruling coalition government; through to the Front National in France that has recently polled over 17 per cent in the presidential elections; including the Austrian Freedom Party (FPO) who obtained over 20 per cent of the vote in the last election which was described as the biggest slap in the face for centrist parties since the Second World War.

Anti-Islam ideology includes the alleged fight against the Islamization of Europe thereby preventing the nightmare of Eurabia (a political neologism which is also the title of a book by Bat Y'Eor) or Londonistan (which in its UK version is published by the *Daily Mail* journalist Melanie Phillips). All European far-right parties have adopted some form of anti-Islam ideology, whose central configuration includes the following. It proposes that Muslims (an economically deprived, politically disorganized, territorially dispersed minority) will seize power from white Europeans (who control all the political institutions and own most of the wealth). How? Some suggest through immigration or revolution. Or, a common obsession is demographic change that Muslims will 'outbreed' whites culminating in the Islamization of Europe because, we are told, every Muslim baby is potentially a 'genetic carrier' of radical Islam. Multiculturalism is blamed: it has emboldened Muslims to make aggressive claims for equality; at the same time it has weakened white liberals who refuse to defend the Enlightenment. Muslims will, it is feared, take over Europe: establishing Islamic law (shariah) that will be forced on all Europeans forced to live as oppressed minorities (dhimmis) in an authoritarian Islamic state (caliphate).[6]

It is true that the far-right political parties, as well as racist movements, have taken a lead in the development of this anti-Islam ideology. Yet, it would be wrong to assume that the creation of this nascent ideology has its sole origin in the populous. A key insight of R. I. Moore's analysis of a European model of persecution is that although the populous did become involved in the mechanics of persecution they were not the originators of the rhetoric of persecution. Moore argues that those who had power (he specifically identifies the literati) were actively involved in creating the false representations about Jews, heretics and lepers that led to the persecution of these groups. More recently, Pnina Webner's analysis also suggests the complicity of 'intellectual elites' in the production of contemporary anti-Muslim racism. Webner has argued that a crucial feature of racism against Muslims is the use of anti-fundamentalist images that provide racists with a legitimizing discourse against Muslims that are used by intellectual elites as well as 'real' violent racists (Webner 2005).

It is also a significant feature of public debates about the face veil that, although ordinary people have anxieties, they have been 'led' by members of the political elite. In the UK, Jack Straw's comments about the face veil led to a heated debate among the media class about Islam and Muslim women, although this public debate did not translate into a political mobilization to prohibit the face veil as it did in other European states. In the Netherlands, Annelies Moors concludes that

> Except for the 2003 case, [which concerned a school's refusal to allow three Dutch girls to attend school with face veils] the other media hypes

---

[6] See M. Malik review of Martha Nussbaum in *Times Higher Education Supplement*, 26 April 2012.

have been due to the effects of statements made and actions taken by politicians, who have at the very least amplified (if not produced) feelings of anxiety and 'being under threat'. Even if tapping into existing feelings of uncertainty and unease, they have directed such sentiments towards a highly specific target, that of face veiling women.

(Moors 2009; see also Chapter 2 in this volume)

In Belgium and France, the two European countries where the wearing of a face veil in public has been criminalized, the creation of false knowledge about Muslim women who wear the facial veil has been a process that has involved not only populist far-right movements (such as the Front National or Vlaams Belang) but also 'intellectual' political elites.

In Belgium, the federal Parliament passed a 'Law prohibiting the wearing of any clothing totally, or principally, hiding the face' (also known as the anti-Burqa Act) almost unanimously. All the representatives of all the mainstream political parties voted to pass the law, except three MPs linked to the Green Party who abstained and Eva Brems (a professor of human rights law at Ghent University and a Flemish Green Party MP) who was the only politician to vote against.

In France, although there was some popular anxiety about the facial veil, including political activity by far-right groups, the issue was introduced into the national public debate after a legal case in 2008 in which the French Conseil d'Etat (the French State Council) refused to grant French citizenship to a Muslim woman (Faiza M.) who wore the facial veil. Faiza M., who was married to a French convert to Islam and had three children, had met all the requirements to be granted French citizenship. Her testimony confirmed that she spoke fluent French, she was voluntarily willing to confirm her acceptance of French values, and that although she wore the facial veil she was fully involved in the domestic management of her house and her family. Faiza M. met all the formal requirements to be granted French citizenship. In normal circumstances the French administrative court would have granted her application. However, since 2003 the French government had the right to intervene in naturalization proceedings to raise non-legal objections. In the case of Faiza M., the Minister for the Interior, Eric Besson, intervened by citing Faiza M.'s failure to assimilate as a reason to deny her citizenship. In their analysis, the State Council agreed with the line of argument that Faiza M. should not be granted citizenship because she had failed to assimilate. As Bowen notes, the main justification for their finding that she suffered from an assimilation deficit was her adoption of the facial veil (rather than her conduct or treatment of others) that was taken to be a sign of her radical practice.

The Faiza M. decision was not just a legal source, it was the outcome of an intervention of Eric Besson, a mainstream politician, which deliberately shifted the terms of the debate. After the decision, there was significant coverage of the issue of the facial veil in the French media. This, in turn, had an effect on the perception and treatment of French women who wore the facial veil. In July 2008, a housing authority in Vénnisieux, Lyon (which has a large Muslim population) refused to allow a family to rent a house because the wife wore a facial veil (Bowen 2011: 335). This incident was reported in Le Monde in 2009. Following these public debates, André Gerin (a French Communist MP) who was former mayor of Vénnisieux raised the issue of the facial veil in April 2009. Nicolas Sarkozy set up a Commission led by André Gerin (despite the fact that he had already made his views clear). Sarkozy also prejudged the issue by speaking out against the facial veil in the French Assembly before the Gerin Commission had reported.

Political elites have mobilized feminism and gender equality as key justifications in creating this rhetoric of persecution. Yet they have done very little to give voice to Muslim women themselves. The Gerin Commission heard from a range of representatives including liberals and feminists and only one Muslim woman (Kenza Drider) who was told to remove her facial veil while giving evidence before the Gerin Commission. The Belgian and French case studies confirm that adult Muslim women choose to wear the full facial veil, yet in many situations feminists involved in public debates or parliamentary processes have questioned the actual choices of adult Muslim women.

In the past, as Moore notes, those who were persecuted included lepers, who were represented as a pollution in the wider political community. Similarly, in the public debates about the full facial veil in France, in her evidence to the Gerin Commission, the prominent French feminist Elisabeth Badinter uses similar images of pollution, sickness and mental illness to explain the fact that adult French women freely chose the veil. Badinter states:

> So when I hear women explaining that the full veil makes them feel good and protected – but protected from what? – I believe that what they say is true, but I think these women are very sick and I do not think we may have to determine ourselves according to their pathology.
>
> (cited in Mancini 2012: 420–1)

Of course, the creation of this false knowledge about Muslim women who wear the full facial veil also required organized political power to translate this rhetoric of French elites into criminal law statute. Within this political process, the presence of far-right political parties provided the motivation for the mainstream politicians (such as Sarkozy) to adopt the rhetoric of the far right (Marine Le Pen's Front National) in order to secure electoral support. Nevertheless, the assumption that the criminalization of the facial veil is an outcome of far-right populism ignores the complicity of political elites in this process. Belgium and French criminal law bans were an outcome of the intervention of political elites (mainstream politicians, media commentators, feminist activists) rather than a response to a popular sentiment that was rising against the facial veil.

Political elites were responsible for creating knowledge about Muslim women who wear the full facial veil. This 'false rhetoric', as Moore calls it, relied on 'democratic' political processes such as the Gerin Commission. This process of creating false knowledge about Muslim women who wear the full facial veil, and denying them a direct political voice in the lawmaking process, was crucial because it allowed political elites to assert that they already knew about the meaning of the facial veil. Having created a false identity for Muslim women who wore the facial veil they were confronted with the problem of what to do when these women spoke out about their actual choices and desires. In Moore's terms, having created a false identity they had to destroy (or at the very least deny) the real identities for Muslim women who wore the facial veil. The mechanism to achieve this destruction was the assumption that Muslim women who wear the facial veil suffer from an 'autonomy deficit'.

4. DENYING MUSLIM WOMEN'S IDENTITY: THE AUTONOMY DEFICIT

In the last decade since 9/11, during the period of the creation of the narrative about Muslim women who wear the veil as oppressed (or paradoxically an aggressive threat to the nation), there was emerging public evidence about the actual choices and desires of Muslim women themselves. It is, indeed, a remarkable feature of legal cases during this period that so many European Muslim women litigated their claims to wear the veil in some of the highest European constitutional courts:

Ferishta Ludin in the German Constitutional Court; Ms. Dahlab (a Swiss convert to Islam) and Leyla Şahin (a young Turkish medical student) in the European Court of Human Rights and Shabina Begum in the UK House of Lords (now the UK Supreme Court). Rather than silent and oppressed, these women's litigating to defend their constitutional and human rights confirms a high degree of intelligence and political courage (Evans 2006: 52).

Some of the legal decisions themselves challenged the use of a reductionist analysis that constructs the headscarf as a symbol of gender inequality or as a symbol of aggressive Islam while ignoring the actual desires of Muslim women. In *Ludin*, the German Constitutional Court refused to automatically categorize the headscarf as a practice of gender inequality.[7] This analysis of headscarves that avoids treating it as a symbol of gender inequality is also strongly endorsed in the dissenting judgment of Judge Tulkens in *Leyla Şahin* where she states:

> As the German Constitutional Court noted in its judgment of 24 September 2004 (the *Ludin* case), wearing the headscarf has no single meaning; it is a practice that is engaged in for a variety of reasons. It does not necessarily symbolise the submission of women to men and there are those who maintain that, in certain cases, it can even be a means of emancipation of women. What is lacking in this debate is the opinion of women, both those who wear the headscarf and those who choose not to.[8]

Judge Tulkens also confirms that what is needed is an analysis of gender that takes up the subjective point of view of the women themselves:

> It is not the Court's role to make an appraisal of this type – in this instance a unilateral and negative one – of a religion or religious practice, just as it is not its role to determine in a general and abstract way the signification of wearing the headscarf or to impose its viewpoint on the applicant. The applicant, a young adult university student, said – and there is nothing to suggest that she is not telling the truth – that she wore the headscarf of her own free will. In this connection, I fail to see how the principle of sexual equality can justify prohibiting a woman from following a practice which, in the absence of proof to the contrary, she

---

[7] *Ludin* BverfG, 2 BvR 1436/02 (24 September 2004; decision of the German Federal Constitutional Court). For a detailed discussion of the *Ludin* case (both the decisions of the Federal Administrative Court and the Federal Constitutional Court), see Mahlmann (2003: 1099).

[8] All references to Judge Tulkens from *Leyla Şahin v. Turkey*, European Court of Human Rights, Decision of 10 November 2005, application no. 44774/98 (§12ff.).

must be taken to have freely adopted. Equality and non-discrimination are subjective rights which must remain under the control of those who are entitled to benefit from them. 'Paternalism' of this sort runs counter to the case-law of the Court.

In the UK House of Lords, in the *Shabina Begum* case (which concerned the right of a British Muslim schoolgirl to wear a long robe to her school) although there was some evidence of involvement of men in advancing the legal case, there was clear evidence that she made her own choice to adopt the religious robe (jilbab). Baroness Hale in *Shabina Begum* in the House of Lords also emphasizes the need for legal analysis to take the views of women who wear the headscarf seriously. At the domestic level, the comments of Baroness Hale in the *Shabina Begum* case endorse a more complex analysis of the headscarf as a matter of individual choice.[9]

Judge Tulkens and Baroness Hale's analysis in these passages pays close attention to the actual voices of Muslim women and it is recognizes that many European Muslim women adopt the headscarf or full facial veil as a matter of individual choice. The case studies in this volume, based on interviews with the French and Belgian women who wear a full facial veil, confirm the analysis of judges such as Tulkens and Hale that these religious practices are not, as assumed by liberals, forced on Muslim women. As the Belgian case study demonstrates, no serious effort has been made to listen to the voices of the Belgian Muslim women who have adopted the full facial veil. The main driver and motivation to start wearing the face veil appears to be religious devotion and piety, with the large majority of women treating it as a voluntary commitment to a higher level of Islamic practice. It is worth noting that three women adopted the facial veil because of their relationships with their present and future husbands. However, although the evidence suggests that there was a desire to 'please their husbands' or preserve their relationship, there is no evidence of coercion by the men on the women. The French case study is very similar in confirming that adult French Muslim women are autonomously choosing to wear the full facial veil. (See Chapter 5, this volume).

Of course, reliance on individual choice is not the end of the story. A feminist or gendered analysis needs to take into account the full context within which these Muslim women choose to adopt the full facial veil. For example, it is important to ask questions about

---

[9] *R v. Headteacher and Governors of Denbigh High School* (*ex parte* Shabina Begum [2006] UKHL 15, §§93–6.

power and authority: who is defining what constitutes the Islamic tradition? How much power do women have to construct and interpret religious sources and norms? Why is the full facial veil presented as the main exceptional pious practice for those Muslim women who want to attain greater proximity to God? Despite these legitimate questions about the gendered aspects of the full facial veil, none of the evidence from the interviews with the Belgian and French Muslim women who adopt the veil justifies the popular representation of them as non-autonomous individuals who are being 'forced to adopt a barbaric practice' as suggested in the public debates preceding criminalization.

Yet, the evidence that Muslim women are choosing to adopt the face veil has had little impact on the drive towards criminalization in Belgium and France.

John Bowen has noted that the French criminalization of the facial veil assumes that the Muslim women who choose to wear it suffer from an autonomy deficit (2011: 343). Attributions of false consciousness to adult Muslim women, verging on illiberal paternalism, is a common recurring argument of feminists such as Elisabeth Badinter who argues that these women are 'sick and I do not think we may have to determine ourselves according to their pathology'.[10] These arguments are also permeating legal analysis. As Bowen notes, the legal decisions of the French Constitutional Council that preceded the French criminal law ban on the face veil included the line of argument that French citizens should be autonomous in private as well as public and, moreover, that some religious practices such as the facial veil weaken this condition for autonomous citizenship. Bowen summarized this attitude towards the women who wear the facial veil, as 'Her clothes were a sign of a basic personal flaw, one that comes from holding the wrong religious views' (*ibid.*: 337).

5. PERSECUTING MUSLIM WOMEN

Moore's analysis of the emergence of a mechanism of persecution is of particular importance in considering state responses to the facial veil, especially the use of the criminal law as the preferred form of regulation. Denmark provides an interesting example of how to address concerns about the full facial veil without falling into patterns of persecution such

---

[10] Quoted and translated in Mancini (2012) (copy on file with the author).

as a general criminal ban. Belgium and France are a contemporary example of 'the return of a persecuting society'.

Moore notes that a range of key religious, political and legal changes during this period laid down the foundations for state formation which included the mechanism for the persecution of vulnerable groups who did not fit into the emerging definitions of what it meant to be Western European (1987: 9–10). This mechanism, Moore argues, was not just limited to that historical period but had the potential to be adapted and applied to a much wider range of victims. Crucially, this period also saw changes in the nature of the legal system from a segmented to a state-based society. Moore identifies the way in which law itself has to take on a different function and form in order to meet the new demands for the identification and sanctioning of those who do not fall within the accepted definition of the Christian community. In segmented societies, a crime is defined and identified when there is an individual victim who complains of a harm that has been caused by another. In the emerging political and legal system in which heresy needed to be identified and sanctions, those in political authority (religious or political rulers) had to develop the mechanisms to seek out and punish those who had committed the new offences of heresy, even if no particular individual in the general public had complained of a harm caused to her.

As Moore observes, the changes that took place that required the prosecution of heresy also required material changes in the nature of state power and law. Although not usually termed as a heresy, the adoption of the face veil, and the response to it in Belgium and France, displays many of these features and it also requires a shift in the mechanism of legal regulation. The criminalization of the facial veil in France and Belgium is no longer about using the criminal law to fulfil its classic liberal function of preventing harm or even about safeguarding gender equality. Rather, as Nadia Fadil argues (see Chapter 12 in this volume) these criminal bans are more like the use of coercive power used for the purpose of preserving majoritarian values and creating properly 'acceptable' subjects who are French Belgian citizens rather than preventing harm to others. The use of criminal law and sanctions also raises questions about the instrumental use (or misuse) of gender equality in justifying the criminalization of the full facial veil. The comparison with Denmark is illuminating. This does not mean that gender equality is always irrelevant or that it may not justify some legal regulation. For example, the Danish rejected a general criminal ban on the full facial veil but they did take gender equality seriously by increasing criminal sanctions against those men who coerce women into wearing a full facial veil.

Moore notes that a persecuting society also developed greater legal powers to initiate inquisitions and to investigate the most private aspects of the life and thoughts of individuals who were 'suspect'. This expansion of the power of the state, as well as the breach of the private and public distinction, is clear in the criminalization of the facial veil that extends a general ban on clothing beyond discrete areas such as schools and employment to all appearances in the public sphere. Such a ban breaches the most fundamental principles of liberal constitutionalism by eroding a range of individual freedoms: not only the right to freedom of religion but also the right to privacy, the right to freedom of speech, the right to freedom of association. As the applicant in *SAS* v. *France* argues in the application to the Grand Chamber of the European Court of Human Rights, these criminal bans are an attack on the core principles of civil and political rights, as well as the right to democratic participation of citizens in a democracy.

In the Faiza M. decision[11] (2008) the Conseil d'Etat used the intimate details of her medical records to discern her public values. This has been a feature of (illiberal) immigration laws for some time. It is significant that the route into this regression of the liberal rule of law was the discretion given to politicians to intervene in citizenship cases for non-legal reasons. What is new and significant, however, is that this form of legal reasoning has wider influence and it is now applied not just to migrants but also to all French Muslims. This values-based reasoning constructs certain religious practices as 'radical' and incompatible with French citizenship. French Muslims who are born in France, speak French as their only language, have jobs, pay taxes and participate fully in mainstream politics may still suffer from a deficit of French values if they adhere to a religious practice that is deemed to be radical. Jean-Marie Le Pen adopted the rhetoric of a 'clash of civilizations' with Islam when the Front National decided to focus its political mobilization on the defence of French Enlightenment values against Muslims (Betz and Meret 2010). The Faiza M. decision and the criminalization of the facial veil suggest that this far-right reasoning is now being mainstreamed into French constitutional law and legal reasoning. As John Bowen notes, the adoption of this line of reasoning by mainstream politicians as well as the highest French courts (the Constitutional

---

[11] Conseil d'Etat, 27 June 2008, no.: 286798.

Council and Council of State) is not just based on the idea that French institutions can coerce Muslims who cause harm to others but it seems to accept a permanent clash of values between French values, Islam and French Muslims.

Bowen concludes:

> The French case suggests a slow appropriation of a set of assumptions associated with 'clash of civilizations' claims, assumptions increasingly shared by public figures in a number of Western European countries. These changes form part of the rise of a new kind of 'nationalist–populist' rhetoric, the new form of National Front self-presentation, and similar developments in the Netherlands, Belgium and Germany. These movements increasingly make Muslim bodily citizenship the problem for which a return to 'shared values' is the answer. Worryingly, they are now being espoused by French high judges, and not only Marine Le Pen. (2011: 345).

The use of the criminal law as the preferred form of legal regulation has obscured the need, or in the most extreme situations made it impossible, to initiate wider dialogue about the facial veil. This dilemma is accurately summarized by Ralph Grillo and Prakash Shah who conclude that the current approaches impose a single normative meaning and solution to the issue of the face veil, thereby 'stifling or impeding what might otherwise be a "natural" conversational and dialogical development among Muslims, and with non-Muslims, about the significance of the face veil' (2012).

Such dialogical conversation, especially with and involving the Muslim women who wear the face veil, is vital to raise more critical questions about the consequences of the face veil for women's autonomy. These Muslim women object to the fact that they have not been invited to participate in these debates. One Belgium woman objected that 'They have not asked for our advice ... they have not asked our opinion, they have not asked the proposals we could make on this, they have forbidden us'. The case studies from Belgium and France confirm that these Muslim women are not only fully capable, but they are in fact eager to participate in such a dialogue, as well as fully participate in democratic processes.

6. CONCLUDING COMMENTS

The French and Belgian criminal bans on face veils in public did not ask Muslim women to give their viewpoint or participate in the creation of the laws that would have such a dramatic impact on their personal freedom. As the Belgian case study concludes, the hasty adoption of the ban, without any effort to enter into contact with the women concerned, is experienced as a breach of democratic principles. Perhaps, however, the paradigm of assuming that political elites want to include Muslim women who wear the full facial veil within democratic processes is itself flawed. If the contemporary criminalization of the facial veil is an example of the return of a persecuting society, then it would be surprising if the victims of persecution were given a voice. Before we can move towards a more reasonable discussion about the face veil in Europe we may need to identify the ways in which the European model of persecution has survived twentieth-century constitutional liberalism and the guarantee of individual human rights. In fact, the use (or misuse) of arguments about autonomy and gender equality in the justification of the criminalization of the face veil suggest we may have to confront the more worrying fact that the European model of persecution has efficiently evolved to the point where it has subsumed Enlightenment values such as autonomy and gender equality into its mechanism for identifying and persecuting new victims, such as Muslim women.

In European debates, the face veil is frequently presented as a medieval practice. It would be a supreme irony if the contemporary twenty-first-century response of European states such as France and Belgium to the face veil shared some similar features to Europe's history between the tenth and thirteenth centuries when, according to R. I. Moore, Europe became, and has since remained, a persecuting society.

REFERENCES

Betz, H. G. and Meret, S. 2010. 'The Political Mobilisation against Muslims in Western Europe', in M. Malik (ed.), *Anti-Muslim Prejudice in the West – Past and Present*. Abingdon, Oxon.: Routledge.
Bowen, J. R. 2011. 'How the French State Justifies Controlling Muslim Bodies: From Harm-Based to Values-Based Reasoning', *Social Research*, 78(2): 325–48.
Brems, E., Janssens, Y., Lecoyer, K., Ouald Chaib, S. and Vandersteen, V. 2012. *Wearing the Face Veil in Belgium: Views and Experiences of 27 Women Living in Belgium concerning the Islamic Full Facial Veil and the Belgian Ban on Face Covering*, Report of the Human Rights Centre, Ghent University.

Evans, Carolyn 2006. 'The "Islamic Scarf" in the European Court of Human Rights', *Melbourne Journal of International Law*, 7(1): 52–74.

Grillo R. and Shah, P. 2012. *Reasons to Ban? The Anti-Burqa Movement in Western Europe*, MMG Working Paper 12-05 (Germany: Max Planck Institute for the Study of Religious and Ethnic Diversity).

Mahlmann, Matthias 2003. 'Religious Tolerance, Pluralist Society and the Neutrality of the State: The Federal Constitutional Court's Decision in the Headscarf Case, *German Law Journal*, 11(4): 1099–1116.

Malik, M. 2008. *Anti-Muslim Prejudice in the West – Past and Present*. Abingdon, Oxon.: Routledge.

Mancini, Suzanna 2012. 'Patriarchy as the Exclusive Domain of the Other: The Veil Controversy, False Projection and Cultural Racism', *I-CON*, 10: 411–28.

Moore, J. R. 1987. *The Formation of a Persecuting Society*. Oxford and New York: Blackwell.

Moors, A. L. 2009. 'The Dutch and the Face Veil: The Politics of Discomfort', *Social Anthropology*, 17(4): 393–408.

Open Society Foundations 2011. *Unveiling the Truth: Why 32 Muslim Women Wear the Full-face Veil in France* (*Report of At Home in Europe project of the Open Society Foundations*), New York.

Tourkochoriti, Ionna 2012. 'The Burka Ban: Divergent Approaches to Freedom of Religion in France and in the USA', *William and Mary Bill of Rights Journal*, 20(79): 791–852.

Webner, Pnina 2005. 'Islamophobia: Incitement to Racial Hatred – Legislating for a New Fear?' *Anthropology Today*, 21(5): 6.

12

ASSERTING STATE SOVEREIGNTY: THE FACE-VEIL BAN IN BELGIUM

Nadia Fadil

How can we understand the fact that a small number of face-veiled women in a country like Belgium, have provoked in a very short amount of time a strong moral consensus which has resulted in the almost unanimous vote of a law that banned public covering of faces in the spring of 2011? This has been the central interrogation of some recent analyses that have sought to unravel the affective layer that the question of the face veil triggers (Moors 2009, 2009). Minorities hold a significant status in the political imaginary of liberal nation states. Whereas the protection of cultural and religious minorities is traditionally considered as one of the cornerstones of such democratic societies, several recent critical contributions have nuanced this perspective by showing how liberal states do not simply defend but rather produce and regulate the political subjectivity of those minorities – this as part and parcel of a process of maintaining and sustaining a cultural and political hegemony within the nation. The affective discourse that undergirds parts of these regulatory processes is, consequently, understood as an anxiety over the potential loss of hegemony in defining the contours of the nation state.[1]

A previous version of this chapter was presented at the Blankensee Colloqium workshop Understanding the Muslim Question: Towards a Genealogy of Multiculturalism and the Minority Question in Western Europe, organized by the Freie Universität Berlin and the KU Leuven in June 2013. I would like to extend my gratitude to all participants of that workshop and to Jogchum Vrielink, Saila Oulad Chaïb, Salman Sayyid, Charles Hirschkind, Eva Brems and Maleiha Malik for their critical feedback and constructive comments.

[1] See in this respect the short, yet well-known essay *Fear of Small Numbers* (2006) by Arjun Appadurai, who tries to grasp the reasons behind the disproportional fears and violence majorities often display towards minorities. Similarly, in her essay 'State of Shame' (1998), the

The practice of face veiling is an illustration of such a minority practice that provokes such anxieties. Even more than their headscarved equivalents, face-veiled women seem to trigger a visceral reaction and to touch upon a sense of 'human dignity' that is seen to be under threat. One of the often-heard arguments on face veiling is that the latter represents a symbol of women's oppression as it forces women into seclusion and encourages a total segregation between the genders in the public sphere. This runs against the various studies on this question, among which those collected in this volume, which have shown that face veiling is understood by many of its wearers as an expression of a deep spiritual commitment which is individually chosen, often against the will of their direct environment. Yet such empirical findings seem to have little effect in the debate surrounding the face veil. The deepness of the visceral reaction on this sartorial practice is striking, and the rapidity with which a legal ban was defended and introduced in a few European countries significant. Belgium represents, together with France, one of the first European countries to have adopted such a national ban on face veiling in spring 2011. The law came right after a communitarian institutional crisis which paralyzed political life at a federal level for more than a year and created large divisions between the francophone and the Flemish political elite. It is therefore striking that the question of face veiling represented one of the first matters that was adopted by the newly elected federal chamber with a very large consensus.

This chapter is an attempt to think through the large unanimity that surrounds this question of face veiling, as well as the 'sense of urgency' that propelled the Belgian legislators to push for a nationwide ban in 2011. In so doing, it is equally an attempt to think through the various reasons why voices like those collected in this volume cannot be heard in the public debate on 'face veiling' (Spivak 1988). One of the striking observations that has been raised by the different authors of the studies in this volume is the clear contradiction that exists between the motivations put forward by face-veiled women and what Brems et al. have described as the 'outsider's society' (see Chapter 4 in this volume). While the different chapters show that Muslim women predominantly made a conscious choice to wear the face veil for religious reasons, the societal discourse surrounding these practices persistently insists on their

anthropologist Elizabeth Povinelli also seeks to account for the moral anxiety that is unleashed by cultural practices that are considered as abject from a liberal standpoint, such as female genital mutilation. She takes the large media uproar that surrounds these practices as a signpost of an anxiety over a loss of a cultural hegemony.

oppression – which also figured as one of the reasons to outlaw this practice in Belgium. In what follows, I will argue that in order to understand this decision to outlaw face veiling, it is not sufficient to only relate it with a widely shared desire to 'liberate' face-veiled women from their 'religious oppression'. Rather, I will argue that through the question of face veiling a number of concerns come to be addressed about the nation, the assertion of state sovereignty through the law and the regulation of the forms of life that can be 'tolerated' or 'allowed' within the political community (and which is ultimately the state's ultimate competence). In order to substantiate this claim, I will pause at two moments in this conflict. The first one concerns the parliamentary debates that took place in April 2010 and 2011. The second episode is the decision by the Constitutional Court in December 2012 to uphold the law. Both cases show how face veiling crystallizes a concern with the law, the operation of the law and the sovereignty of the nation that comes to be expressed through the capacity to consider and define who can be considered as a 'legal subject'.

1. RESTORING NATIONAL PRIDE

When examining the parliamentary discussions, one in 2010 and the other in 2011, as well as the judgment by the Constitutional Court in December 2012, one is immediately struck by the overwhelming consensus that is displayed between the MPs on the need to legislate. These different positions are structured (as has also been shown in Chapter 4 in this volume) a concern over: (1) women's oppression; (2) the 'vivre-ensemble' and how face veiling impedes upon the latter; and (3) the security threat that the face veil poses to the surrounding environment. The legal value of the different arguments offered by the MPs and the Constitutional Court has been amply discussed, and criticized, across several contributions (Brems et al. 2013). My interest, in examining these debates, therefore lies not so much in understanding their substantive value, but rather in accounting for the 'sense of urgency' that seems to speak out from several contributions in these parliamentary debates and the deeply held conviction that a national law was needed to regulate such very minor practices. One of the central triggers behind the enactment of a federal law was indeed a widely shared sentiment that certain practices, such as the face veil, were escaping governmental control. This sentiment became especially reinforced after the Police Court of Etterbeek in January 2011 decided to annul an administrative fine that had been given to a face-veiled woman, arguing that there was no strong legal ground to do so.[2] The different local bans were considered to be legally too weak, the absence of a coherent regulation throughout the national territory was seen to provoke confusion and a strong national legislation was therefore needed to create a certain degree of order. A national law that would prohibit face veiling was therefore considered urgent for it would not only (1) put clear limits on the type of sartorial practices that can be displayed in the public sphere but it would also (2) establish a degree of legal consistency within the national borders. This concern with legal congruity is very explicit in the argumentation offered by Catherine Fonck, MP for the francophone Christian Democratic Party (CdH) in the parliamentary debate of April 2011:

> At this moment, very different rules and regulations are being applied in small geographical zones. In the light of such a fundamental proposition, such a situation is untenable. It is for instance prohibited to wear an all-covering veil in Brussels, while nothing prohibits that in the commune of Ixelles. Other communes prohibit an all-covering veil except in the periods of Carnival and Halloween. In a democratic society, only a law can prohibit one's freedom of circulation.[3]

A coherent legal arsenal, so the argument goes, is considered crucial in order to regulate acts such as the face veil. Two observations stand out in this justification of a nationwide ban. The first one is that the absence of a law would allow for a degree of legal incoherence, which is seen as intolerable – 'untenable' in Fonck's words. The second element is that such a prohibition on face veiling is understood, even by Fonck herself, as a law that comes to curtail a principle that is considered to be essential for citizens, i.e. freedom of circulation. A first way to understand these statements is to view them as being driven by a concern about the legality of a measure sanctioning face veiling. By arguing in defence of a law, the concerned MP seems to insist on the fact that fundamental rights, such as freedom of circulation, can only be suspended by the lawmaker. Yet besides this concern with the lawfulness of a particular measure, I suggest that this argumentation in favour of a law equally reflects a concern with national sovereignty and the capacity to assert such sovereignty through the law. The tradition of legal positivism

---

[2] 'Piqué: wet nodig die de boerka verbiedt', at: www.brusselnieuws.be/artikel/etterbeek-cassatie-tegen-beslissing-politierechter

[3] Belgian Chamber 2010–11, no. 53–219/4.

teaches us indeed that a law does not only establish certain rules of conduct, but it is first and mostly an expression of the will of the sovereign and of the capacity to regulate and rule over a particular political community and territory.[4] It is significant to note how such a legal positivist tenet, which lost its influence throughout a large part of the twentieth century, seems to find a new forceful ground around this particular question. In order to account for the symbolic and affective importance that is attributed for the need of a law, I believe it is therefore important to not only consider the functional reasons that are given to justify such a measure, but also the way in which this question of 'a law' re-emerges as an articulation of the will of the nation in this particular context, as an assertion of national sovereignty through the regulation of otherness within the national territory.

Such affirmations of sovereignty become especially clear as we turn to the moment in which such calls for a national regulation on the face veil were voiced, i.e. at a moment of deep institutional crisis. The ban on face veiling was voted in Belgium for the first time at the very moment when the country faced a deep institutional crisis, which eventually resulted in the fall of the government in April 2010 (see also Chapter 4 in this volume). At a time of deep institutional division, the question of the 'face veil' (or the Muslim question) seems to emerge as a new symbolic ground on the basis of which a national unity becomes articulated and one's political sovereignty becomes expressed. Being able to hold onto the exclusivity of being the first country on a 'worldwide' level to adopt such a law seemed to figure as an important reason behind the 'urgency' for such a law. A concern that becomes very explicit in the following claims of the MP of the Liberal Party (MR), Denis Ducarmes, during the parliamentary debates of April 2010:

> We should also be proud. Can we still be Belgian and proud these days? I must admit that I have more and more difficulties doing so. The image of our country is more and more incomprehensible. But considering the unanimity we will probably have around this proposition in this parliament there is probably a new reason to be proud, as our country will be the first to break women who are enslaved from their barriers. Belgium will be the first country to pass this law, and we hope to be followed by France, Switzerland, Italy, the Netherlands etc. Seeing that

---

[4] For a short account of legal positivism in the field of international law, see Anghie (2004), esp. ch. 2.

such a small country, that is facing difficulties, manages to pass such a law will probably encourage them to do the same.[5]

Asserting the sovereignty of the nation and a degree of 'pride' about the country lie at the heart of Ducarmes's words. A pride that seems to be lost at a period of deep institutional crisis and in the face of various regional conflicts and economic crises that have plagued the country and haunted the European continent.[6] The law on face veiling becomes, therefore, a healing practice. A practice that emerges as an antidote to the fragmented Self, and that also renders the expression of a 'collective will' (through the law) yet again possible.[7] Whereas the hegemonic consensus that is displayed around face veiling remains a unique case in point, it is significant to note how the 'minority question' has emerged as a symbolic ground around which a large degree of political consensus comes to be established in a fractured institutional landscape like Belgium. In the period between 2010 and the time of writing, various laws have been adopted in the federal chamber around these questions.[8] These different cases gathered a large consensus in the otherwise strongly divided federal chamber. The degree of consensus (not to say unanimity) that is displayed around face veiling is, however, exceptional. The question remains, therefore, to understand why the mere act of covering one's face seems to hold such a disruptive power that its wearers are cast out from the polis? In order to

---

[5] Belgian Chamber 2009–10, no. 52–2289/005.

[6] This argumentation is inspired by Hannah Arendt's (1951) well-known work *The Origins of Totalitarianism*, who links the emergence of modern forms of anti-Semitism to the newly established political structures of the nation state in which the figure of the Jew comes to hold a position of outsider that could not fit within the new body politics.

[7] France provides a good example in this case, where a national law was adopted in 2010. The report (Gérin and Raould 2010) that preceded the adoption of the law cites studies that show that Muslim women view face veiling as a particular religious practice. However, the members of the commission that advised a ban referred to the intrinsic significations of face veiling that they essentially associated and linked with new forms of religious radicalism that were deemed incompatible with French values. Whereas the trope of the 'oppressed Muslim woman' did figure as a spearhead in the argumentation, the latter was not detrimental to the proposition to ban the face veil. The fear of religious radicalism, of which face veiling was considered to be a symbol, was more pervasive in the general argumentation.

[8] Some examples are the law of 4 December 2012 on nationality, which rendered the criteria to have access to Belgian nationality more strict, *Wet tot wijziging van het Wetboek van de Belgische nationaliteit teneinde het verkrijgen van de Belgische nationaliteit migratieneutraal te maken*, publication date: 14/12/2012, Effective: 01/01/2013, and the law of 8 July 2011 which tightens the conditions for family reunion with a foreign spouse, *Wet tot wijziging van de wet van 15 December 1980 betreffende de toegang tot het grondgebied, het verblijf, de vestiging en de verwijdering van vreemdelingen wat betreft de voorwaarden tot gezinshereniging*, publication date: 12/09/2011, effective: 22/09/2011.

understand this it is necessary, I believe, to account for the way in which state sovereignty equally entails the capacity to deliberate over the forms of life that are included within political life, and is thus granted legal subjectivity. It is to this observation that I turn to in the next section.

2. PRODUCING INDIVIDUALITY THROUGH THE LAW

The liberal–humanist tradition has taught us to consider human beings as 'natural' carriers of individual rights. Such is a conception that is central to the enlightenment tradition that has found its articulation through the notion of the inalienability of rights. Yet several critical contributions have sought to question this assumption by showing that the notion of the 'self' and 'personhood' that lies at the heart of the legal disposition is not merely pre-given, but rather a matter of negotiation, and in some cases contestation. One of the most recent descriptions of such mechanisms – yet in the context of colonial Egypt – can be found in the work of Samera Esmeir (2012), who offers in her recent book *Juridical Humanity* an account of how positive law installed and codified the very notion of humanity. Set in the context of colonial Egypt, she argues that the category of 'the human' emerged as a residue to the question of 'inhuman treatments' and conditions, thus stating that this concept of the human figured as 'the excess that remains in the law after the inhuman has been expelled' (*ibid.*: 93). Producing the 'human' by expelling the 'inhuman' was seen to be one of the central hallmarks of colonial power within Egypt and its civilizing missions and lay at the heart of its juridical arsenal. Esmeir's work is inspired by the critical line of scholarship as established by Foucault, that has sought to understand how the production of the category of the 'individual' and the 'human' is central to modern forms of governance.[9] Besides regulating over individual bodies, modern power is equally seen to produce the individual subjects it holds at the centre of its operation. Such an account allows for

---

[9] This insight runs throughout Foucault's oeuvre, who has sought to understand how modern forms of power operate through mechanisms of totalization and individualization. An observation that he has started developing in his seminal work *Discipline and Punish* (1975), which explores the production of individual bodies and souls through total institutions (such as prisons) and disciplinary measures that target the 'individual', and which he has continued examining in his work on Sexuality (*History of the Sexuality, Vol. 1. The Will to Knowledge*, 1976) and his lectures at the Collège de France (see especially *Security, Territory and Population. Lectures at the College de France, 1977–1978*). For an introductory essay on this question see especially Foucault (2003 [1979]).

a perspective which understands the law not only as a 'protector' of individual subjects, but also as the very technology through which this individuality comes to be produced. Furthermore, this competence of attributing a legal subjectivity to particular forms of life is considered to be one of the ultimate competences of modern forms of power. This is the central point that lies at the heart of Giorgio Agamben's work *Homo sacer* (1998[1995]), in which he tries to unravel the internal contradictions that lie at the heart of modern state sovereignty. Building upon the work of Schmitt (who defines sovereignty through the capacity to proclaim the rule of exception) and Foucault (who views the inclusion of 'life' – bios – as one of the central hallmarks of modern power), he argues that the production and exclusion of 'bare life' figures as one of the ways through which state sovereignty is asserted. In other words, state sovereignty comes to be asserted through the deliberation of the forms of life that fall outside of political and legal order and are thus subjected to a permanent state of exception. While he uses the metaphor of the camp to geographically situate this distinction, he takes this polarity between 'bare life' and 'political life' as one of the central hallmarks of modern state power: 'The fundamental categorical pair of Western politics is not that of friend/enemy, but that of bare life/political existence, zoē/bios, exclusion/inclusion' (1998: 8). At the heart of Agamben's work lies not only a desire to capture the contradictory tensions that lie at the heart of modern sovereignty, but also – and more importantly – the insight that state sovereignty becomes asserted through a mechanism of selective inclusion and exclusion of the forms of life that can be included within the polis, or within political life.

The case of face veiling is a significant one, for it offers a glimpse into the ways in which state power operates through a continuous deliberation over forms of lives that can be included within its juridical order. This becomes particularly clear as we consider the argumentation offered by the Belgian Constitutional Court in December 2012. The niqab-wearing applicants argued, most centrally, that the ban amounted to a violation of their right to freedom of religion.[10] In responding to this the court relied strongly on the following (and closely related) arguments:

> Considering the fact that the individualization of the person, for which the face constitutes a fundamental element, represents an essential

---

[10] Constitutional Court 6 December 2012, no. 145/2012, B.23.

condition for the operation of a democratic society, of which each legal subject is a member, the legislator can rightfully assume that the concealment of the face can endanger the operation of the society and, consequently, needs to be legally sanctioned.[11]

At the heart of its argumentation lies not only a concern with the emancipation of the concerned face veiled women or the kinds of social interactions face veiling would preclude, but the very 'individuality' and legal subjectivity of these women. It shows, in other words the functionality of the law in not only defending and protecting individual rights but also in determining who is to be considered as an individual subject in front of the law. What is crucial about this argumentation is not only the affirmation of the liberal premise that a society consists of the gathering of individuals ('individualization ... represents an essential condition for the operation of a democratic society'), but equally the insistence on the importance of the face in determining this question. In so doing, the constitutional court takes a step ahead in defining this individuality on the basis of 'recognizability'. The latter becomes even more clear in the following passage.

> Regarding the claim that the law needs to be necessary in a democratic society and needs to correspond with an urgent societal need, such as the Court has noted in B.21, it can be stated that the individuality of every legal subject in a democratic society is unthinkable without the visibility of its face – that figures as a fundamental component of it. Hiding the face in public places, even though it is part of the freedom of expression of the person, has as main consequence that every possibility of individualization of this legal subject, who is a member of the society, is removed, whereas this individualization figures as a fundamental component of what constitutes a legal subject. The prohibition relative to covering one's face, therefore, corresponds to an urgent societal need in a democratic society.[12]

Three elements need to be underscored here. First, we observe how the question of individuality comes to be marked through the face. Whereas other indexes are generally used to determine the legal *personae* (such as age or one's sex) of a particular subject, it is interesting to note how the face emerges here as a new criterion. Uncovering one's face becomes, in other words, essential to the process of legal identification and the condition under which 'individuality' can be

---

[11] *Ibid.*, B.28. [12] *Ibid.*, B.37.2

attributed. This also implies that maintaining one's face covered excludes one from the very category of the 'individual'.[13] Second, this capacity to be recognized as an 'individual' (or what the court describes as 'individualization') is a condition to be granted a legal subjectivity – or to be recognized as a subject within and before the law. Third, this impossibility to individualize emerges as a matter of urgency. This observation seems at first sight striking, for the small number of face-veiled women as well as the absence of clear threat posed by these women cannot account for the sense of urgency that speaks throughout the court's decision. In order to understand this, it is important, I believe, to attend to the sentiment of impotence that speaks throughout this argumentation and the feeling that law cannot 'operate'. Through the act of face veiling, the face-veiled women seem to emerge as elements that escape the individualizing powers of the law – i.e. law's capacity to regulate 'life' within a certain political space. In so doing these women are not addressed as passive objects of regulation, but almost as disturbing 'rebels'. Such observations invite us to consider how such a concern with 'rule of the law' seems to be conditioned by the 'Muslim question', and how regulating Muslim lives (ranging from the capacity to unveil (face) veiled women, monitor mosques, regulate 'halal' meat, etc. ...) has become essential to the operation of state power.[14] It belongs to the state's competence to determine who can be considered as an 'individual' (and thus be included within political life) as it equally belongs to the state's competence to exclude forms of life that fall outside of those scripted notions of the 'individual'. And the question of Islam and Muslim subjects seem to hold a particular position in this regard. Challenging this capacity to determine who is to be considered an 'individual', as face-veiled women are seen to do, implies challenging the state's competence in determining who is to be counted as a legal subject.

[13] The question of the individuality of a subject and the centrality of the face was a matter of thought already in the parliamentary debates, which invoked the argumentation by the French philosopher Elisabeth Badinter and a specific interpretation of Emmanuel Levinas to argue that the 'face' figures as a central condition to be able to establish communication and to identify someone as an individual. For a critical evaluation of this, see Vrielink (2013).

[14] The question, however, remains why face veiling (more than other forms of face covering that can be encountered in everyday life, such as helmets) is met with particular suspicion. Several authors have argued for the need to attend to the historical particularities and the constitutive – yet conflicting – relationship Islam holds to (Christian) Europe. For a further account of this, see Anidjar (2003); Vakil and Sayyid (2010).

3. CONCLUSION

A central paradox has often animated discussions surrounding the (face) veil ban: whereas defenders of the law often argue that such a regulation is needed to 'liberate' women, several studies have documented and shown that Muslim women who decide to face-veil actually 'chose' to do so, and that a ban thereby limits their freedom and autonomy. In accounting for this paradox, several analysts have taken it as a manifestation of 'bad faith' from the side of the defenders of the ban.[15] What the case of the face veil invites us to explore – and what the argumentation by the Constitutional Court shows, however, is that it is here less a matter of 'good/bad' faith, but rather a matter of a discursive (and material) competition over the question of 'individuality' and 'subjectivity'. More than in the case of the veil (where there seems a larger consensus to consider veiled women as liberal subjects), the discussion around face veiling illustrates the construction of a quasi-hegemonic consensus over a specific interpretation of what is to be considered as 'an individual' or as a 'legal subject' – which come to be equated with one another in the case of the face veil ban. A quasi-hegemonic consensus, for the empirical evidence that shows that the women actually chose to face-veil (and by doing so, seek to inscribe these women within a liberal language) seems – so far – to prove unsuccessful and remain 'inaudible'. The recent argumentation offered by the Constitutional Court shows not only that such interpretations find little resonance, but it also shows how the law and state sovereignty figure as a central source in deliberating over the forms of life that can be considered as fully 'human'. It also helps us to understand, I suggest, why 'forms of life' that wilfully refuse this scripted notion of 'the individual' are understood as disturbing rebels. For they enter into an illegitimate competition with the sovereign in deliberating over their own humanity. Such a competition probably figures as one of the biggest sins within a modern state. A sin that needs to be urgently sanctioned: in the best case with a strong reminder (through a fine), in the worst case through imprisonment.

---

[15] Eva Brems, 'Boerkaverbod laat vrouwen in de steek', in *De Standaard*, 29/04/2012 [Burqa law is abandoning women to their fate].

REFERENCES

Agamben, Giorgio 1998. *Homo sacer: Sovereign Power and Bare Life*, Stanford University Press.

Anidjar, Gil 2003. *The Jew, the Arab: A History of the Enemy*, Stanford University Press.

Appadurai, Arjun 2006. *Fear of Small Numbers*, Princeton University Press.

Anghie, Anthony 2004. *Imperialism, Sovereignty and the Making of International Law*, Cambridge University Press.

Arendt, Hannah 2004 [1951]. *The Origins of Totalitarianism*, New York: Schocken, p. 41.

Brems, Eva, Vrielink, Jogchum and Oulad Chaib, Saïla 2013. 'Uncovering French and Belgian Face Covering Bans', *Journal of Law, Religion and State*, 2: 69–99.

Esmeir, Samera 2012. *Juridical Humanity. A Colonial History*, Stanford University.

Foucault, Michel 1991 [1975]. *Discipline and Punish: The Birth of the Prison*, London: Penguin.

Foucault, Michel 1998 [1976]. *The History of Sexuality 1: The Will to Knowledge*, trans. Robert Hurley, London: Penguin.

2003 [1979]. 'Omnes et Singulatim: Toward a Critique of Political Reason', in P. Rabinow and N. Rose (eds.), *The Essential Foucault: Selections from Essential Works of Foucault, 1954–1984*, New York and London: New Press, pp. 180–201.

2007. *Security, Territory, Population: Lectures at the Collège de France, 1977–1978*, Houndmills, Hants.: Palgrave Macmillan.

Gérin, André and Raoult, Eric 2010. *Assemblée Génerale. Rapport d'information fait en application de l'article 145 du règlement. Au nom de la mise d'information sur la pratique du port du voile intégral sur le territoire national*, 26 January.

Moors, Annelies 2009. 'The Dutch and the Face-Veil: The Politics of Discomfort', *Social Anthropology*, 17: 393–408.

2012. 'The Affective Power of the Face Veil: Between Disgust and Fascination', in B. Meyer and D. Houtman (eds.), *Things: Material Religion and the Topography of Divine Spaces*, New York: Fordham University Press, pp. 282–95.

Povinelli, Elizabeth 1998. 'State of Shame', *Critical Inquiry*, 24: 575–610.

Spivak, Gayarti 1988. 'Can the Subaltern Speak?', in C. Nelson and L. Grossberg (eds.), *Marxism and the Interpretation of Culture*, Urbana, IL: University of Illinois Press.

Vakil, Abdool Karim and Sayyid, Salman 2010. *Thinking through Islamophobia: Global Perspectives*, New York: Columbia University Press.

Vrielink, Jogchum 2013. 'De Grondwet aan het gezicht onttrokken. Het Grondwettelijk Hof en het "boerkaverbod"', *Tijdschrift voor Bestuurswetenschappen en Publiekrecht*, 4: 250–60.

13

THE PERFORMATIVITY OF FACE-VEIL CONTROVERSIES IN EUROPE

Schirin Amir-Moazami

> *In our occidental societies the face is the part of the body which carries the heart of the individual, the soul, the reason, the personality. For us this is a cultural secular heritage.*[1]

INTRODUCTION

In this chapter I will take up the discussions in Europe around bans on female face coverings, recurrently labelled as 'burqa', by analysing them as part and parcel of the proliferation of discourses on the 'Muslim question'[2] in Europe. In my view we cannot understand the presumably sudden emergence of discussions around this religious bodily practice without understanding them within their broader discursive repertoire anchored in a liberal–secular matrix.

More specifically, looking at the reasoning undergirding the various measures against female face covering in different parts of Europe and the very act of turning this bodily practice into a discourse, I argue that the controversies are – even if centred on legal questions (banning or not?) – not to be understood in the first place as interventions on the (un)lawfulness of particular styles and forms of veiling. Rather, they

---

[1] Statement by art historian Nadeije Laneyrie-Dagen, articulated during the hearings on the face veil in France. *Mission d'information sur la pratique du port du voile integral sur le territoire national* (8 December 2009, Séance 4.30, Compte rendu no. 16).

[2] It needs to be clarified that the 'Muslim question' could be misunderstood as wrongly drawing linear causalities to past histories, namely to the political, cultural, racial and economic gaze on Jews as a problem in Europe, gradually labelled as the 'Jewish Question' (Arendt, Bauman, Marx in response to Max Bauer). I use the term Muslim question in order to point to the fact that the definite, durable and not temporary presence and active participation of Muslims in Europe has gradually been turned by various actors in society into a 'problem' which requires being addressed and acted upon. The ways in which it is addressed, however, reveals a number of different rationalities and practices. As Gil Anidjar recently argued, the very fact that certain minorities in Europe have been dealt with as a question and/or problem in the first place requires recentring our attention to Europe itself as the question and/or problem (2012).

are embedded in a broader spectrum of discursive production on Muslims in Europe and in a longer history of aversions vis-à-vis gendered Islamic bodily practices in public spaces, unloaded and consensualized through the face veil. I argue that the face veil as a bodily practice with strong religious connotations and as a distinctive marker of gender segregation in public spaces transgresses embodied secular conventions about bodily orders and sexual freedom and thus provokes strong reactions with a markedly affective repertoire.

Without being able to think through secular embodiment carefully in this short chapter, when speaking about the secular I mainly address two interrelated aspects, dwelling on the scholarship around Talal Asad (2003, 2006) and some of his interlocutors (Agrama 2012; Mahmood 2009): first, a set of regulative practices, closely tied to nation-state institutions and discourses, which guide the borders between the religious and the secular in the public and thereby necessarily also in the private, and which form and shape citizens. Second, a more tacit and often unmarked set of secular affects, prevalent in the social practices of secular societies on various levels. I will call these secular embodied politics. The controversies around the face veil in Europe revealingly bring these two dimensions together in a more tangible manner than those we could witness on other forms of veiling such as the headscarf.

I will start by critically addressing the very emergence of the controversies itself and try to place these within their broader discursive repertoire of addressing and targeting the 'Muslim question' in Europe. In a second step, I will highlight ways to understand this emergence in its longer genealogy tracing the discursive regimes of unveiling Muslim bodies back to the colonial past and its post-colonial reconfigurations. Engaging with the empirical material gathered in this volume, I will end my reflections by emphasizing the necessity to embed the women's narratives within this wider discursive framework.

1. THE DISCURSIVE ECONOMIES OF THE 'BURQA' CONTROVERSIES

Taking up Arjun Appadurai's book title (2006), Annelies Moors (2009) in an article on the political controversies around the face veil in the Netherlands speaks about the 'fear of small numbers'. Similarly, all empirical studies in this volume confirm that the number of fully veiled women across Europe was so marginal that it was difficult to even study the phenomenon empirically. Why then, one may ask, has this non-issue turned into a public discourse, invited legal authorities to raise their voices on the case, triggered nationwide hearings of scholars and experts providing their views on the question and finally led to a significant number of legal bans on face veils in various European public spaces?

I ask this question because I think it is important to take this public outcry despite small numbers in its own terms before even arguing for or against bans in the first place. In my view this rise of a 'non-issue' into a public controversy is to be understood as part and parcel of a wider process of the 'discursification' of Muslims in Europe in general and Muslim gender norms and sexuality in particular, which are accounted for, scrutinized, put to the gaze, researched, studied, archived, attempted to be made transparent and governed. To better grasp this process, I suggest looking back at some of the basic assumptions in Foucault's first volume of the *History of Sexuality* (1978) which, even if scrutinizing an entirely different time, context and phenomenon, provides us with some important analytical tools to understand what might be happening here.

In this volume Foucault, more specifically, reminds us that since the inception of Western modernity we could witness an incitement to discourse on sexuality and that this incitement and process of turning sex into a discourse was coupled with the aim to empirically tackle and shape the effects on the pleasures. Foucault relates this 'veritable discursive explosion' (*ibid.*: 17) on sexuality to the regulation of both the individual body and that of the population through modern forms of power, driven by norms instead of direct (physical) sanctions and prohibitions. Foucault calls these the 'polymorphous techniques of power' (*ibid.*: 15, 104) by which he means the scientification of sex, the related medicalization of the body and the psychologicization of sexual practices, entangled with the will to knowledge:

> This is the essential thing: that Western man has been drawn for three centuries to the task of telling everything concerning his sex; that since the classical age there has been a constant optimization and an increasing valorization of the discourse on sex; and that this carefully analytical discourse was meant to yield multiple effects of displacement, intensification, reorientation, and modification of desire itself.
>
> (*ibid.*: 23)

While Foucault relates this to the discovery of the 'population' as a holistic target of state intervention and regulation with modern technologies of power, he also makes clear that the process always entailed what Mitchell Dean calls in his conceptualization of governmentality 'dividing practices' (1999: 157); in this case the division of normal from deviant, licit from illicit sexual practices, and, more generally, the healthy and the pathologic, the criminal and the loyal, etc. The entire process of counting, accounting, managing, regulating, controlling and disciplining bodies and souls was thus according to Foucault essentially a process of selection, distinction and division of the normal and the abnormal. As Foucault makes also clear in other writings (e.g. 1991[1972]), any incitement to discourse is always tied to power relations and mechanisms which also structure and order the discourse, i.e. what can be said, thought and articulated, and what cannot be said, thought and articulated.

Even if developed for an entirely different temporal context and question, I find Foucault's insights useful here as an analytical angle to look at the obsession with which these small numbers of fully covered women across Europe was addressed and articulated and to contextualize this within the technologies of power operative thereby. What we can learn from Foucault's analysis, more precisely, is that what he calls the 'incitement to speak' (of sex) was anchored in specific functionalities (in his case the production of desires) and that the explosion of discourse simultaneously always implied its regulation. The seemingly contradictory assumptions on the shortage of discourse, which Foucault prominently addressed in *The Order of Discourse* and its explosion through incitement are thus intimately bound together by the regulating powers undergirding both the shortage and the incitement of any discourse.

Translated into the field of inquiry surrounding debates on the face veil, since the late 1990s we can observe in Europe an increasing incitement to discourse on the 'Muslim question' (e.g. Parekh 2008). This incitement is anchored in deeper structures of modern techniques of powers as conceptualized by Foucault – in particular modern forms of knowledge production guided by the aim to empirically tackle Muslims' 'inner truths' in order to better govern them (see Amir-Moazami 2011; Peter 2008; Tezcan 2012). This proliferation is of course inscribed in numerous rationalities. The quasi-pedagogical 'rescue narratives' (Bracke 2012), i.e. attempts to safeguard the oppressed Muslim woman through civic education are paralleled by more disciplining practices, as materialized in the creation of new legal rulings which ban various forms of covering in public spaces in various European settings.

It is thus important to locate the underlying rationalities entailed in the process of discursification of the Muslim question in their diverse and partly diverging rationalities and functions. These functions go beyond legal discussions around conflicting norms and principles (in the case under scrutiny religious freedom vs. gender equality) in that these very norms are also produced through the scrutiny on the deviance of the other.

A closer inquiry into the dynamics of these and other controversies on Muslim gender norms and bodily practices would thus need to look at these as more than (mis-)representations but as discursive *practices* which are embedded in a wider range of governmental techniques. Although I am not able to do this at length in this chapter, I would like to highlight two interrelated aspects which seem important to me: first, a critical inquiry of some of the terminology involved in the controversies on the face veil, and second an attempt to think about the longer trajectories of the discourses on veiling in Europe.

To start with, the very labelling of full veiling or face veiling as 'burqa', which then transformed vernacularly into the 'burqa debates', and 'burqa bans' is all but innocent. The burqa, as the Afghan style of veiling, characterized by the mandatory imposition of covering as a medium of male authority and control over women's bodies, provokes an imagery which literally transfers the face veil to a different space and externalizes the bodies concerned. This terminology, in particular, evokes and disseminates emotions of fear, and sometimes also disgust (see Amir-Moazami 2013) vis-à-vis a supposedly exp-anding religious practice that has reached European borders. While it literally neglects women who live within these borders to share the same space, it simultaneously produces feelings of uneasiness, as it suggests that these external forms of veiling along with a whole set of unwanted gender norms and practices have now entered European spaces. We can thus assume that the face veil is not acci-dentally labelled 'burqa', as it stands for something broader – a process of transgression by the other within. I suggest that this terminology, just like the discourse in which it is embedded more broadly, should be looked at in its productivity as well as its contribution to decontex-tualize a religious practice as belonging to a different spatial and normative universe, while at the same time suggesting that this universe is moving closer.

There is an interpellative and largely performative aspect involved in this act of naming, especially if we understand language in the ways in which Judith Butler and others have thought about it, as a political *practice* that always *does* something (e.g. Butler 1990, 1997). In Butler's understanding performativity alludes to the process of generating meaning through the process of naming, of 'producing effects through reiteration' (Butler 1990: 20, see also 1997). What is crucial is the temporal dimension of performativity: The performative can be futural, in that it generates effects by materializing what is 'not yet'. But it also depends on something which has already been said in the past, and its power and authority depend upon how it recalls that which has already been brought into existence.[3]

Instead of innocently representing a social reality – the 'burqa' having intruded European borders – the naming of this complex religious practice thus needs to be understood as part of the practice itself. Even if the effects of any speech act can never be fully anticipated, the pronunciation is part of its production. The performativity in the face-veil controversies and the political practices it has triggered consists in two interrelated aspects: first, the very process of putting to the public gaze a marginal religious practice, taking it up to the level of the state, up to issuing new laws to address it; and, second, the repetitive labelling of this practice through a vocabulary which evokes a whole set of negative emotions and imagery. Read along these lines, the whole process of taking account of the phenomenon, the fact that it is spoken about and how it is spoken about generates more than simply a subject (the one who articulates the speech act) and an object (the fully covered woman to be uncovered).

As Sara Ahmed (2004) reminds us in her thorough analysis of the politics of emotions, the speech act, in which aversion or disgust against the other is publicly articulated also generates a community 'of those who are bound together through the shared condemnation of a disgusting object or event' (*ibid.*: 95). The publicly iterated aversion against what has come to be called the 'burqa' thus should be understood as a process of both casting out and pulling together. It aligns the individual with the collective at the very moment the speech act is articulated.

This is alluded to, for example, in the above quoted statement by the French art historian Nadeije Laneyrie-Dagen, articulated in the course of the French hearings on the face veil ('in our occidental societies', 'for

---

[3] Drawing on Austin, Butler elaborates on these differences particularly detailed in ch. 1 of *Excitable Speech* (1997).

us', etc.). The repetitive scheme of re-emphasizing over and over again the contours of this cultural heritage of 'our' conventions of dress norms, our conventions of public expression of sexuality, in short of a bodily order that is disturbed by the presence of a different bodily scheme needs to be understood as a practice which at the same time recaptures the body of the European self – a body that is both vulnerable and at the same time stabilized through the reiterative practice of embodied conventions that are presumed to differ from non-European experiences (i.e. Islamic bodily conventions).

Moreover, as much as this kind of epistemic intervention constitutes a direct intervention into the body of the face-veiled woman by external-izing her from the spatial, cultural and political experiences of a Western European hemisphere, the very act of iterating the liberal–secular matrix to be incorporated by those who are not yet part of us, is part of a civilizing project of European nation states with a long genealogy (see Anidjar 2003; Bauman 1991; Elias 2002 [1969]). While it is important to critically address the functionality and productivity of this kind of civilizing project, it thus also seems unavoidable to look at the discursive practices of unveiling veiled bodies in their historicity and not just as an effect of post-war migration or more recent processes of securitization, responsive to terrorist attacks in the name of Islam, and global geopolitics.

POST-COLONIAL FANTASIES?

It is especially the desire to 'capture' the Other, and to look inside her, salient in the various debates on veiling across Europe, that finds ante-cedents most notably throughout colonial history. Meyda Yeğenoğlu's (1999) psychoanalytical and feminist critique of Orientalism illustrates this particularly well. Focusing on the politics of unveiling, Yeğenoğlu relates the colonizer's obsession to lift the veil and to look at what is 'hidden' behind it to a specific regime of transparency and control which she relates to Western post-Enlightenment thought and practice. Such an interpretation could shed light, for example, on the question as to why the veil still today is predominantly turned into a symbol, externalizing supposedly unique meanings that are detached from the experiences of the women who wear it (see Asad 2006). Also the wide suspicion that behind the veil the *real* nature of the person is hidden in need to be unveiled is replicated in the current discussions around face veiling throughout Europe. What is particularly interesting in this reading is Yeğenoğlu's focus on epistemological affinities of the search for transparency and the practices of control, which she finds even in Nietzsche's division of 'truth' and 'fantasy'.

Dwelling on the forces of colonial violence Frantz Fanon (1965 [1959]) similarly analyses how at the advent of the independence war, French colonizers tried to mobilize Muslim women to uncover for the sake of 'republican values', driven by the slogan:

> If we want to destroy the culture of Algerian society, its capacity for resistance, we must first of all conquer the women: we must go and find them behind the veil where they hide themselves and where men keep them out of light.
>
> (*ibid.*: 37–8)

Similar to Yeğenoğlu also Fanon makes clear that the effort of conquering Algerian women by literally 'unveiling Algeria' (*ibid.*) was not only a military question. Rather, it was rooted in a broader problematique of power where Algeria was not only considered a territory to be conquered but in which this conquest was established in terms of an epistemological superiority.

Despite my uneasiness with both Yeğenoğlu's and Fanon's psychoanalytical focus (which tends to suggest some kind of 'Western mindset'), I find Yeğenoğlu's conceptualization of the veil to be a transgression of rules and conventions of transparency particularly interesting for the purpose of the controversies on the face veil. It helps us to understand the deeper structures undergirding recurrent publicly articulated aversions against the face veil in Europe within a particular genealogy of transparency and/as control of individual and collective bodies, whose broader genealogy is pointedly illustrated in Foucault's analysis of the Panopticon as the materialization of modern forms of discipline. These deeper structures are (among other things) rooted in the ambivalences inherent in norms of freedom and modern techniques of control of the presumably free body, as well as habitualized conventions of visibility and communication.

The incitement to speak, which I started this chapter with, to articulate, to render one's inner truths visible to the outside can be traced to the same genealogy as the incitement to turn parts of one's body visible and to become publicly legible, turning the private to the public gaze, of becoming a publicly visible, identifiable actor in society and also to be publicly legible. Any notion of transparency and the incitement to turn visible, however, always occurs within limits and conventions as well as institutional conditions so that the visible always simultaneously turns other things invisible (Schaffer 2008).

The above-quoted statement by Laneyrie-Dagen hints exactly at some such puzzled and at the same time reiterated conventions. In the case of the face veil these are about the acceptance of some kind of physical visibility under certain conditions, which the art historian traces back to the triumph of the individual within a linear trajectory from antiquity through Christianity to today's secularized Europe. The face as the noblest part of the body and the dissimilation of the person's emotions and thus her individuality is here narrated as part of a particular Christian/secular trajectory. The very fact that the face veil has turned into an object of public controversies and invited so many actors to publicly voice their aversions despite the factually minor number of covered women, in turn, reveals the performative aspect of the iterative practice of showing the limits *and* stage-managing a particular kind of bodily visibility as part of a secularized Christian imaginary.

There is definitely much more to say about this, and what would be needed is a deeper inquiry into the conventions and regimes of visibility, rendered salient in various past and contemporary politics of unveiling.[4] To start with, one would need to dismantle the social imaginary underpinning the norm of depiction of the face and the gestures through which the 'soul' of the individual and his reason is to be revealed. What I can offer here is, however, not a thorough genealogy of these secular regimes of visibility as tied to bodily conventions and norms of bodily display in public. For the time being my point here is simply to suggest that the aversions against the fully covered female body and face, unloaded, and at times produced and more or less consensualized throughout Europe, cannot be understood as mere expressions of contemporary anti-Muslim sentiments and sudden discoveries of Muslims in Europe as a problem. Rather, they are inscribed in reconfigurations of practices with a much longer political and epistemological history, in this case genealogies of regulations of religion in public life of Europe and related conceptions and conventions of publicness and privacy, notions of bodily display and order in public as well as conventions and norms of bodily visibility.

---

[4] I mentioned already Yeğenoğlu's work which goes in this direction. See also von Braun and Mattes (2007).

2 CAN FACE-VEILED WOMEN SPEAK?

It is within this larger setting as well that the voices of the women – represented in this volume through the voices of researchers – need to be contextualized. All empirical investigations in this volume show how strongly the publicly articulated aversions are echoed microscopically in the women's narratives of encounters of mistreatment and misrecognition in everyday interactions. These experiences make clear that the whole practice of veiling within European publics cannot be grasped solely on the level of its 'internal' logic but has to be placed within the wider discursive framework, including the highly tense and emotional repertoire surrounding it which these women encounter and struggle with on a daily level.

Taking up again some of the remarks on the functionalities, productivities but also shortages of discourse, it is important to recall that the women's voices are not immune from the discursive structures, which undergird not only their narratives but which, more generally, channel what can be said, thought and heard and what cannot. Put differently, the various possibilities and freedoms to speak do not mean also that everything that is articulated is also heard (Asad 2003: 185), as the public sphere is structured by in-built limitations which proliferate, filter but also silence what is heard, and how. In the concrete case of veiling in general and face veiling in particular we thus have to take up again the question raised a long time ago by Spivak not whether the 'subaltern' can speak but whether she is heard within a hegemonic framework structured by an increasingly pre-established set of questions: are Islamic norms and religious practices integratable into the liberal constitutional orders? Are Muslim women oppressed or not? Is veiling a sign of free choice or submission? And so on.

Drawing on Butler's notion of hegemonic frames, Sarah Bracke and Nadia Fadil (2012) make an important observation, relevant for my argument and for the volume in general. In their analysis of veil debates across Europe they critically discuss the one-dimensional direction towards *certain* religious practices alone. This contributes to exceptionalize the veil as well as it normalizes other bodily practices which increasingly escape from view. More importantly, Bracke and Fadil (*ibid.*: 12, 13) argue that the very framing of these debates ('is the headscarf oppressive or emancipatory?') leaves these women in a deadlock. It scrutinizes *their* views on gender roles and relations and *their* agency or lack thereof. Bracke and Fadil show how much scholars as well have become captured by this framing. They revealingly speak about their own discomfort when constantly being manoeuvred into the position to defend the emancipatory character of veiling, although they actually wanted to articulate a critique of the discursive structures undergirding the one-dimensionality of such questions.

Thus, also the emphasis on the emancipatory function of veiling leaves little space for disrupting the discursive structures, as it ultimately participates in the game of exceptionalizing through normalizing, but also because the frame itself leaves little space for critically addressing the liberal–secular matrix within which the emancipatory or submissive character of veiling is put to the public gaze and inspected.

As post-colonial theorists succinctly pointed out, the bottleneck of hegemonic frames like these is rather small, which makes the articulation of minority positions particularly difficult. In the case of the face veil this appeals in particular to a vocabulary which does not easily fit into liberal–secular scripts. Covered women are thereby almost compelled to legitimize their religious practice in a liberal–secular vocabulary (free choice, gender equality and, more generally, liberal freedoms) (see Fernando 2010).

The interview material in this volume clearly reveals the women's attempt to somehow undo their exceptional status. The emphasis on their striving for gender equality, for example, as well as the recurrent emphasis on the free choice of their face veil, can be interpreted along this line. This recurrence to the ideal of individual autonomy, I suggest, should, however, not be taken at face value but should be problematized within the broader discursive framework sketched out above.

To be sure, I am not replicating here the argument of a 'false consciousness', as recurrently spelled out also in liberal feminist critiques of this bodily practice as an expression of 'internalized' modes of oppression.[5] Rather, I argue that these articulations need to be situated within a hegemonized notion of freedom of choice, idealized notions of individual autonomy, and a problematization of gender equality univocally directed towards Muslims. These notions are not to be understood as fixed norms but they are dependent on such reiterations, and they become stabilized through the very process of discursification of non-conformist otherness. The emphasis on the voluntary, individually chosen character of this bodily practice, in other words, is one of the

---

[5] This argument is particularly well documented in the debate initiated by Susan Moller Okin's rhetorical question 'Is Multiculturalism Bad for Women?' (2001).

273

most important features of 'framing' the right to be covered, structured by liberal sensibilities.

The obvious fact – also revealed in the empirical material in this volume – that many women don the veil as an ethically guided bodily practice in order to cultivate piety and submission under God's authority,[6] has become increasingly illegible within this liberal–secular matrix. What is said and articulated and by whom is thus not only filtered by in-built asymmetries of liberal–secular public spheres, despite the promise to be inclusive to all kinds of voices. The justifications themselves are only legible within a specific vocabulary. The frames offered in the controversies over the face veil and the deeper emotional structures undergirding them strongly limit the available repertoire to position themselves and to justify their bodily practices. The heated discussions on various other forms of veiling in different European public spheres, in other words, has shown that the subaltern can speak, that she is even incited to speak through various processes of interpellation. The flip side of this incitement to speak, however, is that speech acts are often reorganized, re-categorized and trimmed along a set of preformatted questions.

3. CONCLUSIONS

What I suggested in a rather explorative and programmatic way is a perspective which might allow us to inquire into what I called with Foucault the 'discursive explosion' on Muslims in Europe in general and Muslim gender norms and sexuality in particular from two perspectives. One axis would be a set of questions about the kinds of epistemological and normative frameworks on which this discursive explosion is premised. The second, and related axis, would be an analysis of the techniques and practices of intervention and regulation which this search for truth about Muslims has currently triggered. Moreover, I have argued that the complex web of interrelated interventions into the Muslim field, including the regulation of gender norms and sexuality, would require a genealogical labour which takes into account the longer histories of the supposed recent occurrence of the 'Muslim question'.

Understanding the face-veil controversies in their functionalities, the public furore about small numbers thus needs to be understood also as a means to reconvene, reorganize to reproduce normative notions of

---

[6] On the most insightful conceptualization of the underlying piety, see Mahmood (2005).

subjecthood, liberal freedoms and regimes of visibility which this bodily practice disturbs and puts into question. What might constitute, if not a break in the reiteration of the preformatted questions which are part of these functionalities, but at least a re-signification, in my view, therefore lies not so much in the women's narratives than in the very act of transgressing a normative bodily regime of visibility and public legibility. It is most notably through the disclosure of embodied secular conventions of communication, bodily conduct in public and notions of visibility through which face-veiled women almost deliberately transgress the position of the 'gaze'. The fact that the fully covered woman can see without being seen provides her with a disturbing agency. The irritation of the bodily act itself – expressed exactly in the fear of small numbers – indeed, also relativizes the reproduced imagery of the passive, and oppressed covered woman, as it disturbs conventions of seeing and being seen. It reverses the panoptical logic of scrutiny, examination and control of the body of each and everyone. In this respect the partly violent outcry against this form of veiling, indeed, could also be understood as an expression of an uneasiness with the loss of control and transparency, as much as it constitutes a rupture with conventional modes of communication and bodily visibility.

REFERENCES

Agrama, H. 2012. Questioning Secularism: Islam, Sovereignty, and the Rule of Law in Modern Egypt, Chicago University Press.
Ahmed, S. 2004. 'Affective Economies', Social Text, 79(2): 117–39.
Amir-Moazami, S. 2011. 'Dialogue as a governmental practice', Feminist Review, 98: 9–27.
2013. 'The Secular Embodiments of Face-Veil Controversies across Europe', in N. Göle (ed.), Islam and Public Controversy in Europe, Farnham: Ashgate, pp. 83–98.
Anidjar, G. 2003. The Jew, the Arab: A History of the Enemy, Stanford University Press.
2012. 'On the European Question', Forum Bosnae, 55, 13–27.
Appadurai, A. 2006. Fear of Small Numbers, North Carolina, NC: Duke University Press.
Asad, Talad 2003. Formations of the Secular: Christianity, Islam and Modernity, Stanford University Press.
2006. 'Trying to Understand French Secularism', in H. de Vries et al. (eds.), Political Theologies. Political Religion in a Post-Secular World, New York: Fordham University Press, pp. 494–525.

Bauman, Z. 1991. *Modernity and Ambivalence*, Cambridge: Polity.

Butler, J. 1990. *Gender Trouble: Feminism and Subversion of Identity*, London and New York: Routledge.

1997. *Excitable Speech: The Politics of the Performative*, London and New York: Routledge.

Bracke, S. 2012. 'From "Saving Women" to "Saving Gays": Rescue Narratives and Their Dis/continuities', *European Journal of Women's Studies*, 19(2): 237–52.

and Fadil, N. 2012. "Is the Headscarf Oppressive or Emancipatory?' Field Notes on the Gendrification of the Multicultural Debate', *Gender and Religion*, 2(1): 36–56.

Dean, M. 1999. *Governmentality: Power and Rule in the Modern Society*, 2nd edn, Los Angeles, London, New Delhi, Singapore, Washington, DC: Sage

Elias, N. 2002 [1969]. *Über den Prozess der Zivilisationen Bd. I*, Frankfurt am Main: Suhrkamp.

Fanon F. 1965 [1959]. *A Dying Colonialism: Freedom for Algeria*, New York: Grove.

Fernando, M. 2010. 'Reconfiguring freedom: Muslim Piety and the Limits of Secular Law and Public Discourse in France', *American Ethnologist*, 37(1): 19–35.

Foucault, M. 1978. *The History of Sexuality. Part I*. New York: Pantheon.

1991 [1972]. *Die Ordnung des Diskurses*. Inauguralvorlesung am Collège de France. 2. Dezember 1970, Frankfurt/Main: Fischer.

Mahmood, S. 2005. *Politics of Piety: The Islamic Revival and the Feminist Subject*, Princeton University Press.

2009. 'Religious Reason and Secular Affect: An Incommensurable Divide?', *Critical Inquiry*, 35: 836–62.

Moller Okin, S. 2001. *Is Multiculturalism Bad for Women?* Princeton University Press.

Moors, A. 2009. 'The Dutch and the Face-Veil: The Politics of Discomfort', *Social Anthropology/Anthropologie Sociale*, 17(4): 393–408.

Parekh, B. 'European Liberalism and "the Muslim Question"', ISIM Paper 9, Amsterdam, at: http://openaccess.leidenuniv.nl/bitstream/1887/12641/1/paper_Parekh.pdf.

Peter, F. 2008. 'Political Rationalities, Counter-Terrorism and Policies on Islam in the United Kingdom and France', in J. Eckert (ed.), *The Social Life of Anti-Terrorism Laws*, Bielefeld: transcript Verlag, pp. 79–108.

Schaffer, J. 2008. *Ambivalenzen der Sichtbarkeit. Über die visuellen Strukturen der Anerkennung*, Bielefeld: transcript Verlag.

Siverstein, P. A. 2004. *Algeria in France: Transpolitics, Race and Nation*, Bloomington and Indianapolis, IN: Indiana University Press.

Sivestri, S. 2012. 'Comparing Burqa Debates in Europe: Sartorial Styles, Religious Prescriptions and Political Ideologies', in S. Ferrari and

S. Pastorelli (eds.), *Religion in Public Spaces: A European Perspective*, Farnham and Burlington, VT: Ashgate, pp. 275–82.

Spivak, G. C. 1988. 'Can the Subaltern Speak?', in Ranajit Guha and Gayatra Chacravorty Spivak (eds.), *Selected Subaltern Studies*, Oxford University Press.

Tezcan, L. 2012. *Das Muslimische Subjekt. Verfangen im Dialog der Deutschen Islam Konferenz*, Konstanz University Press.

Von Braun, C. and Mattes, B. 2007. *Die Frau, der Islam und der Westen*, Berlin: Aufbau.

Yeğenoğlu, M. 1999. *Colonial Fantasies: Towards a Feminist Reading of Orientalism*, Cambridge University Press.

14

PROSCRIBING UNVEILING – LAW: A CHIMERA AND AN INSTRUMENT IN THE POLITICAL AGENDA

Susan S. M. Edwards

1. INTRODUCTION

Since '*l'affaire du foulard*' (Benhabib 2002: 95) three decades ago, when three female pupils (Fatima, Leila and Samira) were expelled from the Gabriel-Havez of Creil school in France for wearing a headscarf (hijab), what some women wear, has come under intense scrutiny at the highest levels, has resulted in legal intervention, compromised rights to citizenship[1] and unleashed rage erupting in physical assaults particularly on women who wear the face veil (niqab). Across Europe, and further afield within Anglo-American jurisdictions, for example, in America and Canada, women's clothing has been a matter for public and legal debate. So important are these particular items of dress (face veil and headscarf) to concerns at both national and local government level that in some European countries restrictions have been imposed by the state through the enactment of law.

WHAT IS IT ABOUT A PIECE OF CLOTH THAT IS SO ENGAGING?

Of course, it is not so much the metre of fabric but its supposed meaning and signification that lies at the epicentre of the fomented discourse. The face veil question and whether women should have a right to wear it

---

[1] *Mabchour* case, no. 286798, Conseil d'Etat séance du 26 May and 27 June 2008. http://eudo-citizenship.eu/caselawDB/docs/FRA%2027%20June%202008%20n%B0286798.pdf. See also Barbibay (2010); Bienkowski (2010); Suvarierol (2012) and Meer *et al.* (2010).

if they so choose has divided public, legal and academic opinion, and divided feminism, even though the latter is committed to a universalist discourse of rights and equality. For example, in France 'pro choice' feminists argue for the right to wear the face veil (Knief 2010), while others argue that the face veil denigrates women and usurps equality. Within Europe, because of its history and strivings for modernization, the Islamic secular state of Turkey has also banned the veil while the hijab (headscarf) is banned in schools, universities and in the workplace.[2] Further, in non-European countries where Islam is the majority religion, for example, Egypt and Syria, the wearing of the face veil has been banned in state schools and places of work.[3] While in the Islamic Republic of Iran the face veil is a matter of choice but the hijab is enforced. Even in jurisdictions which have not imposed restrictions on wearing the face veil, they have nevertheless engaged with this issue at the level of considering whether women should be permitted to wear a face veil as witnesses or defendants in the courtroom (see below). These very different public and legal discourses reveal the extent of the polysemicity of 'covering' and the veil. So how then might the recent developments in Europe to proscribe veiling be understood?

The rationale for such restriction, from wherever it emanates, is driven by very situationally contextualized political agendas. Western proscription, especially in France, is motivated by fears of rising migration from Arab countries, while Egypt, prior to the Arab Spring, feared the increase in a specific configuration of Islamism, and bans were imposed in universities (said to prevent examination cheating).[4] While pre-Arab Spring bans for example for presenters wanting to wear the hijab on state television have been lifted there were fears that such clothing may become a requirement highlighting the tension between the pre-Arab Spring's government of moderate Islam, and, from

---

[2] See *Milliyet Daily*, 'Religion, secularism and the veil in daily life' (2007) KONDA Research and Consultancy, at: www.konda.com.tr/en/reports.php (accessed 28 March 2013).

[3] See www.alarabiya.net/articles/2010/07/19/114244.html, reporting on the Syrian ban in universities in an effort to promote state secularism (19 July 2010) (accessed 28 March 2013). A. England, 'Syria bans niqab at colleges', *Financial Times* (London), 20 July 2010; Droubi (2011).

[4] The presiding judge in upholding the decision to prohibit the wearing of the niqab said 'If niqab is regarded as personal freedom, it is not an absolute one that is beyond all restrictions. The authority concerned shall intervene to temporarily ban in a specific place according to the nature of the circumstances and the public interest.' www.huffingtonpost.com/meedan/face-veil-debate-resurfac_b_412824.html (accessed 28 March 2013).

2012 following the election of Mohamed Morsi, the move to stricter interpretations of Islam.[5] That tension persists in the struggle for power following the demise of Morsi in June 2013. Clearly, the ideological interpellation of the face veil is context specific as it is caught in the battle for modernity while at other moments in the struggle for nationalism or a specific configuration of Islamism, and so on.

The face veil, more than any other item of clothing or religious or cultural symbol is caught in its own web of religious and sectarian struggle and also in a web of politics, power and the law.

While the empirical chapters in Part I of this volume strive to understand the meaning of the niqab for its subjects, this chapter rather explores the deliberate efforts of the West to eschew the search for real meaning in preference for their metanarratives and projections. I do not seek to condone the face veil when its object is part of an imposed ideology. However as contributors to this volume and other academic commentary[6] demonstrate wearing a niqab cannot simply be explained through a monist interpellation by the observer. At the same time, in the West, the face veil debate and discourse is manipulated by conservative and colonial forces as part of a tactic to further marginalize, ostracize and demonize minority communities. The law for its part, as an ideological state apparatus, reflects these representations at several levels of its operation (Althusser 1971). Part of the feminist legal theory project must include inquiry into the ways in which legal reasoning transforms the embodied imaginings from the dominant discourse into the 'objective' form of doctrine which passes for the 'normative'. Elided to this is the importance of exploring the Eurocentric and orientalist imaginings with regard to the function of the face veil as leitmotif or trope through which Muslim women can be constructed.

---

[5] For example, Professor Malak Zaalouk has stated, 'Again during the Arab Spring movements, we saw how young women were not only deeply involved but for example in the case of Egypt they actually ignited the whole youth coalition moving to Tahrir Square on the 25 January and even in prior occasions had moved various labour movements in Mahalla as a prelude to the January revolution. Half way through that glorious magical moment where young boys and girls sat shoulder to shoulder chanting and demonstrating against the old regime, a renewed attitude of exclusion reigned where young women were again being intimidated and asked to withdraw from the public sphere and stay home.' http://blog.ungei.org/?p=1. See also www.al-monitor.com/pulse/politics/2012/09/hijab-egypt-state-television.html (accessed 28 March 2013).

[6] The world-renowned and celebrated feminist lawyer, academic and activist, judge and film director, Dr Jocelynne Scutt provides a lengthy and detailed exposition in her film *Covered: A Video Installation and Booklet* at http://theburqahdebates.com/index.php?option=com_content&task=view&id=55&Itemid=61, which explores the contradictory meaning of 'covered'.

This chapter concentrates on the cultural and legal representation of the face veil in the West, most notably in Europe, and explores the continuing articulation and reproduction of the ideology of orientalism (Said 1978) through the sexual and cultural interpellation of the veil which has become the primary object of interrogation and control. Political and legal debate has excluded the meaning the veil holds for the subject,[7] instead, construing its meaning and symbolism from the standpoint of the society and its ideological state apparatuses that come to define it, while ideology forces meaning on the regulated female (Muslim) subject through interpellation. The polysemicity of the face veil (Young 2003) and its meaning requires a culturally specific interpretation which should also place at its epicentre the meaning that the face veil holds for the wearer, the object of this volume.

I argue that the ideology of the veil is central to the project of the Western nation state's uncompromising condemnation of the increasingly present (Muslim) 'other' at every level of its operation (Nussbaum 2012). Efforts to control the (Muslim) 'other' in public policy and through formalized mechanisms such as substantive law take on attempts to proscribe the most visible form of 'otherness' – the body – through regulating the dress of women. The West represents dress as an oracle, exclusively an expression of extreme Islamic religious symbolism (Salafism or Jihadism), inexorably a standard bearer of women's subordination, eschewing alternate representations and the voice and authenticity of its wearer which, the empirical research in this volume seeks to contest. As Mancini (2012: 413) writes, 'today's appeal to gender equality ennobles anti-Muslim racist bigotry, channeling it in an acceptable discourse that can be upheld by respectable political and institutional actors'.

In turn, women seeking to wear the veil and to challenge what I consider to be acts of gender-based violence at several levels of operation are forced to articulate and defend this choice through the prism of the legally constructed human rights gateways. In this sense claims to dress freedom are articulated almost exclusively in a rights framework, particularly through the conduit of Article 9 ECHR embodying religious rights and claims to defend religious freedom, which must be read alongside Article 14 which promotes the right to be free from

---

[7] Judge Tulkens's dissent in Şahin: 'What is lacking in this debate is the opinion of women, both those who wear the headscarf and those who choose not to' (para. 11); Françoise Tulkens is a Belgian lawyer.

discrimination. Article 9 however, as Strasbourg jurisprudence demon-strates, has served at times as a chimera, since its application by the ECtHR has upheld the position of the member state (whatever that may be) through the application of Article 9(2) and together with arguments of margin of appreciation, subordinated the protection of the claims of minorities to qualifying claims, which are at times, based on highly questionable and specious reasoning.[8]

2. VEILED IN COURT

The recent decision of the Supreme Court of Canada in *R. v. N. S.*,[9] demonstrates that even when the face veil is not prohibited in the street, as it is in France, it continues to inhabit the epicentre of debate across the world. In the courtroom it is said to challenge the fairness of the proceedings and to obstruct the assessment of the credibility and verac-ity of the witness. In this case, the accused, M – d S and M – l S, were charged with sexually assaulting N. S. N. S. was called by the Crown as a witness at the preliminary inquiry. N. S., who wore a face veil and not surprisingly wished to give her evidence wearing the veil and saw no reason to remove it. At the *voir dire*, the judge concluded that N. S.'s religious belief was 'not that strong' and ordered her to remove her face veil. N. S. appealed. The Court of Appeal held that if the witness's freedom of religion and the accused's fair trial interests were both engaged on the facts and could not be reconciled, the witness may be ordered to remove the face veil. The Court of Appeal then returned the matter to the preliminary inquiry judge to decide whether the veil should in the instant case be retained or removed. N. S. wished for a definitive ruling in her favour providing certainty and permitting her to wear the face veil at trial not wishing the issue to be left to the discretion of the trial judge. She appealed to the Supreme Court.

The Supreme Court (*per* McLachlin CJ, LeBel, Deschamps, Fish, Rothstein and Cromwell JJ, Abella J. dissenting) dismissed the appeal

---

[8] See for example the contrasting arguments in *Leyla Şahin* v. *Turkey* (application no. 44774/98) Judgment, Strasbourg, 10 November 2005, where the veil was regarded as an 'active' symbol and while in Grand Chamber, *Lautsi and others* v. *Italy* (application no. 30814/06) Judgment, Strasbourg,18 March 2011, the crucifix was regarded as a 'passive' symbol, and in both instances the position of the state was not interfered with.

[9] [2012] SCC 72, File No.: 33989, 8 December 2011; 20 December 2012, an appeal from the Court of Appeal for Ontario.

and remitted the matter to a preliminary inquiry judge. The matter, as LeBel J. correctly stated, was not one for the Supreme Court:

[79] Because of the way the litigation and the appeals were conducted, I agree with the disposition proposed by the Chief Justice. I would remit the matter to the judge presiding at the preliminary inquiry, the stage at which this case has remained bogged down for years as a result of the incidents that this Court is now trying to resolve.

However, although the court agreed that whether she should be permitted to wear the niqab or not was not a matter for them, they nevertheless went on to express their opinion on the question of niqabs in the courtroom. The Supreme Court ruled that under the Canadian Charter, even where the accused's fair trial rights were engaged, a witness would not be required to remove her niqab. McLachlin CJ (Cromwell JJ Deschamps, Fish) concurring: 'Where evidence is uncontested, credibility assessment and cross-examination are not in issue . . . being unable to see the witness's face will not impinge on trial fairness'. McLachlin CJ went further and said: '[2] A secular response that requires witnesses to park their religion at the courtroom door is inconsistent with the jurisprudence and Canadian tradition.' And, in response to the Crown's submission that the fair trial rights of the accused would be compromised, McLachlin CJ, said: '[19] a niqab-wearing witness's eyes, tone of voice and cadence of speech remain available to the cross-examiner and trier of fact'. However LeBel and Rothstein JJ, did not agree with her reasoning: 'I have reservations about her approach and will propose a different rule . . . [78] A clear rule that niqabs may not be worn would be consistent with the principle of openness of the trial process and would safeguard the integrity of that process as one of communication.' And went on: 'The public must be able to see how the justice system works.'

Madam Silberman Abella (dissenting) took a much more robust position on whether the niqab could be worn in court and rather than leaving the question to any individual set of facts and judicial interpretation and discretion said that unless the witness's face is directly relevant to the case, such as where her identity is in issue, she should not be required to remove her niqab. In her dissent she demolished the arguments of those who opposed the wearing of the niqab in court. She said this:

[82]The court system has many examples of accepting evidence from witnesses who are unable to testify under ideal circumstances because of

visual, oral, or aural impediments. I am unable to see why witnesses who wear niqabs should be treated any differently.

[83] I would, however, make an exception in cases where the accused can demonstrate that the witness' face is directly relevant to the case, such as where the witness' identity is in issue.

[89] With great respect, however, I disagree with the majority that the 'strength' of a witness' belief, while not relevant in assessing the witness' prima facie religious claim, is nonetheless somehow relevant when balancing that claim against trial fairness. It is unclear to me how a claimant's 'strength' of belief – particularly given the highly subjective and imprecise nature of the freedom of religion analysis – affects the protection a claimant should be afforded under the Charter.

[92] As this case demonstrates, courts are engaged in a constant process of reconciling historic expectations and practices with the Charter's vision.

[103] A witness may also have physical or medical limitations that affect a judge's or lawyer's ability to assess demeanour. A stroke may interfere with facial expressions; an illness may affect body movements; and speech impairment may affect the manner of speaking. All of these are departures from the demeanour ideal, yet none has ever been held to disqualify the witness from giving his or her evidence on the grounds that the accused's fair trial rights are thereby impaired.

The matter of veiling in court has been a question considered in several jurisdictions. On 28 October 2011, Judge Stefan Wikmark, in Sweden barred three women from wearing face veils who wished to attend a trial as observers. Gösta Hultén, spokesperson for Charta 2008, responded arguing that the argument that their clothing may be perceived as disturbing order is a broad and subjective interpretation of the Code of Judicial Procedure. She wrote: 'No particular dress code exists in our courts. To wear a fully covering veil is in itself not illegal in Sweden. Whatever we may think about this garment, it may be important to the person wearing it. It may also mirror a certain religious group affiliation. To show this can be seen as part of our constitutional freedom of expression.'[10] This was not the view reached in the UK when HH Judge Peter Murphy at the opening of a trial at Blackfriars Crown Court in London said that 'open justice overrides religious belief' and told a woman defendant that she would not be allowed to enter a plea

[10] www.goteborgdaily.se/complaint-against-court-after-veiled-women-refused-entry (last accessed 29 April 2013).

unless she removed her niqab in court because she needed to be iden-tified.[11] Her counsel argued her case for not removing the niqab on Article 9 claims, following the case of *N. S.* (above).[12] Judge Murphy in delivering his 36-page judgment[13] said the ability for a jury to see a defendant's demeanour during cross-examination was a principal part of the adversarial trial system. He accepted counsel's argument and that of the expert that 'the value of seeing a witness in the process of evaluating her evidence can be overstated'[14] and in considering Article 9 he balanced the defendant's right to manifest religious belief against the court's need to function 'fairly and effectively'.[15] He directed that the defendant remove her face veil when giving evidence[16] and that the defendant may give evidence from behind a screen but not shielded from the judge, the jury and counsel.[17] He also forbade the press to make or disseminate images of the defendant in court.[18] One can only hope that her discomfort in removing her face veil in giving evidence will not result in any additional nervousness being misinter-preted. Her counsel in argument had alluded to this possibility and said that in giving evidence she may cover her face with her hand look away or look down and asked 'How is the court to respond to that?'

3. THE LAW PROSCRIBING THE NIQAB (FACE VEIL)

The prohibition of very specific garments of clothing worn by particular groups in the West has an interesting history. France's statutory prohib-ition of women face veil wearers from its streets is not the first such dress prohibition. England banned 'Scottish Dress' (kilts, the plaid – a shawl thrown over the shoulder, and other aspects of Gaelic culture, etc.) following the Act of 1746,[19] in an attempt to suppress and destroy the Scots as an ethnic group. In 1923, in Turkey, President Ataturk banned the fez and other items of clothing as part of a wider attempt to

---

[11] www.theguardian.com/law/2013/aug/23/judge-refuses-muslim-to-wear-burqa-court
[12] I am grateful to Susan Meek, Furnival Chambers, London, Counsel for D(R) for assistance in this matter.
[13] The Crown Court at Blackfriars, *The Queen v. D(R)*, Judgment of HH Judge Peter Murphy in relation to wearing of niqab by defendant during proceedings in crown court.
[14] *Ibid.*, §34.   [15] *Ibid.*, §47.
[16] www.telegraph.co.uk/news/uknews/law-and-order/10312604/Muslim-woman-Rebekah-Dawson-must-remove-niqab-while-giving-evidence-judge-rules.html
[17] *The Queen v. D(R)*, see above n. 13, §86(4).   [18] *Ibid.*, §58.
[19] See the Disarming Act (1746), or the Dress Act 1746 Abolition and proscription of the Highland Dress 19 George II, Chap. 39, Sec. 17, 1746.

modernize and Westernize the country.[20] In Iran, on 7 January 1936, a royal decree by Reza Shah Pahlavi resulted in banning the veil (Chehabi 2007: 34; Sedghi 2007: 34). The banning of the veil in Western societies has its own development and women in these groups and cultures living within the West are now being targeted who because of their distinctive dress are easily identifiable.

While the legal response of other European countries on this question has been less proscriptive, for example local bans are in existence in Italy and Spain, and a ban is on the political agenda in the Netherlands, Denmark's Prime Minister, Lars Loekke Rasmussen (2009–11), has stated that while the niqab has no place in Denmark's society on equality grounds, nonetheless it has taken a decision not to ban it.[21] This followed in response to the Danish Liberal–Conservative government's original announcement in 2009 that they would develop a policy to ban the niqab in the interests of 'democratic integration' discussed further in Chapter 3 in this volume (see also Warburg et al. 2013). In Sweden, the Equality ombudsman has stated that a ban is not acceptable. On 30 November 2010, the Equality ombudsman stated (contrary to the Danish position above) that if a general ban prohibiting students from wearing a niqab were implemented, it would violate existing discrimination laws.[22] Such a ban is also unacceptable in the UK or in Ireland. In the UK in January 2012, the Face Coverings (Regulation) Bill (Bill 20 55/1), a private member's bill, fell before its second reading. However, the niqab concern has been resuscitated as the Liberal Democratic Home Office Minister, Jeremy Browne, has urged a national debate on the state's role in preventing veils being imposed on girls. Nick Clegg, leader of the Liberal Democrats and Deputy Prime Minister, said he did not believe in issuing 'edicts from Whitehall ... telling people what pieces of clothing they should wear' but said he believed the wearing of full veils was 'not appropriate' in the classroom, but would not support a 'state ban' on doing so.[23]

---

[20] Act No. 671 of 25 November 1341 (1925) on the Wearing of hats; Act No. 2596 of 3 December 1934 on the prohibition of the wearing of certain garments; Act No. 2590 of 26 November 1934 on the abolition of titles and appellations such as efendi, bey or pasa. Act No. 1353 of 1 November 1928 on the adoption and application of the Turkish alphabet.

[21] www.worldnewsforum.net/archive/index.php/t-9366.html (last accessed 29 April 2013).

[22] www.non-discrimination.net/law/selected-case-law/sweden-general-ban-niqabs-unlawful. See Equality ombudsman case 2009/103 of 30 November 2010. See also http://english.alarabiya. net/articles/2010/12/01/128138.html (last accessed 29 April 2013).

[23] www.birminghampost.co.uk/news/regional-affairs/nick-clegg-veil-row-comments-6027044.

Both the Belgian and French bans have been challenged and upheld in court. Yet a case is pending before the ECtHR, *SAS v. France*.[24] In this case it is contended in legal argument that the explicit linkage between race and religion (§3) and the proclaimed basis for the ban including: that the burqa is contrary to republican values; and poses a danger to public safety which constitutes a manifestation of a refusal of ostensible equality between men and women (§ 26). Such legal proscriptions and their rationales have not passed without comment. Lord Stewart in a Scottish case in the Court of Session, High Court of Justiciary, *RQK* (Assisted Person) Petitioner,[25] said this, when speaking of the meaning of public order in its widest sense:

> I note in passing that the Law of 19 May 2010 prohibiting the wearing of the niqab and the burqa in France proceeds upon a ministerial recital: 'the protection of l'ordre public . . . extends to prohibiting conduct which challenges the essential rules of the republican social contract, the basis of our society.' These are drumly waters.
>
> (§ 23)

Such is the strength of feeling for and against the wearing of the niqab on the street and elsewhere that private individuals have publicly engaged on both sides of the debate. In France, Rachid Nekkaz set up a fund to pay the fines of women who choose to wear the veil and are brought before the court.[26] Since the law came into force in France, it is reported that 425 women wearing the niqab have been fined and 66 have received warnings (Erhlanger and Camus 2012). In Belgium, Filip Dewinter, one of the leaders of Vlaams Belang, a right-wing extremist Flemish nationalist party (Erk 2005), styling himself as a vigilante bounty hunter aka the Wild West has offered a reward to anyone who reports a woman wearing a niqab to the police.[27] It is relevant that in 2004 on 14 November the Belgian far-right party Vlaams Blok changed its name to Vlaams Belang since the Court of Cassation confirmed a Court of Appeal ruling which had found Vlaams Blok to be in violation of the law against racism. In his

---

[24] ECtHR *SAS v. France* 43835/11. Written submissions on behalf of Liberty (Intervener). See also Ferrari and Pastorelli (2012).

[25] *RQK* (Assisted Person) Petitioner (Judicial Review of a determination by the Secretary of State for the Home Department in terms of the Immigration Rules (HC 395 as amended) Rule 353, Outer House, Court of Session [2011] CSOH 199).

[26] www.france24.com/en/20110819-french-businessman-pay-all-burqa-fines-belgium-rachid-nekkaz (last accessed 5 April 2013).

[27] www.onislam.net/english/news/europe/457480-belgian-rightists-offer-niqab-bounty.html (last accessed 4 April 2013).

analysis, Cas Mudde has found 'Islamophobia' to be 'the most important aspect of the party's xenophobic propaganda' (2000: 13). One must ask whether anything has changed, since a recent political party propaganda video produced by this party and posted on YouTube ends with a caption 'Stop Immigratie – Stop Islamerising'. It begins with children riding a merry-go-round trying to catch the tassel hanging above them as they ride round. The music of the fairground Wurlitzer playing in the background is light and carefree. Two women, faces and bodies completely veiled, come into view – the music changes abruptly and using all the techniques of the theatre of menace with diminishing and augmenting chords, and instability, a sense of anxiety, alarm and fear is created. One by one, the children hurriedly leave the merry-go-round, as more women in face veils now with openings for the eyes are riding on the merry-go-round until only veiled women ride. The chords then change once again to c and d flat (like in the film *Jaws*) leitmotif notes and the camera focuses on the hand of one of the veiled women which shows a henna pattern – a symbol of 'otherness'. She catches the hanging tassel.[28] The veil here is not presented as a symbol of subordination, which is the publicly proclaimed reason for its restriction, but the veil and its wearer is presented as something demonic and to be feared. Such tactics were used in anti-Jewish propaganda in Nazi Germany and in anti-black propaganda in the Deep South in the United States. Such representations serve to incite and inflame the already existing racial, cultural and religious hatred which is now being fomented and directed against women who wear the veil. The incitement of hatred is reflected in the growing number of assaults against veiled women[29] and acts of vigilantism as in France[30] where a Frenchman who ripped the face veil from a wearer was given a five-month suspended prison sentence and ordered to compensate his victim.

4. DUPLICITOUS RATIONALES

4.1. Gender equality
Western nations that ban the face veil have engaged in duplicity and colonial masquerades (McClintock 1995: 50; also Jacobson 2007). Restricting freedom of choice and imposing anti-niqab bans, they

[28] www.youtube.com/watch?feature=player_detailpage&v=LqjiFrVgX7U
[29] MAMA (Measuring Anti-Muslim Attacks), show that Muslim women were targeted in 58 per cent of all incidents. www.guardian.co.uk/uk/2013/mar/09/muslim-helpline-faith-attacks-women (last accessed 10 April 2013).
[30] *Daily News*, Egypt, 14 March 2013.

claim, are necessary to promote gender equality. Such posturing is duplicitous when promoted by those who have, in all other respects, systematically eschewed the human rights of women from the subaltern and are blinded to the abuses against all women in their midst. Phillips is correct when she writes: 'The critique of polygamy or arranged marriages or the enforced seclusion of women gives the impression that all is well in the heartlands of liberal democracy' and 'people must earn the right to speak out against injustice by first demonstrating their track record closer to home' (2010: 25–6).

In those countries which profess their commitment to gender equality, the media representation, sexualization and objectification of women in film, cinema and pornography, have not been met with the same zealous determination to protect women. Some aspects of the pornography industry are valorized in the West, indeed some countries force what they consider to be expressions of sexual freedom on the would-be citizen from the subaltern that many feminists would regard as exploitative of women. What feminists regard as ambivalent representations, for example the use of women in nudity, are read and inscribed by some countries as an expression of freedom which the subaltern applicant must embrace to satisfy the hurdle of the citizenship test.[31] For example, satisfying citizenship in Holland requires the applicant's acceptance of female nudity (the infamous video of a nude woman emerging from the sea). In addition, acceptance of two men kissing is also a requirement of the citizen applicant.[32] In such ceremonies (rites of passage) the woman from the subaltern must also remove the piece of cloth from her head or face. It is difficult to see how this can promote gender or cultural equality since it is deliberately targeted at women from certain communities. Moors (in Chapter 2 in this volume) argues that attempts to ban face veils are part of the 'culturization of politics' and that in the Netherlands Islam itself has been regarded as incompatible with European values. What seems astonishing from these debates is the blindness of some Western women to their own oppression and the gullibility of the West in its passive acceptance of the sexual

---

[31] www.dw.de/testing-the-limits-of-tolerance/a-1935900-1.

[32] Sebastiaan Gottlieb and Laurens Nijzink in their research found that applicants from the European Union, Norway, Iceland, Switzerland, Australia, Japan, Canada, New Zealand, South Korea and the United States do not have to take the test under the Citizenship Tests Abroad Act (Wet Inburgeringsexamen Buitenland) of 2006) (www.expatica.com/nl/news/news_focus/Human-Rights-Watch-Dutch-citizenship-tests-discriminate_229302.html accessed 22 April 2013).

commoditization of women which is implicit in these arguments of liberation. The West subsists in a false consciousness of its own treatment of women. The arguments of Berger (1972) are relevant here in that the West has manipulated our 'ways of seeing', and language defines the limits of our thinking and meaning such that the sexualization of women and the pornographization of the Western world lead the West not into self-scrutiny or recognition of its own exploitation of women but on a crusading mission to save others from what it perceives to be the expressions of the oppression of women.

There is also a presumption of a 'Western Consensus' (Said 1981: 48) with regard to the meaning of the niqab which is saturated by orientalist rhetoric. This reification and fetishization of Middle Eastern dress is demonstrated in the recent efforts of the feminist group – Femen – to draw the attention of the world to their oppressed Muslim sisters in what they called a 'Topless Jihad' and 'Bare breasts against Islamism!'.[33] Alexandra Shevchenko said 'nobody can use religion ... to abuse women, to oppress them'.[34] At the same time laying one's breast uncovered, in Femen's view, has only one meaning and that is liberation. However, 'Muslim Women Against Femen' rebut this orientalist configuration and state 'Femen stole [our] voice'.[35] As Saadawi has said 'Women in the West wear nudity the way Arab women wear the veil' (Davis 1984: 146).

It is to be remembered too that the politics of forcibly unveiling women has been a deliberate strategy of domination by the colonialist. Fanon (1965) analysed the meaning of forcible unveiling for Algerian women in *Studies in a Dying Colonialism*.[36] So in this act of unveiling how is anyone to be persuaded that the West will deliver liberation to the veiled women?

4.2. The veil's polysemicity

Western nations profess to have a monopoly on the meaning of the veil which they say is to promote Islam or to subordinate women. Many

---

[33] Anonymous, 'Femen storm in a DDcup: stand-by for "topless jihad" Al-bawaba', at: http://femen.info/femen-storm-in-a-dd-cup-stand-by-for-topless-jihad-al (last accessed 4 April 2013).

[34] Anonymous, 'Femen's topless jihad day: bare-breasted activists target Tunisia embassies', *Middle East Online*. At: www.middle-east-online.com/english/?id=57921 (last accessed 4 April 2013).

[35] Bachhi, U., 'Anti-Femen topless jihad day: Muslim women slam "racist" feminist activists', *International Business Times. UK* at: www.ibtimes.co.uk/articles/454131/20130405/femen-muslim-women-protest-topless-jihad.htm (last accessed 4 April 2013).

[36] See also *Frantz Fanon: black skin, white mask* / directed by Isaac Julien (Video Pal Format); Djebar (1996); Gibson (1999).

Muslims in fact contest that Islam requires veiling and as this volume demonstrates women who wear the veil do so for many reasons. Research conducted within and outside Europe categorically challenges mono determinist essentialist meanings, revealing instead the polysemicity of the veil. History, time and the specificities of the cultural context are all relevant to understanding the fluidity of signification of dress and the realization that the cultural sign of the veil is not fixed in its meaning. El Gundi observed, 'the veil is a complex symbol of many meanings. The signifier(s) situates the meaning of the sign in its time and place' (1999). Feminist critiques including from Saadawi (1997), Fischer (1978), Sedghi (2007), Benhabib (2002) and Yeğenoğlu (1998) among others, recognize that while the veil has often, although not always, been a symbol of patriarchal oppression, the veil, and hijab at least for some women, who wear it, can also be a visible symbol of political positionality and an expression of resistance to and contesting of Western foreign policy. So, for example, in the context of Iran's more recent history: 'veiling, unveiling, and re-veiling illuminate the contest for political power in the course of Iran's development' (Sedghi 2007: 34). Bouteldja, in this volume (Chapter 5), points to the multidimensionality of motivations that impact on a woman's decision to wear the niqab. Moors, in her contribution in this volume (Chapter 2), says that of the women she interviewed the only common element was that for them the face veil was part of a commitment to becoming a better Muslim. While Østergaard, Warburg and Johansen, in this volume (Chapter 3), found that women wearing the niqab in Denmark were either Danish converts or Muslims with a cross-ethnic orientation and connected with an affiliation to Salafism. Bouteldja while discovering a multiplicity of motivations behind the decision to wear niqab also found that some wearers had been forced into wearing the full-face veil by male relatives or Salafi groups. And so for Western diaspora perhaps a common thread is indeed the significance of Salafism. But even here we must be wary of imputing a Salafist meaning to niqab wearing and transcend the neo-orientalist projections (Abbas 2007).

5. THE EAST IN THE MIDST OF THE WEST

What is especially significant in these several writings is that the analyses of the veil have usually observed the practice of covering within veiled communities and not among diaspora living in foreign host communities. This volume seeks to make a significant contribution in exploring motivations from diaspora living in the West. Certainly the sight of veiled women in the streets of London, Paris or Ontario is a relatively new phenomenon brought about by recent patterns of migration. Sawchuk (1988: 16) writes, 'events, objects, images, as cultural signs or allegories [which] do not have one fixed or stable meaning . . . derive their significance both from their place in a chain of signifiers, a chain which is itself unstable because of the constant intervention of [this] theoretical change'. Body apparel then, like the body itself, cannot escape being a historical and political and situational construct. Thus, as de Beauvoir has observed, 'the body is a situation' (cited in Moi 1999: 59).

Said revealed how orientalist ideology depicted Middle Eastern women as backward and oppressed. Such ways of seeing and recognition have relevance to the contemporary portrayal of Arab and 'oriental' women which today is vocalized at all levels of ideological operation in the hijab/niqab debates. In this sense, the body of the Arab/oriental woman is examined, inspected, scrutinized, controlled and called to account through her choice of dress in a way that would be intolerable if it were not the Muslim woman who was being so scrutinized. The West essentializes its wearers using the nomenclature 'niqabis' and 'hijabis' reducing women to the mere cloth which covers them; in this way cloth becomes skin. In turn, such ideologies about women like oracles continue to shape and form representations and craft perceptions about Islam and the Middle East. In turn, these perceptions come to have a real impact on reality and political decision making and the West's foreign policy. Ashcroft et al. argue: 'the discourse of Orientalism persists into the present, particularly in the West's relationship with "Islam", as evidenced in its study, its reporting in the media, its representation in general' (1989: 168). The media is a powerful institutional state apparatus constantly depicting the veiled woman as the terror in our midst that threatens. Eastern and Middle Eastern women are captives of Western representation, robbed of agency, robbed of authenticity and self-inscribed meaning. Their religion, culture and reason are appropriated by the West who poses as the grand narrator. Ethnocentricism/anthropocentricism and 'eurocentricism' (Amin 1989: 106) characterize the way in which 'knowledge' on the veil, and to veil, and to unveil, reflects Western values (Copbbah 1987), as the West provides the template for understanding these women in its 'totalising discourse' (Said 1993: xxv, xxvii).

The material reality is that Muslims are under attack (Winter 2006: 279) and the Muslim woman by her very visibility is being targeted in a kind of aggression spreading across Europe from Belgium to Holland, to Spain, to Sweden,[37] where a 'moral panic' is being carefully crafted and orchestrated in assaults at every level of operation on immigrant and second-generation Muslim communities. Assaults on their person and the denial of their right to dress has led to women being forced to flee their own countries. In the UK one such asylum claim (*The Queen on the application of (1)B (2)M v. Secretary of State for the Home Department*),[38] came before the High Court of Justice where an Iranian claimant (B) who arrived from Iran via France claiming asylum with his daughter (M) who wears the burqa, has been refused asylum and ordered to return to France on the basis that France was the first country within EU territories at which the claimant and his daughter arrived. The Secretary of State argued that the claimants could simply be returned to France without considering the merits of their claim notwithstanding the fact that in France M will not be permitted to wear the niqab in public places. The judge upheld the decision of the Secretary of State and also refused permission to appeal although lawyers for the claimants contended that both claimants would be subjected to degrading treatment (Article 3) and on this ground should not be 'returned' to France.[39] The discrimination experienced by women wearing the niqab is evident in the research studies in this volume (see Part I), where contemptuous or condescending attitudes and hostility and aggression characterize others' responses to them. The real motive and intention of he who removes the cloth is not to liberate but to conquer, and this is part of a colonial and racist inspired assimilationist agenda.

6. CONCLUSION

Subaltern women have no being, no personhood – they are veil. The veil fetishizes and reifies their body, soul and authenticity. Across Europe, veiling the face and body is an act, and a performance as Moors demonstrates that women choose, yet only the West is authorized to define, and thus such women are contained and imprisoned within a Western narrative and fiction. The law wrestles with its own heartbeat of freedom and choice, human dignity and equality, as these principles collide with the dictate of national ideologies and political agendas. Minority women stand at the precipice as they are rained down upon by

---

[37] 'Vannais: the assault on migrant communities', *Vk*, 12 May 2009.
[38] [2013] EWHC 2281 (Admin.).   [39] *Ibid.*, §100.

violence of the bane of custom in all its multifaceted complexity and the violence of the state at national and local level which through its repressive and ideological state apparatus, seeks to conquer, crush and destroy. Young articulates their subject position when he asks the question, 'Have you ever felt that the moment you said the word "I", that "I" was someone else, not you. That in some obscure way you were not the subject of your own sentence?' (2003: 1).

REFERENCES

Abbas, T. (ed.) 2007. *Islamic Political Radicalism: A European Perspective*, Edinburgh University Press.
Althusser, L. 1971. 'Ideology and Ideological State Apparatuses', in *Lenin and Philosophy and Other Essays*, New York and London: Monthly Review Press, p. 171.
Amin, S. 1989. *Eurocentricism*, London: Zed Press.
Ashcroft, B., Griffiths, G. and Tiffin, H. 1989. *The Empire Writes Back: Theory and Practice in Post-colonial Literatures*, London: Routledge.
Barbibay, Y. 2010. 'Citizenship Privilege or the Right to Religious Freedom', *Cardozo Journal of International and Comparative Law*, 18: 159.
Benhabib, S. 2002. *The Claims of Culture, Equality and Diversity in the Global Era*, Princeton University Press.
Berger, J. 1972. *Ways of Seeing*, London: Penguin.
Bienkowski, S. 2010. 'Part 2: Note: Has France Taken Assimilation Too Far? Muslim Beliefs, French National Values, and the June 27, 2008 Conseil d'Etat, Decision on Mme M', *Rutgers Journal of Law and Religion*, 11(2): 437–58.
Chehabi, H. E. 2007. 'Staging the Emperor's New Clothes Dress Codes and Nation Building under Reza Shah', *Iranian Studies*, 26(3–4): 209–29.
Copbbah, J. A. M. 1987. 'African Values and the Human Rights Debate: An African Perspective', *Human Rights Quarterly*, 9: 309.
Davis, A. 1984. *Women Culture and Politics*, London: Women's Press.
Djebar, S. A. 1996. 'F. Fanon and R. Faulkner, Women, Veils And Land', *World Literature Today*, 70.
Droubi, L. (2011). 'The Constitutionality of the Niqab Ban in Egypt: A Symbol of Egypt's Struggle for a Legal Identity', *New York Law School Law Review*, 56(2): 687–709.
El Gundi, F. 1999. *Veil: Modesty, Privacy and Resistance*, Oxford: Berg.
Erlanger, S. and Camus, E. 2012. 'In a ban, a measure of European tolerance', *New York Times Europe*, 1 September.
Erk, J. 2005. 'From Vlaams Blok to Vlaams Belang: The Belgian Far-Right Renames Itself', *West European Politics*, 28(3): 493–502.

Fanon, F. 1965. *Studies in a Dying Colonialism*, New York: Monthly Review Press.

Ferrari, S. and Pastorelli, S. 2012. *Religion in Public Places: A European Perspective*, Farnham: Ashgate.

Fischer, M. M. J. 1978. 'On Changing the Concept and Position of Persian Women', in L. Beck, and N. Keddie, (eds.), *Women in the Muslim World*, Cambridge, MA: Harvard University Press, pp. 189–215.

Gibson, N. C. 1999. *Rethinking Fanon: The Continuing Dialogue*, Amherst NY: Prometheus.

Jacobson, K. 2007. *Odalisques and Arabesques: Orientalist Photography, 1839–1925*, London: Quaritch.

Knief, A. 2010. 'Liberté, egalité – de féministes! Revealing the burqa as a pro-choice issue', September /October, *Humanist*.

McClintock, A. 1995. *Imperial Leather: Race, Gender, and Sexuality in the Colonial Contest*, London: Routledge.

Mancini, S. 2012. 'Patriarchy as the Exclusive Domain of the Other: The Veil Controversy, False Projection and Cultural Racism', *International Journal of Constitutional Law*, 10(2): 411–28.

Meer, N., Dwyer, C. and Modood, T. 2010. 'Embodying Nationhood? Conceptions of British National Identity, Citizenship, and Gender in the "Veil Affair"', *Sociological Review*, 58(1): 84–111.

Moi, T. 1999. *What Is a Woman?*, Oxford University Press.

Mudde, C. 2000. *The Ideology of the Extreme Right*, Manchester University Press.

Nussbaum, M. 2012. *The New Religious Intolerance: Overcoming the Politics of Fear in an Anxious Age*, Cambridge, MA: Harvard University Press.

Phillips, A. 2010. *Gender and Culture*, London: Polity.

Saadawi, N. 1997. *The Nawal El Saadawi Reader*, London: Zed.

Said, E. 1978. *Orientalism: Western Conceptions of the Orient*, London: Penguin.

1981. *Covering Islam: How the Media and the Experts Determine How We See the Rest of the World*, New York: Pantheon.

1993. *Culture and Imperialism*, London: Vintage.

Sawchuk, K. 1988. 'A Tale of Inscription: Fashion Statements', in A. Kroker and M. Kroker (eds.), *Body Invaders: Sexuality and the Postmodern Condition*, London: Macmillan.

Sedghi, H. 2007. *Women and Politics in Iran: Veiling, Unveiling and Reveiling*, Cambridge University Press.

Song, S. 2011. 'Three Models of Civil Solidarity', in R. Smith (ed.), *Citizenship, Borders and Human Needs*, Philadelphia, PA: University of Pennsylvania Press.

Suvarierol, S. 2012. 'Nation-Freezing: Images of the Nation and the Migrant in Citizenship Packages', *Nations and Nationalism*, 18(2): 210–29.

Van der Schyff, G. and Overbeeke, A. 2012. 'Exercising Religious Freedom in the Public Space: A Comparative and European Convention Analysis of General Burqa Bans', *European Constitutional Law Review*, 7(3): 424–52.

Warburg, M., Schepelern Johansen, B. and Østergaard, K. 2013. 'Counting Niqabs and Burqas in Denmark: Methodological Aspects of Quantifying Rare and Elusive Religious Sub-cultures', *Journal of Contemporary Religion*, 28(1): 33–48.

Winter, B. 2006. 'Secularism aboard the Titanic: Feminists and the Debate over the Hijab in France', *Feminist Studies*, 32(2): 279–98.

Yeğenoğlu, M. 1998. *Colonial fantasies: Towards a Feminist Reading of Orientalism*, Cambridge University Press.

Young, R. K. C. 2003. *Postcolonialism: A Very Short Introduction*, Oxford University Press.

INDEX

Books in the series

Diseases of the Will
Mariana Valverde

The Politics of Truth and Reconciliation in South Africa: Legitimizing the Post-Apartheid State
Richard A. Wilson

Modernism and the Grounds of Law
Peter Fitzpatrick

Unemployment and Government: Genealogies of the Social
William Walters

Autonomy and Ethnicity: Negotiating Competing Claims in Multi-Ethnic States
Yash Ghai

Constituting Democracy: Law, Globalism and South Africa's Political Reconstruction
Heinz Klug

The Ritual of Rights in Japan: Law, Society, and Health Policy
Eric A. Feldman

The Invention of the Passport: Surveillance, Citizenship and the State
John Torpey

Governing Morals: A Social History of Moral Regulation
Alan Hunt

The Colonies of Law: Colonialism, Zionism and Law in Early Mandate Palestine
Ronen Shamir

Law and Nature
David Delaney

Social Citizenship and Workfare in the United States and Western Europe: The Paradox of Inclusion
Joel F. Handler

Law, Anthropology and the Constitution of the Social: Making Persons and Things
Edited by Alain Pottage and Martha Mundy

Judicial Review and Bureaucratic Impact: International and Interdisciplinary Perspectives
Edited by Marc Hertogh and Simon Halliday

Immigrants at the Margins: Law, Race, and Exclusion in Southern Europe
Kitty Calavita

Lawyers and Regulation: The Politics of the Administrative Process
Patrick Schmidt

Law and Globalization from Below: Toward a Cosmopolitan Legality
Edited by Boaventura de Sousa Santos and Cesar A. Rodriguez-Garavito

Public Accountability: Designs, Dilemmas and Experiences
Edited by Michael W. Dowdle

Law, Violence and Sovereignty among West Bank Palestinians
Tobias Kelly

Legal Reform and Administrative Detention Powers in China
Sarah Biddulph

The Practice of Human Rights: Tracking Law between the Global and the Local
Edited by Mark Goodale and Sally Engle Merry

Judges beyond Politics in Democracy and Dictatorship: Lessons from Chile
Lisa Hilbink

Paths to International Justice: Social and Legal Perspectives
Edited by Marie-Bénédicte Dembour and Tobias Kelly

Law and Society in Vietnam: The Transition from Socialism in Comparative Perspective
Mark Sidel

Constitutionalizing Economic Globalization: Investment Rules and Democracy's Promise
David Schneiderman

The New World Trade Organization Knowledge Agreements (2nd edition)
Christopher Arup

Justice and Reconciliation in Post-Apartheid South Africa
Edited by François du Bois and Antje du Bois-Pedain

Militarization and Violence against Women in Conflict Zones in the Middle East: A Palestinian Case-Study
Nadera Shalhoub-Kevorkian

Child Pornography and Sexual Grooming: Legal and Societal Responses
Suzanne Ost

Darfur and the Crime of Genocide
John Hagan and Wenona Rymond-Richmond

Fictions of Justice: The International Criminal Court and the Challenge of Legal Pluralism in Sub-Saharan Africa
Kamari Maxine Clarke

Institutional Inequality and the Mobilization of the Family and Medical Leave Act: Rights on Leave
Catherine R. Albiston

Authoritarian Rule of Law: Legislation, Discourse and Legitimacy in Singapore
Jothie Rajah

Law and Development and the Global Discourses of Legal Transfers
Edited by John Gillespie and Pip Nicholson

Law against the State: Ethnographic Forays into Law's Transformations
Edited by Julia Eckert, Brian Donahoe, Christian Strümpell and Zerrin Özlem Biner

Transnational Legal Process and State Change
Edited by Gregory C. Shaffer

Legal Mobilization under Authoritarianism: The Case of Post-Colonial Hong Kong
Edited by Waikeung Tam

Complementarity in the Line of Fire: The Catalysing Effect of the International Criminal Court in Uganda and Sudan
Sarah M. H. Nouwen

Political and Legal Transformations of an Indonesian Polity: The Nagari from Colonisation to Decentralisation
Franz von Benda-Beckmann and Keebet von Benda-Beckmann

Pakistan's Experience with Formal Law: An Alien Justice
Osama Siddique

Human Rights under State-Enforced Religious Family Laws in Israel, Egypt, and India
Yüksel Sezgin

Why Prison?
Edited by David Scott

Law's Fragile State: Colonial, Authoritarian, and Humanitarian Legacies in Sudan
Mark Fathi Massoud

Rights for Others: The Slow Home-Coming of Human Rights in the Netherlands
Barbara Oomen

European States and their Muslim Citizens: The Impact of Institutions on Perceptions and Boundaries
Edited by John R. Bowen, Christophe Bertossi, Jan Willem Duyvendak and Mona Lena Krook

Religion, Law and Society
Russell Sandberg

The Experiences of Face Veil Wearers in Europe and the Law
Edited by Eva Brems